WE THE PEOPLE

3

The Civil Rights Revolution

WE THE PEOPLE

3

The Civil Rights Revolution

Bruce Ackerman

THE BELKNAP PRESS OF
HARVARD UNIVERSITY PRESS

Cambridge, Massachusetts
London, England
2014

Library of Congress Cataloging-in-Publication Data
Ackerman, Bruce A.
We the people / Bruce Ackerman.
p.   cm.
Includes bibliographical references and index.
Partial Contents:
I. Foundations.
ISBN 978-0-674-94840-2/0-674-94840-8 (alk. paper)
II. Transformations.
ISBN 978-0-674-94847-1/0-674-94847-5 (alk. paper)
III. The Civil Rights Revolution.
ISBN 978-0-674-05029-7
I. United States—Constitutional history.   2. United States—
Constitutional law.   I. Title.
KF4541.A8 1991
342.73'029—dc20
[347.30229]
91-10725

For Owen Fiss
Insight. Integrity. Commitment.

CONTENTS

ACKNOWLEDGMENTS

I began working on *We the People* in the late 1970s, and I could not have sustained this project over the past thirty-five years without the support of a wonderful circle of friends. From the very beginning, I have talked my way through countless questions with Bo Burt, Guido Calabresi, Mirjan Damaska, Owen Fiss, Al Klevorick, Tony Kronman, Jerry Mashaw, and Alan Schwartz. Over the decades, this conversation circle was enriched by a remarkable community of scholars who have made their way to New Haven: Anne Alstott, Akhil Amar, Ian Ayres, Jack Balkin, Aharon Barak, Rick Brooks, Amy Chua, Drew Days, John Donohue, Don Elliott, Bill Eskridge, James Forman, Heather Gerken, Abbe Gluck, Robert Gordon, Michael Graetz, Dieter Grimm, Oona Hathaway, Christine Jolls, Paul Kahn, Daniel Markovits, Tracey Meares, Nick Parrillo, Robert Post, Cristina Rodriguez, Jed Rubenfeld, Vicki Schultz, Scott Shapiro, Reva Siegel, Alec Stone-Sweet, Patrick Weil, Jim Whitman, and John Witt. All have contributed to this book. More important, they have made Yale Law School into an intellectually vibrant place where serious ideas are taken seriously in day-to-day encounters at lunch, in the hallways, and in an endless stream of faculty workshops.

I am also much indebted to my friends in the Yale political science department. Robert Dahl, Juan Linz, David Mayhew, and Steve Skowronek have been real inspirations, providing detailed comments and larger perspectives that have structured my basic framework. Seyla Benhabib and Ian Shapiro have played a similar role in helping me define my philosophical path. Beyond New Haven, Meir Dan-Cohen, Stephen Gardbaum, Laura Kalman, Ethan Leib, Sandy Levinson, Teemu Ruskola,

John Skrentny, Rogers Smith, and David Super provided extremely helpful commentaries on one or another draft.

Then there are my students, who have critiqued my evolving ideas over more than a decade of courses and seminars. Some followed up with formidable investigations into critical sources, often hidden in the archives. My work with Jennifer Nou culminated in a jointly authored article, and final completion of the larger project greatly depended on a series of remarkable contributions by several generations of Yale law students, including Josef Ansorge, Larry Benn, Arwyn Carroll, Ben Cassady, Eric Citron, Justin Collings, Jesse Cross, Tomas Dombrowski, Blake Emerson, Danieli Evans, Dov Fox, Rob Heberle, Craig Konnoth, Kevin Lamb, Marin Levy, John Lewis, Chris Lynch, John Paredes, Matt Pearl, Nick Pedersen, Alex Platt, Adam Sharpe, Julia Spiegel, Lisa Wang, Victoria Weatherford, and Chan-young Yang.

While I was working on this book, my longtime secretary, Jill Tobey, passed away; she is sorely missed. Lise Cavallaro and Jennifer Marshall have filled a very large gap with distinction. Thanks too to the library staff, and especially Gene Coakley and Sarah Kraus, for searching out obscure legal materials with blinding speed. This made it possible to review large masses of relevant sources at the same time, allowing for a deeper appreciation of their complex relationships.

As you can see, I am a lucky guy. But the greatest gift has been my life with Susan Rose-Ackerman, my wife of forty-five years. She has combined unconditional love with extraordinary intelligence, making it possible to combine work and family in wonderful ways.

Thank you.

———◆———

I introduced some of this project's larger themes in "The Holmes Lectures: The Living Constitution," 120 *Harvard Law Review* 1727 (2007). I am grateful to Elena Kagan, then dean of the Law School, and the Harvard Law faculty for their hospitality and incisive commentary when I visited Cambridge to deliver those lectures. With the permission of the *Review*, Chapters 1–4 are derived in part from this earlier publication. Similarly, a joint essay with Jennifer Nou serves as the basis of Chapters 5 and 6: "Canonizing the Civil Rights Revolution: The People and the Poll

Tax," 103 *Northwestern University Law Review* 63 (2009). That publication has given me permission to reprint relevant excerpts here.

Finally, I deeply appreciate the unstinting support of Anthony Kronman, Harold Koh, and Robert Post during their deanships at Yale Law School—they provided all the help any scholar could hope for. I also thank President Louis Vogel for inviting me as a visiting research professor at the University of Paris (Pantheon-Assas) in the fall of 2011, permitting me a few months' escape from day-to-day distractions when I was rethinking the foundations of this project.

Confronting the Twentieth Century

T HE SUN IS SETTING on the civil rights revolution. The struggle was an unforgettable experience for the generation that lived through it—the stunning news of *Brown v. Board of Education,* the bitter conflict at Little Rock, the passage of the great civil rights laws, and so much more have reverberated in our public life for decades.

All this is ancient history for the rising generation. They may celebrate Martin Luther King Jr. Day, but the civil rights revolution will never have the same living resonances. We are fast reaching a critical moment in the dialogue between the generations that is constitutional law—the moment at which lived experience becomes historical legacy. What the rising generation chooses to remember—and what it chooses to forget—will shape the way it understands America's constitutional choices for the twenty-first century.[1]

This is not a new problem. On July 4, 1826, John Adams and Thomas Jefferson died at almost the same moment—making it painfully clear that the fate of the Republic was in new hands. Americans had two choices. They could follow Jefferson's famous advice that "the earth belongs to the living" and replace the Constitution of 1789 with a new Constitution for a new age. Or they could sustain political order by creating a constitutional tradition, with generation upon generation debating the half-remembered legacy of the constitutional past, using this endless debate to anchor a collective confrontation with the trackless future.

Americans have taken this second path. The elaboration of our tradition has become more demanding over time. Two centuries onward, the Founding is only the beginning of a much longer story of constitutional vision and revision. Our challenge is to fit the civil rights revolution into this larger pattern of constitutional development. What is the best way to understand the relationship between the Second Reconstruction of the

1960s and the first Reconstruction of the 1860s? Does the rise of New Deal constitutionalism in the 1930s help explain why the Second Reconstruction succeeded where the first period of Reconstruction failed? Does it help explain the limits, and the distinctive character, of the egalitarian commitments emerging from the civil rights revolution?

My answers build upon the first two volumes in this series, but don't be alarmed—you won't have to read them before confronting these questions! It's enough to suggest how the basic framework of *We the People* challenges conventional legal wisdom.

The dominant professional narrative is court-centered—the young lawyer is taught from casebooks that focus almost exclusively on judicial opinions stretching from *Marbury v. Madison* to *Brown v. Board, Roe v. Wade,* and beyond. *We the People* is regime-centered. It focuses on the institutional relationships and public values affirmed by the constitutional system as a whole, fitting the courts into this larger framework.

The Founding generated a distinctive governmental constellation during the Early Republic. But the Civil War and Reconstruction revolutionized this pattern to establish the Middle Republic—adding new values and institutional relationships into the Founding mix. The same thing happened during the New Deal, with Americans repudiating key elements of the nineteenth-century constitution to create a Modern Republic to meet the challenges of the Great Depression. The New Deal regime, in turn, set the stage for the civil rights revolution—which ultimately destroyed the coalition of racist southerners and ethnic northerners that had united to form the Democratic coalition established by Franklin D. Roosevelt. During the two decades spanning the Eisenhower and Nixon administrations, liberal Democrats and Republicans joined with the civil rights movement to build a distinctive New Deal–Civil Rights regime that continues to serve as the foundation for the Modern Republic. This book explores the constitutional legacy they left behind.

Early, middle, modern—historians and political scientists have used similar categories to make sense of long-term constitutional developments. Nevertheless, this familiar trichotomy challenges conventional legal wisdom, which focuses narrowly on the Supreme Court at the expense of larger changes in the governing regime.

A change in focus from court to regime has wide-ranging ramifications. In proposing the Constitution, the Philadelphia Convention claimed to speak in the name of We the People, setting up a first fundamental problem: should constitutionalists take popular sovereignty seriously as they study the successive transformations of the American constitution over time?

Many serious scholars have said no. Most famously, Charles Beard and a host of Progressive writers did their best to puncture the Founding myth of popular sovereignty, portraying the Philadelphians as largely motivated by economic self-interest.

I take a different view. Popular sovereignty isn't a myth. The Founders developed a distinctive form of constitutional practice that successfully gave ordinary (white male) Americans a sense that they made a real difference in determining their political future. This Founding success established paradigms for legitimate acts of higher lawmaking that subsequent generations have developed further. Reconstruction Republicans, New Deal Democrats, and the civil rights leadership once again confronted the task of winning broad and self-conscious popular consent for their sweeping transformations of the constitutional status quo—and each time they (more or less) succeeded. The challenge is to analyze the concrete ways in which the evolving constitutional system tested their claims by requiring them to return repeatedly to the voters to earn the very special authority required to create a new regime in the name of We the People.

Conventional constitutional lawyers have failed this challenge. They don't seriously consider how Americans responded to the Civil War, Great Depression, and civil rights movement by creatively adapting the paradigms of popular sovereignty inherited from the eighteenth century. They have indulged a series of legal fictions that obscure the distinctive character of these latter-day exercises in revolutionary constitutional reform. They pretend that the political leadership in each of these eras transformed America's fundamental commitments by obediently following the path set out by the Founding Federalists for formal constitutional amendment.

They are wrong.

Americans have occasionally used the formula for formal amendment laid out by the Founders in Article V—under which Congress proposes, and state legislatures ratify, changes in our higher law. But the great political movements of the past have often displayed far more creativity in gaining popular consent to their new constitutional settlements. In earlier volumes, *We the People* followed Reconstruction Republicans and New Deal Democrats step by step as they built new systems of popular sovereignty to win broad and self-conscious popular support for their transformative initiatives.

To sum up my argument: In writing Article V, the Founders relied on the *division of powers* between the states and the central government to organize debate and decision on constitutional amendments. But Reconstruction Republicans and New Deal Democrats increasingly relied on the *separation of powers* between the presidency, Congress, and the Supreme Court to earn the broad popular consent required for fundamental change in the name of We the People.

This separation-of-powers model has been elaborated in different ways at different times. Most often, the president claims that his successful reelection represents a "mandate from the people," and he successfully convinces Congress and the Court to endorse his new vision of constitutional government. This is the scenario that worked for Lincoln in the case of the Thirteenth Amendment, and for Roosevelt in the case of the New Deal Revolution.

But sometimes another branch has taken the lead. During Reconstruction, John Wilkes Booth's bullet replaced Lincoln with the conservative Andrew Johnson, who tried to enlist the Supreme Court in a joint effort to stop the Republican revolution in its tracks. If Reconstruction was to move beyond the Thirteenth Amendment, the Republican Congress had no choice but to assert constitutional leadership. Although the point is ignored in standard legal accounts, it was a series of dramatic conflicts between Congress, the president, and the Court—not the formal ratification of the Fourteenth and Fifteenth Amendments—that largely determined the constitutional shape of the Middle Republic. If Andrew Johnson, backed by the Supreme Court, had won his struggle for public support, Congress never would have been in a position to force the South, through military means, to ratify the Fourteenth and Fifteenth Amendments. The new Republican regime would have been based on the more modest vision of human rights and national power suggested by the Thirteenth Amendment.

While different branches have taken leadership roles in the struggle for regime change, their challenge is always the same—to gain sufficient public support for their constitutional revision so that, over time, *all three branches* repeatedly endorse the legitimacy of the breakthroughs that initiated the new regime. During the presidential election of 1868, Democratic candidates were still denouncing the legitimacy of the

Fourteenth Amendment. It was only when Ulysses S. Grant won the White House and appointed strong Republicans to the Supreme Court that the validity of the Reconstruction Amendments was put beyond question.

The legitimation of the New Deal proceeded at a similar pace. The Old Court stopped its assault on activist legislation in 1937. But the meaning of this retreat was initially unclear. Was it merely a strategic retreat or the inauguration of a new vision of constitutional government in America? Only Roosevelt's precedent-shattering third term decisively answered this question—enabling him to reconstitute the entire Supreme Court, which then unanimously endorsed the principles of New Deal constitutionalism in ringing terms. By the early 1940s, all three branches had given their repeated support to the New Deal regime—ending serious legal debate about its legitimacy. Critics who sought to restore the Constitution of the Middle Republic found themselves treated as extremists, far outside the mainstream of legal opinion.

The contrast between Reconstruction and New Deal served as the centerpiece of the second volume in this series, *Transformations*, setting the stage for the present study. During the civil rights revolution, the separation of powers once again organized a lengthy process of debate and decision that culminated in a period in which all three branches vindicated a new vision of constitutional government in the name of We the People. But there was one big difference: while the presidency or the Congress had initiated the previous rounds of constitutional politics, this time the Supreme Court initially seized the initiative. *Brown v. Board of Education* put the issue of racial equality at the very center of a great generational debate, forcing President Dwight Eisenhower and Congress to confront questions they happily would have ignored.

Supreme Court leadership wasn't nearly enough to win the precious sense of mobilized and broad support required to gain the assent of We the People. It was only when President Lyndon Johnson and his liberal Congress followed through with a series of landmark statutes that *Brown's* promise became a fundamental premise of the modern republic.

Lyndon Johnson's 1964 victory over Barry Goldwater played a pivotal role, giving him a broad mandate to move beyond the Civil Rights Act of 1964 to win passage of the Voting Rights Act of 1965 and the Fair Housing Act of 1968. By the end of his presidency, all three branches had engaged in a collaborative process that extended *Brown* far beyond the sphere of public education into an escalating series of initiatives that revolutionized the constitutional meaning of equality.

Nevertheless, the future of the New Deal–Civil Rights regime remained in doubt when Americans went to the polls in 1968. A hostile president could have readily used his powers to undercut the emerging constitutional consensus. But Richard Nixon refused to do so. When campaigning in 1968, Nixon made it clear that he was no George Wallace. And he was true to his word after taking office, signing legislation that consolidated the landmark statutes of the 1960s and supporting administrative measures that enhanced their impact. Nixon was not a vanguardist—at crucial moments he actively opposed bureaucratic and judicial efforts to expand the achievements of the preceding decade. But it is a mistake to cast him as a die-hard opponent. Nixon's very real support of the New Deal–Civil Rights regime gave it a bipartisan basis that placed its legitimacy beyond serious question. Southerners who engaged in perfectly respectable constitutional arguments denouncing the Freedom Riders and Martin Luther King Jr. in the early 1960s were faced with some tough choices: they could fall silent, change their opinions, or be treated like cranks.

Most changed their opinions. They were still racial conservatives, but to remain credible, they took a new tack. They no longer denounced the civil rights revolution but rather manipulated its achievements for their own purposes: What did *Brown* really mean? Was it a mandate for sweeping assaults on racial subordination or a more modest ban on differential treatment by the state on racial grounds? Southern conservatives held the second view, but they accepted the legitimacy of *Brown* and the landmark statutes of the 1960s to a degree that would have been astonishing only a decade earlier.

The broad outlines of this story are familiar, but their constitutional implications are suppressed by a lawyerly fixation on Supreme Court opinions as the preeminent source of insight into the constitutional meaning of the civil rights revolution. This focus provides a plausible starting place in understanding developments during the 1950s, when the Warren Court was the only branch of government asserting constitutional leadership. But the mantle of leadership passed to the president and Congress—and, most important, the American people—during the 1960s. It was the People, not the Court, who considered Goldwater's frontal assault on the Civil Rights Act of 1964 and responded by giving Lyndon Johnson a landslide victory. It was the People, not the Court, who gave their sustained support to a broad and bipartisan coalition in Washington, D.C., that followed up with a series of breakthrough statutes in the late 1960s and early 1970s that redefined the constitutional meaning of equality.

Twenty-first-century Americans should no longer allow the Court to monopolize their vision of the civil rights revolution. They should hear the voices of the *primary* spokesmen for the American people—Martin Luther King Jr. and Lyndon Johnson, Hubert Humphrey and Everett Dirksen—as they hammered out the new terms of our social contract in the Civil Rights Act, the Voting Rights Act, and the Fair Housing Act. They should place the collective decision to adopt these statutes within a larger story of popular sovereignty beginning with *Brown* and ending with the efforts by Richard Nixon and Congress to consolidate the landmark statutes during the early 1970s.

To make this point, I will be developing the notion of a *constitutional canon:* the body of texts that law-trained professionals should place at the very center of their constitutional understanding. When modern lawyers want to gain a sense of the legacy left behind by the Early Republic, they focus on the original Constitution, the *Federalist Papers,* and famous Marshall Court decisions such as *Marbury v. Madison.* But up to now they haven't deployed a similarly broad canon when dealing with the civil rights revolution. They have been content to rely on their own half-remembered experiences to provide the context for interpreting particular Supreme Court decisions. As lived experience fades, however, the profession must confront the pastness of the past.

Like the first period of Reconstruction and the New Deal, the civil rights revolution will be accessible only through the printed words and flickering images of an ever more distant age. While a few lucky historians can spend a happy lifetime exploring the archives, lawyers and judges and legislators have no such luxury. They are in the practical business of decision making: the achievements of the past must be packaged into easily readable form for the very busy men and women who are charged with sustaining our constitutional tradition. Canonization is a professional necessity.

It is also a professional peril. By putting a few texts at the center of the legal conversation, practical decision makers leave countless others in obscurity, inevitably distorting the meaning of the past. Constitutionalists should be aware of this danger and make self-conscious efforts at self-correction over time. Part One urges the rising generation to expand the canon beyond cases such as *Brown* and include the debates and decisions surrounding the landmark statutes of the era. It makes this case by developing three convergent lines of argument.

Chapter 1 explores a more conventional alternative to the inclusion of landmark statutes. If we wish to move beyond court cases, the most obvious place to look isn't the statute books but the formal constitutional amendments passed in recent times. Under our official theory of canon formation, these modern amendments are privileged expressions of We the People. So why not rely on them, ignoring the landmark statutes, to fill out our understanding of the legacy of the twentieth century?

For starters, there have been few formal amendments since the birth of the New Deal regime. This might not be a problem if the ones that were passed accurately reflected the fundamental changes that occurred during the twentieth century. But as Chapter 1 suggests, if lawyers did take these amendments seriously, they would only succeed in generating deeply misleading accounts of the constitutional principles that guide the modern republic.

Systematic miscommunication is a very serious flaw in the construction of a canon. The aim of the entire exercise is to enable law-trained folk to use a small set of texts to generate deep and broad insights into our governing arrangements. This won't happen if we focus our analytic searchlight on texts that lead down blind alleys. Although the modern amendments are undoubtedly a part of our official canon, they can't function as a source of insight without a great deal of supplementation.

Modern lawyers already recognize this point. Despite their official status as solemn commitments by We the People, the modern amendments are generally ignored by lawyers—even most professors of constitutional law would flunk a pop quiz on, say, the Twenty-Fourth Amendment. (Nope, that's not the one that gives residents of the District of Columbia the right to vote in presidential elections!)

In contrast, lawyers *do* take the landmark statutes of the civil rights era very seriously—only they don't treat them as a source of *constitutional* principles. After all, they say to themselves, the Civil Rights Act calls itself a statute—and mere statutes simply don't deserve the special standing of higher law reserved to formal Article V amendments.

My second argument rejects this formalist prejudice. Constitutionalists must recognize that certain landmark statutes are indeed rooted in considered judgments of the people, and that it is these statutes, not formal amendments, that provided the primary vehicle for the legal expression of popular sovereignty in the twentieth century.

I have already made the key point: while Article V depends on a dialogue between national and state assemblies to revise the Constitution, the civil rights era relied on the separation of powers between Congress, the presidency, and the courts to express the sovereign will of We the People.

But it will take a lot more work to make this point persuasive. Chapters 2 through 4 consider each stage of the process of collective debate and decision—from the Supreme Court's intervention in *Brown* through the central debates of the 1960s to the final acts of consolidation during the Nixon years—and provide a blow-by-blow comparison with the efforts of earlier generations to speak for the People through the separation of powers.

Here is where my earlier studies are useful. They contains a sustained analysis of the historical precedents left behind from Reconstruction, the New Deal, and other crucial turning points in American history, in which the separation of powers was used effectively to earn the constitutional authority to speak in the voice of We the People. When judged by these precedents, the civil rights revolution emerges as one of the most successful exercises in constitutional politics in American history. The lawyers, judges, and statesmen of the twenty-first century dishonor this achievement if they refuse to canonize the principles of the landmark statutes that express it.

My first two arguments deal with a central problem in canon formation. Every canon is necessarily selective and offers the legal profession the prospect of both insight and blindness. The challenge is to maximize the first and minimize the second. A civil rights canon that emphasizes the formal amendments of the modern era condemns us to blindness (argument 1), but a canon that embraces the landmark statutes focuses professional conversation on the right question (argument 2): what were the principles emerging from the ongoing efforts by the likes of King, Johnson, Nixon, and Dirksen to earn the institutional authority to express the will of the People?

Asking the right question doesn't mean that we will all agree on the same answer. Nevertheless, it's a lot better than arguing about the wrong question—one that blinds us to the greatest achievements of the civil rights generation. This is my first punch line.

Part One concludes with a final argument for the canonization of landmark statutes. Up to this point I've been considering a fundamental predicament that will confront thoughtful lawyers of the twenty-first century. As they grow to professional maturity, they are thrown into a rich tradition of constitutional achievement stretching back over the centuries. If they wish to carry this tradition forward, they must come to understand it. They can't hope for the sound development of constitutional doctrine if they condemn themselves to blindness from the outset by casting the landmark statutes of the civil rights revolution into the shadows.

My third argument takes an originalist turn. It does not deal with the interpretive predicaments of the rising generation. Rather, it focuses on the perplexities of twentieth-century Americans who mobilized in support of the sweeping egalitarian breakthrough of the 1960s. What did *they* think they were doing in hammering out the terms of their landmark statutes? Did they suppose that the great civil and voting rights acts could legitimately serve as the functional equivalents of Article V amendments?

Great questions—but just because they are important to the canonizers of today doesn't mean they were important to the lawmakers of the twentieth century. Originalism's original sin is to forget this simple point. It is easy to march through the archives collecting random statements on one or another issue that is important to us. But it's wrong to suppose that scattershot opinion played a central role in an earlier era's debate. When this obvious point is ignored, the result is "law office history": the scholar emerges with a string of individual remarks that he wrongly supposes to represent the *considered* judgment of We the People of the United States reached at some earlier period of epochal change. Serious constitutionalists should reject this temptation. They should face up to the fact that the past didn't even try to answer many of our most important questions.

But sometimes a particular struggle of an earlier day *does* manage to cast some light. Sometimes the originating generation focuses on a current interpretive problem with the requisite constitutional seriousness—and when this occurs, we should certainly pay attention.

I have found a civil rights struggle that meets these stringent standards, and it serves as the basis for my final argument for canonizing landmark statutes. It involves the successful effort to abolish poll taxes, which had barred millions of blacks and whites from the polls for generations without raising serious constitutional complaint. Poll taxes were then swept away in the 1960s through the joint action of Congress, the president, and the Supreme Court.

The story is important in its own right, but that's not the reason I've put it at center stage. It deserves attention because, through a remarkable concatenation of events, the problem of the poll tax forced the leading figures of the time to confront our central analytic question: to what extent may a landmark statute function as a legitimate alternative to a formal Article V amendment in expressing the considered judgments of We the People?

As we shall see, this question held the key to the passage of the Voting Rights Act of 1965—the statute that would revolutionize southern democracy. As a consequence, a broad range of protagonists took it very, very, seriously—ranging from Martin Luther King Jr. to Lyndon Johnson, from the National Association for the Advancement of Colored People (NAACP) to the Justice Department, and from southern Democrats to racial liberals in Congress. With the fate of their revolutionary reform hanging in the balance, the president and Congress, with the critical assistance of King, reached an answer of large importance: they self-consciously repudiated the idea that Article V should monopolize higher lawmaking, choosing instead to use their landmark statute to function as an engine of constitutional change in the name of the American people.

By rediscovering the original significance of this fateful choice, Part One concludes with a three-part punch line: not only do the formal amendments of the modern period fail to illuminate basic constitutional principles of the New Deal–Civil Rights regime (Chapter 1), but the landmark statutes do indeed represent the considered judgments of We the People as they were mediated by the operation of the separation of powers over the course of two decades (Chapters 2–4), and finally, the leaders of the civil rights revolution understood this and affirmed that landmark statutes were a legitimate alternative to Article V in expressing the considered judgments of We the People (Chapters 5 and 6).

So isn't it past time for constitutionalists to follow through and give these statutes a central place in the civil rights canon?

———————◆———————

Part Two takes the next step and uses the landmarks as a springboard for reflection on the animating constitutional principles that we have inherited from the twentieth century. As before, my foil will be a judge-centered definition of the canon, which looks exclusively to the opinions of the Warren and Burger Courts as the definitive source of legal understanding.

For Court watchers, the enduring meaning of the civil rights revolution is a series of precedent-shattering reinterpretations of the Reconstruction Amendments, beginning with *Brown* and ending (more or less) with *Roe*. The other key actors in the regime—presidents, Congress, voters—enter as bit players, supporting or opposing the path of constitutional transformation marked out by the Court.

My emphasis on landmark statutes provides a different perspective. While there can be no denying the Court's leadership role in the 1950s, its relationship to the principles hammered out in the landmark statutes is more complex—in ways unrecognized by Court-centered accounts.

Under the standard story, *Brown* kicks off a great debate among the Justices, as the Court moves far beyond *Brown* to later cases that generate much grander theories of equal protection. We follow the majority and minority over the decades as they argue whether the Constitution is concerned with discriminatory purpose or discriminatory effect, whether it is color-blind or allows for affirmative action.

For all the bitter disagreement, the leading protagonists agree on one point: the right answers, whatever they are, should apply across the board, regulating all aspects of the state's engagement with the larger society.

Once we bring the landmark statutes into the picture, this one-size-fits-all approach seems very dubious. These statutes self-consciously divide the world into different spheres of life: public accommodations, education, employment, housing, voting. They impose different regimes on different spheres—focusing on statistical patterns that suggest unequal treatment when it comes to voting, relying on an intent-based standard in regard to restaurants, and developing intermediate positions in other areas. They insist on a far more contextual understanding of the constitutional meaning of equality in different spheres of social and political life.

The judge-centered story also emphasizes a key limitation on the scope of America's constitutional commitment to equality (however it is understood). Relying on Supreme Court decisions of the nineteenth century, constitutionalists continue to tell themselves that the Equal Protection Clause extends only to actions by the state and doesn't constrain the acts of private parties.

This legal truism is immediately challenged by the landmark statutes. The Civil Rights Act of 1964, for example, *only* imposed a ban on discrimination by private employers and didn't change the law governing the public sector. This is precisely the reverse of standard doctrine, which insulates private actors from egalitarian principles but imposes them rigorously on all state actors. The Fair Housing Act of 1968 raised the same challenge to conventional wisdom, imposing a sweeping ban on discrimination in the private housing market that makes a mockery of traditional limitations.

The state action restriction simply doesn't make sense of the living Constitution, as expressed in the landmark statutes. As we shall see, the Warren Court understood this point. It was on the verge of dispatching the state action doctrine in its 1964 decision in *Bell v. Maryland*—but it refrained at the last minute since Congress was poised to take leadership on this issue with the Civil Rights Act. The current legal community uses *Bell*'s deference to Congress as an excuse for pretending that the state action doctrine of the nineteenth century remains intact.

A new canon for the twenty-first century opens up a different view. We shall hear Humphrey, Dirksen, Johnson, and King develop new constitutional principles that the Warren Court, and its successors, failed to pass on to us. These political leaders placed the problem of *institutionalized humiliation* at the heart of the problem of racism in America. The practice of segregated schooling was just a special case of a more general evil—the systematic perpetration of "feelings of inferiority," to recall Warren's famous formulation in *Brown*. During the 1960s, the landmark statutes generalized Warren's logic by banning institutionalized humiliation in other crucial spheres of life, striking down exclusionary practices in public accommodations, private employment, and the private housing market. In taking these decisive actions, Congress and the president moved far beyond the narrow version of state responsibility inherited from Republican Reconstruction—requiring private actors as well as state officials to accept wide-ranging responsibilities to realize the principles of constitutional equality.

Recovering this distinctive concern with humiliation serves to introduce a larger aspect of the civil rights legacy—its effort to build a genuinely sociological jurisprudence. The Second Reconstruction didn't content itself with the creation of abstract legal rights. It intervened decisively in the real world to eliminate systematic humiliation. If the next generation is to remain faithful to this great achievement, it should reflect more deeply on the meaning of institutionalized humiliation and its relationship to law. My discussion in Chapter 7 aims to kick off this much-needed conversation.

I then move to another distinctive feature of the landmark statutes. Call it "government by numbers": instead of relying on the verbal formulae of the classical legal tradition, the statutes often relied on technocrats and numerical targets to achieve real-world egalitarian gains. At times this concern with hard-edged quantitative indicators clashed with the more qualitative emphasis on humiliation that also served as an organizing leitmotif; as we shall see, this conflict was most acute in the sphere of public education. But at a deeper level, concerns with quality and quantity expressed the same overarching aspiration—to bridge the yawning gap between the law on the books and the law of ordinary life in ways that made a real difference in social life.

The constitutional roots of "government by numbers" go deep, beginning with railroad regulation by the Interstate Commerce Commission in 1887. With the New Deal, major economic actors had gotten into the habit of submitting vast quantities of data to the Civil Aeronautics Board, Federal Communications Commission, Securities and Exchange Commission, and countless other expert agencies. But there continued to be silence on one crucial matter—the treatment of blacks and other minorities. So long as white southerners played a key role in the New Deal coalition, race issues were off the legislative agenda. But the landmark statutes of the 1960s blew the New Deal coalition apart, with northern liberal Democrats and Republican racial moderates joining together to break the back of racist resistance led by southern Democrats.

In making this breakthrough, the emerging civil rights coalition adapted the New Deal tradition of "government by numbers" to achieve their egalitarian objectives. Consider voting rights. Since the New Deal, the federal courts had been struggling to ensure black voting rights in the South—and they had failed miserably. If the Voting Rights Act of 1965 had continued in this tradition, it would have failed as well. So its draftsmen took a different course, specifying hard numerical criteria that pinpointed states and localities that had systematically denied blacks the ballot, and providing administrative as well as judicial mechanisms to force the polls open to all eligible citizens. "Government by numbers" did not merely play a technocratic function—it operated as a symbol of determination to get the job done.

This symbolic affirmation was deeply rooted in the constitutional culture of the New Deal. In the same way that a technocratic focus enabled the Securities and Exchange Commission or Social Security Administration to achieve breakthroughs in the real-world economy, the Voting Rights Act's exercise in "government by numbers" achieved a breakthrough in southern democracy. We shall see similar developments in employment discrimination and other spheres: time and again, government by numbers served as a token of constitutional seriousness in the rising New Deal–Civil Rights regime.

The courts played a complex role in this development—sometimes promoting the new regime, sometimes undermining it. But I reserve these complexities for Part Two, which will compare and contrast developments in four spheres of inequality marked out by the landmark statutes—public accommodations, voting, employment, and housing. Congress and the president, along with the courts and executive agencies, confronted different problems in rooting out systematic humiliation in each of these spheres, and used different mixes of legal and technocratic principle to achieve equal treatment in the real world.

This principled complexity, however, is not reflected in the one-size-fits-all formulae that sum up today's conventional wisdom. Current judicial doctrine increasingly focuses on state actions categorizing people by race or other "suspect classifications." If government officials avoid the use of such classifications, they can expect to evade judicial scrutiny. It's only the use of suspect categories that triggers a demand for the elaboration of a compelling state interest. These pat formalisms fail to do justice to the distinctive achievements of the Second Reconstruction, which committed American government to move beyond abstract equality and achieve real-world results in crucial spheres of political and social life.

But if I am right about existing doctrine, this only raises a further puzzle: how did it come about that lawyers and judges have managed to displace the central meanings of the Second Reconstruction?

Part Three answers this question by turning to doctrinal developments in two key (and interrelated) domains—public education and interracial marriage. In contrast to the spheres surveyed in the previous part, the president and Congress refused to take constitutional leadership on these matters at any point in the civil rights era. They raised issues that were too hot for the politicians to handle, and they were happy to let the Court take the heat as it searched for solutions that might gain popular consent. We shall follow the winding path pursued by the Justices in this quest—and show how their turn to legalism helped insulate them from political backlash that could well have destroyed their judicial independence.

Fifty years onward, reasonable people continue to disagree on the ways in which the Warren and Burger Courts resolved the paradoxes of constitutional leadership. But we should not allow these disagreements to divert us from one large point: there were many other areas in which the early steps of the Warren Court did *not* remain controversial but served to provoke a broad popular movement that expressed itself in the passage of the landmark statutes of the civil rights revolution. Chapter 14 reflects on the larger constitutional legacy left behind by Earl Warren and Dwight Eisenhower, Martin Luther King Jr. and Lyndon Johnson, and Hubert Humphrey and Richard Nixon as they sought to express the will of We the People. But for now, it is more important to reflect on a fundamental roadblock that prevents the profession from taking on this great mission. Quite simply, lawyers and judges have gotten themselves into the habit of portraying twentieth-century Americans as political pygmies whose greatest achievements cannot compare with those of their illustrious ancestors. I will call this *the problem of the twentieth century* and urge you to consider it as an urgent issue meriting sustained debate.

To see my point, contrast the conventional treatment of the Founding and Reconstruction with the New Deal and the civil rights revolution. Lawyers and judges have no trouble saying that James Madison and George Washington led the People to endorse the revolutionary reforms set out in the original Constitution, or that Abraham Lincoln and John Bingham did the same in framing the Reconstruction Amendments. But they currently deny a similar status to Franklin Roosevelt and Robert Wagner, or Lyndon Johnson and Martin Luther King Jr. It is not We the People but We the Judges who are given the starring roles in the stories we tell about these latter-day revolutions. Rather than studying the words and deeds of the nation's political leaders, lawyers focus on the remarkable ways in which the Supreme Court of the 1930s and 1960s managed to give new meanings to the texts handed down by the giants of the eighteenth and nineteenth centuries.

Yet the subtlety and complexity of this debate have made it easy for them to forget its basic premise: somehow or other, Americans lost their

constitutional voice during the course of the twentieth century, leaving it
to courts to speak for them.

Popular sovereignty is dead in America: this is the unspoken assumption
that guides lawyerly debate over the constitutional inheritance of the
twentieth century.

A bitter truth—if it were true.

But it isn't.

I do not deny the very real accomplishments of the Founding Federalists and Reconstruction Republicans. But the modern era doesn't represent a period of decline from the great popular achievements of the distant
past. It is marked instead by episodes in which America's greatest political
leaders managed to renew the country's constitutional tradition of popular sovereignty. Indeed, in many respects, the New Deal and the civil
rights revolution were more successful in generating broad popular consent for their radical reforms than their predecessors.

Begin with the obvious: We the People were represented in earlier times
by white men. It was only in the twentieth century that first women and
then blacks took a large role in constitutional construction. No less important, the Founding Federalists and Reconstruction Republicans won
the mobilized consent of their fellow Americans by the narrowest of electoral margins. Although they talked the talk of We the People, they barely
managed to walk the walk. It will never be clear whether the voters who
went to the polls to elect delegates to state ratifying conventions gave a
majority of their votes to Federalists or Anti-Federalists.[2] Similarly, Reconstruction Republicans had only a narrow majority of their countrymen behind them as they rammed the ratification of the Fourteenth and
Fifteenth Amendments through southern legislatures with the help of the
Union Army and a wide assortment of heavy-handed techniques.[3]

Contrast the New Deal Revolution. If there was any political movement in American history that spoke decisively in the name of We the
People, it was the Democratic Party led by Franklin Roosevelt. The New
Deal's repudiation of laissez-faire and its affirmation of an activist national government gained the mobilized consent of overwhelming majorities in every region and every class—not just once, not just twice,
but repeatedly, in election after election throughout the 1930s and 1940s.
While the movement led by King and Johnson never gained the same
overwhelming support, its majorities were far larger and more broadly

based than anything achieved by the party of Lincoln in the aftermath of the Civil War. Under any realistic approach to popular sovereignty, the twentieth-century revolutions represent greater successes than their eighteenth- and nineteenth-century predecessors.

The same is true when we judge these revolutions by their ultimate success. The Founders tried to build a stable Union of free and slave states that could jointly control the economic development of the New World. After staggering through a series of crises, this Founding enterprise collapsed amid the bloodiest war in the Western world between 1815 and 1914. The descent into civil war, moreover, was exacerbated by features hardwired into the Founding design.[4]

The central aspirations of Reconstruction were shattered even more quickly. Within a single generation, the cause of black civil rights had been remitted to the tender mercies of southern whites. By the early twentieth century, the Fourteenth and Fifteenth Amendments mocked the hopes of the Reconstruction Congress to commit the people to a new era of equality.

In contrast, the central achievements of the New Deal have now sustained themselves for seventy-five years. Social Security and the regulatory agencies of the New Deal have served as precedents for the further development of the activist welfare state, with Medicare joining Social Security and the Environmental Protection Agency joining the Securities and Exchange Commission and a host of other expert agencies that seek to check the abuses of free market capitalism.

By the same token, the Second Reconstruction has already stood the test of time better than its nineteenth-century predecessor. Fifty years after its passage, the Civil Rights Act of 1964 remains a centerpiece of the living Constitution; at a comparable moment in history, the Civil Rights Act of 1875 had already been declared unconstitutional by the Supreme Court. What is more, the decisive triumph for racial justice in the 1960s has set the stage for further egalitarian movements by women, gays, and the disabled over the last generation.

Nevertheless, the New Deal–Civil Rights regime is currently under assault. The Roberts Court barely allowed the Affordable Care Act to survive, and it has directly attacked a key provision of the Voting Rights Act, requiring Congress to revive the statute if it wishes to remain faithful to the legacy of the civil rights era.

Such decisions would be unthinkable if the legal community recognized the New Deal and civil rights revolutions for what they are: the greatest higher lawmaking achievements of the American people during the twentieth century. Only a professional commitment to formalism blocks an encounter with this commonsense truth. On this familiar view, the only way We the People can speak is through the forms specified by Article V. If Americans and their elected representatives choose to redefine their fundamental constitutional commitments in a different way, so much the worse for them. It is the form, not the substance, of popular sovereignty that really matters. Given the absence of Article V amendments, formalists are prepared to defend Roberts Court decisions that ignore the fundamental contributions of We the People of the twentieth century.

Part One confronts this formalist prejudice. We will be playing a high-stakes game. It is a very serious thing for the legal profession to tell a story of the decline and fall of popular sovereignty in America, when in fact the twentieth century saw its rebirth and revitalization. Not only does this story distort our past, but it impoverishes our future. If Americans have indeed lost their capacity to speak for the People in the twentieth century, why should the twenty-first century be any different?

This is the larger question raised by school of constitutional originalists led by Justices Antonin Scalia and Clarence Thomas on the Supreme Court. If taken seriously, their call to purify the canon by focusing exclusively on the 1787 text and its amendments under Article V does not merely reinforce the formalist tendencies already apparent in modern case law; it represents nothing less than an elitist effort to erase the constitutional legacy left behind by our parents and grandparents as they fought and won the great popular struggles of the twentieth century.

This book points the way to a different future.

PART ONE

Defining the Canon

CHAPTER I

Are We a Nation?

T HE TELEPHONE RANG, and a familiar conversation began. Since 1989, the State Department had been badgering me to serve on delegations to advise one or another country on its constitutional transition to democracy. I had refused, and refused, and refused: no junketing for me, no ignorant professing in front of politicians I did not know in countries I barely understood.

Once again I heard an earnest midwestern voice at the end of the line, speaking self-importantly in the name of the Special Assistant to the Assistant to the Deputy Assistant Secretary of State. This time, he assured me, it was going to be completely different.

The State Department wasn't asking me to help write a constitution in a language I couldn't read. It was inviting me to engage in a one-on-one tutorial with the great Akhil Alfarabi, a master of both the European and Islamic legal traditions, who wished to extend his understanding to American constitutional law. Nothing but mutual enlightenment, the cheery voice guaranteed: it was past time to bridge the fearsome cavern separating the great legal systems of the world. And they were asking for only a week of my time.

Why not? I asked, and soon I found myself, jet-lagged, greeting a smiling Alfarabi at an undisclosed location. After drinking endless cups of tea, we began a serious conversation where I always begin: with the written Constitution, starting from the words "We the People" and working our way to the end of the text.

A Dialogue

Alfarabi was indeed a master of the art of elaborating profound legal principles out of lapidary texts, and he listened intently as I presented the famous words left behind by the American Founding and Reconstruction. After a couple of days of joyful conversation, we moved into our final lap: the texts of the twentieth century. But Alfarabi was getting impatient, and a bit resentful, at my treating him like a brilliant first-year student. "How about changing places," he suggested, "and let me take the lead in interpreting the last few constitutional amendments?"

Truth to tell, I was a bit doubtful: for all his learning, he didn't have the foggiest idea of American history. But after all, I didn't have any idea of his country's history either, and that hadn't stopped us from having a great conversation.

Why not? I asked myself, glimpsing the ghost of John Dewey energetically nodding his approval. "We have reached the Twenty-First Amendment. What do you think it means?"

"Well, the year is 1933, and Franklin Roosevelt is coming into office—he's the one who announced the New Deal, no?"

I responded enthusiastically, as is my habit, and was greatly relieved to learn that the guy knew more about my country's history than I knew of his.

"And looking at the amendment," said Akhil, "I can see why they call it the New Deal. As a Muslim, I find it deeply regrettable that the ban on alcohol is repealed, but from the perspective of a lawyer, it's obvious that something very new is happening: We the People are demanding a sharp cutback in overly ambitious federal regulatory schemes. The larger constitutional principle is clear: the era of big government is over," Alfarabi said with confidence, for great lawyers never lack self-confidence.

Before I could figure out what to say, Akhil was moving on to the next amendment. "This Twenty-Second Amendment," he explained triumphantly, "only confirms my interpretation. It was enacted when Harry Truman was in the White House—wasn't he a loyal follower of Roosevelt?—and the text shows that the people are moving right along in the direction marked by Roosevelt's New Deal. In 1933, they repudiated big government; now they are cutting back the imperial presidency by limiting incumbents to two terms in office. There can be no doubt about the larger point: goodbye big government, goodbye imperial presidency—a New Deal indeed."

He beamed brightly, secure in his mastery of the interpretive techniques I had taught him when reading the great American texts of the eighteenth and nineteenth centuries. But I paused once again before responding, and Alfarabi raced ahead.

As he mumbled something about the District of Columbia, I glanced apprehensively at the Twenty-Fourth Amendment, prohibiting the states and the national government from imposing poll taxes in federal elections. This is the only modern text that hints at the civil rights revolution's preoccupation with racial justice. Would Alfarabi catch the point?

Yes, nothing escaped his inquiring mind, but his reading emphasized the plain meaning of the text. For the only time in American history, this amendment explicitly condemns wealth discrimination, and Alfarabi took the ball and ran with it: "If the government can't impose a tax when it comes to voting, surely it can't burden other fundamental rights of citizenship. So the key question raised by Twenty-Four is obvious: how to define the range of basic interests protected against invidious economic discrimination?"

"Never thought of that," I muttered, but Akhil was already moving on, and when he encountered the Twenty-Sixth Amendment, guaranteeing the right to vote for eighteen-year-olds, he began to connect the dots in the great American fashion. "What," he asked, "is the common thread linking the ban on voting discrimination against teenagers with the ban on voting discrimination against poor people?"[1]

His eyes darted forward to see whether the remaining amendments contained the answer, but he was shocked to find that he had arrived at the end of his journey. Almost a half century has passed since the enactment of the Twenty-Sixth Amendment in 1971, and the American people have added absolutely nothing to the text—unless you count an odd little provision, initially proposed in 1789, forgotten for almost two centuries, and then revived and ratified by the states in 1992, forbidding members of Congress from immediately raising their own salaries.[2]

"Hmm," said Alfarabi, "I guess nothing much has happened since the teenagers' historic struggle for voting rights. Nevertheless, I can now formulate the basic question left by the modern era of development: how can a weak federal government, with a chastened presidency, do justice to the People's repudiation of wealth discrimination and its ringing endorsement of teenage rights?"

"That's not quite how we Americans think about our twentieth-century legacy," I said gently.

"Really?" said Alfarabi. "Where have I gone wrong?"

"In taking these amendments so seriously and looking upon them as the source of grand new principles."

"But that's precisely what you Americans always do. The First Amendment doesn't explicitly guarantee freedom of association, but you derive this right from the principles underlying the written text. Sometimes you call it a penumbra, sometimes you call it an emanation, sometimes—as in the case of freedom of association—you almost forget that the words aren't in the Constitution. But you do it all the time with your ancient texts, and that's just what I've been doing with your modern amendments. Aren't they even more important, since they were passed more recently?"

"A good question, but no American asks it."

"That's curious," said Alfarabi. "What accounts for such blindness?"

"Maybe your brilliant interpretations suggest a paradoxical answer: if we treated the recent amendments as important statements of principle, we would be falsifying the great truths about the constitutional achievements of the twentieth century. You see, the New Deal did not represent a repudiation of big government but its sweeping popular affirmation. And the civil rights era revolutionized America's commitment to racial equality and wasn't centrally concerned with discrimination against the poor or the young."

"You may say anything you like, my dear Professor Ackerman, but if you will forgive me, you seem to be making up your story out of thin air. With the greatest respect, it is simply impossible to read the constitutional text to support your claims."

THE PATH TO MODERNITY

A funny thing happened to Americans on the way to the twenty-first century. We have lost our ability to write down our new constitutional commitments in the old-fashioned way. This is no small problem for a country that imagines itself living under a written Constitution.

Eighty years of false notes and minor chords, culminating in a symphony of silence—and the twenty-first century will be no different. When Republicans controlled Congress between 1994 and 2006, they provoked great debates over abortion and religion, federalism and the war powers of the presidency. But they did not try to resolve these issues through new constitutional amendments—we saw only failed gestures on matters such as flag burning and gay marriage.

When they got serious about constitutional change, they pursued the paths marked out by the New Deal and civil rights revolutions. They demonstrated their commitment to the right to life, for example, by passing a statute that banned partial-birth abortions. This law did not express the sweeping ambitions of the Civil Rights Act or the Social Security Act. But if the Republicans had continued to dominate the presidency and Congress through 2012, they would have claimed a popular "mandate" to enact a landmark statute directly repudiating *Roe v. Wade,* challenging the Supreme Court to strike it down.

At the same time, Republican presidents John McCain and Mitt Romney would have continued adding right-thinking Justices to form an overwhelmingly conservative majority on the Roberts Court. Depending on the accidents of timing, it might not have been necessary for the McCain-Romney Congresses to pass a landmark statute affirming the right to life. The Roberts Court might have done the job itself, denouncing *Roe* as "wrong from the moment it was decided." On this scenario, the McCain-Romney-Roberts Court would have followed in the footsteps of its New Deal predecessor—treating *Roe* in the same way modern courts have treated *Lochner* since 1937, as a symbol for a discredited era of unbridled "judicial activism."

Recent Democratic victories have halted this dynamic for the moment. The only question is whether the conservative majority on the Court will use its remaining years in power to stage a full-scale assault on the twentieth century.

The danger signs are clear enough. In confronting the Affordable Care Act, the five conservative justices thundered their disapproval of the New Deal's revolutionary reinterpretation of the Commerce Clause.[3] But Chief Justice Roberts lacked the courage of his convictions and devised an alternative rationale to support the statute, saving his Court from a dangerous confrontation with a resurgent Obama during an election year. Having avoided a high-stakes conflict reminiscent of the struggle between President Roosevelt and the Old Court during the New Deal, the Chief Justice has now renewed the conservative offensive—striking down a key provision of the Voting Rights Act. I will be discussing this remarkable decision in Chapter 14. It remains an open question whether the five conservatives will seize short-term opportunities to broaden their assault on the New Deal–Civil Rights regime before death and disability loosen their grip on power.

Whatever the future may hold, one thing is clear: don't expect big changes through formal amendments. We the People can't seem to crank out messages in the way described by Article V of our Constitution. Our writing machine has gone the way of the typewriter.

Why?

There are three possibilities: there is something wrong with the machine, something wrong with the American people, or nothing wrong with either. Conventional wisdom gives the happy answer: it's a good thing that formal amendment is so hard, for otherwise the Constitution would become a mess, full of details signifying little.

The happy answer is half right: yes, it should be hard to amend the Constitution, but there are plenty of different ways to make things hard. The question is whether the Founders' way makes sense.

My answer is yes and no: it made sense for them, but it no longer makes sense for us. After two centuries of development, America's political identity is at war with the formal system of constitutional revision left by the Framers. We understand ourselves today as Americans first and Californians second. But the Founders wrote Article V for a people who thought of themselves primarily as New Yorkers or Georgians. We have become a nation-centered people stuck with a state-centered system of formal revision.

This tension between state-centered form and nation-centered substance serves as the dynamic force behind the living Constitution. Although Americans may worship the text, they have not allowed it to stand in the way of their rising national consciousness. Since the Civil War, they have given decisive and self-conscious support to national politicians and their judicial appointees to redefine constitutional values through landmark statutes and superprecedents. The great challenge is to develop historically sensitive categories for understanding these developments.

Alfarabi is a creature of my own imagination, and our dialogue is purely fictional, but there are many flesh-and-blood thinkers and doers who actually believe that Americans are operating on the basis of the formal Constitution.[4] This has caused all sorts of mischief as they use the world hegemon as a model for their own constitutional arrangements—the fiascos in Afghanistan and Iraq are only the last in a line of formalist failures. Yet it is one thing to fool the rest of the world, quite another to fool ourselves. We won't be able to define, let alone resolve, our fundamental constitutional problems until we confront the long and complex transformation in American political identity that has turned our written Constitution into a radically incomplete statement of our higher law.

Begin by seeing the Framers as they saw themselves. Fifty-five men went to Philadelphia, but only thirty-nine signed the document. Almost all had forged continent-wide bonds during and after the Revolution. Time and again they had shown that they were prepared to die for the Union. Compared to the average citizen, they were revolutionary nationalists, and they proved it when they emerged from their secret meetings in Philadelphia to propose their Constitution in the name of We the People *of the United States*. In taking this step, they shattered the Articles of Confederation, which the thirteen states had ratified only six years before, in 1781. Although the Articles required all thirteen states to approve all amendments, the Framers declared that nine states would suffice. Going further, they cut the existing state governments out of the ratification process, demanding that each state hold an extraordinary ratifying convention unknown to its constitutional law.[5]

To appreciate the magnitude of these moves, compare them with recent efforts in Europe to follow the Philadelphia example. In 2002 and 2003, the Brussels convention hammered out a new Constitution for the European Union—only to confront the same problem their predecessors faced in Philadelphia in building "a more perfect Union." Like the Articles of Confederation of 1781, EU treaties required the unanimous consent of member states for any revision. But in contrast to Philadelphia, the Brussels convention refused to break this rule. It did not declare that their proposed constitution would come into effect if two-thirds of the member states consented, nor did it call for ratifying conventions to meet in each state. Instead Brussels accepted unanimity and allowed each state to design its own ratifying procedure. As a consequence, when voters in France and the Netherlands rejected its initiative in 2005, the entire project went down to defeat.

The American Constitution would have suffered the same fate if the Philadelphia convention had been equally respectful of established legal forms. North Carolina and Rhode Island played the roles of France and the Netherlands, flatly rejecting the Federalists' bold constitutional proposal and continuing their boycott even as President Washington and the First Congress began operations in 1789.[6] If unanimity had been the rule, these two vetoes would have set back the Federalist campaign for "a more perfect Union" for a decade, perhaps forever.

The Founding Federalists were revolutionary nationalists, but they were also realists. They knew they couldn't get away with a ratification or amendment process that was entirely nation-centered. As the High Federalist John Marshall explained in *McCulloch v. Maryland,* "No political dreamer was ever wild enough to think of breaking down the lines which separate the States, and of compounding the American people into one common mass."[7] As a consequence, the revolutionary break marked by Article V remained state-centered: central institutions could merely propose, but not ratify, constitutional revisions, leaving the final decision to a supermajority of the states.

Only the bloodbath of the Civil War gave birth to a stronger national identity. In contrast to the Founders, Reconstruction Republicans won the authority to declare, in the Fourteenth Amendment, that national citizenship was primary and state citizenship was secondary. With these words, the Republicans aimed to transform the Federalists' state-centered federation into a nation-centered federation.

This revolution turned out to be a paper triumph. It would be a very long time before national citizenship gained a central place in the living Constitution. For starters, Reconstruction Republicans failed to create nation-centered structures for future constitutional development. Instead they pursued their short-term aims by stretching the state-centered forms of the Founders' Constitution beyond the breaking point.

The crisis reached its climax when the southern states refused to ratify the Fourteenth Amendment, thereby depriving it of the three-fourths majority required by Article V. Instead of accepting defeat, Congress responded with military force—destroying the dissenting state governments, constructing new ones, and unconstitutionally keeping the reconstructed states out of the Union until they gave their consent to the new nationalizing amendments.[8]

These revolutionary activities led to short-run success, but they required such enormous political energy that they exhausted the constitutional ambitions of the Republican Party and the American people. Once the Fourteenth and Fifteenth Amendments were ratified by the reconstructed southern governments, the country's political attention moved elsewhere, and nobody was prepared to consider whether the new nation-centered understanding of American citizenship required a nation-centered system of constitutional revision.

The same thing happened in response to the presidential election crisis of 1876. The dispute between Hayes and Tilden was resolved through extraconstitutional means without confronting the larger question: did it still make sense for the country to elect its primary national leader through the fiction of a state-centered Electoral College?[9]

It happened again in 1873, when the Supreme Court's decision in the Slaughterhouse Cases transformed the great promise of the Fourteenth Amendment's grant of national citizenship into a mockery, virtually reading it out of the Constitution.[10] It would take much more than a formal amendment to make the primacy of the American nation into a living constitutional reality.

Too bad for us. If the Civil War generation had followed through, Americans would have been in a better position to confront the great crises of the twentieth century. At various points, we have been in dire need of nation-centered systems of constitutional revision, presidential selection, and citizenship entitlement.

There was a very good reason why the nineteenth century didn't help us out. Despite the brave words of the Fourteenth Amendment, nineteenth-century Americans remained uncertain about the primacy of their commitment to the nation. Everybody recognized that secession was no longer legitimate, but it would require the transformative events of the twentieth century before ordinary Americans unequivocally put the nation first.[11] The First World War, followed by the Great Depression, followed by the Second World War, impressed an entire generation with the need to address the great questions of war, peace, and economic welfare on the national level. The sense of American community became stronger with the next generation's struggle for civil rights at home and liberal democracy abroad. And it has been reinforced once again by the tragedy of September 11.

This deepening national consciousness was supported by broader transformations in social and cultural life. A century ago, the United States remained a European settler republic looking to the Old World for cultural leadership. Now it speaks to the world in its own distinctive accents—attracting and repelling, but very much the great cultural force of the age. America may not be a very civilized place, but it is a civilization. And its inhabitants find themselves at the center of revolutions in transportation, communications, education, and business, which combine to teach one great message: though you may be living in Montana today, you or your children may be making a life for your family in Florida or Oregon the day after tomorrow. And if you do put down roots elsewhere in this great country, you will find that, despite regional variations, they speak American out there.

No need to exaggerate. Even today, Americans don't think of themselves as citizens of a unitary nation-state on the model, say, of nineteenth-century France. We remain Texans or Pennsylvanians as well as Americans, but the textual promise of the Fourteenth Amendment has finally become a living reality: we are Americans first. As national citizenship has come to the fore in the living Constitution, the inadequacy of other state-centered forms inscribed in the text, and unchanged since the Founding, has become a very serious problem on those occasions when ordinary Americans try to redefine their fundamental commitments.

DEFINING THE CANON

This is the point of my fabulous conversation with Alfarabi. Since he is blissfully unaware of the living Constitution, he supposes that the official amendments express the key changes in America's constitutional identity during the twentieth century.

He has made a perfectly natural assumption. It just happens to be wrong. As a consequence, his interpretations are eccentric because every American intuitively recognizes that the modern amendments tell a very, very small part of the big constitutional story of the twentieth century—and that we have to look elsewhere to understand the rest.

But where? A blur of legal landmarks whiz by in the collective consciousness: the Social Security Act and *Brown v. Board of Education,* the Civil Rights Act and *Miranda v. Arizona*—the list goes on and on. Whichever cases and landmark statutes you might or might not add, I am pretty certain of one thing: all the texts you propose have been produced by national, not state, institutions, as befits the constitutional conclusions reached by We the People of the *United* States.

The trouble comes when we compare the cases and landmark statutes on our lists. Mine might contain the Administrative Procedure Act, but yours might not; yours might include *Roe v. Wade,* but others emphatically disagree. Is there any way to resolve these disputes, besides pounding on the table with increasing vehemence? Is it possible to elaborate criteria, rooted in basic constitutional principles, that allow lawyers and judges to separate the wheat from the chaff in a disciplined fashion?

This is the problem of canon formation. To state it crisply, begin with the idea of an *official* constitutional canon—this is the body of texts that conventional legal theory emphasizes as central. In America today, the official canon is composed of the 1787 Constitution and its subsequent formal amendments. But a yawning gap divides the official canon from the nation-centered self-understanding of the American people. The legal profession has been trying to fill this gap with an *operational* canon that promotes landmark statutes and superprecedents to a central role in constitutional argument. These attempts have proceeded in an ad hoc fashion, but it is past time to consider the problem more self-consciously and reconstruct an official canon that makes sense of the constitutional achievements of *all* generations since 1776—including Americans who lived in the twentieth century. Without a disciplined acknowledgment of the great legal texts of the modern era, constitutional law will fail to provide Americans the guidance they need as they confront the challenges of the future.

The redefinition of the constitutional canon is proceeding apace. The Senate confirmation hearings of recent Supreme Court nominees provide a telltale benchmark. Senators of both parties spent hours and hours trying to pin the nominees down on a variety of key twentieth-century texts—repeatedly asking whether they recognized *Roe,* or some other case, as a superprecedent especially entrenched in our law. The nominees bobbed and weaved in response, but the very questions marked a significant step. They suggest that the operational canon presently contains at least two components: one part is composed of the official canon, the other of judicial superprecedents. Like the formal text, superprecedents crystallize fixed points in our constitutional tradition: the Court has no authority to trivialize their significance as it goes about developing legal doctrine.

Indeed, superprecedents often deserve much greater weight than principles canonized in the official text. *Brown v. Board of Education* is a much more important reference point than, say, the Founding guarantee of "a republican form of government." While no Supreme Court nominee could be confirmed if he refused to embrace *Brown,* he could safely confess great puzzlement about the meaning of "republican" government and gain a seat on the bench—despite the fact that this textual provision was absolutely central to the Founding generation.[12] When we look away from our official theories for a moment, we see that the living Constitution is organized on the basis of an operational canon that does not accord primacy, much less exclusivity, to the official canon.

And yet we are presently reshaping the operational canon in a haphazard fashion.[13] Though the notion of a superprecedent has become familiar, we have not yet begun to consider seriously whether landmark statutes also deserve a central place in the modern constitutional canon. This will be a central thesis of this book.

My thesis isn't terribly novel: Abraham Lincoln repeatedly claimed that the Missouri Compromise should be accorded a "sacred" status comparable to the Constitution itself.[14] During the twentieth century, a series of important writers have called on the profession to treat major statutes, in Justice Stone's words, as "a source of law, and as a premise for legal reasoning."[15] William Eskridge and John Ferejohn have recently propelled this argument further in pathbreaking work that seeks to win "quasi-constitutional" status for "super-statutes" that have shaped the American legal tradition.[16] And Cass Sunstein has pointed in similar directions.[17]

I am taking the next step, urging you to discard the residual *quasi*s and other hesitations and grant full constitutional status to the landmark statutes of the civil rights revolution. Otherwise, our view of this great American triumph will be profoundly distorted.[18]

Sustained reflection on the statutes will not only enrich the ongoing enterprise of constitutional interpretation. It will also highlight the high stakes involved in the effort by Justice Scalia, and many others, to challenge the very notion of a living Constitution. We will come to see Justice Scalia's challenge as an invitation to cut ourselves off from the American people's great constitutional achievements of the twentieth century.

That would be sheer folly. I do not propose to worship at the shrine of the twentieth century. From the Founding to the present day, each generation of Americans has contributed to our constitutional legacy—some more, some less—and each generation has made its share of mistakes. But to cut ourselves off from almost a century of popularly driven change simply because Americans expressed their new constitutional conclusions through national institutions and not through the state-centered institutions envisioned by the Founders—*that* would be folly.

I want to emphasize the historicist character of my critique. For me, the "living Constitution" is not a convenient slogan for transforming our very imperfect Constitution into something better. While the effort to make the Constitution into something truly wonderful is an ever-present temptation, the problem with this high-sounding aspiration is obvious: there are lots of competing visions of a better America, and the Constitution shouldn't be hijacked by any one of them. The aim of interpretation is to understand the historical commitments that have *actually* been made by the American people, not those that one or another philosopher thinks they should have made.[19] On this key point, I am closer to Justice Scalia than to Professor Ronald Dworkin.[20] I part company when Scalia joins Alfarabi in assuming that the formal text contains the *complete* constitutional canon, thereby cutting himself off from the last eighty years of constitutional achievement.

Justice Scalia is not the only one making this mistake. Almost everybody does, albeit in a watered-down form. To see my point, distinguish two issues: canon definition and canon interpretation. The first seeks to identify the key texts of our tradition; the second, to figure out what they mean.

Almost all constitutional debates center on the second question. Some think that the grand abstractions of the formal Constitution should be limited to the particular understandings of the generation that enacted them; others, that it is up to the living to fill in the best interpretation of the First Amendment, the Equal Protection Clause, or the Due Process Clauses.[21] But both sides focus on the same official canon—the formal text running from Article I through the latest twentieth-century amendment. To be sure, the advocates of a living constitutionalism more readily grasp the significance of twentieth-century transformations as they elaborate the modern meaning of ancient texts. But they do so in ways that sometimes distort these more recent achievements, and they sometimes use the official canon as a springboard for elitist efforts to revolutionize American values.

Hard-line originalists, in contrast, lack the courage of their convictions. Perhaps Justice Thomas is willing to question the constitutionality of paper money, but I suspect that even he would find this prospect a bit daunting. Certainly Justice Scalia proudly declares himself a reasonable originalist and tempers his fidelity to Founding understandings when they are too out of line with existing precedents and contemporary realities. But Scalia lacks principles to explain when he will be reasonable and when he will be originalist.[22]

It is time to question the premise organizing these familiar debates. Rather than focusing myopically on the great texts of the eighteenth and nineteenth centuries, we must redefine the canon to permit a deeper understanding of what Americans did, and did not, accomplish over *all* of our history, including the part that is closest to us.

By taking up the problem of canon definition, we shall be preparing the way for a breakthrough in the current impasse over interpretation.

Once we get clearer about *what* we should be interpreting, the debate over *how* to interpret the canon will take a different shape. Many disagreements that sound fundamental today will turn out to be arguments over the proper weight we should give to principles derived from twentieth-century texts as opposed to those inherited from earlier centuries.[23] In contrast, proponents of similar-sounding positions may sometimes find that they have deeper disagreements than they had previously imagined.

If my proposal is adopted—and stranger things have happened—legal debate would take on a different shape. Nowadays, slogans such as "originalism" and "living constitutionalism" often serve as sound bites that advertise competing positions on a wide range of hot-button political issues. But a redefined canon would create a host of strange allies in the ongoing conversation that is our Constitution. Not that participants would magically come to universal agreement on the one true meaning of the reformulated canon, but at least they would be talking to one another, rather than shouting at one another, about the contributions made by different generations over the course of the past two centuries.

My ultimate aim, in short, is to deny that law is politics by other means and that constitutional interpretation is mere pretense. Since the time of *Marbury v. Madison,* our legal culture has managed to provide Americans with a common reference point even as they waged an unceasing effort to transform the constitutional baseline for succeeding generations. And if we allow this culture to disintegrate into a partisan shouting match, we will lose a great deal.

But we will never construct a solid foundation for legal interpretation by pretending that the American people have accomplished nothing important over the past eighty years. The life of the law, somebody once said, is not only logic but experience.[24] The time has come to build a canon for the twenty-first century based on the truth of the entire American experience.

CHAPTER 2

The Living Constitution

CONSTITUTIONAL HISTORY goes in cycles. Since 1776, each rising generation has looked up at the political heights to find that the government of the day was hell-bent on oppression. Time and again, the same response: organize an oppositional movement in the political wilderness, reclaim corrupt government in the name of the people, and redefine America's constitutional future.

In the beginning, the revolutionary cry was "no taxation without representation," but once the struggle against King George III had been won, the Jeffersonian Republicans were soon leading the charge for a second American revolution. A generation later, the Jacksonians were denouncing the Bank of the United States and its stranglehold on ordinary Americans—only to see their political hegemony destroyed by the rising Republican Party rallying the people against the Jacksonian defense of the slave power. A generation after that, the Republicans had become the spokesmen for the status quo, provoking a Populist crusade.

Something different happened this time around. Every great protest movement since 1776 had finally succeeded in scaling the commanding heights, but the Populists failed to win the Bryan-McKinley elections of 1896 and 1900, and a period of stuttering followed, with a host of middle-level movements achieving midlevel successes of very different kinds. With the Great Depression, New Deal Democracy broke through this impasse with its vindication of activist government. This decisive transformation frames the central problem for this book—how to assess the next great cycle of popular sovereignty that culminated in the civil rights revolution?

With each turn of the wheel, the oppositional movement proposes a revisionist diagnosis of the public and its problems—sometimes gaining massive support from the American people, sometimes falling short. Whatever the fate of particular movements, the cyclical pattern recurs and recurs—the brainchild of America's shotgun marriage between Revolutionary Enlightenment and Protestant Christianity.[1] The living Constitution is a product of these cycles of popular sovereignty—and sets the stage for our own generation's struggle to speak in the name of the People.

Our study requires careful attention to themes and variations elaborated over the course of two centuries. History is full of surprises. No cycle is an exact replica of any other. If we are to understand the real and existing American Constitution, we must put each cycle in the context of the others, summing up the constitutional conclusions reached by the American people over two centuries of struggle. We cannot blindly suppose that the formal constitutional text tells us all—or even most—of what we need to know.

MOVEMENT, PARTY, PRESIDENCY

Begin by reflecting on the great institutional divide separating the Founding model of popular sovereignty from the recurring patterns that have emerged over the past two centuries. The Philadelphia Convention did not want or expect presidents to claim popular mandates for sweeping constitutional change. This plebiscitary theme begins only with Thomas Jefferson and ends, for the moment, with Barack Obama.[2] The Founders' failure to foresee the rise of plebiscitarianism was entirely understandable: there weren't any presidentialist systems around at the time, and past history pointed to popular assemblies as the privileged forum for popular sovereignty. During the Glorious Revolution, it was the Convention Parliament of 1689 that spoke for the people, definitely not the king, and this scenario had just been repeated during the American Revolution as colonial assemblies rose up against their royal governors.

The Philadelphia Convention was part of this citizen-assembly tradition and projected it into the future.[3] One of the Founders' great aims was to prevent the presidency from becoming a platform for demagogues. They not only excluded it from any role in the system of constitutional amendment but designed the Electoral College to make it especially difficult for presidents to claim a direct popular mandate. Their Whiggish history had taught them that the great enemies of republics were demagogues such as Julius Caesar, and they were determined to block this particular path to tyranny.[4]

But when tested by events, their constitutional machinery shattered with spectacular speed. The ink was hardly dry before the partisan struggle between Adams's Federalists and Jefferson's Republicans destroyed the original understanding of the presidency during the election crisis of 1800.[5] This basic change is only dimly reflected in the revised election mechanics established by the Twelfth Amendment.[6] It involved the transformation of the presidency into an office that would episodically speak in the name of the American people and would claim a large role in the ongoing process of higher lawmaking.

The victorious Jeffersonians created a three-part pattern of popular sovereignty that would reverberate through American history. I call it the movement-party-presidency pattern, and its dynamic is at the heart of the living Constitution. Since this pattern wasn't anticipated by the Founders, we must study its development in common-law fashion, comparing each great cycle of presidential leadership with the others. There is no other way to understand how the American people have in fact sought to maintain control over their government over the past two centuries.

Movement, party, presidency—definitions would be helpful. The defining feature of a movement is its activists, a large body of citizens who are willing to invest enormous time and energy in the pursuit of a new constitutional agenda. Jeffersonian Republicans weren't blowing smoke in asserting that a "second American revolution" was required to save the Republic from the "monocrats" (crypto-monarchists) in the Federalist Party. Whatever you or I might think about their diagnosis, *they* really believed it; no less important, they acted on it. The same is true of Lincoln's Free Soil Republicans, Roosevelt's New Deal Democrats, and, more recently, Ronald Reagan's Republicans.

Which leads to the idea of a movement party. Most movements don't get off the ground, and most that do don't form a new party or colonize an old one. But as the Jeffersonians taught, a movement party can be a powerful thing, since it provides a home for conviction-politicians who view their election as a popular mandate for fundamental change. It also sharply reduces the costs of engagement for sympathetic members of the public: the party label tells them which politicians embrace the new agenda, and voting is an easy and obvious way to demonstrate democratic support.

Movement parties are in a race against time. Idealistic motivations fade because some problems get solved, others go away, and new problems arise that defy the movement's ideology. Power begins to corrupt movement politicians, and the party increasingly serves as a magnet for opportunists who couldn't care less about its originating ideals. The broad popular movement for constitutional change inexorably becomes a memory.

Call this the *normalization of movement politics*.[7] It gives added importance to the third element in the pattern: the plebiscitarian presidency.[8] By virtue of his strategic position, a movement president has the organizational resources to win the race against time by mobilizing a winning coalition in Congress in support of landmark legislation and by winning the confirmation of movement judges to the Supreme Court.

All of this defied the expectations of the Framers. Yet our twentieth-century experience requires us to confront it squarely, because it provides the key to the constitutional dilemma presented in Chapter 1. Our problem, you will recall, is that the formal system of amendment no longer marks the great changes in constitutional course ratified by the American people since the New Deal. I argued that this failure was the product of an increasing mismatch between the federalist framework of formal amendment and the rising national consciousness of the American people.

Given this mismatch, it no longer made sense to allow a small minority of the states—which might contain less than 5 percent of the country's population—to veto new fundamental commitments by sustained national majorities. If popular sovereignty was going to have a future in the twentieth century, Americans would have to develop a credible constitutional vocabulary that allowed We the People of the *United* States to address, and sometimes resolve, the fundamental questions tossed up by history.

Here is where my next thesis enters: precisely because the movement-party-presidency pattern goes back to the days of Jefferson, it provided a deeply familiar language of popular sovereignty that filled the void left in the public mind by the marginalization of the Article V system.

The movement-party-presidency dynamic that produced Franklin Roosevelt was the watershed—successfully legitimating the activist welfare state in landmark statutes such as the National Labor Relations Act and the Social Security Act, and in superprecedents such as *Wickard v. Filburn* and *United States v. Darby*. Since I have already explored this breakthrough in *Transformations,* I take up the story again in the 1950s, at the dawn of the civil rights revolution.

The rising New Deal generation had now reached political maturity. No longer radical reformers, they were leading members of the political and judicial establishment. Yet their memories of the New Deal legitimation crisis remained vivid and served as models for resolving the fundamental issues raised by the civil rights struggles in the years ahead.

At decisive moments, constitutional precedents set during Roosevelt's presidency served as critical reference points. We will see the old New Dealer Lyndon Johnson claiming that his landslide victory over Barry Goldwater in 1964 provided him with the same kind of mandate from the people that Roosevelt had won by defeating Alf Landon in 1936. We will see the Warren Court looking back to the New Deal's victory over the Old Court as it confronted the shattering implications of the Civil Rights Act of 1964. We will watch the entire political leadership—from Martin Luther King Jr. to Lyndon Johnson to Everett Dirksen—following Roosevelt in rejecting the need for formal Article V amendments to codify a constitutional revolution as they hammered out the landmark Voting Rights Act of 1965.

But as always, the institutional grammar inherited from the past did not survive unchanged. The challenge is to integrate the new and old elements into a New Deal–Civil Rights model of constitutional legitimation, based on a rich account of the institutional dynamics through which the American people debated, and ultimately resolved, the key issues placed before them by the civil rights movement. It is this model, not the New Deal archetype, that frames the constitutional dilemmas confronting the present generation.

The Question of Popular Sovereignty

Before proceeding to a blow-by-blow account, step back and consider the basic framework that will guide discussion.

Begin with the very idea of popular sovereignty—and its harsh treatment at the hands of modern political science. On the skeptical view pioneered by Joseph Schumpeter, "popular sovereignty" is a mythic fig leaf covering the harsher realities of elite rule. The masses are ignorant and manipulable.[9] At best, the democratic election ritual allows ordinary people to replace one ruling elite with another—sometimes because the opposition party's candidate has a more winsome smile, sometimes because the incumbent party has presided over a great disaster, and sometimes for no discernible reason.

This doesn't imply, the critics are quick to add, that they are bitter-end opponents of democracy. To the contrary, it is only their realistic view that permits us to identify the truly valuable function of regular elections. Although the voters may be lashing out blindly, the occasional upending of the political establishment is a good thing. It makes it tougher for the reigning elite to impose a hard-edged dictatorship on the masses—and for that we should be grateful, even if an electoral changeover merely leads to the ascendancy of a new elite.

But let's not get teary-eyed about democracy and suppose that the People (with a capital *P*) can do more than change elites from time to time. We should dismiss the notion that ordinary men and women can participate affirmatively in their own self-government. This mythic stuff isn't worthy of a high school civics class. It is not only bad political science but positively dangerous—encouraging politicians to present themselves as genuine tribunes of the people and demonize their opponents in a desperate effort to seize and maintain power. Such claptrap only makes it easier for megalomaniacs to destroy fundamental liberties, paving the way for a genuinely oppressive dictatorship.

To which I reply, it all depends on what you mean by "popular sovereignty." I definitely don't want to conjure up an ecstatic moment at which the capital-*P* People magically appear, speak, and then just as magically retire from the scene. The American Constitution creates a formidable obstacle course for transformative political movements, providing opponents with a series of electoral opportunities to challenge a rising movement's vision of revolutionary reform. If the system is working, these repeated challenges and responses will generate an extraordinary level of public discussion and awareness.

Even when public controversy reaches its height, ordinary Americans won't be on top of the ins and outs of the detailed debate in Washington, D.C. Nevertheless, something quite remarkable will be happening: a large proportion of the electorate *will* recognize that the country is reaching a constitutional crossroads, they *will* understand that the leading candidates for public office are pointing the country in very different directions, and they *can* explain the basic outlines of the collective choice at stake. Within this setting, popular sovereignty isn't a myth—ordinary Americans know what they are doing when they repeatedly support candidates espousing fundamental change. When these elected representatives come to Washington to carry out their mandate from the people, the result of their labors deserves an honored place in the constitutional canon.

This is, at least, the theory of popular sovereignty laid down at the Founding and developed further at later turning points in the life of the Republic. The question is whether the spirit of popular sovereignty was once again redeemed during the civil rights revolution.

One thing is clear: we can't find compelling evidence of constitutional achievement by looking at the formal amendments passed during the period. This was the point of my imaginary conversation with Alfarabi. If—and it's a big if—the Constitution continues to provide a credible framework for the modern exercise of popular sovereignty, we must look elsewhere: to the operation of the separation of powers between the presidency, the Senate, the House, and the Supreme Court. To see why, consider how this system can function to create the kind of mobilized public debate and broadly based decision making required for the people to express their will.

The key here is the staggered terms of office created under the separationist system—two years for the House, four for the presidency, six for the Senate, life tenure for the Court. This makes it virtually impossible for a political movement to ram its transformative initiatives into law on the basis of a single electoral victory—in contrast, say, with a British-style parliamentary system, where a single election can indeed generate dramatic changes. In America, however, a comparable movement must undertake an arduous march through the presidency, Congress, and the Court before it can legitimately enact sweeping changes. This means that a movement for radical reform must pass a series of electoral tests before it can gain the broad and self-conscious support required for any credible claim to speak in the name of the American people. Many have tried, but few have succeeded in sustaining popular support over this formidable obstacle course. I shall be distinguishing six phases in this dynamic process of popular sovereignty.

Begin with stage zero, *normal politics*. During such periods, the separate power centers established by the Constitution are controlled by disparate political coalitions with different priorities. Nevertheless, they share one large point in common: none is prepared to challenge the status quo. President and House, Senate and Court are all in the business of intelligently adapting the basic values of the regime to meet the demands of a changing world—sometimes finding common ground, sometimes reaching frustrating impasses. But no major political force is interested in challenging fundamental premises.

Neither are the voters, who look on at the wheeling and dealing in Washington, D.C., with relative indifference. Political junkies aside, they have better things to do with their time than follow the struggle over the latest farm bill or highway program. They sit on the sidelines while well-organized interests struggle over particular initiatives—supervised (one hopes) by moderate politicians with common sense and decent respect for the common good. This ongoing process of give-and-take simply isn't compelling enough to command much attention from ordinary men and women living beyond the Beltway. They may heed the call on Election Day and take the trouble to vote. They may even take time to listen to a debate or two, or scoff at a political advertisement. But the center of their attention is elsewhere—work and family, sport and religion, hobbies and vacations. These are the spheres of life that really matter, not politics.

Even at its most banal moments, there is another political reality swirling on the periphery. A glance beyond Washington reveals a host of movements calling on Americans to put aside their petty concerns and confront fundamental problems looming on the horizon. But few are listening, and even fewer are devoting significant chunks of their lives to the cause. What is more, there are lots of causes—each offering up different, often competing, diagnoses of the public good.

Little wonder, then, that normal politicians generally respond to the cacophony of ideological chatter with cautious gestures—no need to antagonize these folks unnecessarily, but the American public just isn't interested in screamers, thank you, and so let's get on with the business of passing the next tax bill.

Then the valence of politics begins to change. The appeals of one or another reform movement gain a decisive response from one or another institution in the separation of powers—the House of Representatives during Reconstruction, the presidency during the New Deal, the Warren Court during the civil rights revolution. This inaugurates the first stage in the popular sovereignty dynamic: *signaling*.

The signaling institution's assertion of the need for sweeping reform soon puts it at loggerheads with the branches still dominated by constitutional conservatives, requiring them to respond to fundamental questions they would vastly prefer to avoid. The initial round is often confused—one or another branch may choose to make concessions to the signaling institution, while others may issue blistering attacks on the false prophets seized with weird ideas who have gained control of a key branch in the separation of powers.

Federalism enriches the escalating debate. While Article V may be obsolete, the states play a large role in the national debate. Governors, legislators, and state courts will use their authority to advance or block the initiatives of the signaling institution; senators and representatives will vigorously press the conservative or reformist line that dominates in their districts.

Here is where the electoral system kicks in. The results of each passing election will lead both sides to recalibrate their institutional strategies and political rhetoric. Conservative victories may oust reformers from their signaling institution(s), returning the system to normal mode and resulting in a failed constitutional moment. But if the reform movement keeps on winning elections, the system will move into the *proposal phase*. In this, the second stage, the House, Senate, and president are finally prepared to pass landmark statutes that break sharply with the constitutional status quo.

This triumph changes the nature of public debate, concentrating the public mind yet further. The clear and present prospect of fundamental change encourages ordinary Americans to take politics with a new seriousness. If they don't like what they are hearing from their newly ascendant spokesmen in Washington, surely this is the time to throw the rascals out?

This gives a distinctive meaning to the next election—stage three in the evolving process. If the conservatives win, the forward momentum stops dead in its tracks, with repeal or evisceration of the landmark statutes a distinct likelihood. But if the movement for revolutionary reform wins big at the polls, I will call it a *triggering election*: the winners not only claim a mandate from the people for their recent reforms but begin to push other sweeping initiatives onto their action agenda.

This inaugurates the fourth stage in the dynamic, *mobilized elaboration*. Now that the revolutionary reformers have crushed the opposition at the polls, the separation of powers no longer operates as an overwhelming roadblock for further transformative initiatives. The rising movement is now largely in control of all the key institutions—House and Senate, presidency and Supreme Court. With its accelerating series of electoral victories, its claim of a popular mandate has a credibility lacking under normal political conditions. The movement's challenge is to redeem its mandate by churning out a stream of landmark statutes, judicial superprecedents, and (perhaps) formal amendments that transform its mandate from the people into an enduring constitutional legacy.

Such creative periods never last. Popular support may slacken as the reformers get more ambitious, and movement leaders may clash as they try to redefine the cutting edge of the action agenda. After an election or two or three, conservatives may begin to make an electoral comeback—leading to the next key question: how seriously should the lawmaking system take this backlash?

Perhaps very seriously. Perhaps it indicates a widespread popular determination to repudiate the very premises of the constitutional reforms that have so recently gained ascendancy. Or perhaps it simply indicates that the time has come to call a halt to the accelerating period of elaboration.

The next presidential election provides a critical test: is there a serious contender who advocates all-out repudiation? If so, and if he wins, the new regime is in deep trouble—its landmark statutes and superprecedents have not yet entrenched themselves into the constitutional culture and remain vulnerable to decisive acts of congressional repeal and judicial overruling. But if the new president has pledged his support to the recently constructed landmarks, the result is stage five, a *ratifying election,* which generates a collective sense that the old regime is a thing of the past. The challenge instead is to refine the terms of the new constitutional consensus in a further series of statutes, executive initiatives, and judicial decisions. During this *consolidating phase,* many bitter-end opponents of the rising regime transform themselves into new-regime conservatives. They abandon their effort to return to the "good old days" and try to structure the terms of the emerging constitutional consensus in ways that express their concerns. They are only partially successful, since the now entrenched reformers have a powerful role to play in defining the new constitutional settlement.

The system then returns to stage zero: normal politics. The partisans of the old regime have been pushed to the sidelines while the House, Senate, presidency, and Supreme Court generate furious disputes over secondary issues. With the old passions displaced by the new regime consensus, ordinary citizens return to the sidelines, focusing more emphatically on the pursuit of private happiness.

This return to normal politics is temporary—after a decade or three, a new call for revolutionary reform will echo through the land, and new leaders will confront the rigors of another long march through the separation of powers—signaling, proposing, triggering, elaborating, ratifying, and consolidating new constitutional meanings in their own voice. Or perhaps the effort will be blocked at one or another of these stages, generating a stuttering series of failed constitutional moments.

The question before us in the early twenty-first century is how to place the civil rights revolution within this recurring institutional cycle. Should we see it as a failed constitutional moment—and if so, can we locate precisely the phase at which it failed?

Or should we see it as a paradigmatic achievement of popular sovereignty in the twentieth century and give full constitutional recognition to the landmark statutes and judicial superprecedents that mark its enduring legacy?

CHAPTER 3

The Assassin's Bullet

FROM THE DAYS OF Thomas Jefferson to the days of Barack Obama, it has been the sovereign prerogative of a president, backed by a movement party, to place a revolutionary agenda for constitutional reform at the center of American politics. But things were different at midcentury: it was the Supreme Court, not the presidency, that initiated the great debate. The present chapter explores the many paradoxical consequences of this institutional substitution.

The Court's role was fundamental but limited. *Brown* served as a constitutional signal, provoking an escalating debate among ordinary Americans about the need for a Second Reconstruction. The Court couldn't win this argument on its own. *Brown*'s fate hung in the balance until President Johnson and Congress gave it decisive support in the landmark statutes of the 1960s.

This could not happen without a fundamental reorganization of American politics. A successful attack on racial segregation inevitably disrupted the reigning New Deal coalition of southern whites and northern ethnics that had supplied the Democratic Party with its governing majority.[1] Successful politicians don't readily give up on a winning formula, and so it is no surprise that latter-day New Dealers viewed *Brown* with trepidation. What overcame their resistance?

The civil rights movement is part of the answer. But constitutional structure and sheer accident were also important. As in the first Reconstruction, the assassination of a sitting president played a crucial role. The vice presidents who moved into the White House in the 1860s and 1960s pushed the constitutional process in very different directions—Lyndon Johnson to the left, Andrew Johnson to the right. These shifts affected not only the substance but also the form of the two constitutional revolutions: Andrew Johnson's move to the right explains why Reconstruction ex-

48

pressed itself through Article V amendments in the 1860s, and Lyndon Johnson's move to the left explains why the Second Reconstruction took the form of landmark statutes. Given the importance of the assassin's bullet, the chapter concludes with some reflections on the role of contingency in American constitutional law.

Chapter 4 follows the story from the rise of Lyndon Johnson in 1963 to the fall of Richard Nixon in 1974. Here we will find ourselves in more familiar historical territory, with presidential leadership replacing judicial leadership as the primary engine of constitutional change. Nevertheless, the distinctive politics unleashed by *Brown* generated important variations on presidentialist themes.

This will require a reappraisal of Richard Nixon's place in history. Court-centered accounts emphasize how his conservative judicial appointments slowed the momentum of the Warren Court's civil rights revolution. I will be emphasizing a different part of the story: Nixon will appear as a crucial agent in the consolidation of the New Deal–Civil Rights regime, placing a bipartisan seal of approval on the fundamental principles expressed by the landmark statutes of the new order and putting their repeal beyond the pale of political possibility. This allowed the American people to move on to other challenges with a confident sense that there would be no return to the old regime that governed race relations during the first half of the twentieth century.

NORMAL POLITICS AND ITS DISRUPTION

The Second Reconstruction was a product of generations of activism, which began long before *Brown* and continues onward into the twenty-first century. But this book does not try to contribute directly to this rich history.[2] It focuses instead on the two decades between 1954 and 1974, when ordinary Americans—white as well as black—centrally engaged with their national institutions to confront and resolve fundamental issues of racial justice. From this constitutional perspective, there is no gainsaying *Brown*'s decisive importance.

To see my point, turn the clock back to May 16, 1954, the day before Earl Warren announced his famous opinion. A glance at the Washington scene serves as a textbook example of normal politics. By the early 1950s, every major institution had embraced New Deal premises, leaving no obvious institutional opening for a serious challenge to its constitutional achievements.

Dwight Eisenhower was in the White House. The Republicans had chosen him as their presidential candidate over Robert A. Taft, aka "Mr. Republican." Taft was eager to wage a renewed campaign against the New Deal, calling upon the people to repudiate the Roosevelt legacy. But the Republican National Convention knew that an all-out attack on the New Deal was a sure loser. It turned instead to a popular war hero to break the New Deal's grip on the White House. Eisenhower's victory over Adlai Stevenson represented a final stage in the consolidation of the New Deal regime. While the Republicans had finally captured the presidency, Eisenhower's brand of "modern Republicanism" accepted Roosevelt's constitutional legacy. Indeed, his principal domestic initiative was the greatest public works program in history: the interstate highway system. While Harry Truman had famously desegregated the armed forces by executive decree, there was zero chance that Eisenhower would follow up by placing civil rights at the center of his political agenda.[3]

Congress presented a similar picture. The Republicans won narrow majorities in the wake of Eisenhower's victory in 1952, but Democrats regained control in 1954. Since southern Democrats controlled many key committee chairmanships, Congress would not be in the vanguard of any campaign for racial justice. To the contrary, it was the anti-Communist movement led by Joseph McCarthy that dominated the constitutional stage.[4]

The NAACP and its Legal Defense Fund had been hard at work for decades, but its steady stream of small political and judicial victories was hardly enough to trigger a massive national conversation. Normal politics in America is *always* a scene of intense interest group activity, with countless groups pushing mightily in different directions and jubilating in their small successes. But nothing in the postwar years hinted at the mass mobilizations that would soon be exploding into the national consciousness—the Birmingham bus boycott began only in late 1955, and Martin Luther King Jr. was just graduating from divinity school.

Within this context, *Brown* hit like a bombshell, forcing all sides to confront an issue that threatened to rip up the framework of normal politics.

Brown as a Signal

In calling *Brown* a constitutional signal, I take a middle path between legalists who exaggerate *Brown*'s significance and political scientists who trivialize it.[5] For legalists, the Warren Court appears at the center of the story throughout the entire civil rights era, leading a reluctant nation to heed, at long last, the commands of the Reconstruction Amendments. Political scientists are right to scoff at this judge-centered vision—*Brown* remained very vulnerable until the Court was reinforced by the constitutional politics of the Johnson presidency. But while *Brown* failed to integrate many southern schools during the 1950s, it did catalyze an escalating debate that ultimately penetrated the nation's workplaces, churches, breakfast tables, and barrooms in a way that is rare in America (or any other country, for that matter).[6]

Trivializers don't do justice to this point, but it is central. Higher lawmaking in America is never a matter of a single moment; it is an extended process, lasting a decade or two, that begins when a leading governmental institution inaugurates a sustained period of extraordinary political debate, and it culminates with all three branches generating decisive legal texts in the name of We the People. *Brown*'s role in precipitating this dynamic is a big deal. It ensured that fundamental change, if it ever came, would arrive not as the result of diktat from above but as the consequence of debate and decision from below.

But *would* Americans ever make a decisive break with Jim Crow?

Only one thing was clear: the political system would have a special difficulty answering this question.[7] When Lincoln and Roosevelt used their election to raise equally fundamental questions, their political parties had already gained sufficient coherence to carry the country in a national election. But now that the Court substituted for the presidency in asserting signaling authority, the parties would have to scramble in response to the profound constitutional crisis that *Brown* was generating.

The early advantage went to the Republicans. As the minority party in the New Deal regime, they had a golden opportunity to exploit an issue that could split the northern and southern sections of the dominant political coalition. As the "party of Lincoln," the Republicans could never compete with white Democrats in pandering to racist sentiment in the South. But they were well positioned to appeal to the burgeoning black vote in the North. During the 1930s, northern blacks had switched to the

Democrats in support of the New Deal. *Brown* put this recent switch to the test: Warren was a Republican, appointed by the first Republican president since 1932, and blacks responded by giving almost 40 percent of their votes to Eisenhower and Nixon in 1956. Throughout the 1950s, American voters—both black and white—consistently identified the Republicans as the racially liberal party, albeit by narrow margins.[8]

Although Eisenhower himself was unenthusiastic, the Republican leadership was broadly antiracist in orientation. While their main concern was to make economic regulation more business-friendly, *Brown* didn't require a wrenching recombination of the party's DNA.

Not true for the Democrats. When Adlai Stevenson campaigned for the presidency in 1956, he confronted the standard New Deal predicament. He had to attract the votes of both southern whites and northern ethnics (among whom blacks were only one of many significant groups). He responded by adopting a remarkably weak position on civil rights—as did presidential hopeful John F. Kennedy.[9]

A vignette from the 1956 Democratic National Convention brings the point home. Stevenson broke with the past by asking the convention to choose his running mate. Kennedy threw his hat in the ring along with Senator Estes Kefauver of Tennessee, who had recently gained notoriety by refusing to sign on to his colleagues' Southern Manifesto denouncing *Brown.* As a consequence, racist delegates flocked to Kennedy: "Bizarre though it was to see segregationists cheering on a Roman Catholic Harvard graduate, Mississippi's twenty delegates whooped rebel yells as they cast their votes for the New Englander, while Strom Thurmond's South Carolina delegation kept up a steady chant throughout of 'We Want Kennedy, We Want Kennedy.' "[10]

Similar party dynamics were on display as the president and Congress turned to civil rights issues. Though Eisenhower was personally lukewarm, his attorney general, Herbert Brownell, was a strong racial liberal. He not only made sure that Supreme Court nominees gave their unconditional support to *Brown* but also pushed a steady stream of racial moderates onto federal courts in the South. When the president hit the campaign trail in 1956, Brownell convinced him to endorse his department's plan for the first serious civil rights act since Reconstruction.[11]

Brownell's proposal was modest, but its passage was symbolically important: Republicans were once again reappearing on the stage as the party of Lincoln.[12] With southern Democrats threatening a filibuster against the specter of Yankee domination, Vice President Richard Nixon launched a preemptive strike at the southerners' scorched-earth strategy. As the Senate organized itself for business in 1957, Nixon addressed an abstruse constitutional question with very concrete implications: Since two-thirds of its membership carried over from its previous session, did the Senate have to organize itself from scratch? Or was it instead a continuing body that was bound by the rules that governed the previous session?

There is no right answer to this metaphysical question, but it was practically important. If the Senate was a continuing body, this meant that the filibuster rule, requiring a two-thirds vote for cloture, applied automatically. If not, a simple majority of forty-nine Republicans and northern Democrats could sweep away the two-thirds requirement on opening day.

Senate presidents had traditionally proceeded on the premise that the Senate was a continuing body. But Nixon stunned the South by declaring otherwise, opening the way for the smooth passage of Brownell's legislation.[13]

This created a big problem for Lyndon Johnson. As Senate majority leader, he had refused to sign the Southern Manifesto and alienate his northern colleagues. But he was also entirely unwilling to cut all links to his fellow southerners. Using all of his political skills, Johnson managed to deflect Nixon's assault on the filibuster through some parliamentary pyrotechnics of his own.[14] Yet Johnson's procedural victory only underscored the Republicans' renewed claim to racial liberalism: in the filibuster fight, Nixon was standing with Lincoln, while Johnson was championing the cause of southern racists.

Johnson could not afford such typecasting if he ever hoped to be president—especially since he had generally voted the standard southern line on race issues since his arrival in Congress in 1937.[15] Unless he could change this image, he would never gain sufficient northern support to win the Democratic presidential nomination. So after preserving the filibuster, Johnson reversed course. He went to work convincing his fellow southerners to accept "compromise" civil rights legislation that would have no serious impact on the real world of Jim Crow. To succeed in this maneuver, he needed key northern Democrats, such as Senator Kennedy, to put their seal of approval on his hollowed-out "compromise."

This put Kennedy on the spot. His state, Massachusetts, was a hotbed of civil rights groups, which lobbied fiercely against any compromise that would eviscerate the statute. But when push came to shove, Kennedy rejected these home-state pleas and voted with Johnson to fatally weaken the bill. His decision reflected the perplexities of all Democratic candidates for the presidency: just as Johnson needed symbolic civil rights legislation to pacify the North, Kennedy needed to reassure the white South by showing that he wasn't interested in a Second Reconstruction. At the end of the day, Johnson and Kennedy cobbled together a weak civil rights bill. But it fell to Richard Nixon to assume the mantle of righteousness in condemning the compromise as "one of the saddest days in the history of the Senate, because it was a vote against the right to vote."[16]

The political difficulties confronting future Democratic presidents were heightened by the southern backlash against *Brown*. Since the New Deal, there had been a gradual amelioration of race-baiting, with a new generation of southern Democrats emphasizing government-sponsored economic improvements such as the Tennessee Valley Authority and rural electrification and soft-pedaling harsh white-over-black appeals. But *Brown* provoked a strong pushback from southern whites, who repudiated well-known moderates at the polls.[17] The rising generation of politicians was quick to take notice. After losing his first election as a racial moderate, George Wallace swore that nobody "will ever out-nigger me again."[18]

The politics of border-state Arkansas served as a sign of the times. After Eisenhower famously sent the 101st Airborne Division in response to Democratic governor Orval Faubus's defiance at Little Rock, the voters of Arkansas rewarded their governor with a landslide victory. While racial liberals chastised Eisenhower for his obvious reluctance in taking military measures, the scenes in Little Rock reinvigorated historical definitions of the racial policies of the two parties: as in the days of Reconstruction, a Republican president was overriding the fierce protests of white Democrats.

As the presidential election of 1960 approached, *Brown*'s fate remained very much in doubt. Martin Luther King Jr., with the assistance of a timely order by the Supreme Court, had led Montgomery blacks to victory in their 381-day boycott of segregated buses in December 1956.[19] But his subsequent campaigns ended more equivocally.[20] In contrast, southern racists flocked to chapters of the White Citizens' Council by the hundreds of thousands, encouraging vicious acts of violence and waves of state legislation aimed at destroying black organizations. Massive resistance put desegregation on hold throughout wide areas of the South.[21]

The Kennedy-Nixon campaign did nothing to resolve the impasse. The priorities of both men lay elsewhere—most notably foreign policy, with each claiming to be the superior cold warrior. On the domestic front, it was the economy, not race, that commanded central attention. As the 1960 campaign reached its climax, Kennedy famously telephoned Coretta King when Georgia threw her husband into jail, and he used his (white) Democratic Party contacts to procure the civil rights leader's release. This gesture won black votes, but a single phone call was hardly enough to mark a decisive turn from Kennedy's "southern strategy" of the 1950s.

Election Day was a cliff-hanger. Only 100,000 votes—a margin of 0.1 percent—separated the two candidates.[22] If Nixon had won, he could have built on his civil rights record to encourage black Americans to rejoin the party of Lincoln.

Under this scenario, our hypothetical Nixon would have greeted the wave of sit-ins sweeping the South in 1960 as a great political opportunity, urging Congress to pass a strong voting rights bill that would enable black voters to create a powerful Republican Party in the South for the first time since Reconstruction. This achievement would also encourage racial liberals in the rest of the country to move decisively into the Republican column, leaving the Democratic Party to racist bitter-enders.

The presidentialist dynamics of the 1960s would have resembled those of the 1930s. Roosevelt's treatment of the labor movement provides a useful reference point. The New Deal broke sharply with the old regime by recognizing collective bargaining as a fundamental right.[23] Its statutory initiatives provoked massive unionization campaigns, with organizers marching under signs proclaiming, "The President wants YOU to join a Union!"[24]

Nixon could have responded similarly, pushing for strong civil rights laws that expressed both the principles and the political interests of the modern Republican Party. But for Kennedy, the Freedom Rides and sit-ins were a problem, not an opportunity. For the most part, he managed these tensions between northern and southern Democrats by focusing on other matters—the challenge posed by the Soviet Union abroad, the need to ensure economic prosperity at home through Keynesian tax cuts. There were no grand initiatives for racial justice during Kennedy's first hundred days—or the first nine hundred, for that matter. The classic movement-party-presidency strategy for constitutional change threatened political suicide for New Deal Democracy, as everybody was perfectly aware.

Things changed only in the spring of 1963. Civil rights demonstrations in Birmingham provoked a violent racist response. When police lashed out brutally against peaceful demonstrators, a wave of national revulsion led Kennedy to deliver his first moral condemnation in a television address. He followed up with a presidential proposal for a decisive legislative breakthrough on civil rights.[25]

Martin Luther King Jr. then brought movement politics to a new level at the March on Washington in late August. Standing before a quarter of a million activists at the Lincoln Memorial, King did not merely dream about the distant future. He presented an action agenda:

> There are those who are asking the devotees of civil rights, "When will you be satisfied?" We can never be satisfied [1] as long as the Negro is the victim of the unspeakable horrors of police brutality. We can never be satisfied [2] as long as our bodies, heavy with fatigue of travel, cannot gain lodging in the motels of the highways and the hotels of the cities.
>
> We cannot be satisfied [3] as long as the Negro's basic mobility is from a smaller ghetto to a larger one.
>
> We can never be satisfied as long as [4] our children are stripped of their selfhood and robbed of their dignity by signs stating "for whites only."
>
> We cannot be satisfied as long as [5] a Negro in Mississippi cannot vote and a Negro in New York believes he has nothing for which to vote.[26]

King is anticipating the concerns of the landmark statutes that would shortly establish the constitutional canon of the civil rights revolution: the Civil Rights Act of 1964 marks a decisive response to his demands to end Jim Crow in public accommodations (point 2 in the quote) and public schooling (point 4), as well as the Voting Rights Act of 1965, which swept away barriers to black voting (5), and the Fair Housing Act of 1968, which opened up the white suburbs (3). King doesn't explicitly target workplace discrimination—also a high priority of the Civil Rights Act— but recall that he was addressing the March on Washington for Jobs and Freedom.[27]

Despite King's rhetorical success at the Lincoln Memorial, Kennedy's support remained shaky. The white South had supplied his margin of victory in 1960. If he publicly backed a breakthrough bill, this would guarantee a lengthy Senate filibuster, full of southern denunciations, just as he was gearing up for reelection. All this sound and fury would be particularly toxic if Barry Goldwater became his Republican opponent and made his opposition to federal civil rights laws a centerpiece of the campaign.[28] Looking back, King later remarked that if Kennedy had lived, "there would have been continual delays, and attempts to evade [civil rights legislation] at every point, and water it down at every point."[29]

This was, after all, precisely what had happened to the first civil rights law in 1957, and it also happened in 1960, when Lyndon Johnson seriously weakened a House civil rights bill before he pushed it through the Senate.[30]

Indeed, it is precisely because he was anticipating further roadblocks that King did not stop with his action program: "I say to you today, my friends, so even though we face the difficulties of today and tomorrow, I still have a dream."[31] King's dream is a response, at least in part, to his recognition that the movement-party-presidency dynamic was stalled—at least until 1965, and possibly forever.

What, if anything, could break the impasse?

ASSASSINATION AND CONSTITUTIONAL CHANGE

The assassin's bullet: Lee Harvey Oswald created a constitutional space for decisive legislative action, opening a path for Lyndon Johnson to save the civil rights revolution at the cost of destroying the New Deal coalition.

There are multiple paradoxes here, but all have their roots in the Constitution's misconceived creation of the office of the vice presidency. The existing system of selection gives presidential candidates powerful incentives to balance the ticket by naming a running mate from a different region who speaks with a different ideological accent.[32] This means that an assassin's bullet generates a double shock: the nation not only mourns a fallen leader but deals with a replacement eager to push politics in a different direction. This pattern has repeated itself time after time: the progressive Teddy Roosevelt was, to put it mildly, an odd replacement for the reactionary William McKinley, and similar dislocations occurred in most other cases of vice presidential succession.

Reconstruction provides the most illuminating precedent. In 1864 Lincoln selected a southern War Democrat, Andrew Johnson, to balance the ticket, enabling John Wilkes Booth's bullet to put a racial conservative in the White House at a moment when Republicans were preparing their great leap forward after the Civil War. When Congress first met in December 1865, the Fourteenth Amendment wasn't a high priority. Republicans were preparing to use the recently ratified Thirteenth Amendment as a platform for a series of landmark statutes vindicating the nation's new commitment to equality. It was only Johnson's repeated vetoes that forced the Republicans to make the Fourteenth Amendment their 1866 election platform as they struggled against Johnson's fierce campaign to remove them from power.[33]

If Booth had missed his mark at Ford's Theatre, lawyers would be telling themselves a different story about Reconstruction. If Lincoln had remained safe in the White House, he would have proudly signed the landmark statutes that Johnson vetoed—and filled Supreme Court vacancies with strong Republican Justices whom he could count on to vindicate these statutes in eloquent judicial opinions overruling *Dred Scott*.[34] With landmark statutes and superprecedents on the books, it would have been unnecessary for the Republicans to go further and propose the first section of the Fourteenth Amendment. The Reconstruction of the 1860s would have looked more like the Reconstruction of the 1960s, with formal amendments playing a smaller role while landmark statutes and judicial opinions bulked large in the Republicans' constitutional legacy.

But John Wilkes Booth intervened, exposing the vice presidency's structural flaw at the worst possible time. Although Americans had voted for Lincoln, Andrew Johnson subsequently transformed the presidency into the great institutional foe of an egalitarian revolution. Once the presidency was lost, Republicans could no longer count on the Court to overrule *Dred Scott*. If they wished to secure the full rights of citizenship for black Americans, there was now only one way to do it, and that was to use their last remaining bastion in Congress to propose constitutional amendments that explicitly contained these guarantees.

Even these initiatives confronted formidable roadblocks. Article V required the approval of three-fourths of the states, and white southern legislatures were fully prepared to reject the Fourteenth and Fifteenth Amendments, thereby depriving them of legal validity. When faced with this prospect, congressional Republicans used military force and other desperate constitutional expedients to ram their amendments through southern legislatures. These heavy-handed methods contributed to the alienation of the white South for generations. Given the assassin's bullet, however, military reconstruction was necessary for putting the American people on record on the question of black citizenship.[35]

Now fast-forward to the 1960s. Kennedy, like Lincoln, balanced his election-year ticket with a southerner named Johnson.[36] But this time the assassin's bullet shifted the presidency sharply to the side of the civil rights revolution. While Andrew Johnson repudiated the egalitarian Republicans of the 1860s, Lyndon Johnson rejected Kennedy's conservative approach to race relations.[37]

Part of the shift was the result of personal conviction—Johnson simply had stronger egalitarian commitments than Kennedy. But the presidents were also responding to two very different strategic problems. For Kennedy, a Senate filibuster of a strong civil rights bill was a political nightmare, alienating white southerners just when he needed their votes in his reelection campaign. For Johnson, a filibuster provided a golden opportunity to demonstrate that he was not a stereotypical southern racist and deserved nationwide support.[38] As he put it: "I knew that if I didn't get out in front on this issue [the liberals] would get me. . . . I had to produce a civil rights bill that was even stronger than the one they'd have gotten if Kennedy had lived. Without this, I'd be dead before I could even begin."[39]

As the first southern president in the White House since Andrew Johnson left in disgrace in 1869,[40] he could count on a powerful "favorite son" vote from his native region even if he took the high road on racial equality.[41] With the civil rights movement reaching its peak, the new president joined with King to propel the Civil Rights Act into law on July 2, just as the 1964 presidential campaign was heating up.

Before exploring this exercise in presidential leadership further, it's best to pause. What to make of the remarkable conjunction that permitted a southern Democratic president to redeem the promise of *Brown v. Board of Education*?

MASTERING FATE

I have been emphasizing special institutional features that distinguish the civil rights revolution from earlier transformations in American history. The first was the Court's decision to push the race issue into the center of American politics—forcing the political party system to reorganize itself in ways that would permit Americans to express their constitutional will on the race question.

Republicans were the obvious change agent. *Brown* represented no threat to their traditions, and the party had a compelling interest in splitting the dominant New Deal coalition. But when Nixon lost in 1960, the constitutional order faced a deeper challenge. It was one thing for King to demand a breakthrough at the March on Washington in 1963, quite another for Kennedy and his Democratic Congress to deliver the goods without ripping their party apart.

Democrats might have responded to their political predicament by enacting another round of minimalist legislation, like the bills passed in 1957 and 1960. But given the rising civil rights movement, minimalism threatened to generate mass alienation. Movement leaders would predictably denounce the political establishment as apologists for racism; establishment politicians would respond with their own denunciations of extremism and anarchy. The escalating estrangement would threaten bridge builders on both sides of the divide. If King failed to achieve legislative breakthroughs, his Gandhian ideals of civil disobedience would have been utterly displaced by more radical appeals to black power.[42] With the movement taking a more violent turn, racial conservatives would have been in a better position to exploit white backlash, undercutting efforts by liberals in Congress and the administration to move beyond minimalism and enact breakthrough legislation that would visibly lead to real-world improvements in everyday life.

Call this the *political blockage problem*. Over the past two centuries, it has destroyed many democratic constitutions throughout the world— sometimes through the seizure of power by the extraparliamentary movement, sometimes through an authoritarian coup by the forces of law and order. But in America of the 1960s, this didn't happen.

Tragically, paradoxically, it was an act of violence—the assassination of President Kennedy—that eliminated the political blockage separating the movement in the streets from the existing party system. By replacing Kennedy with Johnson, Lee Harvey Oswald awarded the presidency to a man with the political interest and political abilities to make an alliance with another great bridge builder, Martin Luther King Jr., despite the damage it would do to the reigning New Deal coalition. Working together, Johnson and King managed to channel the energies of constitutional politics into enduring landmark statutes. While there would be plenty of violence and backlash ahead, these legislative achievements sustained the sense that the American people were the masters of their own destiny and could steer the nation onto a new and better track.

Yet the role of the assassin's bullet in achieving this precious victory raises disturbing questions about the very nature of constitutional order.

Indeed, is there any order at all in a system that depends on such tragic contingencies?

My answer is yes, but it cannot be discovered by looking upon the Constitution as an Enlightenment machine that can operate flawlessly without the ongoing creativity of later generations.[43] The question is not whether the passions and misfortunes of the real world will regularly disrupt this Enlightenment fantasy; they have in the past, and they will in the future. It is whether future generations can master the complex arts of statesmanship required to conquer fate and reinvigorate the Founding tradition of popular sovereignty—or whether they will allow these tragedies to overwhelm them and permit the tradition to degenerate in a destructive cycle that undermines the confidence of Americans that they can indeed govern themselves.

When judged by this standard, the civil rights era should count as one of the greatest successes in American constitutional history—greater by far than the nineteenth-century Reconstruction that gave us the Fourteenth and Fifteenth Amendments. The Republicans of the 1860s also conquered fate by enacting the Fourteenth and Fifteenth Amendments despite the shattering consequences of an assassin's bullet. But their use of constitutionally irregular methods, including military occupation, greatly contributed to the white backlash that followed. In contrast, the leaders of the 1960s managed to achieve a more lasting sense of constitutional legitimacy despite the alienating outbreaks of violence that threatened to tear the country apart.

There was nothing inevitable about this. Our next task is to consider how Americans avoided constitutional disintegration. We will be following the institutional dynamic through which political leaders, in dialogue with the voters, built up a more constructive alternative. Step by step, Democrats and Republicans in Congress and the presidency, together with civil rights activists and ordinary voters, created a constitutional framework through which the American people gave their sustained and self-conscious consent to a series of landmark statutes marking an egalitarian breakthrough.

The study of this institutional process provides the best argument for my larger thesis, urging the full acceptance of the landmark statutes of the civil rights era into the constitutional canon. If we honor the Fourteenth and Fifteenth Amendments, we should honor these landmark statutes even more. They were hammered out in a way that was far more inclusive and

democratic than their nineteenth-century predecessors. They did not involve the exclusion of the southern states from Congress, or the southern
ratification of the amendments under northern military occupation. They
represent a far more authentic expression of popular sovereignty than anything the previous century has to offer.

CHAPTER 4

The New Deal Transformed

In framing their debates and decisions on civil rights, Americans relied heavily on the patterns of constitutional legitimation built up during the New Deal Revolution.

This was hardly surprising. Most participants had lived through the dramatic political and institutional standoffs of the 1930s. They vividly recalled Roosevelt's Hundred Days, the Old Court's dramatic invalidation of the National Industrial Recovery Act, the New Deal's second wave of landmark statutes, and the Court's retreat in response to Roosevelt's sweeping victory of 1936. These memories provided constitutional paradigms that guided their own generational struggle over civil rights.

History never repeats itself. While collective memories of the 1930s provided constitutional reference points, two variations on New Deal themes appear and reappear throughout the Johnson and Nixon presidencies.

Both have their roots in the Warren Court's initial act of leadership. While the New Dealers confronted a hostile Supreme Court, the rising civil rights coalition had the opposite problem: even when the president and Congress were ready to take constitutional leadership, the Court was reluctant to cede its primacy. This sometimes led to forms of political-judicial struggle that were very different from anything seen in previous periods of American history.

No less important, the Court's early leadership split the New Deal coalition, requiring President Johnson and Martin Luther King Jr. to reach out to liberal Republicans to pass the landmark statutes of the civil rights era. The need to construct a bipartisan coalition of liberal Democrats and modern Republicans contrasts sharply with the classic movement-party-presidency dynamic on display during the New Deal revolution. During the 1930s Roosevelt integrated the labor movement into the Democrats' struggle against a Republican Party and Supreme Court initially committed

63

to the old regime. In contrast, the mediating institution of a movement party was absent during the 1960s. While there was plenty of presidential leadership and a powerful mass movement, it would take lots of creative statecraft to channel all this energy into landmark legislation. Nevertheless, the protagonists proved equal to the challenge, with Nixon and his liberal Congress codifying Johnson-era breakthroughs in ways that made the landmark statutes an enduring part of America's constitutional legacy.

But we are getting ahead of ourselves. Let's pick up the story at the point where Lyndon Johnson assumes the presidency.

PHASE TWO: PROPOSAL

The new president wasted no time. Five days after Kennedy's assassination, he went before Congress to commit himself to his predecessor's project.

But what precisely was that project?

> No memorial oration or eulogy could more eloquently honor President Kennedy's memory than the earliest possible passage of the civil rights bill for which he fought so long. We have talked long enough in this country about equal rights. We have talked for one hundred years or more. It is time now to write the next chapter, and to write it in the books of law.
>
> I urge you again, as I did in 1957 and again in 1960, to enact a civil rights law so that we can move forward to eliminate from this Nation every trace of discrimination and oppression that is based upon race or color. There could be no greater source of strength to this Nation both at home and abroad.[1]

In Johnson's telling, civil rights was Kennedy's highest domestic priority. This was pious mystification, but the message was clear: after a decade of procrastination and half measures, the presidency was prepared to take constitutional leadership in civil rights.[2]

Or was it?

Johnson's speech proudly recalled his role in leading the Senate to enact civil rights legislation in 1957 and 1960. But there was a darker side to Johnson's Senate record. On both occasions he had weakened the strong civil rights bill coming out of the House—rendering it palatable to his fellow southerners, who were threatening to filibuster it to death.[3] On both occasions House Republicans had reacted bitterly, and for good reason: they had taken political heat in joining liberal House Democrats in support of a strong bill, and then they saw the Democrat Johnson betraying them in the Senate while hypocritically presenting himself as a heroic leader in the civil rights struggle. What chutzpah!

Never again, declared William McCulloch, the pivotal House Republican on civil rights.[4] While he was prepared to join liberal Democrats to back a breakthrough bill, he wanted a guarantee against a repeat of Johnson's performances in 1957 and 1960. He demanded the right to veto any future Senate "compromise" that represented yet another capitulation to southern Democrats. This was a truly extraordinary request: I can't think of another case in which a member of the minority party in the House claimed the right to control the terms of a bipartisan deal in the Senate.

Nevertheless, the administration accepted this remarkable demand.[5] As we have seen, Johnson had a very different strategy for winning the upcoming election than Kennedy had. He could still count on much of the South to deliver for its favorite son, and he hoped that a breakthrough Civil Rights Act would provide compelling evidence to the North that he was not just another southern racist. Not only was McCulloch's support essential for this strategy to succeed in the House, but it also served as a preliminary to the main act—persuading Everett McKinley Dirksen, the Republican minority leader, to break the inevitable southern filibuster of a strong civil rights bill.

This would be tough but not impossible: though Dirksen was not as committed to modern Republicanism as Eisenhower and Nixon, he very much identified himself as a member of the party of Lincoln. He recognized the legitimacy of federal regulation of private enterprise—especially when the states had fallen down on the job. With national polls registering 70 percent support for a strong bill,[6] Dirksen declared that a landmark statute represented an "idea whose time had come."[7] Collaborating with McCulloch, he struck a "compromise" with the Democratic leadership that represented a decisive breakthrough. "Who would have thought a year ago that this could happen?" asked Attorney General Robert Kennedy as the bill headed for passage.[8]

Constitutional leadership had decisively passed from the Court to the presidency and Congress, with the New Deal experience providing the key precedents. In 1936, Roosevelt had returned to the people with a series of landmark statutes that expressed a new constitutional vision of activist government, including the National Labor Relations Act, the Social Security Act, and the Securities and Exchange Act. This time around, Johnson came into the 1964 election with a single landmark statute, the Civil Rights Act, but one that included employment, public schools, public accommodation, and voting in a sweeping redefinition of egalitarian values.

If you will forgive my jargon, the higher lawmaking system was shifting gears—moving from the signaling stage to the proposal stage. By passing their breakthrough statute, the president and Congress put their fellow Americans on notice that the time for talking had passed and that the moment had arrived for hammering out a broad legal framework designed to endure for generations.

But would the voters agree?

PHASE THREE: A TRIGGERING ELECTION?

At similar moments in the past, there was a straightforward way to answer this question. Consider 1936, when the Republicans nominated Alf Landon to oppose Franklin Roosevelt, or 1864, when the Democrats offered George McClellan to counter Abraham Lincoln. On both occasions, the opposition candidates denounced the revolutionary proposals emerging from the presidency and Congress, and called upon the people to repudiate these revolutionary efforts at transformation and to reassert the basic soundness of the old regime.

In nominating Landon and McClellan, the opposition party played a crucial function in the dynamic of higher lawmaking. If it had chosen me-too candidates who embraced the radical initiatives of the rising regime, the voters would have been deprived of a crucial choice, leaving it to political elites, not We the People, to wheel and deal their way to a new settlement.

The opposition party rose to the occasion again in 1964: the Republicans nominated Barry Goldwater, who denounced the Civil Rights Act and urged the American people to repudiate it as unconstitutional. But this nomination occurred only with great difficulty.

During earlier cycles, the party out of power had previously been the dominant party of the previous regime: the Democrats before 1860, the Republicans before 1932. But after the first term of the movement-party presidencies of Lincoln and Roosevelt, establishment Democrats (nineteenth century) and establishment Republicans (twentieth century) were fighting for their political lives, and they knew it. It's no surprise that they chose presidential candidates who urged the people to repudiate the revolutionary initiatives streaming out of Washington, D.C., and return (as much as possible) to the tried-and-true ways of the past.

The party dynamic was different in the 1960s. With the Court and the civil rights movement taking the lead, both parties were split on the proper way to respond. I have been emphasizing the threat to the Democratic Party of the New Deal, but the civil rights movement was also splitting the Republican Party, with libertarian Goldwaterites squaring off against modern Republicans who endorsed the need for a federal breakthrough. If Republicans had rejected Goldwater for a me-too candidate, the voters would have lost a critical opportunity to choose between fundamental change and the status quo.

As the campaign began, this me-too scenario seemed to be unfolding. The early favorite was Nelson Rockefeller, an emphatic racial liberal who came to the table with lots of political assets. Not only had he piled up an impressive record as governor of New York, but he was also a Rockefeller—whose campaign contributions had built up a national network of supporters over the years. He was prepared to spend even more lavishly in an all-out effort to win.

But his forward motion was disrupted by his divorce and quick remarriage, generating a scandal that alienated many Republican traditionalists. Just as the moralizing was dying down, news of the birth of the Rockefellers' first child revived the scandal at the worst possible time—hitting the front pages when Rockefeller and Goldwater were bitterly contesting the crucial California primary.[9] Goldwater's victory there gained him the nomination and provided the American people with "a choice, not an echo," on the Civil Rights Act.

Perhaps Goldwater would have come out on top even if his rival had not defeated himself by scandalizing traditionalists—the neoconservative movement was already on the rise, and its mobilized followers might well have overcome Rockefeller's establishment connections and megadollars. My point is to emphasize the exceptional fragility of the higher lawmaking dynamics that prevailed during the civil rights revolution. Since the movement-party presidencies of Lincoln and Roosevelt had taken the lead in shaping the rising constitutional agenda, the succeeding presidential election provided an obvious focal point for the opposition party to make a desperate appeal to the people to halt the juggernaut before it was too late. But in the 1960s the rising movement had split both parties, leaving it open for the Republicans to nominate either a Nelson Rockefeller or a Barry Goldwater.

The die was cast on June 18, 1964. Ignoring the pleas of Everett Dirksen, Goldwater rose on the Senate floor to denounce the Civil Rights Act, which was triumphantly moving to final passage. In a speech reported on front pages throughout the nation, Goldwater's real enemy turned out to be New Deal constitutionalism. He saw the new statutory effort to regulate "private enterprise in the area of so-called public accommodations and . . . employment" as another step down the road to serfdom.[10] Goldwater condemned it as flatly unconstitutional. On his view, only a formal constitutional amendment, ratified by the states under Article V, could legitimate this radical expansion of activist national government.[11] This hard-line position would have doomed the civil rights movement to failure, since Article V gave thirteen southern legislatures a veto. But in Goldwater's view, that was a price worth paying for protection against the looming Leviathan.

Lyndon Johnson presented a starkly different vision. With only a week remaining before the election, he traveled to the progressive southern city of Memphis, Tennessee, to define the mandate he was seeking from the American people. He began by defending classic New Deal programs from Goldwater's assault, and then turned to the future:

> The settled issues of the 1930's are not the issues of the 1960's, and that is really the choice you have to make. Do you want to go back to the thirties or do you want to go forward with the sixties? . . .
>
> If I take my compass or my ruler and take a direct line down the center of this crowd and divide you, we can do little; but united, as we are, there is little that we cannot do. And you know one of the things that I think we ought to do, and I say this as a man that has spent all of his life and cast his every vote in Texas, and as the grandson of two Confederate veterans, I think one of the things that we are going to have to do is wipe away the Mason-Dixon line across our politics.
>
> And because we are good people and because we are fair people, and because we are just people, and because we believe in the Good Book, we are going to have to follow the Golden Rule, "Do unto others as you would have them do unto you," and when we do that, we are going to wipe away the color line across our opportunity.
>
> The mandate of this election is going to be a mandate to unite this Nation. It is going to be a mandate to bind up our wounds and to heal our history, and to make this Nation whole as one nation, as one people, indivisible, under God.[12]

The dynamic of debate was leading Johnson to transcend the limits of the New Deal regime. With Goldwater attacking Social Security as well as the Civil Rights Act, Johnson was urging Americans to move beyond the 1930s and break down the racial barriers that New Dealers had accepted as a price for social progress in the 1930s.[13] As he later explained: "If Goldwater wants to give the voters a choice, I concluded, then we'll give them a *real* choice. . . . We were now engaged in a colossal debate over the very principles of our system of government."[14]

Barry Goldwater was also up-front in his campaign for a sweeping mandate from the people. Ever since Roosevelt crushed Landon in 1936, Republicans had nominated a series of me-too candidates who accepted basic New Deal premises—Wendell Willkie, Thomas Dewey, Eisenhower, and Nixon. These modern Republicans earned nothing but Goldwater's contempt.[15] His aim was to lead the people to reverse the New Deal and embrace classical Republican principles of limited powers and laissez-faire.

The living Constitution was passing a vital test: the presidential candidates were talking to each other, rather than past each other, on the great issues that divided them. And it was providing the nation with a benchmark—the New Deal landslide of 1936—for determining whether one side had won the argument decisively.

These basic points reveal a breach between the practice and theory of modern American constitutionalism. As a matter of real-world practice, each presidential election inexorably generates a great popular debate about the nature of the winner's "popular mandate"—with some denying the new president has won any mandate at all, others exaggerating its scope. But you would never guess this from the writings of constitutional lawyers, who never confront the notion of a "mandate," much less try to apply it in a disciplined fashion to particular elections.

This is a shame, since we can't even begin to assess the canonical status of the landmark statutes of the era without confronting Lyndon Johnson's landslide victory. Does it represent, like the Democratic triumph of 1936, the kind of "triggering election" that is central to the modern practice of popular sovereignty in America?

AN ELECTORAL MANDATE?

It is easy to be skeptical of the very idea that national elections can trigger popular mandates.[16] After all, voters always have a variety of disparate concerns. Yet talk of a "popular mandate" for one or another "break-through initiative" seems to falsify this point.

Call it the bundling problem: for example, Goldwater not only opposed the Civil Rights Act but also rejected the Great Society's vision of economic justice. Johnson responded by bringing foreign policy into the mix, portraying Goldwater as a "trigger-happy" militarist.[17]

Issue bundling leads to skepticism. If many Americans were using their ballots in 1964 to support Johnson's promise of prudent moderation in foreign affairs, it seems wrongheaded to view the Democratic landslide as a mandate for racial justice.

Despite its intuitive appeal, I reject the bundling objection. It is too broad legally and too shallow philosophically.

On the legal side, notice that bundling doesn't only challenge modern forms of constitutional revision through presidential leadership. It is equally troublesome when it comes to Article V amendments: voters generally don't focus on candidates' positions on potential amendments when casting ballots for Congress or state legislatures. They concentrate instead on a host of other issues. Yet the official canon treats a new formal amendment as an unproblematic expression of We the People.

Which leads to a deeper point. Some constitutional systems do indeed respond to the bundling objection by trying to remove the resolution of constitutional matters from the hands of elected politicians. Since the Progressive era, special referendum procedures have become a familiar part of state constitutional practice—and a fixture in many foreign countries as well. But the American Constitution is different. When operating in its federal mode (under Article V) or in its national mode (under the living Constitution), the system leaves it to our political representatives to determine when the time is ripe to hammer out enduring constitutional texts in the name of the people. When the system is operating in the federal mode, these texts take the form of Article V amendments; when operating in the national mode, the canon is constituted by landmark statutes and superprecedents. To put the point in a single sentence, the American system relies on the forms of *representative* democracy, not *plebiscitary* democracy, to determine the credibility of a popular mandate.

Direct and representative systems have different strengths and weaknesses, but both face the same problem—talk is cheap, and it is all too easy for elected politicians to claim a mandate from the people under inappropriate conditions.[18] As a consequence, the rival systems make it hard for political claims of a mandate to gain institutional credibility. But they try to achieve this result in different ways.

Under the direct system, mandates are tested through a specially structured referendum procedure that gives voters the final say. Under the representative system, mandates are tested through the operation of the separation or division of powers. Ordinarily, different political coalitions are dominant in the different branches and the different regions of the country, but if the same transformative movement keeps winning elections long enough, it will dominate the federal or national system so decisively as to speak credibly in the name of the people.

The American Constitution is firmly committed to the representative system and imposes rigorous tests on a reform movement before it can earn the authority to claim a mandate. When operating in its federal mode, the classic system requires the movement to win the support of two-thirds of both houses of Congress and three-quarters of the states to validate a formal amendment. When operating in its national mode, the living Constitution requires a movement to maintain its electoral momentum in the face of vigorous dissent by the conservative branches until finally the movement wins sustained support from all three branches of government, enabling it to consolidate landmark statutes and judicial superprecedents.

These two systems have different strengths and weaknesses. Under direct democracy, the questions put before the people in referenda may be misleading, and voters may be poorly informed about the real stakes involved. Under the representative system, political and judicial leaders will have a better understanding of the key issues, but they may express new constitutional principles in legal texts that diverge significantly from popular understandings.

Neither system is perfect—but that's life. While both can be greatly improved, my task is to interpret the American Constitution as it is, not as it ought to be.[19] From this perspective, the bundling objection is simply inapt: it falsely supposes that our Constitution seeks to test claims of a mandate by isolating single issues for focused decision by the voters. Instead, our national tradition of popular sovereignty tests claims of a mandate in a different way—by engaging the voters and their representatives in a series of elections, and awarding a mandate to constitutional movements that survive a rigorous institutional obstacle course that gives their opponents repeated opportunities to defeat their initiatives at the polls. The point of my six-stage analysis is to describe that obstacle course and determine whether the partisans of civil rights managed to make it across the finish line.

Within this framework, the landslide victory of 1964 had a very different significance for each of the three great issues raised in the campaign. President Johnson had proclaimed his War on Poverty earlier that year, in his State of the Union address, and so his landslide victory served only as an institutional signal that inaugurated a period of popular debate.[20] But in contrast to the civil rights revolution, the American people never followed up on this signal by giving the War on Poverty their sustained electoral support. The anti-poverty campaign was unable to sustain political momentum over the next decade, and its fate was sealed when its champion, George McGovern, was decisively defeated by Richard Nixon in 1972. From that moment on, the partisans of economic redistribution pursued their aims—with little success—through normal political means.

While Johnson's War on Poverty was a failed signal, his war policies in Vietnam had no constitutional significance whatsoever. Rather than proclaiming a new beginning in foreign policy, the president was seeking to reassure Americans that he would operate well within the bipartisan consensus established by Harry Truman and Dwight Eisenhower. It was Goldwater, not Johnson, who was proclaiming the need for a fundamentally new approach—and the voters sided with Johnson.

In contrast, the civil rights agenda was at a different stage of development. It had been the subject of heated debate in courts, in legislatures, at dinner tables, and in workplaces for a decade, and the conflict between Johnson and Goldwater over the Civil Rights Act made it clear that the country was at a turning point.[21] By winning a landslide on the scale of 1936, Johnson and his Congress were on solid ground in claiming that the voters had given them a Roosevelt-style mandate for moving forward with the civil rights revolution.[22]

This is my point in calling 1964 a triggering election. While it represents a crucial phase in the popular sovereignty dynamic, I do *not* suggest that it sufficed to transform the Civil Rights Act immediately into a central element of our constitutional canon. Despite Johnson's sweeping victory, it still remained possible for conservatives to beat back the liberal assault on the status quo.

But it became more difficult. Suppose, for example, that the Goldwaterites had experienced a remarkable political revival during the elections of 1966, 1968, and 1970—sweeping into power a new president and Congress that repealed the 1964 act and went further to repudiate the foundational principles of New Deal constitutionalism. Under this scenario, today's lawyers would look back on 1964 as a blip, representing nothing more than a momentary collective shock at the death of Kennedy.

This thought experiment helps refine the significance of triggering elections. Before the 1964 election, the great debate between civil rights and states' rights was in relative equipoise, with neither side clearly ascendant in the struggle for public support. But once Johnson and the racially liberal Congress swept the polls, even bitter-end racial conservatives recognized that the main current of national opinion was moving against them and that they had better turn back the tide quickly before it became the constitutional mainstream.

PHASE FOUR: MOBILIZED ELABORATION

At this point, the Supreme Court's response to the Civil Rights Act became all-important. If it had invalidated the act's more revolutionary features, Johnson, King, and their congressional allies would have squandered much of their electoral mandate dealing with the intransigence of the Court, rather than following through with the Voting Rights Act of 1965 and the Fair Housing Act of 1968.

This is what happened to Roosevelt: despite his decisive victory over Landon, he could not translate his triggering election into a great harvest of New Deal legislation. There was a lot of mobilized deliberation in 1937, but it centered on the president's attack on the Court—and for good reason. Unless Roosevelt managed to overcome continuing judicial resistance to New Deal breakthroughs, the constitutional crisis threatened to escalate out of control. The Old Court finally responded to this danger by executing its famous "switch in time," giving its approval to key elements of the president's program. Nevertheless, its post-election confrontation with Roosevelt deprived him of a great deal of political momentum.

In contrast, the Warren Court allowed the president and Congress to make more constructive use of their period of mobilized deliberation. This was no accident. Liberal or conservative, there was one proposition on which all members of the Warren Court could agree: that the Old Court of the 1930s had made a tragic mistake in opposing the New Deal, and that this mistake should never again be repeated.

The Court didn't keep the country waiting to make its message clear. President Johnson signed the Civil Rights Act on July 2, and the Justices accelerated cases that challenged its constitutionality, rendering judgment on December 14—only a month after the voters had given the president and his liberal Congress their sweeping victory. The decisions in *Heart of Atlanta Motel* and *McClung* not only repudiated Goldwater-style arguments against the Civil Rights Act but also gave the breakthrough statute the Court's unanimous endorsement.[23]

The appearance of unanimity was deceiving. Confidential records show that the Justices had real difficulties with the act. Their problem was *stare decisis*. In the aftermath of Reconstruction, the Court had famously struck down a public accommodations statute in the Civil Rights Cases of 1883. If the Warren Court followed this important precedent, it would have been obliged to strike down central provisions of the act.

To be sure, the Justices hadn't allowed *stare decisis* to stop them from overruling *Plessy* as it applied to education in *Brown*. But it's a mistake to exaggerate Warren Court activism. In searching the archives, I've found evidence that a narrow five-man majority was indeed prepared to eviscerate the Civil Rights Cases if this had been the only way to uphold the new statute. (I'll provide a blow-by-blow account in Chapter 7.) But Justice John M. Harlan made it clear that he would respond with a strong dissent— and others might well have joined him.[24] If the Court had announced a split decision, the dissent would have greatly enhanced the constitutional respectability of a ferocious campaign against the 1964 act.[25]

Here is where New Deal constitutionalism came to the rescue. Justice Harlan was an Eisenhower appointment—and like all modern Republicans, he had long since made his peace with the broad reading of the Commerce Clause inherited from the 1940s. He was prepared to join *Heart of Atlanta* and *McClung*—so long as the opinions relied exclusively on the New Deal reading of the Commerce Clause without challenging established equal protection doctrine inherited from the first period of Reconstruction.

Within the short-term context, it made sense for the rest of the Court to go along. By adding its unanimous voice to the judgments rendered by the president, Congress, and the voters, it deprived die-hard opponents of authoritative-looking support for their constitutional objections.[26] Nevertheless, in speaking for the Court, Justice Tom Clark treated the great purposes of the landmark statute almost as an embarrassment, remarking that Congress's authority under the New Deal Commerce Clause is "no less valid" when it is "legislating against moral wrongs."[27] Instead, he blandly explained that the act should apply to a remote restaurant because its owner purchased "$150,000 worth of food, $69,683 or 46% of which was meat . . . bought from a local supplier who had procured it from outside the State."[28] Whatever the pragmatic foundations for these banalities, they reinforce my main points: if lawyers of the twenty-first century really want to understand the greatest egalitarian achievement in modern history, they must look beyond the *United States Reports*. To learn the real constitutional aims of the Civil Rights Act, they must listen to the voices of Martin Luther King Jr., Lyndon Johnson, Hubert Humphrey, and Everett Dirksen as they hammered out this landmark statute in the name of the American people.

That will be the aim of Part Two of this book. For now, it suffices to emphasize the pervasive role that New Deal constitutionalism played in shaping the higher lawmaking system of the 1960s. Not only did the Roosevelt-Landon campaign of 1936 serve as the crucial reference point for Lyndon Johnson's claim to a mandate in 1964, but the Supreme Court's reliance on New Deal doctrine was central in framing the next phase of the higher lawmaking dynamic, mobilized elaboration.

To put the point functionally: In the modern regime, the Supreme Court plays a gatekeeper role in controlling the dynamics of the elaboration phase. If it tries to keep the gate shut, as in the 1930s, a lot of political energy will be spent prying it open, but if the Court opens the gate wide, as in the 1960s, the constitutional movement can spend all its energies elaborating its vision in a series of landmark statutes.

This basic point helps explain a striking difference between the New Deal and civil rights eras. Despite Roosevelt's sweeping victory of 1936, the pace of statutory achievement slowed noticeably during his second term. Landmark statutes passed between 1933 and 1935 continue to shape the living Constitution of the twenty-first century—think of the Securities and Exchange Act, the National Labor Relations Act, and the Social Security Act. But despite his landslide victory over Landon, Roosevelt couldn't follow through with comparable victories in his second term—largely because he was diverted by his court-packing campaign, intended to bring the Old Court into line with the New Deal.[29] Over the middle run, Roosevelt resolved this crisis by appointing a series of sympathetic Justices who decisively canonized the New Deal vision in a series of superprecedents.[30]

But the short-term struggle against the Old Court made it impossible for the president to use his 1936 landslide as a springboard for an ambitious series of landmark statutes.

Constitutional transformation proceeded at a different pace in the 1960s. There were only modest achievements during the Kennedy years, with the first great landmark statute gaining enactment only after his assassination.[31] But in contrast to the New Deal, Johnson's November landslide opened the floodgates for the passage of the Voting Rights Act of 1965 and the Fair Housing Act of 1968. While other factors contributed to this distinctive dynamic, it is easy to miss the significance of the Supreme Court's exercise of its gatekeeping power.

But we have not yet come to the end of our story. Despite the triggering election of 1964, despite the Supreme Court's green light, it remained perfectly possible for the American people to withdraw its mandate and repudiate the landmark statutes.

The key test would come in 1968. When Americans returned to the polls, would they pick a president and Congress that remained committed to the newly established New Deal–Civil Rights constitution? Or would they vote to turn back the clock?

PHASE FIVE: THE RATIFYING ELECTION

Once again, the New Deal experience provides comparative perspective. As they faced the presidential election of 1940, the Republicans had a tough choice to make: they could continue to wage all-out war against the New Deal or they could accept the legitimacy of the rising constitutional order. After a good deal of agonizing reappraisal, the party took the second path. Its candidate, Wendell Willkie, was hardly a Republican at all—he had been a registered Democrat as late as 1938.[32] Despite the party's gesture of accommodation, the voters gave Roosevelt a decisive 55–45 percent victory in November.

This was a good deal smaller than the 61–39 percent landslide of 1936, but the popular verdict was clear enough. With the Republicans withdrawing their implacable opposition to the New Deal, it was obvious that the American people were not about to return to the Hoover-Landon vision of limited national government. The vote of 1940 served as a ratifying election.

Was the same thing true in 1968?

The question requires a rethink of familiar stereotypes of Nixon. He is the guy liberals love to hate—from his Red-baiting rise to fame in the 1940s to his disgraceful fall after Watergate in the 1970s, his career serves as an endless provocation for moralizing psychobabble. But I want to focus attention more narrowly on his role as a presidential candidate in 1968. So far as the landmark civil rights statutes were concerned, the record is remarkably clear: Richard Nixon was the Wendell Willkie of 1968, expressing the Republican Party's affirmation of the most recent constitutional revolution.

Only this time, Willkie won.

To elaborate: Goldwater's crushing defeat in 1964 forced the Republican Party into another period of agonizing reappraisal—and, as in 1940, the party refused to choose a candidate who would continue hard-edged denunciations of the new regime. In this case, it was Ronald Reagan who denounced the landmark statutes of the civil rights revolution and Richard Nixon who supported them.[33] The Republican National Convention chose Nixon, a man with a long-standing commitment to civil rights— recall his early efforts, as Senate president in 1957, to destroy the filibuster rule. As Part Two will explain, Nixon also played a key role in ensuring the passage of the Fair Housing Act of 1968, encouraging congressional Republicans to join with liberal Democrats to break the southern filibuster against this landmark initiative.[34]

Nixon's commitments were tested further during the fall campaign. With Hubert Humphrey making a dramatic comeback in the polls and George Wallace registering support as high as 21 percent, he was in grave political peril. If he had been a sheer opportunist, he could have pandered to Wallace voters, allowing them to suppose that he would tolerate major erosion of the civil rights acts.[35]

But this didn't happen. Nixon *did* run a law-and-order campaign, but he never wavered in his support of the landmark statutes.[36] Nixon's moment of truth came in October 1968, as public opinion polls showed Humphrey making a strong comeback. A more dedicated opportunist would have shifted gears to indicate some flexibility on the landmark statutes to attract millions of potential Wallace voters into his column. Instead, "Nixon conspicuously, conscientiously, calculatedly denied himself all racist votes, yielding them to Wallace," as Theodore White put it in his classic *The Making of the President*.[37]

Nixon—dare I say it?—was a man of principle. He appealed to the silent majority on a host of racially coded issues, but he refused to join

Wallace in denouncing the statutes—and he won his gamble, gaining a razor-thin victory over Humphrey.[38] As in 1940, both Republican and Democratic candidates were converging on a new constitutional consensus. Nixon would not be leading the country back to the days of Jim Crow any more than Willkie urged Americans to return to the days of Herbert Hoover.

Nineteen sixty-eight, like 1940, marked the date of a ratifying election.

With a bipartisan consensus behind the new civil rights regime, the higher lawmaking system entered its final phase: consolidation. Though Nixon was no Barry Goldwater, let alone George Wallace, he had no plans for further decisive breakthroughs on civil rights. As the civil rights movement splintered after King's assassination, politics began to return to a more normal key, with liberal congressional leaders cutting deals with a president whose priorities were elsewhere. The days of a movement presidency speaking in the name of the people were over.

Nevertheless, Nixon played a major role in hammering out the terms of the new constitutional settlement. As Part Two explains, the president failed to satisfy many liberal demands, especially when it came to the escalating controversies over school busing. But he endorsed many others—including affirmative action—with remarkable vigor, and he signed a series of consolidating statutes that significantly enhanced the landmark statutes of the Johnson administration. By the end of the Nixon years, all three branches had worked together in complex ways to entrench the New Deal–Civil Rights regime. At a comparable stage in the nineteenth-century Reconstruction, the Grant administration was failing to follow through on the promises of the Fourteenth and Fifteenth Amendments.[39] But this was not happening the second time around—the law on the books was becoming a powerful reality throughout the land.

The Second Reconstruction did not signify America's final triumph over its racist legacy. But compared to the first Reconstruction, it was a relative success. When Booker T. Washington and W. E. B. Du Bois confronted the Reconstruction Amendments at the dawn of the twentieth century, they could only view them as grim parodies of constitutional pretension. We stand at the same distance from the civil rights era, and the scene is very different. While the landmark statutes are threatened by an increasingly aggressive Roberts Court, they remain central realities of the living Constitution, and that is no small matter.

FROM MOVEMENT PARTY TO MEDIA POLITICS

We have been putting the civil rights revolution in historical perspective, exploring its relationships to past cycles of popular sovereignty—most notably Reconstruction and the New Deal. This has allowed us to pinpoint differences as well as similarities: how the Court, rather than the presidency, served as the key signaling institution; how an assassin's bullet transferred constitutional leadership to a movement presidency in the 1960s, as opposed to a movement Congress in the 1860s; how New Deal precedents allowed Lyndon Johnson to claim a Rooseveltian mandate from the people in 1964 and encouraged the Supreme Court to defer to this mandate by upholding the Civil Rights Act.

Each of these contrasts is worth more reflection. But I want to focus on a key difference that can easily escape attention, because it involves the dog that didn't bark. In contrast to every constitutional turning point since the days of Thomas Jefferson, the civil rights era does not involve a movement party serving as the principal engine of popular sovereignty.[40] While King and others definitely gained the support of millions of followers, both black and white, they neither dominated the established political parties nor formed an insurgent party of their own. Since the New Deal, the Democratic Party had a split personality, with liberal northerners and racist southerners in an uneasy political coalition. The same was true of the Republicans, with anti–New Dealers such as Barry Goldwater rejecting civil rights initiatives that were perfectly acceptable to modern Republicans including Richard Nixon and Lincolnians such as Everett Dirksen. This split between the movement and the party system made the translation of constitutional politics into constitutional law an especially tricky business.

Most obviously, it was particularly difficult for the movement to pressure the president and Congress into an ambitious legislative program, since this would generate severe political tensions that threatened to rip both parties to shreds. This meant that a great deal would depend on the movement leadership's political skills—most notably on King's mix of high Gandhian principle and shrewd media politics. King planned his southern campaigns with the aim of provoking horrendous television images of racist brutality.[41] These dramatic pictures shocked the national conscience, encouraging racial liberals of both parties to take the high road on civil rights.[42]

To put the point in a single line, King used media politics to substitute for a movement party as an engine for higher lawmaking—and it worked. But there were dangers lurking. King was making himself hostage to the calculations of the media business: if TV producers believed that black militants made for better broadcasts, King's version of nonviolence could readily be overwhelmed by scenes of the Watts riots. Although movement parties lose momentum over time, they don't lose it nearly as quickly as media movement leaders.

The absence of a movement party also caused serious problems for ordinary voters. If Americans disapproved of the Fourteenth Amendment in 1866 or the New Deal in 1936, they had an easy way to say no—they could simply throw the nineteenth-century Republicans or twentieth-century Democrats out of office. But if a modern Republican such as Nelson Rockefeller had gained the Republican presidential nomination in 1964, the voters would have been deprived of a clear yes-or-no choice at a decisive turning point.

As luck would have it, the right kind of Republican came to the fore at the right moments in the higher lawmaking process—Dirksen joining with the Democrats to pass the Civil Rights Act, Goldwater presenting a clear choice in 1964, and Richard Nixon supporting the new regime in 1968 and consolidating it thereafter.

It could have been different. The nation's hopes for a new beginning in race relations might have been overwhelmed by race riots, party bickering, and legislative impasse. The absence of a movement party placed an extraordinarily heavy burden on particular acts of political leadership to push the process onward to a collective sense of resolution. The paradoxical combination of Earl Warren, Dwight Eisenhower, John Kennedy, Martin Luther King Jr., Lyndon Johnson, Everett Dirksen, Barry Goldwater, and Richard Nixon allowed the American people to organize a meaningful process for debating and deciding their constitutional destiny. Despite the challenges and tragedies, Americans had managed to transcend the pettiness of normal politics and the chaos of mass action to affirm their support for a series of landmark statutes that broke the back of Jim Crow in this country.

Canonizing the Civil Rights Revolution

The question is whether today's Americans are equal to the lesser challenge of honoring this collective achievement. Will the legal profession grant the landmark statutes a central place in the constitutional canon for the twenty-first century?

The partisans of the formalist Constitution say no. They cannot transcend the fact that the Article V amendments of the 1960s and 1970s fail to express the central constitutional achievements of the civil rights revolution. At best, formalists tell a Whiggish story portraying the era as fulfilling the constitutional commitments made a century before by the Reconstruction Amendments. At worst, they may denounce parts of the landmark statutes as unconstitutional because they go beyond the Reconstruction framework inherited from the nineteenth century.

My aim has been to provide common-law tools that will permit the profession to recognize the Second Reconstruction for what it was—one of the greatest acts of popular sovereignty in American history. In making their grand refusal, the formalists are worshipping at the shrine of John Wilkes Booth. They fail to appreciate that it was Booth's bullet that disrupted the standard pattern of presidential leadership that has been at the heart of constitutional politics since the age of Jefferson. If Booth had missed his mark in Ford's Theatre, the formal Constitution never would have been amended to include the Equal Protection and Due Process Clauses of the Fourteenth Amendment. Instead, the Republicans would have spent the next few years elaborating the constitutional meaning of citizenship and equality largely through landmark statutes and judicial superprecedents.

In other words, it is the 1860s, not the 1960s, that represent the historical oddity in constitutional development. The civil rights era is simply one more variation on the great theme of presidential leadership, with movement support, for constitutional change in the name of the American people. The legal landmarks emerging from this moment of popular sovereignty should not be denigrated merely because they took the form of statutes and superprecedents.

To be sure, the leading principles of the civil rights legislation could be repealed by a simple majority of Congress if supported by the president. But a sufficiently determined national majority could also reverse

Marbury v. Madison and decisively undermine the current practice of judicial review. Yet this formal point does not deprive *Marbury* of a canonical place in our tradition. As with *Marbury,* an all-out assault on the landmark statutes could not occur without a massive popular mobilization equal in force, but opposite in effect, to the civil rights movement that generated these landmarks in the first place.

This suffices for my argument. I have no interest in constructing a constitutional canon for eternity. It is hard enough to define one that makes sense at the dawn of the twenty-first century. I do not stand before you with a crystal ball: if some future generation does indeed make the collective effort to repeal the landmarks of the 1960s, Americans will then be living in a different constitutional world, and they will have to define a very different constitutional canon for themselves. It's enough for us to do justice to our own past and to present our successors with a worthy understanding of their constitutional inheritance.

CHAPTER 5

The Turning Point

THIS PART OF THE book is presenting a three-step argument—and we are now moving into the home stretch.

Step 1: My dialogue with Alfarabi established that lawyers can't really understand the civil rights revolution by staring at the formal amendments generated under Article V (Chapter 1).

Step 2: We can come to terms with this great constitutional achievement only by following the six-stage process through which the American people and their leaders hammered out, and consolidated, the great landmark statutes of the Second Reconstruction (Chapters 2 through 4).

Now for the third step, which demonstrates that Martin Luther King Jr., Lyndon Johnson, and many other leaders were well aware that they were using landmark statutes to amend the constitution—and that *they publicly defended this choice as a legitimate alternative to the path set out by Article V.*

The moment of truth came as part of the struggle over the poll tax, one of the great symbols of southern racism and an early target of reformers. From the 1930s onward, racial liberals repeatedly tried to enlist the federal government in a campaign to abolish the tax—with no lasting results until the dikes broke between 1962 and 1966. During four short years, the Twenty-Fourth Amendment, Section 10 of the Voting Rights Act, and *Harper v. Virginia State Board of Elections* swept away the poll tax.

Today's lawyers remember only one of these texts—and, curiously, it is *Harper.* I say "curiously" because Twenty-Four is an Article V amendment—according to the official canon, it should have pride of place. But in fact nobody takes Twenty-Four seriously. Many leading law professors would flunk a pop quiz on its commands. Section 10 of the Voting Rights Act is even further off the radar screen: the most enthusiastic election law junkies will stumble before they can recall Section 10, which has no current legal significance. In contrast, lawyers can readily identify *Harper* as famously condemning wealth-based restrictions on the suffrage.

Call this the poll tax puzzle, and it is a striking testimony to the Court-watching tendencies of the profession. Even though the *official* canon places Twenty-Four at the forefront, the *operational* canon consigns it to the shadows. I will be calling for a reorganization of the operational canon, placing Twenty-Four and Section 10 into the legal foreground.

Yes to Twenty-Four, I hear you say, *but why promote the forgotten Section 10? It's merely a statute, not a constitutional amendment, and so does not have a place in the official canon. Isn't its present obscurity entirely deserved?*

That's not the way it seemed in the 1960s. Twenty-Four and Section 10 are a unique pair in our history. Both aim at the same problem—the poll tax. Both condemn the tax—the amendment in federal elections, the statute in state elections. Both were enacted at about the same time—the amendment in 1964, the statute in 1965. But it was the statute, not the amendment, that inaugurated the constitutional revolution. Twenty-Four's ban on poll taxes in federal elections was a halfway measure that could have been accomplished by statute. In contrast, Ten attacked a core principle of federalism that granted states the right to determine voting qualifications (except in cases explicitly barred by the Fifteenth and Nineteenth Amendments, which addressed blacks and women). If anything required an Article V amendment, it should have been the ban on state poll taxes.

This point was well understood at the time. Indeed, the revolutionary effort to use a statute to make an end run around Article V endangered the passage of the entire Voting Rights Act. But Johnson refused to let that happen. Fresh from his landslide victory over Goldwater, he joined with King, Everett Dirksen, and Nicholas Katzenbach to hammer out a statutory ban on all poll taxes and vindicate the popular mandate for a revolutionary transformation of southern politics. With the broader public following each move, the president and Congress finally came to a clear and public decision: yes, the time *had* come to supplement the classical form of constitutional amendment with the modern system of landmark statutes.

This story should be of the highest interest. After all, it isn't every day that the debate over constitutional fundamentals spills out of courtrooms and classrooms into the very center of American public life. Generally speaking, politicians have better things to do with their time than talk

constitutional theory. But there are moments when the question of legal
form becomes central to the capacity of the constitutional system to deliver fundamental change in the name of the American people.

This was such a moment.

WHY TWENTY-FOUR?

To set the stage, consider the paradoxical origins of the Twenty-Fourth
Amendment. Begin with its leading sponsor, Senator Spessard Holland of
Florida. One would suppose that the senator leading the charge against
the poll tax would be a strong supporter of Martin Luther King Jr.

Wrong. Holland was a lifelong segregationist.[1] He signed the Southern
Manifesto and voted against the Civil Rights Acts of 1957 and 1960.[2] He
would vote against the Civil Rights Act of 1964 and, even more remarkably, the Voting Rights Act of 1965. What led him to make an exception
and successfully convince Congress to propose Twenty-Four in 1962?

The NAACP also acted against type. It strongly opposed the amendment, arguing that the federal government already had ample power to
ban poll taxes in federal elections. It feared that a congressional decision to
take the Article V route would create "an immutable precedent for shunting all further civil rights legislation to the amendment procedure."[3] A host
of other liberal groups joined to denounce Holland's initiative, including
the American Jewish Congress, Americans for Democratic Action, the
Anti-Defamation League, and the United Automobile Workers.[4]

These protests were not enough to stop Holland. Before pushing onward to the micropolitics of the amendment's passage, we pause to consider the bigger question: despite Holland's unembarrassed racism and the
emphatic opposition of the NAACP, how could two-thirds of Congress,
and the larger public, perceive Twenty-Four as a step forward in the struggle
for voting rights?

New Deal Roots

The answer is the New Deal. The popular understanding of poll tax abolition was rooted in a generation of political and legal campaigning that
began in the 1930s. It would take more than a burst of last-minute lobbying to transform the entrenched public meaning of this decades-long
effort.

New Deal progressives framed their opposition to the poll tax as an issue of class, not race.[5] It played a key role in Roosevelt's larger campaign
to purge the Democratic Party of its reactionary southern leadership.[6]
When southerners joined Republicans to defeat his court-packing plan in
1937, Roosevelt struck back by supporting liberal challengers in the party's
southern primaries of 1938.[7] Poll tax reform was central to this larger effort. As he explained to a southern confidant, "I think the South agrees
with you and me. One difficulty is that three quarters *of the whites* in the
South cannot vote—poll tax etc" (emphasis added).[8]

When Roosevelt went public with his purge campaign he denounced
the southern leadership as representatives of "Polltaxia."[9] Nevertheless,
liberal insurgents failed to oust them in the primaries, and Roosevelt beat
a hasty retreat, publicly refusing to support federal legislation that might
"deprive states of their rights directly or indirectly to impose the poll
tax."[10]

Yet his loud declamations against "Polltaxia" were not forgotten. They
served to make their abolition an enduring priority: if liberalism had a
future in the South, it was essential for poor whites to gain access to the
ballot box. Over the succeeding decades, progressive campaigns continued on a state-by-state basis, with significant success.[11]

Repeal of poll taxes helped break down the class barrier, but its impact
on blacks was less dramatic. It did have a positive impact in urban areas,
where racism was less intense.[12] Yet voting registrars in the rural South
were notorious for flunking blacks on literacy tests even if they paid their
tax.[13] As it emerged from the New Deal, the poll tax was a class issue first
and foremost.

We are now in a position to solve the riddle of Spessard Holland: why
would a proud racist seize the chance to push for poll tax abolition in the
early 1960s? Holland's views were not a response to the rising civil rights
movement. They were rooted in his early days as a Florida politician. He
was a state senator in 1937, when the campaign to repeal the state's poll tax
was cresting.[14] As an up-and-comer, he was all for enabling poor whites to
vote for the party of FDR.[15] When a political opening appeared in the
early 1960s, the elderly Holland was reenacting one of his early triumphs
in pushing for an amendment on the federal level—but the sit-ins and
Freedom Rides were then generating a very different political dynamic on
the national stage.

The New Deal legacy also shaped the Warren Court's understanding of the issue. A big poll tax case, *Breedlove v. Suttles*, came to the Supreme Court in 1937—a moment when even the most liberal justices were in no mood to undertake new ventures in judicial activism. They signed on to a unanimous decision by Justice Pierce Butler that dismissed the challenge in a cursory opinion.[16]

The New Deal echoes continued to resonate when the poll tax question returned to the Court in the 1960s. *Breedlove* was one of the first cases that Hugo Black decided as a Justice, and he would issue a ringing dissent when *Harper* overruled *Breedlove* in its great egalitarian leap forward.[17] Just as Spessard Holland was reenacting his New Deal vote in the Florida state senate, Hugo Black was reenacting his New Deal vote in the United States Supreme Court.

Interregnum

The NAACP and other liberal groups responded to *Breedlove* by turning to Congress. They created a single-issue lobbying outfit, the National Committee to Abolish the Poll Tax,[18] to "avoid confusing their movement with the related struggle for Negro voting rights."[19] Although the NAACP was a leading player, the committee's very existence testified to a continuing determination to define the issue in class terms.[20]

In crafting their political strategy, the abolitionists also changed their legislative objective. Since *Breedlove* had unanimously rejected a Fourteenth Amendment foundation for federal intervention, reformers turned to the first article of the 1787 Constitution, giving Congress the power to control the "manner" of conducting federal elections. This new textual focus implied a narrowing of statutory concern: since Article I concerned only federal elections, the reformers' initial statutory initiatives ignored state elections. Once they narrowed their goals, they were soon making real progress.

Pearl Harbor provided the opening. Despite southern resistance, Congress passed a statute prohibiting states from imposing poll taxes on absentee ballots mailed in by the servicemen and women fighting for America.[21] Looking ahead to the postwar period, Eleanor Roosevelt saw this initiative as inaugurating a new era of federal intervention.[22]

Her husband was more skeptical. Sobered up by his failed campaign against Polltaxia, he was "walking a delicate tightrope," balancing his

concern for equal suffrage with his desire to sustain the support of southern conservatives. His private correspondence made clear that "a constitutional amendment [was] the only practical way to eliminate the [tax]
assessment."[23]

The president was the better prophet. While the Democratic Party remained silent on the poll tax, the 1944 Republican platform supported
prohibition in federal elections—but only through an amendment, not a
statute.[24]

So matters stood in 1946, when the newly elected Senator Spessard Holland began his long struggle for an Article V amendment. Holland's first
initiative passed the House but was defeated by a filibuster in the Senate.[25]
Holland regularly reintroduced his measure in each new Congress but
succeeded only in provoking two more filibusters over the next dozen
years.[26]

His failed campaign was important in the long run. It entrenched the
poll tax amendment in the liberal reform agenda, prepackaging it for use
when political conditions became favorable. While the amendment's symbolic salience was increasing, its practical significance was decreasing. The
New Deal coalition slowly succeeded in its state-by-state repeal campaign.[27]
By 1960, only four states from the Deep South retained the tax, with Virginia joining as the fifth holdout.[28]

The New Deal aim had been largely achieved—poor whites could vote
and the major obstacle to black suffrage was now the discriminatory use
of literacy tests. If the rising tide of public opinion required southern senators to engage in a strategic retreat in defense of Jim Crow, Holland's
amendment had obvious attractions: most southerners could sacrifice the
poll tax without changing political realities at home, enabling them to
concentrate their energies on a last-ditch battle to save literacy tests.

The Sixties

Beware anachronism. Although the Democratic Party is associated with
minority rights today, this wasn't true in the early 1960s.

President Kennedy held conventional liberal views on civil rights, but
his passions were directed elsewhere—to the struggle with the Soviet Union
abroad and to the pursuit of prosperity through Keynesian tax cuts at home.
From his perspective, sit-ins and Freedom Rides presented a political problem of the first magnitude, risking destruction of his relationship to south-

ern Democratic committee chairmen and threatening his reelection chances in 1964.

As a consequence, Kennedy largely contented himself with rhetorical support for serious civil rights legislation. His State of the Union address for 1962 emphasized that "the right to vote should no longer be denied through . . . literacy tests and poll taxes." But anonymous White House sources immediately reminded reporters that he had made "no urgent request" for new legislation.[29]

Within this context, Holland's continuing agitation for the poll tax amendment was a godsend. If the senator from Florida gained his fellow southerners' reluctant support, the administration would be happy to jump on Holland's bandwagon and claim credit for a civil rights win, which would delight its northern supporters. And if the amendment was ratified before November 1964, it might even help Kennedy win reelection by increasing the black vote in the poll tax states.

Holland was on the move before Kennedy took office. He tacked his amendment onto a larger bill that passed the Senate on February 2, 1960—the first time the measure had ever cleared this critical barrier. This set the stage for another blur of parliamentary maneuvering in the House, all of which led nowhere except to a promise from Emanuel Celler, the liberal chairman of the House Judiciary Committee, to push a separate poll tax amendment through the House at some later point.[30] Armed with Celler's commitment, Holland returned to the Senate to obtain sixty-seven co-sponsors, and after more parliamentary razzle-dazzle the amendment made it to the floor, sparking a ten-day filibuster. With the civil rights movement on the rise, proponents finally pushed the initiative through by a vote of 77 to 16.[31] On the bill's return to the House, Representative Celler proved to be a man of his word: taking a series of extraordinary parliamentary steps to overcome southern resistance, he pushed the matter to a final vote, where it gained the requisite two-thirds majority needed to send the initiative to the states.[32]

These procedural details may seem tedious today, but they had a powerful meaning to a twentieth-century audience. For generations, southern barons had been master manipulators of parliamentary procedures to kill efforts to achieve racial justice. Now it was the liberals, led by a southerner, who were beating the southerners at their own game.

This was not the first such triumph. Majority leader Lyndon Johnson had accomplished similar feats in passing the Civil Rights Acts of 1957 and 1960. As on these occasions, success came at a large price.[33] To overcome southern resistance, progressives had to water down their initiative and accept a ban that applied only in federal, not in state, elections. But surely it was yet another small step forward down the path of progress?

No, replied the NAACP and many other liberal groups preparing for a great leap forward in the struggle for civil rights.[34] As the NAACP's Clarence Mitchell explained at a House hearing, "To accept the amendment method of elimination . . . would be a bad precedent, inasmuch as the constitutional issue is raised whenever a piece of civil rights legislation is considered. Once this concession is made . . . [s]uch a course would give lukewarm supporters of civil rights a chance to avoid making a strong battle, and would give opponents an opportunity to block amendments in the States."[35]

In declaring war on Article V, the NAACP and its allies were not indulging in cheap talk. Since three-fourths of the states were likely to approve Twenty-Four, the civil rights leadership was sacrificing progress on the poll tax to make a stand on principle: the federalist premises of Article V were no longer adequate to express the national commitments to racial equality at the heart of their movement's campaign for a Second Reconstruction.

The movement's show of constitutional seriousness was beginning to reach a broader audience. As Holland's amendment approached its final vote in the Senate, liberal Republican Jacob Javits of New York moved to substitute a landmark statute prohibiting poll taxes, emphasizing Mitchell's concerns about a formal amendment's devastating implications for future progress.[36] Senator Paul Douglas, a major Democratic figure, joined in condemning Holland's maneuver as a "booby trap."[37]

The Kennedy administration was unmoved. Assistant Attorney General Katzenbach firmly endorsed the Article V approach:

> While we think that the recent trend in decisions [suggests] that the courts would ultimately uphold such a statute, the matter is not free from doubt. In any event, as a practical matter and in view of the widespread support offered by the many sponsors of Senate Joint Resolution 58, the poll tax may possibly be laid forever to rest faster by constitutional amendment than by attempt to enact and litigate the validity of the statute. All of us know that long delays are inherent in litigation generally, and this is particularly true when important constitutional issues are at stake. Accordingly, the Justice Department

supports the proposed amendment as a realistic technique which seeks the early demise of the poll tax.[38]

Katzenbach conceded that the Supreme Court might well overrule *Breedlove* and uphold a statute striking down the poll tax. But practical politics drove him away from the statutory option. Given the "widespread support" for Holland's initiative, an Article V amendment was the only "realistic" path to a quick victory. What is more, everybody recognized that Holland would lead a southern filibuster if Congress took the statutory course—and that Kennedy wasn't willing to make an all-out effort to close off debate.[39] When faced with the choice of an easy victory or a costly defeat, the administration remained on the sidelines while Javits's statutory initiative lost by a vote of 59 to 34, clearing the decks for approval of Holland's amendment.[40]

From Holland's angle, the short-term politics were equally compelling, as the senator made clear in this letter to an outraged segregationist constituent:

> How do you think we got the 53–43 vote against cloture on the literacy bill which I think we will finally defeat Monday? One of the strong factors was the poll tax amendment against which you seem to have a bad aversion but which has allowed many Senators to cast a Constitutional vote on a relatively non-important matter which gave them an out on vastly more important matters like the literacy test bill.
>
> It is rather disappointing to have such reactions as those contained in your letter when I have been fighting night and day against an ultra-liberal Administration and an ultra-liberal majority for the preservation of the most worthwhile values in the American system.[41]

The amendment was smart politics for both Holland and Katzenbach, but the Javits motion emphasized the long-term problem they had shoved under the rug: if future initiatives against Jim Crow were consigned to the Article V track, even massive popular mobilizations by the likes of Martin Luther King Jr. would not suffice to overcome vetoes from thirteen southern state legislatures.

Perhaps it seemed safe to defer these issues to the indefinite future in August 1962, when Congress approved Twenty-Four and sent it on to the states for ratification. This was a moment when King had not yet led his March on Washington and Johnson was a powerless vice president. As the Kennedy administration struggled to propitiate southern conservatives and northern liberals, few sober politicians imagined how different the political world would appear in three short years.

THE DARKENING SHADOW

Once the voters gave decisive majorities to Lyndon Johnson and his liberal Congress in the fall of 1964, the question of voting rights returned to center stage—and with it the symbolically charged issue of the poll tax. Twenty-Four had gained the support of three-fourths of the states in February 1964, but the civil rights leadership would now settle for nothing less than total abolition. Only by ending state poll taxes as well as literacy tests could blacks gain easy access to the ballot and revolutionize the politics of the Deep South. Predictably, Senator Holland and other southerners used Twenty-Four as a precedent to denounce any statutory move beyond federal elections.[42] The key question was whether Holland could detach northern constitutional conservatives from the civil rights coalition.

This was precisely the anxiety that had led the NAACP and liberal congressional leaders to oppose Twenty-Four in 1962. Their fears were fully vindicated in 1965—but not in the way they had anticipated. It was Lyndon Johnson's own attorney general, Nicholas Katzenbach, who gave broad respectability to Holland's constitutional concerns. While the president was celebrating the civil rights "frontlash" that contributed to his landslide victory over Goldwater, his own Department of Justice was creating a legalistic backlash to block forward movement on a landmark statute.[43]

Nevertheless, these forces could not check the momentum generated by King's campaign for voting rights on the streets of Selma, Alabama. This crisis propelled President Johnson into action, leading him to propose a revolutionary Voting Rights Act in his famous "We Shall Overcome" speech to Congress.[44] Caught between frontlash and backlash, Congress teetered uncertainly, struggling to reach a new constitutional equilibrium. But when push came to shove, Congress repudiated the precedent set by Twenty-Four, self-consciously displacing Article V with the modern higher lawmaking system based on landmark statutes and judicial superprecedents.

Now that he had won a sweeping mandate from the voters, would Lyndon Johnson make voting rights a key priority for 1965?[45] King didn't get a clear answer when he visited the White House on his return from Oslo as the winner of the Nobel Peace Prize.[46] King pressed for a commitment, but the president was evasive, suggesting that Great Society legislation would do more to improve the conditions of blacks. King was determined to change the political equation: "I left the mountaintop of Oslo and the mountaintop of the White House, and two weeks later went down to the valley of Selma, Alabama."[47]

In the meantime, Johnson considered his options. Shortly after King's visit, he told Katzenbach to "undertake the greatest midnight legislative drafting session" to guarantee black voting rights.[48] If effective legislation ran up against constitutional barriers, the Department of Justice should break through the roadblock by drafting an Article V amendment.

On December 28, Katzenbach sent Johnson a memo urging him to take the Article V path, following up with a proposed amendment with grand ambitions. The department's draft did not merely plug the poll tax gap left by Twenty-Four. It created an entirely new foundation for voting rights. The Constitution notoriously failed to guarantee Americans the right to vote—leaving it up to the states, provided that they didn't engage in race or gender discrimination. But the Justice Department's proposal changed the baseline. It swept away literacy tests and poll taxes and forbade the use of other exclusionary devices, leaving intact only a few relatively uncontroversial exceptions.[49]

There was an obvious problem—the overwhelming obstacle course imposed by Article V. Katzenbach wasn't optimistic:

> It is difficult to estimate the extent of the opposition to this kind of constitutional amendment. In addition to resistance from the South, there may be opposition from sources genuinely concerned about federal interference with a fundamental matter traditionally left to the States. One possible alternative—to follow the poll-tax amendment precedent and limit the reach of the new amendment to federal elections—would tend to decrease the magnitude of the opposition, but it would also impair the effectiveness of the measure.[50]

Note the Justice Department's legalistic response to Johnson's political problem: if opposition to its proposed Twenty-Five became too intense, the best strategy was *not* to abandon the classical amendment system but rather to keep on the Article V track and split the opposition between southern die-hards and serious conservatives who were "genuinely" concerned about states' rights. The proper fallback was to cut the amendment's scope to include only federal elections. This had worked for Twenty-Four; why not for Twenty-Five?

Though Katzenbach strongly favored a formal amendment, his memo also explored alternatives. Option two involved "legislation vesting in a federal commission the power to conduct registration for federal elections."[51] Since this statute did not target state elections, it received a clean bill of health, but Katzenbach was "more dubious" when it came to a statute that would "assume direct control of registration for voting in both federal and state elections in any area where the percentage of potential Negro registrants actually registered is low." He put this in last place. It was both constitutionally questionable and politically problematic: "a somewhat similar proposal" had been rejected by key Republican moderates in 1963.[52]

Johnson would ultimately choose option three, including it in the Voting Rights Act he proposed in a special March 15 address to Congress. But a couple of months is an eternity in politics, and in early January the administration was vacillating between the first and second options.[53] When the president delivered his State of the Union address on January 4, he announced that he would submit a detailed proposal on voting rights "within six weeks."[54] At the same time, his spokesman, Bill Moyers, emphasized that the administration had not yet made a definitive choice between an amendment and a statute.[55] More precisely, the Katzenbach memo suggests that at that moment the live options were an amendment that would decisively end "racially-discriminatory manipulation" in both state and federal elections and a statute that limited itself to registration of blacks in federal elections. What accounted for the rapid shift to option three over the next two months?

The campaign for voting rights in Selma. By early January, King was gaining national media attention and broad public support for a decisive congressional breakthrough. In a January 15 telephone conversation, King appealed to Johnson's political instincts, pointing out that the president had failed to carry only those southern states that "have less than forty percent of the Negroes registered to vote." He urged Johnson to build a "coalition of the Negro vote and the popular white vote that will really make the New South."

Said Johnson, "That's exactly right. I think it is very important that . . . we take the position that every person born in this country when they reach a certain age, that he have [sic] a right to vote, just like he has the right to fight."[56] Three weeks later, King flew from Selma to Washington for a "very successful" meeting with the president, after which he praised Johnson's "deep commitment" to voting rights.[57]

But the Department of Justice was slow to follow up. On January 18— the date of the first Selma march—Katzenbach promised the president a draft statute within a week.[58] Yet nothing was forthcoming. With every passing day, a statute limited to federal elections (option two) seemed an increasingly inadequate response to the rising public demand for decisive action. But the department was still struggling with its constitutional doubts about a more sweeping statute (option three). With civil rights leaders and liberal congressmen pressing for a statutory breakthrough,[59] Deputy Attorney General Ramsey Clark told Johnson in mid-February "that a constitutional amendment would not be a satisfactory approach."[60]

The Justice Department followed up with a month of feverish activity, submitting its draft bill to Congress on March 18.[61] The administration's proposal targeted the worst southern states for extraordinary treatment—suspending literacy tests and authorizing federal registrars to intervene and register blacks for full participation in both state as well as federal elections.[62] Even more remarkably, the statute stripped the offending states of any pretense at sovereignty. They could no longer change the rules regarding their own electoral systems. They were instructed to seek the prior approval of a panel of federal judges before their election law changes could go into effect. Nothing like this shattering assault on federalism had been seen since the days of Reconstruction.

Compared to requirements for preapproval and the prospect of an invasion of federal registrars, the statute's proposed ban on state poll taxes seemed like small potatoes. Nevertheless, Twenty-Four transformed the poll tax controversy into a great cause célèbre in the months that followed.

"We Shall Overcome"

The Selma campaign reached its climax on "Bloody Sunday," March 7, when a peaceful march was shattered by a brutal display of police violence on the Edmund Pettus Bridge.[63] Many more vicious acts had been perpetrated during the past century, but television made all the difference, transforming the terrible scenes into an ugly symbol that shocked viewers throughout the nation.[64] The indignant response was overwhelming, yet Lyndon Johnson was not in a position to respond with a pointed public pronouncement. His Justice Department was still laboring mightily on the revolutionary architecture of the Voting Rights Act, and the president could not go forward without a serious-looking proposal.[65]

After a week had gone by, he was in danger of losing the political initiative. When he announced plans to give a special address to Congress, the *Christian Science Monitor* explained that he was "trying rather desperately to keep one jump ahead of national indignation over the civil rights crisis in Selma."[66] As the president drove down Pennsylvania Avenue to the Capitol on March 15, the Justice Department was still burning the midnight oil. Though he had promised congressional leaders draft legislation before his speech, Justice only presented a formal proposal a couple of days later—and even then, it reserved the right to continue tinkering.[67]

All this was utterly irrelevant to the 70 million Americans who turned on their television sets to hear their president offer up a diagnosis of the current crisis:

> What happened in Selma is part of a far larger movement which reaches into every section and state of America. It is the effort of American Negroes to secure for themselves the full blessings of American life.
>
> Their cause must be our cause, too. Because it is not just Negroes, but really it's all of us who must overcome the crippling legacy of bigotry and injustice.
>
> And we shall overcome.
>
> As a man whose roots go deeply into Southern soil I know how agonizing racial feelings are. I know how difficult it is to reshape the attitudes and the structure of our society.
>
> But a century has passed, more than a hundred years, since the Negro was freed. And he is not fully free tonight.
>
> It was more than a hundred years ago that Abraham Lincoln, a great president of another party, signed the Emancipation Proclamation, but emancipation is a proclamation and not a fact.
>
> A century has passed since the day of promise. And the promise is unkept. The time for justice has now come.[68]

These great lines anchored the meaning of the crisis within the constitutional past—but not through the standard narrative known to lawyers. When they look to Reconstruction, their eyes seek out the texts of the Thirteenth, Fourteenth, and Fifteenth Amendments. But when Johnson turned to the past, the key figure was Abraham Lincoln and his Emancipation Proclamation.

As any lawyer knows, the Proclamation failed to guarantee civil equality to blacks, let alone the right to vote; it is even doubtful whether Lincoln had the constitutional authority to issue his edict.[69] But these legalistic quibbles were unimportant to Johnson's audience. For them, Lincoln was the Great Liberator, and Johnson was following in his footsteps. The way forward was through a collective commitment to the civil rights movement—to see it as something more than the work of just southern protestors or black Americans, because "really it's all of us who must overcome the crippling legacy of bigotry and injustice." The "we" in "We Shall Overcome" was becoming "We the People of the United States."

This appeal to popular sovereignty propelled the president to call upon Congress to "join with me in working long hours—nights and weekends if necessary—to pass this bill." While he welcomed suggestions "to strengthen this bill," he insisted that "[t]his time, on this issue, there must be no delay, or no hesitation, or no compromise with our purpose."

But when the administration submitted its bill a couple of days later, it did "hesitate" and "compromise" on one large matter: the Justice Department pulled its punches when it came to the poll tax. Though its proposal suspended literacy tests and "other tests and devices,"[70] it merely proposed an institutional mechanism that made it easier for blacks to pay their poll taxes.[71] The Twenty-Fourth Amendment was casting a long shadow.

This became plain at the first round of House hearings:

THE CHAIRMAN: As you know, we have a constitutional amendment which abolishes payment of poll taxes as a condition precedent in Federal elections? Do you believe that poll taxes should be abolished even in State elections . . . ?

MR. KATZENBACH: Yes; I would like to get rid of poll taxes.

THE CHAIRMAN: Can we do this by statute without a constitutional amendment?

MR. KATZENBACH: I think it is very difficult, Mr. Chairman, to do it by statute. There is presently pending in the Supreme Court a case which the Supreme Court will hear at its next session and may do that job. A constitutional argument can be made that the poll tax, as a condition precedent to voting, is a restriction against voting which is unwarranted by the Constitution, whether applied discriminatorily or not. That argument is being made to the Court. Of course, if the Court should come to the conclusion, as I think it might, then poll taxes would be eliminated at State elections.[72]

Congress, in short, was just looking for trouble if it tried to abolish the poll tax. It should simply stand on the sidelines and leave it to the Court to decide whether to overrule *Breedlove*. According to Katzenbach, the literacy test had displaced the poll tax as the crucial obstacle: "Negroes who cannot register because of other tests have not had any incentive to pay their poll tax."[73] While the Civil Rights Commission had found that poll taxes also played an exclusionary role, Katzenbach said the commission's data were too weak to support a statutory ban.[74]

Liberals were unimpressed. With Emanuel Celler and Ted Kennedy taking the lead, the judiciary committees in both chambers added an unconditional poll tax ban to their proposals.[75] But these moves only served to trigger a complex process of give-and-take.

THE BREAKTHROUGH

The committee's bill hit a roadblock when southern Democrats launched their predictable filibuster. For more than a month, as the filibuster droned on, the Democratic and Republican leaders of the Senate—Mike Mansfield and Everett Dirksen—went to work on a compromise that could win the two-thirds majority needed for cloture. As part of their deal, they stripped the poll tax ban from the bill.[76]

When asked to explain this glaring omission, Dirksen said that Katzenbach had emphasized the "constitutional risks [involved] if we adopt the Kennedy amendment. The Attorney General says the constitutional approach—like that taken by the Senator from Florida [Mr. Holland]—is the proper approach."[77] While Dirksen and Katzenbach were determined to respect the precedent established by Twenty-Four, they recognized that a do-nothing response undercut Johnson's insistence that "there must be . . . no compromise" in fulfilling King's demand for the elimination of *all* roadblocks to full political participation in the South.

Caught between conservative constitutionalism and movement pressure, there was only one way out: legal creativity. Katzenbach provided Mansfield and Dirksen with a completely unprecedented path out of their dilemma—one that simultaneously preserved the Justice Department's constitutional scruples against a statutory ban while allowing Congress to take a strong stand against the tax.[78]

To grasp its distinctive logic, recall Katzenbach's initial presentation before the House Judiciary Committee, when he claimed that the data on the discriminatory impact of the poll tax were too weak to support a statutory ban. But the Justice Department's doubts now became the springboard for some legal jiu-jitsu. Katzenbach provided Dirksen and Mansfield with a new provision that enabled Congress to exercise a novel form of constitutional leadership:

> Sec. 9 (a) *In view of the evidence presented to the Congress* that the constitutional right of citizens of the United States to vote is denied or abridged in certain States by the requirement of the payment of a poll tax as a condition of voting, *Congress declares* that the constitutional right of citizens of the United States to vote is denied or abridged in such States by the requirement of the payment of a poll tax as a condition of voting. To assure that such right is not denied or abridged in violation of the Constitution, the Attorney General shall forthwith institute in such States . . . actions for declaratory judgment or injunctive relief against the enforcement of any poll tax.[79]

Section 9 proposes a distinctive institutional dynamic for constitutional revision—with Congress announcing aggressive constitutional findings on the basis of weak data, and the Court using these findings to overrule its well-established established precedents. This "collaborative" model has no precedent in our history, and I'll comment on its larger significance in Chapter 6.[80] But we haven't yet gotten to the end of our story.

Liberal Counterattack

Katzenbach's legal fireworks helped deliver the Republican votes needed to break the filibuster, but Senate liberals quickly went on the counterattack. Senator Clifford Case derided the Justice Department's maneuver, asking Jacob Javits whether "in his many years of experience as a lawyer [he had] . . . ever seen an animal of the kind that the so-called substitute amendment would set up . . . Ha[d] he ever seen anything like it in all the years of his experience?"

Javits's response was that the "Mansfield-Dirksen poll tax provision is a rare bird, indeed. We would be saying to the Attorney General, 'We have heard some evidence. We are sorry that we cannot make up our own minds. So, Mr. Attorney General, please ask the Court to make up our minds for us.' "[81]

Javits was exaggerating, since the provision actually "declares" that "the constitutional right of citizens" had been "denied or abridged" by "the payment of a poll tax." Nevertheless, he was correct in emphasizing that Congress was speaking in a distinctive voice—announcing a constitutional judgment without following up in the ordinary way, by legislating against the practice. In his view, this effort to speak in a purely constitutional voice was pointless because the attorney general obviously could "go into court" and make his legal arguments without statutory reinforcement.

Javits missed the point. Congress was urging the Court to revolutionize the law with a new "superprecedent"—to use a phrase that is now common but was unknown at the time. The statute's special mandate to the attorney general was a means of expressing the significance it attached to this new mode of Congress-Court collaboration. From this vantage, Javits and his fellow liberals were legal traditionalists, determined to condemn the Justice Department's "rare bird" to immediate extinction.

Here was one matter on which a racist southerner such as Strom Thurmond could agree with his liberal antagonists: "[T]o direct the Attorney General to challenge the constitutionality of a specific State law could establish a precedent which may well be regretted in future years."[82] There was only one way in which Congress could speak in a constitutional voice, Senator Holland added, and that was by proposing a constitutional amendment.[83]

But Javits had had enough of Holland's advice. He called upon his fellow liberals to "learn[] our lesson": "[A]fter being led down . . . the garden path of the [Twenty-Fourth] amendment, it is high time for us to have the courage to face our responsibilities and now, at long last, ban the poll tax, lock, stock, and barrel, root and branch."[84]

Senator Kennedy joined the chorus by invoking Johnson's "We Shall Overcome" speech. Without a flat statutory ban, he explained, there was no guarantee that blacks would be in a position to vote against the George Wallaces of the world and prevent future tragedies at Selma.[85]

All these protests were in vain. The Kennedy amendment lost 45–41, and Katzenbach's unconventional "third way" beyond a constitutional amendment and a statutory ban made it through the Senate.[86]

Meanwhile . . .

In the meantime, Emanuel Celler, chairman of the House Judiciary Committee, was confronting a Republican substitute—which did not contain a poll tax ban.[87] He refused to compromise on this matter of principle, leading King to phone the president to pressure him to consider "what we can do to really block it [the Republican alternative]."[88]

Johnson responded by redefining the issue. He told King that both Celler and his House antagonists had got it wrong and that King should instead support Katzenbach's Senate compromise. If Celler's amendment was passed, he warned, it might so antagonize the courts that they might "nullify[] the whole law." He also made it clear that Katzenbach's legalistic worries were decisive. Even if the civil rights leadership didn't "have much confidence in the Attorney General," he continued, "they're going to be in trouble anyway because he's the man we have to try to rely on to help us. . . . Now you asked for my advice and I'm just telling you, you will either have confidence in me and in Katzenbach, or you'll pick some leader that you do have and then follow [him]."[89]

Johnson's message couldn't be clearer: it was "my way or the highway." Instead of second-guessing Katzenbach, the president urged King to look ahead to the critical moment when the House-Senate conference committee would try to reconcile the competing positions of the two chambers. Together, they would beat the South's "smart parliamentarians" at their own game:[90]

> Then we go to conference. Suppose we get them all in a room and you come and talk to them and everyone talks to them, and say, "Please get your agreement, we're willing to follow the attorney general. . . . If you can trust me, if you can trust the attorney general . . . I'll give every ounce of energy and ability in me that I have to passing the most effective bill that can be written."[91]

The ball was in King's court: would he back Celler and his liberal allies or swing his support to Katzenbach and the creative constitutionalists in the Justice Department?

The Katzenbach-King Compromise

King's moment of truth would not long be delayed. Chairman Celler successfully preserved his poll tax ban by a House vote of 215 to 166.[92] He then led a strong liberal delegation to the conference in an attempt to kill Katzenbach's compromise. Everything depended on the Senate delegation. Its judiciary chairman, James Eastland of Mississippi, had brought along his fellow segregationist Russell Long, leaving room for only two liberal Democrats—Thomas Dodd and Philip Hart. The two remaining slots went to Minority Leader Dirksen and his fellow Republican Roman Hruska, giving Dirksen a decisive influence over the result.

Since the Voting Rights Act represented such a sweeping assault on federalism, the conferees had their hands full in resolving a host of conflicts. Nevertheless, they proceeded with remarkable dispatch until they hit a stone wall on the poll tax.[93] Celler was a formidable force, but Dirksen couldn't be ignored. He (and Hruska) could veto any House-Senate agreement. Although the NAACP and their Senate allies turned up the heat, they could not repeal the laws of addition. Dirksen stood firm.[94] An irresistible force was confronting an immovable object—unless some third party intervened as mediator.

Katzenbach was the obvious choice. When the crunch came, Celler would have a tough time opposing a Democratic administration. And Dirksen had already publicly relied on Katzenbach when making his deal with Mansfield.[95] As the conferees deadlocked during the week of July 19, Katzenbach returned to the Department of Justice to come up with a new formula that would banish the ghost of Twenty-Four from the living Constitution.

He was ready the following week. His new proposal retained the two-step structure of the Senate bill—Congress would continue to speak in a constitutional voice condemning the poll tax, and it would direct the attorney general to bring special lawsuits to convince the Supreme Court to overturn *Breedlove*.

But now Congress would express its condemnation in even stronger terms. Katzenbach's revised provision, labeled Section 10, found not only that the tax had a racially discriminatory impact in some states but that it invariably imposed an "unreasonable financial hardship" without "a reasonable relationship to any legitimate State interest."[96] At a private meeting on July 27, Dirksen and Celler signed on to this tougher version.[97]

Dirksen's consent guaranteed a majority from the Senate delegation, but when the conference committee met later in the day, Celler confronted a rebellion from a majority of House conferees, forcing the leadership to take desperate measures. With the NAACP and congressional liberals heavily invested in the statutory ban, there was only one civil rights leader with the moral authority to break the logjam: Martin Luther King Jr.

Katzenbach reached King on the phone late Wednesday night. With the fate of the act in the balance, King went down the path marked out by President Johnson in his earlier phone call. Katzenbach reported his success in a letter to Celler on the following day:

> Late last night I discussed with Martin Luther King the proposed voting rights bill as it now stands in conference, and particularly the new poll tax provision. Dr. King strongly expressed to me his desire that the bill promptly be enacted into law and said that he felt this was an overriding consideration. . . .
>
> With respect to the poll tax provision he expressed his view to me thusly: "While I would have preferred that the bill eliminate the poll tax at this time—once and for all—it does contain an express declaration by Congress that the poll tax abridges and denies the right to vote. In addition, Congress directs the Attorney General 'to institute forthwith' suits which will eliminate and prevent the use of the poll tax in the four states where it is still employed. I am confident that the poll tax provision of the bill—with vigorous action by the Attorney General—will operate finally to bury this iniquitous device."[98]

Celler immediately convened the conference, read the letter, and gained the consent of the remaining liberal holdouts.[99] He then went to the House floor to present the committee's report—only to confront a maelstrom of indignation.

The sense of betrayal was palpable. Representative Robert McEwen from New York moved to recommit, accusing the conferees of "watering down" the voting bill to only "half a loaf."[100] Representative Delbert Latta denounced the compromise: "[W]e are against the poll tax . . . [and] [w]e do not want to prolong and perpetuate this problem just to carry it over to another campaign."[101]

But Celler was steadfast and pushed the bill through the House by a margin of 328 to 74.[102] During the floor debate, Celler kept King's last-minute intervention confidential.[103] But it was headline news in the *Washington Post* on the following day,[104] and Katzenbach's letter was immediately reprinted in the *Congressional Record*.[105]

The truth was there for all to see: the Voting Rights Act had gained passage through a combination of constitutional creativity by the Justice Department and King's decisive support. "We shall overcome"—President Johnson spoke better than he knew in adopting the slogan of the civil rights movement in his great speech to Congress. It took the authority of Martin Luther King Jr. to bury the ghost of Article V and blaze a new path to constitutional transformation.

In signing the landmark statute, President Johnson took special note of this achievement. Here's part of his nationally televised address:

> The Members of the Congress, and the many private citizens, who worked to shape and pass this bill will share a place of honor in our history for this one act alone.
>
> There were those who said this is an old injustice, and there is no need to hurry. But 95 years have passed since the [Fifteenth Amendment] gave all Negroes the right to vote.
>
> And the time for waiting is gone.
>
> There were those who said smaller and more gradual measures should be tried. But they had been tried. For years and years they had been tried, and tried, and tried, and they had failed, and failed, and failed.
>
> And the time for failure is gone.
>
> There were those who said that this is a many-sided and very complex problem. But however viewed, the denial of the right to vote is still a deadly wrong.
>
> And the time for injustice has gone . . .
>
> This good Congress, the 89th Congress, acted swiftly in passing this act. I intend to act with equal dispatch in enforcing this act.
>
> And tomorrow at 1 p.m., the Attorney General has been directed to file a lawsuit challenging the constitutionality of the poll tax in the State of Mississippi. This will begin the legal process which, I confidently believe, will very soon prohibit any State from requiring the payment of money in order to exercise the right to vote. . . .
>
> So, we will move step by step—often painfully but, I think, with clear vision—along the path toward American freedom.[106]

But would the Court take the next step down the path blazed by Martin Luther King Jr., the president, and the Congress of the United States?

CHAPTER 6

Erasure by Judiciary?

THE STRUGGLE OVER the poll tax catapulted Article V to the center of the political stage—could it properly serve as the exclusive mode of constitutional change in the Modern Republic?

The answer was no: in rejecting Article V, the Voting Rights Act was expressing the broad popular commitment to sweep away *all* devices barring blacks from southern politics. In hammering out Section 10 of the Voting Rights Act, Congress and the president weren't engaging in just another last-minute technicality. They were repudiating a fundamental constitutional obstacle to the vindication of popular sovereignty in the Modern Republic.

Section 10's constitutional significance has been lost in the mists of time—unknown to most voting rights experts, let alone the broader professional community, let alone the larger public. How to account for this remarkable erasure?

Collective amnesia is the paradoxical legacy of Warren Court activism. In *Harper v. Virginia Board of Elections,* the justices completed the mission assigned to them by the Voting Rights Act, striking down all remaining poll taxes in the name of the Constitution. But the majority opinion, written by that paradigmatic activist William O. Douglas, refused to rely on either Section 10 or the Twenty-Fourth Amendment in reaching its judgment. Douglas wrote *Harper* as if it were entirely up to the justices to resolve the question.

Recall that the New Deal Court had upheld poll taxes in *Breedlove* by a vote of 9 to 0. In striking down *Breedlove,* Douglas did not claim it had been incorrectly decided when it came down in 1937. Instead, he proudly denied that the Court could be "shackled to the political theory" of the nineteenth-century Americans who enacted the Equal Protection Clause. In interpreting the contemporary zeitgeist, he entirely failed to mention the fifty-year political campaign against *Breedlove*'s narrow reading of equal protection. To the contrary, he presented the Court as the unique spokesman for We the People of the twentieth century, striking down Virginia's poll tax for failing to comply with *his* understanding of contemporary constitutional understandings.

Later generations of lawyers have taken Douglas at his word, awarding the Warren Court all the credit (or the blame) for its activist reinterpretation of the Fourteenth Amendment. Focusing entirely on the *United States Reports*, they have allowed Douglas to erase the efforts of King, Johnson, Dirksen, Mansfield, and Celler in finally breaking through the old constitutional barriers in the name of twentieth-century Americans.

Collective amnesia is especially wrongheaded in this particular case. Douglas's opinion made its way into the *United States Reports* through the sheerest of accidents. During early Court deliberations on *Harper,* Justice Arthur Goldberg took the lead, writing a draft opinion that moved beyond the Fourteenth Amendment to emphasize the constitutional judgments of We the People of the 1960s. But President Johnson then persuaded Goldberg to resign from the Court to lead a Vietnam peace initiative as ambassador to the United Nations—leaving Douglas to fill the vacuum with a very different opinion. Given the accidental character of Douglas's erasure, modern lawyers have a special responsibility to remember the historical role that modern Americans, and their political leaders, played in redefining the constitutional meaning of equality.

Our visit to the archives in *Harper* will pave the way for a reinterpretation of a second great case involving the Voting Rights Act: *Katzenbach v. Morgan.* This time around, Justice William J. Brennan wrote the opinion for the Court. In contrast to Douglas, he celebrated the power of Congress, in its landmark statutes, to take the lead in defining the modern meaning of equality. What is more, *Morgan* retains an important place in the professional canon, serving as a reference point in the ongoing debate over congressional power. This will allow us to use *Morgan* as a springboard for reintroducing the poll tax story into the modern constitutional canon.

This chapter's microanalysis of a couple of court cases looks very different from my macro-level efforts, in earlier chapters, to characterize the institutional shape of the higher lawmaking dynamics over the period between 1954 and 1974. But micro and macro pathways ultimately lead to the same destination: constitutionalists of the twenty-first century have an obligation to their fellow citizens to elaborate the great achievements of the civil rights revolution by moving beyond Supreme Court decisions to the transformative principles expressed by the landmark statutes. Part Two then proceeds to a more careful study of these landmarks and how they enrich our understanding of the constitutional legacy left behind by the twentieth century.

THE COLLABORATIVE MODEL

Begin by putting *Harper* under the microscope—starting with the landmark statute that it erased from the *United States Reports*. Section 10 marked a new stage in the evolution of the modern system of higher lawmaking.

When Franklin Roosevelt elaborated the modern model of presidential leadership during the New Deal, it took a straightforward form. Backed by a powerful mandate from a mobilized electorate, the president and Congress enacted landmark statutes that directly challenged constitutional orthodoxy.

These enactments set the stage for a stark choice by the Supreme Court. Either it could continue to defend the old constitutional orthodoxy or it could execute a "switch in time." The Court famously made its switch in 1937, upholding breakthrough New Deal legislation in a series of superprecedents that continue to shape constitutional law today. Call this the *challenge model*—the president and Congress challenge the Court to revolutionize its constitutional jurisprudence or risk an escalating assault on its legitimacy.[1]

Section 10 takes a different approach. It offers the prospect of collaboration instead of confrontation. Under this model, Congress simply announces its revisionist constitutional views and "directs" the attorney general to use these judgments to make an effort to persuade the Court to reject its old jurisprudence and create a new superprecedent that expresses the rising generation's transformative constitutional commitments.

Section 10 was breaking new ground: over the centuries, no previous statute had made the attorney general into a congressional messenger to the judiciary. After all, the attorney general is a member of the executive branch: if anybody bosses him around, it is the president, not Congress. Ordinarily, a congressional effort at "direction" would signal an all-out war between Congress and the president for supremacy. But 1965 was no ordinary moment. Katzenbach himself played a key role in getting Congress to issue its marching orders. Instead of signaling bitter conflict, Section 10 expressed an extraordinary level of cooperation between the political branches as they sought to enlist the Court in their project of redefining the meaning of equality.

Here is how the section proposed to establish new doctrinal foundations for the civil rights era:

> The Congress finds that the requirement of the payment of a poll tax as a precondition to voting (i) precludes persons of limited means from voting or imposes unreasonable financial hardship upon such persons as a precondition to their exercise of the franchise, (ii) does not bear a reasonable relationship to any legitimate State interest in the conduct of elections, and (iii) in some areas has the purpose or effect of denying persons the right to vote because of race or color. Upon the basis of these findings, Congress declares that the constitutional right of citizens to vote is denied or abridged in some areas by the requirement of the payment of a poll tax as a precondition to voting.[2]

These "findings" crystallized commitments rooted in two generations of constitutional politics. The first two subsections represent the culmination of the New Deal struggle to enable the poor to gain access to the ballot box. The third brings the contemporary civil rights movement to the fore.

Although Congress expresses these judgments in terms of findings, we are not dealing with ordinary fact-finding here. Congress's first two findings—the New Deal legacy—speak in the ostentatiously normative key of constitutional law: poll taxes impose "*unreasonable* financial hardship" and bear "no *reasonable* relationship to any *legitimate* State interest in the conduct of elections" (emphasis added). The third finding—the contribution of the civil rights revolution—was more fact-based: its assertion of a racist "purpose or effect" was, in principle, falsifiable.

Section 10 concludes on a normative note: it "declares" that the three findings implied that the "constitutional rights of citizens" had been denied "in some areas." This conclusion doesn't follow from the statute's premises. If Congress's first two findings are valid, then the tax is unconstitutional in *all* areas, not just some. Only the third finding—dealing with racist purpose or effect—could plausibly be restricted to some areas of the South. So what was Congress really saying: "some" or "all"?

When set in collaborative context, this ambiguity framed a fundamental question for the Court. On one hand, it could write a (relatively) narrow opinion emphasizing the civil rights movement's contribution to the living constitution. Under this civil rights option, the opinion would emphasize Congress's third finding and instruct the lower courts to investigate the "purpose or effect" of the poll tax in the states that still imposed it.

On the other hand, a more ambitious decision would rely on the first two findings to repudiate *all* poll taxes as "unreasonable financial hardship[s]" on the right to vote. This opinion would view Section 10 as culminating a popular campaign that began with Roosevelt's effort to open up the ballot box to all Americans, regardless of their wealth, and finally led to the King-Johnson-Dirksen-Mansfield collaboration that yielded the Voting Rights Act. In contrast to the civil rights option, call this the New Deal–Civil Rights synthesis.

Which would it be: narrow or broad?

Whatever the Justices' answer, only one thing was clear: Congress and the president wanted a ringing repudiation of *Breedlove* and were providing the materials to do the job according to the rule of law.

ACCIDENTS OF LITIGATION

This message never reached the Court. It was deflected by the American Civil Liberties Union (ACLU), which had begun a judicial challenge to Virginia's poll tax almost two years before Congress started hammering out the Voting Rights Act. With *Breedlove* on the books, the ACLU challenge went nowhere in the lower federal courts, which thought they had no business second-guessing a unanimous decision by the 1937 Court. These predictable rebuffs led the ACLU, in late 1964, to ask the Court to take jurisdiction over *Harper* and overrule its old decision upholding the poll tax.[3]

The matter came before the Justices in February 1965—just when King was flying from Selma to Washington to demand voting rights legislation from President Johnson, and a month before Johnson presented the Voting Rights Act to Congress.

Yet even at this late date, the Court refused to take the ACLU's challenge seriously. In its initial discussion, six Justices voted to reaffirm *Breedlove* summarily, without even hearing plenary argument. During their cursory conversation, somebody mentioned the recent enactment of Twenty-Four, but merely to suggest that the poll tax was dying and that there was no need for the Court to join in the burial. Only Warren, Douglas, and Goldberg briefly demurred.[4]

The majority's decision might be less remarkable if *Harper* had come up on a writ of certiorari, which gives the Court complete discretion in granting or denying jurisdiction. But the case arrived as an appeal, and technically speaking, the six-man majority had no authority to avoid deciding it on the merits. If the majority had stuck to their guns, the Court would have summarily upheld *Breedlove* on the merits a month before the president's "We Shall Overcome" speech kick-started the successful campaign to repudiate the poll tax. Only Arthur Goldberg's intervention stopped his colleagues from offering a ringing endorsement of the constitutional status quo. He asked them to wait until he could write a full-blown dissent, and they, of course, deferred to his request for more time.

This episode challenges the prevailing stereotype of the Warren Court: its initial response was not judicial activism but legalistic caution. The same approach was also prevailing at the Justice Department. Recall that Katzenbach had been advising the president that the best way to overrule *Breedlove* was through a new Article V amendment. As Goldberg was writing his opinion, Justice was finally dropping its formalist fealty to Article V and getting to work on a revolutionary draft of the Voting Rights Act. The legal mandarins on the commanding heights were beginning to catch up with the dynamics of constitutional politics.

Goldberg's draft combined two strands of argument—one drawn from the Warren Court's recent "one-person, one-vote" decisions, the other from congressional debates surrounding the Twenty-Fourth Amendment. He relied on these debates to dismiss Virginia's claim that its poll tax served a legitimate interest in determining whether a voter "took sufficient interest in the affairs of the State." Goldberg emphasized that the House Judiciary Committee confronted an "identical contention" in reporting out Twenty-Four. He took the same tack in denying that the poll tax discharged a significant revenue-raising function.[5] He circulated his draft, which Warren and Douglas joined, on March 4—three days before Bloody Sunday at Selma.[6]

The day after Selma, *Harper* returned to the conference, revealing that Black, Brennan, and Byron White had switched sides—voting to set the case for plenary argument for the Court's next term.[7] In making this decision, they couldn't have guessed that within five short months Section 10 would create a special test-case procedure for the express purpose of repudiating the poll tax. By the time *Harper* came up for plenary consideration, the lower courts were already invalidating poll taxes under Section

10.[8] It was the ACLU's job to emphasize how the statutory arguments endorsed by these cases reinforced the more traditional claims it had previously made to the lower courts in *Harper*. After all, it's never easy to get the Supreme Court to overrule its own precedents, so Section 10 was a godsend, making the ACLU challenge to *Breedlove* a lot easier. But alas, the ACLU entirely failed to incorporate Section 10 into its attack on the Virginia statute. For the past two years its lawyers had relied exclusively on the Equal Protection Clause, and they lacked the intellectual agility to overcome the forces of legalistic inertia.

This might not have been serious if Goldberg had remained on the bench to follow up on his draft opinion, which had already emphasized the importance of considering contemporary constitutional developments. But Goldberg resigned before *Harper* came up, leaving it up to others to raise the issue as the Court began to confront the poll tax problem in earnest.

Would anyone fill the intellectual void?

———————

The answer was yes. Once the Voting Rights Act passed, Solicitor General Thurgood Marshall was invited to intervene in *Harper* to state the government's views. While Marshall didn't have access to Goldberg's unpublished opinion, his office submitted a brief that developed similar lines of argument—only now it moved beyond Twenty-Four to stress Section 10's centrality to the case.

Written largely by the young Richard Posner, then an assistant in the solicitor general's office, the brief turned the spotlight on Congress's invitation to the Court to engage in a collaborative enterprise.[9] It emphasized Section 10's finding that the tax failed to bear "a reasonable relationship . . . [to] the State's legitimate interest," and showed how similar "findings had earlier been made by Congress in proposing the Twenty-fourth Amendment."[10] Posner concluded: "The problem of the poll tax has been before the Congress for some years. Congress has studied it and concluded, with ample basis in fact and experience, that the poll tax is not a justifiable exercise of State power to establish voting qualifications. *Without going so far as to suggest that this judgment is binding upon the Court, we submit that it is entitled to great weight.*"[11] The government's message was loud and clear: Twenty-Four and Section 10 deserved a central place in any decision repudiating *Breedlove*.

But when Solicitor General Marshall made his oral presentation in *Harper,* he didn't pursue this line of argument. The issue did come up, however, when the Court turned to *Harper's* companion case, *Butts v. Harrison.* According to the official transcript, one of the justices (probably Harlan)[12] noted that "somebody"—presumably Katzenbach—had testified at the congressional hearings that the constitutionality of "legislation might be dubious . . . but they didn't seem to have any doubts . . . that the Court could do it, even though the Congress couldn't."[13] Marshall had left the podium by this point, leaving it to Butts's lawyer, Robert L. Segar, to respond.

Segar did not rise to the occasion. He failed to explain that Congress had responded to Katzenbach's problem by condemning the poll tax in Section 10, and he failed to follow up on the solicitor general's brief by arguing that this congressional judgment was entitled to "great weight." Instead, he expressly repudiated the landmark statute: "I was not [at the congressional hearings]. We don't base our argument on what Congress said. . . . In fact, our case was started prior to the 1965 Voting Rights Act . . . and that Act is not cited in our brief, incidentally."[14]

The conversation then moved from Section 10 to the Twenty-Fourth Amendment, but, once again, in an unhelpful fashion:

THE COURT: Under your argument, the Twenty-fourth Amendment would have been surplusage.

MR. SEGAR: Would have been what?

THE COURT: Surplusage; you wouldn't have needed it.

MR. SEGAR: Oh, that's right; absolutely.[15]

Segar had fumbled a second time. He failed to urge the Court—in the manner of Justice Goldberg and the government's brief—to view the amendment's recent repudiation of poll taxes as a reason to rethink its position in *Breedlove.* In an act of stunningly poor advocacy, he accepted the hostile suggestion that his equal protection argument required the Court to view Twenty-Four as absolutely pointless.

———————

Microaccidents were piling up at an alarming rate. If Goldberg hadn't initially asked for extra time to write his dissent, the Court would have affirmed *Breedlove* summarily in 1964—requiring it to reconsider the issue in 1965 or 1966 in the context of the Section 10 lawsuits that would then be reaching its docket from the lower courts. Once it ordered plenary consideration in *Harper,* Goldberg's departure from the Court left it to the solicitor general to bring Section 10 back onto center stage—but Thurgood Marshall failed to drive the point home during oral argument. This left it up to the ACLU to fill the void. However, its lawyer instead went out of his way to proclaim the utter irrelevance of the constitutional politics of the 1960s to the test case before the Court.

The stage was set for judicial erasure.

ERASURE

Justice Douglas spoke for the Court in *Harper* and refused to rely on Twenty-Four or Section 10 in overruling *Breedlove.* He based his decision entirely on texts left behind by the first Reconstruction:

> [T]he Equal Protection Clause is not shackled to the political theory of a particular era. In determining what lines are unconstitutionally discriminatory, we [the Justices] have never been confined to historic notions of equality. . . . Notions of what constitutes equal treatment for purposes of the Equal Protection Clause *do* change. . . . This Court in 1896 held that laws providing for separate public facilities for white and Negro citizens did not deprive the latter of the equal protection and treatment that the Fourteenth Amendment commands. Seven of the eight Justices then sitting subscribed to the Court's opinion, thus joining in expressions of what constituted unequal and discriminatory treatment that sound strange to a contemporary ear. When, in 1954—more than a half-century later—we repudiated the "separate-but-equal" doctrine of *Plessy* as respects public education we stated: "In approaching this problem, we cannot turn the clock back to 1868 when the Amendment was adopted, or even to 1896 when *Plessy v. Ferguson* was written."[16]

If *Harper* had come before the Court between 1954 and 1965, Douglas's reliance on *Brown* would have been entirely sensible. Warren's famous refusal "to turn the clock back" did indeed serve as the most obvious authority for repudiating *Breedlove.* But it was now 1966, and the enactment of Twenty-Four and Section 10 had radically transformed the legal landscape.

Douglas was having trouble grasping this point. Like a general fighting the last war, he was deeply invested in the old judicial strategies developed when the Court dealt with a president and Congress unprepared to take the constitutional lead against racism. Yet he could have written a much more powerful opinion if he had demonstrated Goldberg's intellectual agility.

There is an obvious problem with "unshackl[ing]" equal protection from "the political theory of a particular era": why is Douglas so sure that he is speaking for the zeitgeist? Perhaps the Court is talking only for a tiny minority of judicial do-gooders.

Douglas encourages the charge of elitism by blandly declaring that *Breedlove*'s support for the "unequal and discriminatory treatment" imposed by the poll tax "sound[s] strange to a contemporary ear"—as if this were a matter of music appreciation. His argument would have been far more compelling if he had invoked Section 10's "findings" to justify rethinking *Breedlove*'s premises.

Section 10's erasure becomes all the more puzzling when we turn to Douglas's precise reasoning: "To introduce wealth or payment of a fee as a measure of a voter's qualifications is to introduce a capricious or irrelevant factor. The degree of the discrimination is irrelevant. In this context—that is, as a condition of obtaining a ballot—the requirement of fee paying causes an 'invidious' discrimination that runs afoul of the Equal Protection Clause."[17] In asserting that the poll tax introduces "a capricious or irrelevant factor," Douglas was merely repackaging Section 10's finding that the tax bore no "reasonable relationship to any legitimate State interest"; in condemning the financial payment as "invidious," he was tracking Congress's finding that it imposed "unreasonable financial hardship."[18] So why didn't he mention that Congress had just affirmed the very same constitutional views he was expressing?

Recall that Section 10 invited the Court to choose between the civil rights option, which condemned only poll taxes that had a racist "purpose or effect," and the New Deal–Civil Rights synthesis, which condemned all poll taxes. Douglas's choice of the broader option was bound to be controversial—yet, perversely, he deprived himself of the rich history of popular struggle that gave Section 10 its deeper constitutional meaning.[19]

Paradoxically, the voice of We the People of the twentieth century was heard only by the dissenters. John Harlan, joined by Potter Stewart, rejected Douglas's claim that the tax failed to serve a "rational" purpose in promoting "civic responsibility":[20]

These viewpoints, to be sure, *ring hollow on most contemporary ears.* Their lack of acceptance today is evidenced by the fact that nearly all of the States, left to their own devices, have eliminated property or poll-tax qualifications; *by the cognate fact that Congress and three-quarters of the States quickly ratified the Twenty-Fourth Amendment.* . . . However, it is all wrong, in my view, for the Court to adopt the political doctrines popularly accepted at a particular moment of our history and to declare all others to be irrational and invidious, barring them from the range of choice by reasonably minded people acting through the political process.[21]

Harlan and Stewart viewed Twenty-Four as if it were a strict rule of limitation: We the People banned the taxes in federal elections, and the Court had no authority to go further. Since Douglas did not even bother to mention the amendment, he was in no position to challenge this restrictive interpretation.

Douglas's silence also made life easy for Justice Black, whose dissent predictably declaimed against the entire theory of living constitutionalism: "[W]hen a 'political theory' embodied in our Constitution becomes outdated, it seems to me that a majority of the nine members of this Court are not only without constitutional power but are far less qualified to choose a new constitutional political theory than the people of this country proceeding in the manner provided by Article V."[22] Despite this paean to Article V, Black fails to mention Twenty-Four, let alone consider whether its enactment had significantly undermined *Breedlove.*

If Justice Goldberg had remained on the bench, he never would have allowed this chatter to go unchallenged.[23] His unpublished opinion had already blazed the way toward a more sophisticated approach. It recognized that Twenty-Four did not explicitly abolish state poll taxes, calling it a "compromise necessary . . . to get some progress in this area."[24] With Section 10 on the books, and the solicitor general's brief urging that it deserved "great weight," Goldberg could have developed his argument more forcefully. I suggest the power of this constitutional move by inserting a few italicized sentences at the appropriate place in Goldberg's draft:

> Finally, nothing in the language or history of the Twenty-fourth Amendment, which was an affirmative effort to eliminate the poll tax in federal elections, even suggests that in so doing, Congress and the state legislatures attempted impliedly to repeal the operation of the Fourteenth Amendment in this fundamental area. *To the contrary, the constitutional judgments made by the Voting Rights Act invite us to extend the principles expressed by the recent amendment to*

state elections. We agree with Congress in finding that these taxes impose an "un-reasonable financial hardship" on "persons of limited means," and that they do "not bear a reasonable relationship to any legitimate State interest." As a conse-quence, we condemn the tax as a constitutionally invidious form of wealth discrimination.

Under this "Goldberg scenario," lawyers and judges of the twenty-first century would have learned a very different lesson from *Harper.* Gold-berg would have presented the decision as the culmination of a popular-sovereignty dynamic in which Americans of the 1960s played the key pro-pulsive role—first by expressing their constitutional judgments through the antique form of Article V, then through the modern method of a landmark statute, and finally through a Supreme Court opinion that translates these new constitutional judgments into foundational principles of the New Deal–Civil Rights regime.

It didn't happen that way. But it's past time for the profession to transcend the accidents of history and elaborate on Goldberg's deeper insights.

Collaboration Regained

The task is made a lot easier once we turn to a second great Warren Court decision, *Katzenbach v. Morgan.*[25] While it came down only three months after *Harper,* Justice Brennan's opinion for the Court refused to follow Douglas's lead. He used *Morgan* to propel modern equal protection law down Goldberg's path—emphasizing the key role of collaboration be-tween Court and Congress in elaborating the constitutional meaning of the Second Reconstruction. What is more, *Morgan* retains a central place in the professional canon, permitting us to use the poll tax story to deepen already existing understandings of the potential for collaborative consti-tutional change.[26]

Begin with some striking similarities: *Morgan* and *Harper* were both judicial responses to the Voting Rights Act's revolutionary breakthroughs, with *Morgan* focusing on a different exclusionary device. When Spanish-speaking Puerto Ricans moved to the mainland, they were often barred from the ballot box by state laws requiring literacy in English. Section 4 of the Voting Rights Act banned this practice—despite a recent Supreme Court decision upholding it. *Lassiter v. Northampton County Board of Elections* had been decided in 1959, making it an even more formidable obstacle to congressional action under the Equal Protection Clause than the Court's 1937 decision in *Breedlove*.[27]

Congress refused to be deterred. As with Section 10, Section 4 broke down this barrier to voting, but it employed a different technique. While Section 10 devised a pathbreaking cooperative model to destroy poll taxes, Section 4 issued a straight-out ban on English-only literacy tests.[28]

This set the stage for a familiar challenge-model confrontation in the Supreme Court, with proponents of the landmark statute calling on the justices to overrule *Lassiter*, while its critics urged them to follow established precedent. Brennan responded by transcending this standard dichotomy with a "third way" solution to the problem of constitutional change: his opinion for the Court stood by *Lassiter*, yet collaborated with Congress's landmark redefinition of voting equality.

The Voting Rights Act, Brennan explained, had dramatically changed the institutional equation defining the scope of judicial review. *Lassiter* had merely determined that *individual states* had complied with the requirement for equal protection by insisting on English-only voting. But the Fourteenth Amendment grants an additional power to Congress to enforce its commands, and Brennan defined this power broadly enough to allow it to intervene to protect Spanish-speakers on its own authority.

Brennan anchored his reading of the enforcement clause in a famous formulation by John Marshall: "Let the end be legitimate, let it be within the scope of the constitution, and all means which are appropriate, which are plainly adapted to that end, which are not prohibited, but consist with the letter and spirit of the constitution, are constitutional."[29]

Under the Brennan-Marshall test, the landmark statute readily received a passing grade. In his view, Congress did more than afford individual Spanish-speakers access to the ballot; it provided "the Puerto Rican community" with a vital tool to ensure nondiscriminatory treatment "in the provision . . . of public schools, public housing and law enforcement."[30] Given the link between voting and public provision, Brennan had no trouble finding that the Voting Rights Act represented "appropriate" enforcement.

Justice Harlan was unconvinced. In a dissent joined by Potter Stewart, he emphasized the remedial character of the enforcement clause. Before it authorized a remedy, Congress had to show there was a substantive constitutional problem: no wrong, no remedy. But according to *Lassiter*,

English-only literacy tests were okay—so there was nothing wrong to remedy.

Harlan was also unimpressed with Brennan's link between Puerto Rican exclusion from the polls and the threat of discriminatory provision of public services. Congress, he pointed out, had made no factual investigation on this point; its ban on English-only literacy tests was based merely on a "legislative announcement that Congress believes a state law to entail an unconstitutional deprivation of equal protection."[31] In rubber-stamping this pronouncement, Brennan was allowing Congress to revise "this Court's constitutional decisions under the Fourteenth . . . Amendment."[32] Despite its brave invocations of John Marshall, *Morgan* was a monument of judicial abdication.

Not guilty, replied Brennan—adding a footnote explicitly denying Harlan's charge that he was giving Congress carte blanche. He insisted instead that the Justices would ensure that Congress could use its *Morgan* powers only to "enforce," rather than "dilute," the Court's substantive interpretations of equal protection.[33]

This riposte begged an obvious question: how were the Justices to tell the difference between "dilution" and "enforcement"?[34] Different theories of equal protection draw this distinction differently. If Brennan's opinion grants Congress authority to choose between them, *Morgan* does indeed allow it to replace the Court's judgment with its own; if not, his Marshallian gestures notwithstanding, Brennan's "third way" could turn out to be a narrow path or a royal highway, depending on how later Courts defined the meaning of "enforcement."

The Brennan-Harlan confrontation has provoked much debate over the last half century, but judges and scholars have generally addressed the question in ahistorical fashion, providing a one-size-fits-all answer to the scope of Congress's power, under *Morgan,* to move beyond the Court's case law.

This is a mistake. *Morgan* was a response to a very special situation. During the 1964 election, Barry Goldwater had insisted that the Civil Rights Act and similar initiatives were constitutionally valid only if they were passed as Article V amendments. Despite these objections, President Johnson, the civil rights movement, and their congressional allies had won a landslide victory at the polls, earning a decisive popular mandate for further breakthroughs.

What is more, in hammering out the Voting Rights Act, the civil rights coalition confronted the Goldwater objection in its most emphatic form, with Spessard Holland pointing to the Twenty-Fourth Amendment as a fundamental precedent limiting the legitimate scope of statutory power. The civil rights leadership did not brush this objection aside but confronted it with high seriousness, self-consciously asserting congressional authority to use the Voting Rights Act as a substitute for a constitutional amendment.

Within this context, we can see that both Brennan and Harlan contributed crucial insights in their famous debate. Harlan was right to insist that *Morgan* was breaking new ground in recognizing Congress's authority to move beyond *Lassiter* on the basis of a "legislative announcement" of a new equal protection doctrine. But he failed to recognize that the president and Congress had *earned* the authority to speak in a constitutional voice—even in the case of the poll tax, where this claim was hardest to make.

Brennan's opinion has the great merit of recognizing this point. Indeed, his invocation of John Marshall is itself expressive of the extraordinary character of the constitutional moment. But his more particular rationale doesn't do justice to the situation. Congress was doing more than "enforcing" the equal protection clause; it was *redefining* it—and inviting the Court to join in a partnership by writing a series of superprecedents worthy of the Second Reconstruction.

But Brennan was determined to maintain the Court's position as senior partner in this collaboration. This was the point of relegating Congress to the role of "enforcer" and insisting that it did not have the authority to "dilute"—whatever that might mean—the reigning case law on equal protection. Within its historical context, Brennan's anxieties were perfectly understandable: between 1954 and 1964, the president and Congress had given *Brown* only lukewarm support, leaving it an open question whether southern backlash would prevail and effectively destroy the Court's claim to ultimate constitutional authority. After a decade in the trenches, it must have been tough for the Court to recognize that it was actually winning the decisive support of We the People; Brennan's concerns about "dilution" expressed this residual anxiety.

These fears deserved to be taken seriously. Writing in 1966, Brennan could not know whether the fundamental changes expressed by the Civil

Rights Act and Voting Rights Act were irreversible: perhaps the Republicans would nominate another Goldwater in 1968; perhaps he would sweep into the White House and gain congressional support for a repeal of the landmark statutes?

On this scenario, the Court would have been forced into a last-ditch defense of *Brown* against its "dilution" or complete evisceration. To put the point in the macro-level terms developed in earlier chapters, Brennan was writing *Morgan* during a period of mobilized elaboration after a triggering election. He could not know whether a ratifying election would authorize a final period of constitutional consolidation.[35] Within this setting, it was only prudent to prepare for the worst-case "dilution" scenario while celebrating the remarkable character of the statutory breakthrough.

Taking all these historical contingencies into account, *Morgan* deserves the high place that the profession awards it in the constitutional canon. Nevertheless, the passage of a half century should give us a deeper perspective on its enduring significance. After all, we now know something that Brennan and Harlan couldn't be sure about when they crossed swords in 1966. Despite Brennan's reasonable fears of a backlash, the American people did indeed reject George Wallace in 1968, and Richard Nixon did indeed redeem his campaign pledges by signing a renewal of the Voting Rights Act in 1970. Since Brennan's anxieties about a sweeping backlash proved to be unfounded, we should read his third-way opinion in *Morgan* as gesturing toward a larger truth: that the coordinate model of constitutional revision in which the president, Congress, and the Court collaborate with landmark statutes and superprecedents—serves as a legitimate substitute for formal Article V amendments under modern conditions.

This reading of *Morgan* is reinforced by our excavation of the poll tax story concealed by Douglas's opinion in *Harper*. While the political exclusion of Spanish-speaking Puerto Ricans was a serious injustice, it gained a place on the action agenda only by attaching itself to the central struggle of the era: the movement for black civil and political rights. Since the poll tax story was a key element in this struggle, it provides the best window into the development of landmark statutes and superprecedents as an Article V alternative. Once we place *Morgan* against the poll tax story concealed by *Harper*, we can bear witness to the way in which President Johnson, King, and the congressional leadership used the Voting Rights Act to hammer out the terms of the modern higher lawmaking system, which relied on landmark statutes and superprecedents to express the will of We the People.

As the keeper of the nation's constitutional memory, the legal community owes it to its fellow citizens to convey the larger message left behind by *Morgan* and *Harper:* the Second Reconstruction was not the gift of the Warren Court but the product of a great popular movement of ordinary Americans, who supported the creation of new methods of higher lawmaking that may serve as precedents for future generations as they confront the constitutional crises of the coming decades.

◆

Chapters 5 and 6 have focused on the Voting Rights Act and its judicial reception, since these case studies provide the most institutionally sustained and politically self-conscious elaboration of my thesis. But these precedents didn't come out of nowhere—they were foreshadowed by themes developed by protagonists engaged in the earlier struggle over the Civil Rights Act of 1964.

So let me conclude this part of the book with a speech by Senator Everett Dirksen at a decisive moment in the passage of the 1964 act. With southern Democrats engaged in an endless filibuster, the fate of the bill was in Dirksen's hands. Liberal Democrats could not supply the sixty-seven votes needed to stop the filibuster without Republican support; only Dirksen, the party's leader in the Senate, could supply the extra votes for the requisite supermajority. After striking a substantive compromise with the Democratic leadership, Dirksen finally swung his Republicans behind the cloture vote that ensured the bill's final passage. Here is how he explained his move on the floor of the Senate:

> There are many reasons why cloture should be invoked and a good civil rights measure enacted.
>
> First. It is said that on the night he died, Victor Hugo wrote in his diary, substantially this sentiment:
>
> Stronger than all the armies is an idea whose time has come.
>
> The time has come for equality of opportunity in sharing in government, in education, and in employment. It will not be stayed or denied. It is here. . . .
>
> Second. . . . Since [the Supreme Court struck down the Civil Rights Act of 1875], America has changed. The population then was 45 million. Today it is 190 million. In the Pledge of Allegiance to the Flag we intone, "One Nation,

under God." And so it is. It is an integrated Nation. Air, rail, and highway transportation make it so. A common language makes it so. A tax pattern which applies equally to white and nonwhite makes it so. Literacy makes it so. The mobility provided by 80 million autos makes it so. The accommodations laws in 34 States and the District of Columbia make it so. The fair employment practice laws in 30 States make it so. Yes, our land has changed since the Supreme Court decision of 1883.

As Lincoln once observed:

The occasion is piled high with difficulty and we must rise with the occasion. As our cause is new, so we must think anew and act anew. We must first disenthrall ourselves and then we shall save the Union. . . .

America grows. America changes. And on the civil rights issue we must rise with the occasion. That calls for cloture and for the enactment of a civil rights bill.

Third. [Each party has made a covenant with the people through its civil rights plank.] . . .

Fourth. [After citing other ideas whose "time had come"—pure food and drug legislation, civil service and merit systems, work hours legislation, popular election of senators, women's suffrage, federal income tax—Dirksen continues:] . . . These are but some of the things touching closely the affairs of the people which were met with stout resistance, with shrill and strident cries of radicalism, with strained legalisms, with anguished entreaties that the foundations of the Republic were being rocked. But an inexorable moral force which operates in the domain of human affairs swept these efforts aside and today they are accepted as parts of the social, economic and political fabric of America.[36]

An idea whose time has come: the accents of higher lawmaking are unmistakable, but the speaker should not be confused with the likes of Martin Luther King Jr. or Lyndon Johnson.[37] Dirksen was the spokesman for a generation of mainstream conservatives who were centrally preoccupied with opposing New Deal expansions of the activist regulatory state. But he was now calling upon his fellow Republicans to rise to the historic occasion and reassert their identity as the party of Lincoln. His proud declaration that the "time has come" was front-page news.[38]

In rallying his fellow conservatives, Dirksen made his case in terms that explicitly addressed our major theme. In citing a series of twentieth-century efforts at fundamental reform, he did not limit himself to those, such as the income tax, that involved constitutional amendments. He emphasized that landmark statutes, such as the federal minimum wage law, also serve as compelling precedents: they were propelled by "an inexorable moral force" that had "swept . . . aside . . . strained legalisms" and had now gained acceptance "as parts of the social, economic and political fabric of America."

Dirksen saw himself as participating in yet another of these cycles of constitutional politics, and rejected the "strained legalisms" with which southern senators were trying to bind Congress to the constitutional past.

Our next task is to confront these legalisms and consider the extent to which they continue to rule us from the grave, despite Dirksen's emphatic resolution to the contrary.

PART TWO

Landmarks of Reconstruction

CHAPTER 7

Spheres of Humiliation

S UPPOSE YOU WERE CONVINCED. Suppose you agreed that Americans did not lose their constitutional voice in the twentieth century. Suppose you treated the Second Reconstruction as a genuine act of popular sovereignty. Suppose you recognized that the landmark statutes of the 1960s, no less than the amendments of the 1860s, expressed the will of the American people. Suppose you joined in the effort to construct a new constitutional canon for the twenty-first century.

You would still have a long way to go. In revising the canon, the legal community is not writing on a clean slate. It has already developed a set of categories and stories that express the meaning of the civil rights revolution. The existing account contains a great deal of insight, and it would be silly to lose hard-won wisdom in the pursuit of a broader understanding. The challenge is to integrate old and new into a deeper synthesis of the civil rights legacy.

This chapter begins with the traditional starting point: *Brown v. Board of Education*. But it has an untraditional objective. In the standard court-centered story, *Brown* serves as the prelude to a wide-ranging judicial effort to confront discrimination based on race, ethnicity, religion, gender, and sexual preference. My account emphasizes how *Brown* shaped the constitutional politics of the next decade, defining the terms within which Hubert Humphrey and other legislative leaders made the case for the Civil Rights Act of 1964. After linking *Brown*'s logic to the central arguments for the landmark statute, I return to the Court's complex response to this congressional debate. By moving from the Court in 1954 to Congress in 1964 to the Court's response to the popular affirmation of the landmark statute, we will be building a new canon that recognizes how the judiciary, the political branches, and the American people worked together to build new foundations for a Second Reconstruction.

The new civil rights canon permits a host of new perspectives, beginning with a reinterpretation of *Brown* itself. While the lawyerly debate over equal protection rages on, there is something very curious about *Brown*'s current status: none of the protagonists takes Chief Justice Warren's opinion seriously. Whatever else they disagree about, lawyers and judges all fail to study Warren's words with care, choosing instead to see the opinion as a way station on the route to some far more glorious principle. This is the point at which the real argument begins. Different legal schools bitterly disagree about the doctrinal "truth" that Warren and his companions somehow failed to announce as they set out on their great mission to vindicate the Fourteenth Amendment to their complacent countrymen.

Speaking broadly, two contending camps dominate doctrinal discussion.[1] One school cites *Brown* for an anti-classification principle: no statute or regulation, they say, should sort people out on the basis of racial or other suspect categories without compelling justification. On this view, the spirit of *Brown* urges the state to judge each individual on his or her own merit, without regard to race or other suspect classifications.

The anti-categorization school has not (yet?) decisively vanquished its longtime competitor, which focuses on the fate of groups, not individuals. On this approach, blacks living under Jim Crow serve as a paradigm example of a much broader problem that continues to afflict many groups in the twenty-first century. This is the problem of pervasive societal discrimination. On this reading, *Brown* is concerned with the systematic subordination of powerless groups and requires class-based remedies, most notably affirmative action, to root out historically entrenched injustices.

Anti-classification versus anti-subordination: as we shall see, Warren's opinion refuses to embrace either of these principles, which is precisely why neither school takes Warren's text seriously. This dismissive treatment is downright odd. We are dealing, after all, with the opinion that marks the greatest moment in the history of the Court. Doesn't its message deserve to be considered carefully on its own terms?

There is great wisdom in Warren's opinion, but a single master insight will suffice for now: the Court's emphasis on the distinctive wrongness of institutionalized humiliation. I will be contrasting *Brown*'s anti-humiliation principle with the two traditional approaches, showing how Warren's words provided a constitutional framework for the larger exercise of popular sovereignty culminating in the landmark statutes of the

1960s. This will, I hope, encourage lawyers and judges to break out of their current doctrinal impasse and develop the distinctive implications of a concern with institutionalized humiliation. It also suggests the larger interpretive promise of the new canon: emphasizing landmark statutes doesn't lead to a trivialization of the Supreme Court but often gives its contribution a deeper meaning. As we shall see, this is true of many other great opinions contributed by the Court to the larger process through which Americans made higher law during the civil rights era.

THE LOST LOGIC OF *BROWN V. BOARD*

Both anti-classification and anti-subordination have comprehensive aspirations. Anti-classification challenges *all* state actions that use suspect categories such as race; anti-subordination interrogates *all* pervasive forms of status inferiority. As a consequence, both approaches have trouble with Warren's opinion, which famously limits itself to a declaration that *Plessy* has no place "in the field of public education."[2] Because *Brown* leaves *Plessy* standing in other areas, both anti-classification and anti-subordination can only treat it as a way station en route to their more comprehensive visions.

Brown's sphere-by-sphere approach deserves a more sympathetic reading. Its distinctive focus is symptomatic of a sociological jurisprudence that provides the framework for the entire opinion: first, in defining the nature of the problem; second, in emphasizing the inadequacy of traditional legalistic approaches to social life; third, in explaining why the public schools are an especially strategic sphere for constitutional concern; fourth, in exploring the significance of humiliation; and fifth, in explaining why social science should play a role in constitutional law.

On the first point, it was sociological jurisprudence that led the Court to reject originalism as a plausible approach. Warren explained that when the equal protection clause was enacted, "the movement toward free common schools . . . had not yet taken hold [in the South]. . . . Even in the North, the conditions of public education did not approximate those existing today . . . the school term was but three months a year in many states; and compulsory school attendance was virtually unknown. As a consequence, it is not surprising that there should be so little in the history of the Fourteenth Amendment relating to its intended effect on public education."[3]

But by 1954 public education had become a full-blown sphere of lived experience, with a distinctive set of practices and expectations that set it apart from the family, the workplace, and other zones of daily life. This sociological point, according to Warren, made it silly to treat the occasional remarks of nineteenth-century debaters as if they provided the last word on the subject; it is merely punning to suppose that when they spoke of "public schools," they were soberly addressing twentieth-century realities.

The sociological critique of originalism required a fundamental revision of inherited patterns of legal thought. For Reconstruction Republicans, only three spheres of life were worth distinguishing: the political sphere, which involved voting and the like; the civil sphere, which involved the legal protection of life and liberty, including rights of property and contract; and the social sphere, which involved everything else.[4] Within this traditional trichotomy, the Reconstruction Amendments protected political and civil rights but not social rights.

Here is where Warren made a second fundamental contribution: he proposed to pluralize the social realm into a series of more discrete spheres. The key to step two of *Brown*'s logic is that Americans live out their lives in a multiplicity of social institutions, each with its own practices and expectations. The social world of the school, for example, is organized on principles different from those we encounter at home, work, church, or the neighborhood bar. As a consequence, the same action that may be deeply meaningful at home may be radically wrongheaded at school or work, and vice versa. Rather than pointing vaguely at the social aspect of life, *Brown* is urging us to confront the multiplicity of social spheres, each with its own normative shape, and ask how our constitutional commitment to equality affects the real-world meanings Americans encounter as they move from sphere to sphere in everyday life.[5]

This leads to a third step: now that courts recognize the plurality of social spheres, they must begin to assign priorities. Which spheres are central for the guarantee of equal protection, and which aren't?

Brown's answer:

Today, education is perhaps the most important function of state and local governments. Compulsory school attendance laws and the great expenditures for education both demonstrate our recognition of the importance of education to our democratic society. It is required in the performance of our most basic public responsibilities, even service in the armed forces. It is the very foundation of good citizenship. Today it is a principal instrument in awakening the child to cultural values, in preparing him for later professional training, and in helping him to adjust normally to his environment. In these days, it is doubtful that any child may reasonably be expected to succeed in life if he is denied the opportunity of an education. Such an opportunity, where the state has undertaken to provide it, is a right which must be made available to all on equal terms.[6]

Warren's argument for singling out public education focused on its relationship to other crucial spheres: "citizenship," "military service," "professional training"—each constituted, once again, by distinctive sets of practices, expectations, and models of meaningful action.

In making its case against "separate but equal," *Brown*'s logic certainly doesn't apply to all social relationships across the board. Step three requires the law to single out crucial spheres for the vindication of equality through a complex calculus that assesses both the intrinsic importance of a particular sphere and its strategic relationship to other sociologically significant domains.

We can now proceed to step four. Since public education is a crucial sphere, the Court's next task is to determine whether dominant norms and practices operate to humiliate black children: "To separate them [blacks] from others of similar age and qualifications solely because of their race generates a feeling of inferiority as to their status in the community that may affect their hearts and minds in a way unlikely ever to be undone."[7] These famous lines are indelibly etched into the nation's consciousness. In writing them, did Warren break new methodological ground?

In contrast to the first three moves, the answer here is no. Warren was simply calling upon judges, and the rest of us, to make commonsense judgments about the prevailing meaning of social practices. One of the greatest legal thinkers of the era, Karl Llewellyn, persuasively argued that judges couldn't decide the most humdrum case without relying on this capacity, which he famously called "situation-sense."[8] Without using their common sense, they couldn't determine whether a defendant was a charlatan who had defrauded an innocent victim or whether he was acting reasonably under the circumstances. Warren's contribution in this phase of the argument involved constitutional principle, not judicial method. He was insisting that the Constitution called upon the Justices to use their situation-sense to determine whether segregated schools systematically humiliated black children.

This is precisely the point at which *Brown* departed from *Plessy*. The earlier decision had identified "the underlying fallacy of the plaintiff's argument to consist in the assumption that the enforced separation of the two races stamps the colored race with a badge of inferiority. If this be so, it is not by reason of anything found in the act, but solely because the colored race chooses to put that construction upon it."[9] For Warren, judges must move beyond the language "found in the act" to explore the social meaning of real-world practices. These meanings are generated by the dominant norms that prevail in particular spheres of life. The judicial task is to interpret these norms, not to indulge *Plessy*'s misleading suggestion that they are up to individual "choice." Warren emphasized this point by promoting some lower court findings to a central position in his text: "Segregation of white and colored children in public schools has a detrimental effect upon the colored children. The impact is greater when it has the sanction of the law; *for the policy of separating the races is usually interpreted as denoting the inferiority of the negro group.*"[10] The key phrase is "usually interpreted": Warren was relying on judicial situation-sense to determine whether school segregation "denot[es] the inferiority of the negro group." If it does, the equal protection clause condemns it; if not, not.

In this particular case, only a Martian would have trouble figuring out the right answer: southern-style school segregation was indeed "usually interpreted" by schoolchildren and their parents as humiliating. Judicial situation-sense was enough to vindicate this key conclusion—a point emphasized by Professor Charles Black at the time, but too often missed by an undue emphasis on the fifth and final step in *Brown*'s argument.[11]

In this last move, the Court buttressed its commonsense conclusions with the findings of social science. This move made perfect sense in an opinion concerned with real-world stigma, not legal categorization. But Warren famously got into trouble by relying so heavily on Kenneth Clark's psychological studies of schoolchildren. While Clark's work couldn't bear all this weight, this shouldn't undermine the more general appeal of Warren's final argumentative move.

It was Louis Brandeis, not Thurgood Marshall, who first used social science to convince courts to consider the real-world impact of their doctrines. As early as 1908, the Supreme Court relied heavily on his famous "Brandeis Brief" in upholding maximum-hours laws for women.[12] During the following decades, law schools became centers of sociological and economic critique of the regnant legal formalism, with Frankfurter and

Pound at Harvard, and Douglas and his fellow legal realists at Yale, gaining special prominence. With the triumph of the New Deal, the Progressive use of social science was transformed into jurisprudential bedrock—expertise was the lifeblood of the new administrative state, and New Deal courts recognized the relevance of social science on a broad front. *Brown* was continuing this tradition. Although Clark's studies were inadequate, the answer was to generate better work while relying in the meantime on judicial situation-sense to tell the commonsense truth that southerners were humiliating black children by refusing to allow them to attend common schools with their white peers.

To sum up: in limiting its decision to education, the Court wasn't engaged in a timid evasion of some grand legal theory attacking societywide subordination or racial categorization. It was proceeding sphere by sphere in a sociological spirit, challenging constitutionalists to make the principle of equality meaningful to ordinary Americans as they engaged in critical spheres of social life.

If public education wasn't such a sphere, what was?

And if segregated schools didn't humiliate, what did?

These questions no longer dominate legal debate, but they were very much at the center of constitutional politics of the 1950s and 1960s. In hammering out their landmark legislation, Congress and the president were not aiming for a one-size-fits-all solution. They followed Warren's path. Step by step, they identified additional spheres of social life that were strategic sites for constitutional intervention: public accommodations, private employment, and fair housing. They then set about achieving real-world equality in ways that were tailored to each sphere's prevailing practices and meanings—sometimes successfully, sometimes less so.

In short, *Brown* not only represents the unanimous judgment of the Supreme Court at a great moment in its history. It also expresses the animating logic for the landmark statutes supported by the American people at one of the greatest moments in their history. Given all this, isn't it past time for the legal community to reclaim *Brown*'s lost logic?

This part of the book provides a framework. Different chapters will deal with different spheres, revealing different aspects of the struggle against humiliation and the pursuit of "spherical equality," as I will call it. But first let's consider in more detail *Brown*'s contribution to the larger debate that culminated with the passage of the landmark statutes of the 1960s.

BROWN'S VINDICATION

Warren made an additional gesture to sociological jurisprudence in writing his opinion: he targeted the general public, not the legal profession, as his primary audience. He avoided legalistic discussions of prior case law, presenting his arguments in short, accessible paragraphs. His effort to reach out to ordinary Americans was especially important, since President Eisenhower was not prepared to take the lead and Congress was bitterly divided over the Court's initiative. As a consequence, *Brown*'s commonsense prose helped anchor the next decade's constitutional debate—serving as a target for opponents as well as a rallying point for defenders. This wouldn't have happened if Warren had written in complex legalisms that only the profession could understand.

Which leads to a paradox: while Warren's words inaugurated a great constitutional debate over the next decade, the Court didn't participate on an ongoing basis. The Justices returned to center stage in the Little Rock crisis, demanding obedience to their commands, but they refused to elaborate *Brown*'s reasoning—despite many opportunities to do so. During the 1950s, lower courts were regularly invoking *Brown* in decisions striking down segregation in more and more spheres of life—public transportation, parks, golf courses, beaches. While the Court upheld these judgments, it refused to explain why. It simply published one-line affirmances in the *United States Reports*.

Worse yet, the Court upheld state bans on interracial marriage in decisions that will command our sustained attention in a later chapter. But for now it will be enough to confront the mind-bending paradoxes generated by the Court's checkered jurisprudence: as the law stood in the late 1950s, Virginia couldn't prohibit interracial couples from swimming on public beaches, but it could criminalize their efforts to get married. These tensions led leading academics such as Herbert Wechsler to condemn the Court's race cases as utterly unprincipled—provoking *Brown*'s academic defenders to respond with (conflicting) efforts to provide a compelling rationale.[13] Despite the professional uproar, the Court made no attempt to elaborate or revise *Brown*'s logic.

The general public ignored these academic squabbles. So far as it was concerned, Warren's original statement continued to define the constitutional issues raised by the civil rights struggle. Consider the Montgomery bus boycott. When Rosa Parks's arrest sparked mass action in December

1955, the only thing she "knew" was "that it was the very last time that I would ever ride in humiliation of this kind."[14] At some other time and place, Parks's remark might have simply conveyed a courageous commitment to justice. But Warren's opinion transformed her refusal to "ride in humiliation" into the obvious foundation for a constitutional claim—one that the Court upheld the following year, when it intervened in Montgomery to ban segregated busing.[15] Wechslerians complained that the Justices' Montgomery bus opinion consisted of a single sentence invoking *Brown*. Yet this citation was enough for Parks and millions of others to expand their struggle against institutionalized humiliation into other crucial spheres of social life.

The struggle reached new heights in Birmingham, Alabama, in 1963. When a group of young activists led a campaign of civil disobedience, Sheriff Eugene "Bull" Connor responded with mass arrests. As a shocked nation viewed the violent scenes on television, Martin Luther King Jr. joined the demonstrations—only to find himself incarcerated as well. His great "Letter from Birmingham City Jail" called upon Americans to confront the fundamental issues:

> I guess it is easy for those who have never felt the stinging darts of segregation to say "Wait." But . . . when you suddenly find your tongue twisted and your speech stammering as you seek to explain to your six-year-old daughter why she can't go to the public amusement park that has just been advertised on television, and see tears welling up in her little eyes when she is told that Funtown is closed to colored children, and see the depressing clouds of inferiority begin to form in her little mental sky, and see her begin to distort her little personality by unconsciously developing a bitterness to white people; when you have to concoct an answer for a five-year-old son asking in agonizing pathos: "Daddy, why do white people treat colored people so mean?"; when you take a cross-country drive and find it necessary to sleep night after night in the uncomfortable corners of your automobile because no motel will accept you; when you are humiliated day in and day out by nagging signs reading "white" and "colored"; . . . when you are forever fighting a degenerating sense of "nobodiness"; then you will understand why we find it difficult to wait.[16]

King's open letter was a response to a critique signed by eight white "liberal" Alabama clergymen, so much of his argument was couched in theological terms. But his emphasis on institutionalized humiliation supported King's larger claim that "[w]e have waited for more than 340 years for our constitutional and God-given rights" and that the moment for a decisive breakthrough had come.[17]

With the Court and the movement propelling it forward, the anti-humiliation theme played a central role as congressional leaders made their case for the Civil Rights Act in 1964. The Senate was the central forum for this national great debate. The floor leaders were Democrat Hubert Humphrey and Republican Thomas Kuchel, and they were well aware of its historic significance: not only did they present elaborate speeches introducing the larger purposes of the entire initiative, but similar presentations were advanced by the Democratic and Republican senators who served as floor managers for each important part of the act. This remarkable set of speeches deserves a central place in our understanding of the Second Reconstruction. Just as lawyers ponder the words of John Bingham or Charles Sumner in elaborating the meaning of the Fourteenth Amendment, they should listen to Hubert Humphrey as he tells us about the Civil Rights Act:

> It is difficult for most of us to comprehend the monstrous humiliations and inconveniences that racial discrimination imposes on our Negro fellow citizens. If a white man is thirsty on a hot day, he goes to the nearest soda fountain. If he is hungry, he goes to the nearest restaurant. If he needs a restroom, he can go to the nearest gas station. If it is night and he is tired, he takes his pick of the available motels and hotels.
>
> But for a Negro the picture is different. Trying to get a glass of iced tea at a lunch counter may result in insult and abuse, unless he is willing to go out of his way, perhaps to walk across town. He can never count on using a restroom, on getting a decent place to stay, on buying a good meal. These are trivial matters in the life of a white person, but for some 20 million American Negroes, they are important considerations that must be planned for in detail. They must draw up travel plans much as a general advancing across hostile territory would establish his logistical support.[18]

"Monstrous humiliations"—this is the evil that the public accommodations provisions aim to eradicate. Humphrey returns to this theme in a particularly revealing colloquy with Florida's George Smathers:

> I should like to ask the Senator if he thinks that either the Senator from Florida or the Senator from Minnesota knows what it feels like to be a Negro and to be told he cannot come into a restaurant, to be told he cannot come into a hotel, to be told he cannot send his children to school. . . . How does the Senator think people feel under those circumstances?

What is happening is not so much economics, even though it amounts to economic deprivation. It is not so much education, even though we know people have been denied education. *What is happening is humiliation, the lack of a sense of dignity which has been imposed upon people.*[19]

Going further, Humphrey insisted that "freedom from indignity" should rank along with Franklin Roosevelt's "four freedoms"—freedom of speech, freedom of conscience, freedom from fear, and freedom from want.[20] One month later, Lyndon Johnson followed up: "We cannot deny to a group of our own people, our own American citizens, *the essential elements of human dignity* which a majority of our citizens claim for ourselves."[21]

This stress on humiliation and its relationship to human dignity may surprise American constitutional lawyers. While the idea of dignity serves as the foundation of constitutional rights in Europe and elsewhere, American lawyers generally derive their basic principles from the ideas of equal protection and due process.

This is a misconception—based on a failure to appreciate how *Brown*'s lost logic was reinforced during the struggle for the landmark statutes of the 1960s. It is past time for America's lawyers to hear the voices of the Second Reconstruction, and treat them with the same respect they accord to the likes of Bingham and Sumner when they spoke for the People during the First Reconstruction. Once we choose to listen, we will find that constitutional appeals to dignity abound.[22]

Dignity is a notoriously protean notion, but Humphrey and Johnson were following Warren and King in giving it a distinctive shape, requiring the elimination of the "humiliation" that had been systematically "imposed on people." Over the course of a decade, the initial rendering of this principle in *Brown* moved far beyond the ambit of courts to gain deliberate assent by leading representatives of the American people—and that is no small matter.

ON HUMILIATION

Humiliation is something that almost all of us have experienced. So we can consult our own personal experiences to gain a firmer grasp on the distinctive features of the concept. Once we reflect on everyday examples, we will be in a better position to understand the particular evils of the institutionalized humiliation that *Brown* and the statutes condemn.[23]

Begin with a garden-variety case: You are at work, and you've done a lousy job. You were supposed to fix the machine but you've only managed to make it worse, or you were supposed to prepare a report but you've produced gibberish, or whatever. The day of reckoning has arrived: either you tell your boss and fellow workers or they are going to find out anyway.

As you confront this moment of truth, you may feel embarrassed; after all, you know you haven't performed up to standard. But this is not inevitable. Maybe you are tough or cynical and successfully suppress such fluttery emotions. In any event, embarrassment isn't the same thing as humiliation—which can arise only at the next stage.

Your fellow workers learn of your failure, and what they do next matters decisively. They may respond sympathetically: "Look, everybody makes mistakes. Let's see how you can avoid this problem the next time around." Under this scenario, you haven't been humiliated even if you remain acutely embarrassed. But of course, the response may not be so friendly: "You jerk. How in the world could you have let that happen?"

We have reached the moment of humiliation, which I define as *a face-to-face insult in which the victim acquiesces in the effort to impugn his standing as a minimally competent actor within a particular sphere of life.*

These terms need unpacking, beginning with the "face-to-face" proviso. Suppose that your boss doesn't insult you in the presence of your fellow workers. After responding sympathetically in your presence, he returns to his office and immediately files a terrible job report—"John Doe is a total incompetent!" If the boss had said this face-to-face, you would have been humiliated. But he didn't, and the report doesn't qualify under my definition.

Perhaps my definition is too narrow. As a test, suppose that the boss's report convinces the firm's higher-ups to deny you the promotion you are pining for. You are summoned to the chief executive's office, and the chief gives you the bad news in the nicest possible way: "Your work was fine, but your rival's work was even better. Maybe you'll get the next big opening." No humiliation, by my reckoning, since your "standing as a minimally competent actor" hasn't been impugned.

Yet this conclusion may only strengthen the force of the objection. By hypothesis, you failed to get promoted because your boss stigmatized you as an "incompetent" in his report to the chief executive. Suppose further that you leave the chief's office bitterly disappointed—you *really* wanted that job. Worse yet, despite the chief's sweet talk, you sense that your career has hit a dead end. This recognition shatters your sense of self-worth. Given its devastating impact, why not say that the boss humiliated you in filing his report?

Because humiliation isn't a catchall phrase describing any and all actions generating bitter disappointment. It points to a special harm: even if people are saying harsh things about us behind our back, we can still go about our business in the normal way and receive the standard responses from our peers: "Good morning. See you at the meeting after lunch." But a face-to-face show of contempt stops us in our tracks: however much you'd like to pretend it isn't happening, your boss is degrading you to your face, leaving you with the hard choice: either acquiesce in this profound insult or directly defy the insulter.

It's only if you go along that your humiliation is complete. If you defy your boss instead, he hasn't succeeded in humiliating you. Of course, he may respond to your act of defiance by firing you on the spot—in which case you may face crushing financial burdens as you leave with your head held high. In contrast, if you acquiesce, you may get to keep your job, or even get ahead in the long run. The key point is that humiliation isn't just another psychological or economic "cost" of operating in the world. It is, first and foremost, a form of intersubjective encounter.

We must keep this in mind in clarifying the meaning of "acquiescence." As you stand silent before the boss's stream of insults, many things may be going on inside you. You may be steaming with rage, vowing revenge at the first opportunity; you may be bitterly resigned to the injustices of life; you may even affirmatively endorse the boss's right to expose you to public disparagement. Whatever your psychological response, the fact remains that you are acquiescing in your own degradation. When the boss puts you in this position, he is doing something that is wrong in itself, regardless of the psychological or economic consequences.

Up to now, I've been telling stories of personal humiliation that occur against the background premise of shared social competence. The reason my scenarios are damaging is that they operate to strip the victim of this ongoing presumption of competence, thereby degrading him in the eyes of the relevant community. In contrast, humiliation is institutionalized by social practices that strip an entire group of this ongoing presumption. The imposition of a systematic degradation ritual is even worse than the individualized form—once again, regardless of the consequences.

This is the point Rosa Parks was making in her reflections on Montgomery. At the moment she defied the bus driver's command, she could not know the ultimate consequences of her action; perhaps white Birmingham would successfully crush the boycott and make it even tougher for blacks to travel around the city. The only thing she could "know" was that "it was the very last time that I would ever ride in humiliation."

There was a face-to-face aspect to Parks's humiliation before she engaged in her act of defiance. She might have tried to ignore the stares of whites as she moved down the aisle to the back of the bus. But she knew that they knew that she was acquiescing in a dignity-stripping ritual as she walked to her "proper place" on the bus. The same was true in many other segregated contexts. Consider workplaces where blacks were restricted to menial roles. In countless interactions with white superiors, they were obliged to show in word and deed that "they knew their place." If they refused, they would be fired—signaling to others the dangers of being "uppity."

Nevertheless, when humiliation is institutionalized, it may often occur without a direct face-to-face encounter. Consider, for example, the hotel or restaurant in the Jim Crow South that publicly proclaimed: "No Negroes Allowed." If a black entered anyway, he was sure to confront an emphatic humiliation ritual, culminating with the police dragging him off as trespasser. These threats were often so potent that for decades nobody dared challenge the sign, rendering the prospect of humiliation invisible. This is why the lunch counter sit-ins of the early 1960s played a role similar to Rosa Parks's act of defiance at Montgomery—signaling to the world that blacks would no longer be intimidated by threats of humiliation.

I labor this point to emphasize that institutionalized humiliation may continue long after the restaurants take down their signs and employers no longer explicitly restrict blacks to menial jobs. Even if they are formally accepted into the give-and-take of life within one or another social sphere, they may confront a steady stream of humiliating encounters with fellow participants, generating the same disparaging institutional message. Even if obvious forms of racial insult are minimized, the same pathologies may arise in subtler form.

Suppose, for example, that our hypothetical boss reacts very differently to worker blunders. When white guys make mistakes, he calls them into his private office for sympathetic chats. When black women make similar errors, he publicly humiliates them before their peers. It won't take long before everybody in the office picks up the obvious message: "Watch out, black women. The slightest mistake you make will turn you into an object of ridicule."

From this perspective, the existence of superachieving group members in one or another sphere is hardly enough to disprove the existence of institutionalized humiliation. During the darkest days of racism, men such as Ralph Bunche or Jackie Robinson could decisively establish their competence within their social realms. But this did not lift the presumption of incompetence that exposed countless others to daily humiliation.

As with its individualistic counterpart, institutionalized humiliation is a spherical affair. It may no longer be a serious reality when blacks enter a hotel or restaurant—yet it may remain deeply entrenched in many workplaces and public schools throughout the nation. The only way this can be determined, as *Brown* suggests, is by assessing whether the particular spherical patterns are best "interpreted as denoting the inferiority of the negro group."

This will be a recurring theme in later chapters, but one point suffices for now. While blacks may not encounter institutional humiliation in some spheres of twenty-first-century life, this was definitely not true of the Jim Crow South. To the contrary, they confronted a series of sphere-by-sphere humiliations that cumulated in a totalizing disparagement of their standing as competent adults. This left them—in King's words—in a condition where they were "forever fighting a degenerating sense of 'nobodiness.'"

King's "Letter from Birmingham City Jail" raises a fundamental issue: Did the constitutional regime created by the civil rights revolution emphasize the totalizing character of black subordination? Or did the landmark statutes of the 1960s follow *Brown*'s lead and seek only to eliminate institutionalized humiliation in a selected number of strategic spheres?

Sphericality

Begin with the very organization of the Civil Rights Act. The statute does not contain a statement of abstract principles for general application. It explicitly embraces sphericality: Title II deals with public accommodation, Title IV with public education, Title VII with employment, and so forth.

Let's focus on public accommodations, since later chapters will deal with other spheres at greater length. The debate over "Mrs. Murphy's boardinghouse" is particularly revealing. For Senator Dirksen and others, Mrs. Murphy was a not-so-imaginary landlady who supplemented her meager income by renting out a few rooms of her own house—but experienced visceral disgust at sharing her living space with Negroes. Should Title II require her to overcome these racist instincts and henceforth proceed on a nondiscriminatory basis?

No, explained Hubert Humphrey, using *Brown*'s spherical logic to justify a "Mrs. Murphy exemption":

> The purpose of this exclusion is self-evident: Title II, like the bill as a whole, is designed to reach the most significant manifestations of discrimination. It is carefully drafted and moderate in nature. There is no desire to regulate truly personal or private relationships. The so-called Mrs. Murphy provision results from a recognition of the fact that a number of people open their homes to transient guests, often not as a regular business, but as a supplement to their income. The relationships involved in such situations are clearly and unmistakably of a much closer and more personal nature than in the case of major commercial establishments.[24]

Once again, sociological jurisprudence provided the framework for Humphrey's rationale: he was presenting "the home" as a distinctive sphere for "personal" relationships, and found it "self-evident" that Mrs. Murphy's home remains a special place even though she has decided to make a little money "by opening up her home to transient guests." Her relationship to her visitors will "unmistakably" be "more personal" than that obtained in a "major commercial establishment."

Contrast Humphrey's solicitude for Mrs. Murphy with his refusal to tolerate the "humiliation" imposed on a Negro who is told that "he cannot come into a hotel." It was clear to him that the two exclusions carry different social meanings. While a tired black family might bitterly resent Mrs. Murphy's decision, they would understand themselves as victims of her personal choice—and this is categorically different from the institutionalized humiliation imposed by a hotel clerk who rejects them as part of his standard operating procedures.

Note Humphrey's confidence that the difference between these cases is "self-evident," "unmistakable"—nobody with the slightest situation-sense would deny it. In coming to this conclusion, Humphrey reinvigorated Earl Warren's logic in *Brown*, retracing steps three and four of his great opinion.

In contrast, Humphrey's defense of the "Mrs. Murphy exemption" is an embarrassment for conventional views that look upon *Brown* as a way station on the road to grander theories of equal protection. Begin with anti-subordination. The problem here is that the cumulative impact of the "personal" decisions of lots of Mrs. Murphys can impose a very substantial burden on blacks as a group. Yet these aggregate effects aren't sufficient to convince Humphrey to expand the scope of statutory concern: so long as they arise through personal rather than institutional decisions, they are beyond the concern of the landmark statute.

While Humphrey's rationale is more narrowly focused than anti-subordination, it is far broader than the anti-classification approach traditionally viewed as the alternative. The landmark statute prohibits discrimination by hundreds of thousands of privately owned facilities even when the laws and governmental officials refuse to endorse their racist practices.[25] In contrast, anti-classification only scrutinizes the actions of the state and its representatives when blacks are singled out for special treatment. But, speaking for his colleagues, Humphrey swept away this fundamental restriction—precisely because a hotel clerk is humiliating a black customer when he denies him a room just as much as a government official does when he refuses to allow a black person to enter a meeting hall owned by the public.

Note how this fundamental commitment against institutionalized humiliation only comes into play under spherical presuppositions. Suppose, for example, that a black person is penniless because his former employer fired him for blatantly racist reasons, in violation of Title VII. Nevertheless, Title II doesn't allow the employment victim to raise this legitimate grievance when he moves into the sphere of public accommodations. If he doesn't have the money to pay his bill, the hotel can lawfully deny him service. It's only if he *does* have the cash that Title II comes into play.

WILL THE COURT INTERVENE?

As Congress was hammering out the terms of Title II in the spring of 1964, the Justices were confronting the very same issues in a pending case. *Bell v. Maryland* offered an opportunity to reconsider the Court's epochal decision, in 1883, to strike down the Civil Rights Act of 1875, the nation's first public accommodation law. In these Civil Rights Cases,[26] Justice Joseph P. Bradley had famously declared that Congress could not legislate against "every act of discrimination which a person may see fit to make as to the guests he will entertain, or as to the people he will take into his coach or cab or car, or admit to his concert or theater, or deal with in other matters of intercourse or business."[27]

Speaking for the majority, he declared that the equal protection clause applied only to states, not to private individuals operating under neutral laws. His decision codified a basic trichotomy emerging from the First Reconstruction, which understood the recent amendments to guarantee civil and political equality, not social equality.

The nineteenth-century Court's principal tool for differentiating the civil from the social was private property. Each citizen had a fundamental civil right to go to court and protect his private property from the depredations of others. But so long as his property was legally secure, he could pursue his ends in the social realm without the federal government forcing him to deal with blacks on a nondiscriminatory basis.

We have already heard Senator Dirksen urging Congress to move beyond the Civil Rights Cases in his filibuster-breaking speech of June 1964.[28] But starting in the New Deal, the Court had begun undermining Bradley's line between public and private,[29] and it had continued to extend the scope of state responsibility in a series of sit-in cases in 1963.[30]

Bell v. Maryland involved another sit-in, but it was the toughest case by far. The Maryland court had simply enforced a race-neutral criminal trespass statute against protesters who had refused to leave a Baltimore restaurant upon the manager's request. If this was enough to qualify as state action, property owners could no longer call upon the police without accepting an obligation to respect the Equal Protection Clause. The Civil Rights Cases would be buried at long last.

The case came up for oral argument on October 15, 1963. Arguing for the United States as amicus, Deputy Solicitor General Ralph Spritzer emphasized that "the President is seeking . . . legislation which . . . would be directed at the very problems which underlie this kind of litigation."[31] He urged the Court to give Congress wide leeway by disposing of the case on narrow grounds.

This plea for restraint met with a cold reception in conference. Justices Brennan, Warren, Douglas, and Goldberg wanted to strike a decisive blow against the "state action" doctrine propounded by the Civil Rights Cases.[32] This was unacceptable to Justice Black, who assembled a five-judge majority to uphold the sit-in convictions: "[T]he mere fact that a privately owned business serves a large segment of the public does not mean that it is constitutionally required to serve all."[33]

Finding themselves in the minority, the four liberals became enthusiastic partisans of judicial restraint. Here is Goldberg at the next conference:

> [I]f we allow public discrimination in public places, I am convinced that we will set back legislation indefinitely. Our society will then have an evil virus inside it that will keep it frozen on racial lines. It would be a great disservice to the nation to decide this issue 5–4. There is legislation pending. The federal government's argument is not implausible.[34]

When this plea failed, Brennan led the four liberals in a series of delaying actions to give Congress a chance to pass the Civil Rights Act.[35] He first bought time by persuading Justice Stewart to join the four liberals in a request for a supplemental brief from the solicitor general on "the broader constitutional issues which have been mooted."[36] When the conservatives were unmoved by the new brief, the liberals began bombarding Black with dissenting opinions that required him to revise his draft repeatedly to shore up his slim majority.[37] But by May 1964, Black was finally in a position to hand down a ringing reaffirmation of the Civil Rights Cases— only to see Justice Clark defect at the very last moment.[38]

By early June, Clark was circulating a draft that sounded the death knell for the state action doctrine:

> [A]s Mr. Justice McLean stated in United States v. McDaniel, 7 Pet. 1, 15 (1833), "Usage cannot alter law, but it is evidence of the construction given to it; . . . usages . . . which have become a kind of common law . . . regulate the rights and duties of those who act within their respective limits." We know of no usage that has grown any more into "a kind of common law" than that recognized by all men with respect to public restaurants. . . . [M]illions of our people go to them with the expectation and realization of service. Nothing has stronger support in experience. The well-behaved are always welcome. In some communities the only exceptions are those of color. This customary treatment has, therefore, in some communities, grown into a standard, foreign to the Equal Protection Clause.[39]

Clark was following the path blazed by Warren in *Brown* (recall step four). Just as the Chief Justice found that school segregation was "usually interpreted as denoting the inferiority of the negro group," Clark appealed to "expectations" grounded in everyday "experience" that public restaurants "always welcome" customers who are "well-behaved." By denying service to blacks, the Baltimore restaurant was disparaging their standing as grown-ups capable of fulfilling normal adult standards of conduct. This disparagement of basic social competence is, as we have seen, the very essence of institutionalized humiliation.[40] It is no surprise that Warren enthusiastically signed on to Clark's opinion, predicting that it would "be a classic."[41] After all, it was declaring that institutionalized humiliations arising in the private marketplace could, like those condemned by *Brown,* give rise to common-law violations of the Equal Protection Clause.

By June 11, Clark had won a majority.[42] This was a watershed moment: by a vote of 5 to 4, the Court was on the verge of moving decisively beyond the First Reconstruction, with Clark urging Congress to take the "necessary steps" to enact clear rules that would "meet the necessities of the situation."[43] Almost at the same moment, on June 10, Dirksen and his Republicans were breaking the southern filibuster. With the prospects of final passage looking bright, Clark's opinion for the Court would have provided Title II with a constitutional foundation worthy of the Second Reconstruction, sweeping away the remnants of the limited notions of state responsibility inherited from the nineteenth century.

But at the last moment, William Brennan defected from Clark's majority and led the Court in a different direction. His fear was that "if we came down with *Bell v. Maryland* on constitutional grounds, it would kill the civil rights act."[44] Quite simply, there was a risk that southern senators might use Clark's opinion to persuade fence-sitters to block final passage: why push forward with Title II, they would argue, when the Court had done Congress's job for it?

If this gambit had succeeded, it would have grievously demoralized the civil rights movement and political leadership just as they were on the verge of redeeming the demand of the American people for a new beginning in race relations. Worse yet, a 5-to-4 Supreme Court decision would have been far less effective than a congressional command in breaking the back of Jim Crow—especially since segregationists could have used Black's fiery dissent to mobilize yet another round of bitter-end opposition.

Nothing was certain, of course: the momentum behind the act was sufficiently great that it might well have overcome this last barrier to passage. Nevertheless, the risk was serious enough to lead Brennan to defect from

Clark's opinion. In a final strategic swerve, he joined forces with Justice Stewart, who had previously adopted Black's conservative line, to build a new majority for an opinion that said *absolutely nothing* about the future of the state action doctrine.[45] His new opinion seized on the fact that Baltimore had recently passed a local ban on discrimination in public accommodations, opening up the possibility that the state courts would invalidate the demonstrators' criminal convictions under the now-repealed regime. By remanding the case to Maryland to find out, Brennan's opinion kept the Court on the sidelines as the president and Congress came to their own constitutional conclusions.

This blow-by-blow account gives you a sense of the exceptional fluidity of the Court-Congress relationship at a key moment in the higher law-making process. To put my point in a nutshell: the Court didn't eviscerate the Civil Rights Cases in *Bell v. Maryland* only because it self-consciously decided that it was better for the political branches to do the job instead.

The Justices were right to remain on the sidelines. Their restraint meant that President Johnson and his liberal Congress had to take full responsibility for their assault on Jim Crow—leaving it open for Barry Goldwater to raise his constitutional critique in the presidential campaign. This left it up to the voters to decide on the nation's future, endorsing either Johnson's vision of the New Deal–Civil Rights regime or Goldwater's sweeping critique of New Deal premises. In contrast, if Clark's opinion had carried the day, the egalitarian breakthrough in the sphere of public accommodations would have appeared as a gift of We the Court, not We the People—putting Goldwater in the unfair position of attacking the Court, and not only Johnson, in calling upon the voters to repudiate the rising civil rights vision of the constitution.

Nevertheless, the Court's exercise of self-restraint imposes special responsibilities on today's Americans as we look back half a century on our civil rights legacy. So far as the Justices were concerned, the *only* way to strike down private sector discrimination was to expand the range of the Equal Protection Clause beyond the limits of state action established by the Civil Rights Cases. But once they retreated from the fray, they opened the way for Congress to accomplish the same objective by taking an alternative doctrinal path: it could appeal to the New Deal Commerce Clause to sweep away the classical barrier insulating private enterprise from egalitarian responsibilities. Just as Roosevelt's Congress used this power to enact a national minimum wage law, Johnson's Congress could make the same appeal to guarantee black Americans equal access to public accommodations. After all, restaurants and hotels invariably have connections to the interstate economy, both in the products they buy and in the customers they serve. Although individual businesses might have very slight interstate linkages, even the thinnest connection was sufficient under leading precedents left behind by the New Deal Court.[46] This meant that Congress did not have to reject the old Civil Rights Cases to support its new Civil Rights Act. The alternative route had a great pragmatic advantage: congressional liberals could be 100 percent sure that the Court would uphold their landmark statute on Commerce Clause grounds, since none of the sitting Justices showed any inclination to challenge the New Deal decisions. In contrast, as the then secret history of *Bell v. Maryland* reveals, Congress would have taken a big chance if it had relied exclusively on its claim that private restaurants and hotels were violating equal protection in denying blacks accommodation. So why run the risk of a judicial veto when the Commerce Clause was a sure thing?

This pragmatic imperative fueled the strategy pursued both by the administration and by congressional liberals throughout the legislative process. In defining the scope of Title II, the landmark statute codified a broad interpretation of state action that had a basis in recent Court decisions, but it did not go further and repudiate the entire doctrine.[47] To achieve universal coverage, it added another provision that enthusiastically embraced the expansive New Deal definitions of commerce— covering, for example, restaurants and hotels that "*offer[] to serve inter-state travelers*" (emphasis added) or theaters and stadiums that "customarily present[] films, performances, athletic teams, . . . or other sources of entertainment which move in [interstate] commerce."[48]

Congress's emphasis on commerce had fateful consequences when the Supreme Court turned to consider the constitutionality of the Civil Rights Act in its landmark decisions *Heart of Atlanta Motel* and *McClung*. The Court's encounter with the fundamental issues came with blinding speed: President Johnson signed the bill into law on July 2, and by October 5 the Justices were already hearing final arguments; by December 14 they were handing down unanimous decisions upholding the act—little more than a month after Goldwater's constitutional objections had been buried in the electoral landslide of November.

What a difference five months makes! Justice Brennan's bland opinion in *Bell v. Maryland* had been announced the previous June, disguising the majority's last-minute retreat from Clark's opinion eviscerating the state action doctrine. Since then, Congress had decisively destroyed this long-standing limitation by imposing egalitarian obligations on a host of private firms in the name of the New Deal Commerce Clause. In passing constitutional judgment in December, would the Warren Court follow through on the promise of Clark's opinion and use the occasion to create new foundations for equal protection appropriate for the Second Reconstruction?

It all depended on how the Court weighed short-term expediency versus long-term development. If the Warren majority used *Heart of Atlanta Motel* to repudiate the Civil Rights Cases, only one thing was clear: their opinion would draw a heated dissent from Justice John Harlan, and perhaps the other justices who had dissented in June.[49] This could have serious short-term consequences, as southern racists were continuing their violent campaign against the act's commands, and a strong dissent would encourage bitter-end resistance to continue. In contrast, Harlan had long since made his peace with the New Deal Commerce Clause. He was perfectly willing to join a unanimous opinion upholding the civil rights revolution on the basis of the Roosevelt revolution. Given the pragmatic imperatives of the moment, there is no great mystery about why the Court chose unanimity and relied exclusively on the Commerce Clause in upholding the act's public accommodations provisions—leaving it to Justices Douglas and Goldberg to explore equal protection implications in concurring opinions.

But from the long-term perspective, the Court's strategic swerve generated remarkably superficial opinions.[50] When today's lawyers turn to the *United States Reports* to consider the enduring meaning of the twentieth century's greatest egalitarian breakthrough, they encounter texts treating the landmark statute as if it involved humdrum commercial regulation. While I can understand the pragmatic imperatives that led to this ironic result, it is past time for us to consider an alternative opinion— one that traveled further down the path established by *Brown*, reaffirmed by King and Humphrey and Dirksen in their successful struggle for the Civil Rights Act, and pursued by Clark in his unpublished opinion in *Bell:*

The Civil Rights Cases of 1964 (*Heart of Atlanta/McClung*)
Mr. Justice Brennan delivered the opinion of the Court:

In *Plessy v. Ferguson*, the majority of this Court refused to recognize that racial segregation "stamp[ed] the colored race with a badge of inferiority." It declared that the humiliation imposed upon Negroes did not have its source in "anything found in the act [establishing segregation], but solely because the colored race chooses to put that construction upon it."

Brown repudiated this view. It rejected the myth that school children and their parents voluntarily "choose" the dominant social meanings imposed upon them by the institutions they inhabit. We held that the Fourteenth Amendment required us to look beyond the statute books to recognize the daily humiliations generated by segregated schools on black children.

Brown's approach has now been reaffirmed and extended in the public accommodations provisions of the recent Civil Rights Act. As Senator Humphrey explained:

> It is difficult for most of us to comprehend the monstrous humiliations and inconveniences that racial discrimination imposes on our Negro fellow citizens. If a white man is thirsty on a hot day, he goes to the nearest soda fountain. If he is hungry, he goes to the nearest restaurant. If he needs a restroom, he can go to the nearest gas station. If it is night and he is tired, he takes his pick of the available motels and hotels.
>
> But for a Negro the picture is different. Trying to get a glass of iced tea at a lunch counter may result in insult and abuse, unless he is willing to go out of his way, perhaps to walk across town. He can never count on using a restroom, on getting a decent place to stay, on buying a good meal. These are trivial matters in the life of a white person, but for some 20 million American Negroes, they are important considerations that must be planned for in detail.[51]

As floor manager of the bill, Humphrey is speaking for a Congress determined to put an end to this pervasive pattern of "insult and abuse" imposed on our fellow citizens. Just as *Brown* condemned institutionalized humiliation in the public schools, the Civil Rights Act condemns it in public accommodations. But in generalizing *Brown*'s anti-humiliation principle to new spheres of social life, the new statute requires us to reconsider another nineteenth century precedent that, like *Plessy*, has thus far restricted the prevailing interpretation of the equal protection clause.

The *Civil Rights Cases* of 1883 struck down Congress' first effort to enact a public accommodations law on a national basis. In the majority's view, the equal protection clause only authorized Congress to act against discrimination by state officials, not private inn-keepers. So long as private businesses used color-blind trespass laws to keep Negroes in their place, Congress couldn't stop them. This decision has profoundly shaped subsequent understandings of the Reconstruction Amendments. On the now-traditional view, these amendments had limited ambitions: they only sought to guarantee political and civil rights, and did not demand equality within the larger sphere of social life. But as Senator Dirksen declared in endorsing the new Civil Rights Act, "our land has changed since the Supreme Court decision in 1883."[52]

We agree. Given our respect for *stare decisis,* we may well have paused before overruling the *Civil Rights Cases* on our own. But given Congress' primary motivation in passing its new statute, we can no longer accept the nineteenth century's restrictive understanding of the nation's constitutional commitments. Like *Plessy,* the *Civil Rights Cases* failed to appreciate the evil of institutionalized humiliation—these are just as real whether they be generated by privately owned restaurants or publicly operated schools. Despite the *Civil Rights Cases,* the equal protection clause provides Congress with a solid foundation for its decision to impose sweeping egalitarian obligations on private firms offering their services to the general public in the marketplace.

As a technical legal matter, we could also uphold the new public accommodations law on the basis of the commerce clause. Yet this provision does not adequately express the constitutional ideals that inspired Congress and the President, speaking for the American people, to enact this statute. Throughout the twentieth century, the commerce clause has served as the foundation for a series of legislative efforts to correct a variety of market failures that undermine the public welfare. But the present statute has a different aim: it is a decisive advance in this nation's long struggle for racial equality, and we can only do justice to its significance by considering its relationship to fundamental principles of equal protection.

In upholding Congress' authority to expand the scope of equal protection to the marketplace, we fully recognize the importance of preserving spheres of private life reserved for free choices that seem arbitrary, and even despicable, to the citizenry at large. But over the course of the twentieth century, it has become increasingly apparent that only some kinds of private property are sites of truly personal relationships. In the present case, for example, Congress carefully exempted homeowners who had a legitimate interest in safeguarding their privacy when renting out a spare room to travelers. Yet there is no similar interest involved when the clerk at the Heart of Atlanta Motel refuses a Negro a room that is otherwise available. There is only the insulting implication that the Negro isn't good enough to be served.

We join with Congress in finding that such an assault on dignity is constitutionally unacceptable, and that the state is responsible for bringing it to an end.

I have designated Justice Brennan as the author of this hypothetical opinion, because it builds on the collaborative model of constitutionalism he developed in *Katzenbach v. Morgan*.[53] It is precisely this collaborative model that serves as the foundation of my proposed reformulation of the civil rights canon.

My version of the Civil Rights Cases of 1964 also crystallizes three themes for further elaboration in the rest of the book—which moves beyond public accommodations to devote separate chapters to developments in the spheres of voting, employment, housing, public education, and marriage.

A first theme confronts the limits of the anti-humiliation principle. Generally speaking, it serves to define a minimum baseline, banning characteristic forms of institutionalized degradation. But eliminating humiliation hardly guarantees equal opportunity, let alone equal outcomes.

We have already seen, for example, that a boss might well deny a worker equal opportunity for a job promotion even if he never publicly humiliates him before his peers. We will be elaborating this point in undertaking our sphere-by-sphere analysis. While the law in each area moves beyond anti-humiliation, it adopts a variety of legal and technocratic methods to achieve its egalitarian ends. In elaborating the diversity of these approaches, I hope to redeem one of the book's basic claims: that the civil rights revolution cannot be summed up by a single one-size-fits-all formula. It has left us a complex legacy of anti-humiliation and more ambitious egalitarian principles requiring a sophisticated array of legal techniques for their successful realization.

A second theme interrogates my master premise. While the sphere-by-sphere approach is central to my presentation, does it really do justice to the landmark statutes and great court decisions of the period? Did the constitutional moment culminate in a decision by the president, Congress, and the Court to reject sphericity on behalf of something grander—perhaps anti-subordination, perhaps anti-classification?

A third theme confronts another fundamental claim—that the landmark statutes deserve a central place in the civil rights canon. Even if this is conceded, my methodological turn won't clarify some big interpretive issues. While Congress and the president did take constitutional leadership in many spheres, their landmark statutes left it to the Warren and Burger Courts to confront key issues in other spheres without legislative guidance. This basic point requires us to divide the rest of the book into two chunks. The current part deals with the spheres in which the landmark statutes played a decisive role in defining America's constitutional commitments; Part Three considers the spheres in which the Justices were obliged to fill in key gaps.

CHAPTER 8

Spheres of Calculation

EVERYBODY UNDERSTANDS HUMILIATION. It doesn't take a college degree to see how systematic discrimination in restaurants or sports arenas can strip people of their dignity. When the Court in *Brown*, and Congress in the Civil Rights Act, banned these practices, they were translating the Constitution into a commonsense command: *Thou shalt not humiliate*. While racists might resist, they would not disagree about the point of these degradation rituals—to the contrary, they would recognize them as essential for keeping blacks in line.

But a simple ban on institutionalized humiliation would not suffice. Consider voting: It was true, of course, that southern blacks historically encountered a humiliating reception if they had the courage to enter their county's voting registry. Yet even if officials treated them with dignity in the future, those same officials could manipulate literacy tests and similar devices to bar them from the ballot box. It's easy to develop similar scenarios in other spheres—think of the racial steering that goes on when real estate agents politely guide black buyers into "appropriate" neighborhoods, and so forth.

These pervasive realities pushed the landmark statutes beyond antihumiliation to more ambitious goals, most notably the pursuit of real equality of opportunity. This goal couldn't be achieved without a shift from courts to administrative agencies as the principal change agents. Just as the New Deal created the National Labor Relations Board (NLRB) and the Securities and Exchange Commission to accomplish its regulatory missions, the civil rights statutes relied on a new set of "alphabet agencies" to achieve racial justice: the Equal Employment Opportunity Commission (EEOC), the Department of Housing and Urban Development (HUD), the Department of Health, Education, and Welfare (HEW). In creating these new agencies, the landmark statutes did not slavishly imitate New Deal models. Rather, they displayed great creativity in crafting different administrative setups for different spheres of political and social life. These different designs led to the development of different rules and principles in different spheres.

We shall be exploring these differences in the chapters that follow. But for now, I want to emphasize a broad similarity. The civil rights regime fostered a distinctive administrative style involving *government by numbers.* This technocratic form represented a fundamental challenge to standard legal discourse, which traditionally addressed constitutional issues in qualitative terms—and the resulting tensions will serve as a recurring leitmotif.

Government by numbers had deep roots in the past. As early as 1887, the Interstate Commerce Commission was looking at numbers to determine whether the railroads were exploiting shippers and consumers—and New Dealers famously emphasized the expertise of their new agencies, which often framed regulations in quantitative terms. Nevertheless, the 1960s gave the enterprise a new shape and a new legitimacy. This was the dawn of the computer age, which vastly increased the bureaucratic capacity to collect systematic data on an ongoing basis. What is more, agency experts could now build mathematical models that would transform their data into hard economic and social indicators.[1]

These modeling efforts gave technocracy a new credibility throughout government—from Robert McNamara's Defense Department to Walter Heller's Council of Economic Advisers. But it generated special promise—and special problems—for civil rights.

On the bright side, government by numbers provided a new path beyond the endless technicalities and obfuscations of traditional legal language and lawsuits. It offered the prospect of clean-cut numerical indicators that could dispassionately pinpoint the most serious real-world problems and provide an objective measure of progress in their eradication.

The flip side was that *Brown's* anti-humiliation principle was meaningful only when framed in qualitative terms. This required judges and administrators to engage in textured interpretations of social meaning to determine whether a social practice systematically stigmatized blacks or other groups. Such qualitative judgments predictably escaped technocracy's number-driven assessments of measurable outcomes, generating a distinctive conundrum: how to manage the emerging tension between quantity and quality, between technocracy and situated judgment, in achieving the more equal society demanded by the American people?

It is hardly surprising that Congresses, presidents, agencies, and courts had a hard time synthesizing quality and quantity in satisfying fashion. Different landmark statutes reached different accommodations in different areas with different degrees of success—with the Supreme Court playing a particularly disastrous role at the end of *Brown*'s second decade in the landmark case of *Milliken v. Bradley*. I will defer the darker side of the story to Part Three, and focus first on spheres where technocratic government achieved greater success—starting with voting rights.

I begin with a revisionist perspective on the Reconstruction Amendments, emphasizing how the absence of a bureaucratic apparatus contributed to their failure in the nineteenth century. I then consider how modern administrative government helped ensure the Second Reconstruction's greater success, and I will use this framework to organize an account of the voting rights breakthroughs achieved by the landmark statutes of 1965 and 1970.

The Failure of Republican Reconstruction

According to the conventional legal account, there was nothing fundamentally wrong with the way the three great Reconstruction Amendments aimed to guarantee equality to the liberated slaves. The real problem arose later when the Supreme Court, and the nation's politicians, betrayed the commitments made by the people in the aftermath of the Civil War.

I take a darker view: the amendments were doomed from the start. The heart of the problem was their formalist approach. Give the freedmen the formal right to vote, give them the formal right to defend themselves in court, and they would have all the tools they needed to protect their interests against their former white masters—or so the amendments suggested. There was no need for a more sweeping economic and social transformation.

This key premise was famously denounced by Radical Republicans such as Thaddeus Stevens and Charles Sumner, who urged Congress and the country to move beyond such shallow formalisms. Since the slaves had been the foundation of southern wealth, the freedmen should finally get their fair share—"forty acres and a mule." Since it had previously been a crime for slaves to learn to read, they were now entitled to free public education.[2]

On the Radical view, it would take at least a generation before a new breed of educated and property-owning freedmen could effectively confront their former masters. The Reconstruction Amendments were fated to fail—their proud legalisms disguising the reality of black subordination behind a formal promise of equal citizenship. Here is Thaddeus Stevens denouncing his House colleagues just as they were about to vote for the Fourteenth Amendment:

> In my youth, in my manhood, in my old age, I had fondly dreamed that when any fortunate chance should have broken up for a while the foundation of our institutions, and released us from obligations the most tyrannical that ever men imposed in the name of freedom, that the intelligent, pure and just men of this Republic, true to the professions and their consciences, would have so remodeled all our institutions as to have freed them from every vestige of human oppression, of inequality of rights, of the recognized degradation of the poor, and the superior caste of the rich. In short, that no distinction would be tolerated in the purified Republic but what arose from merit and conduct. This bright dream has vanished "like the baseless fabric of a vision." I find that we shall be obliged to be content with patching up the worst portions of the ancient edifice, and leaving it, in many of its parts, to be swept through by the tempests, the frosts, and the storms of despotism.[3]

Stevens was right, yet modern-day constitutionalists aren't interested in his diagnosis. Their unspoken premise is that the Reconstruction Amendments were fundamentally sound. They reserve their criticism for the later decisions by the Court in *Plessy* and other cases that consolidated Jim Crow in the South. Behind their harshest critique lies the Pollyannaish notion that better Supreme Court opinions might have overcome the deeper economic and educational failures of Reconstruction.

But if the Radicals were right, we must reflect on *why* they failed to carry the country with them. Despite their immense standing as moral and political leaders, Stevens and Sumner confronted a great stumbling block. The federal government of the 1860s lacked a serious civilian bureaucracy capable of protecting the freedmen during the long period in which they couldn't protect themselves. This meant there was only one way to implement the Radical plan: since the only federal bureaucracy then in existence was the military, the only way to protect blacks was to put the South under military occupation for decades.

This grim prospect shocked millions of Republicans who otherwise might have endorsed the Radical program. Continuing military occupation shook republican ideals of self-government to the very core. While Stevens eloquently denounced the old constitutional order as the "most tyrannical" ever "imposed in the name of freedom," was he threatening to substitute a militaristic form of tyranny that was even worse? Nineteenth-century Americans confronted a tragic choice: either military occupation in the name of real freedom for the emancipated slaves or republican self-rule in which whites would use their economic power and cultural authority to make a mockery of the Reconstruction Amendments.

The fateful moment of decision did not come when Union troops were withdrawn from the South as part of the Compromise of 1877. It came in 1868 when the Republican Congress readmitted the southern states as part of the deal that put the Fourteenth Amendment on the books. Once white southerners began exercising real political power in Washington, it was only a matter of time before they would force the removal of Union troops, creating a political vacuum that they would then fill. The federal government simply lacked the civilian bureaucracies required to enforce the amendments in hostile territory; a tiny band of federal judges, backed by a bunch of federal marshals, didn't have a chance.[4]

All this was ancient history a century later, when Americans gave their mobilized support to a Second Reconstruction. The national government had by now developed administrative resources that permitted it to reshape everyday realities while relying on federal troops only at moments of crisis. What is more, the American people were not inclined to question this New Deal inheritance—as Barry Goldwater learned on Election Day in 1964. As a consequence, it was only natural that the new landmark statutes frequently used an administrative approach to the pursuit of racial justice. So let's consider, in general terms, how this option invited fundamental moves beyond the first Reconstruction.

BEYOND COURTS

Before the law on the books is translated into real-world outcomes, three things must happen: somebody must complain, somebody must decide that the law requires redress, and somebody must get the violator to stop. The first problem is *identification;* the second, *interpretation;* the third, *enforcement.*

Courts can interpret, but they depend on individual parties to identify and enforce. Agencies, however, can discharge the identification and enforcement functions without private assistance. Furthermore, their ongoing efforts to interpret their statutory mandates also shape the way courts and legislatures ultimately define governing constitutional principles.

The agency advantage at the enforcement stage is pretty obvious—court proceedings are expensive, and agencies may deliver the goods at lower cost. But the distinctive agency contributions to the identification and interpretation problems are more complex.

Begin by considering a hypothetical agency as it confronts a vast regulatory universe. Since its budget is finite, it can't afford to investigate every potential violation. It must devise an identification strategy that focuses on the most serious problems. How to proceed?

The New Deal tradition had a clear answer: the agency should develop its expertise by deploying the best available social science.[5] And by the 1960s, the computer revolution was giving new credibility to data-driven policy making.

But not in every domain. Sometimes it made perfectly good sense to continue to rely primarily on the courts. Take the realm of public accommodations: A black man sits down at a lunch counter, but the waitress ignores him, instead serving whites who come in later. He has no trouble recognizing that he's a victim of discrimination; nor is legal interpretation a big issue in standard cases. If he has serious trouble, it's at the enforcement stage.

Identification and interpretation can become very serious problems in other social spheres, however. When a black man is politely denied a job, how can he tell whether he's failed because of race or because a rival applicant is more qualified?

More generally, modern societies are full of institutions whose internal logics of decision are opaque to the people affected by them. Here is where government by numbers emerges to penetrate the black box. If the numbers reveal remarkably low voter turnouts from heavily black constituencies, or if a major firm reports a remarkably low rate of minority hires, it is only reasonable to investigate further.

This technocratic response to institutional opacity can also give a distinctive shape to the interpretive enterprise. Law is a problem-solving project: if you define your problem in quantitative terms, it may seem sensible to define the legal solution with numbers as well, using technocratic indicators to allocate burdens of proof and distribute scarce resources among contending claimants. The key point is to see that government by numbers has played a fundamental role in interpreting the law, not only in implementing it.

This requires us to move beyond the traditional view that features the Supreme Court as the "forum of principle."[6] During the civil rights revolution, both the Court and the political branches also engaged in an ongoing dialogue with the bureaucracy—modifying constitutional principles in the light of experience, as revealed by numerical indicators.

I introduce these points through a study of the Voting Rights Act (VRA). Initial passage of the act in 1965 provoked a series of creative administrative and judicial responses over the following years. These decisions set the stage for a second round of political reappraisals culminating in the renewal of the VRA in 1970. During this period of high-visibility activity, President Nixon and Congress endorsed many of the administrative innovations of the previous five years, cementing government by numbers into the very foundations of the constitutional order.

The VRA story sets the stage for the study of different feedback loops in other spheres, ranging from employment to the public schools.

The Voting Rights Act of 1965

Before 1965, Congress had passed a series of statutes relying on the courts to break the back of southern exclusion of black voters. They required the Justice Department to prove that voting registrars had engaged in a "pattern or practice" of discriminatory treatment.[7] But these lengthy lawsuits merely generated cycles of resistance, with southern registrars responding to court orders with new evasive techniques, provoking further rounds of lawsuits.

After the dramatic scenes at Selma, this charade became intolerable: Congress, the president, the movement, and the voters were all demanding decisive action. The new landmark statute responded by framing its demands in technocratic language, abandoning the qualitative verbalisms of the law. If a county used a literacy test or similar device to restrict access to the polls, the key question was whether voter registration or participation fell below 50 percent at the 1964 elections. Once the Census Bureau found that this threshold had been breached, the statute suspended all restrictive devices for five years and authorized the Justice Department to dispatch federal voting registrars to short-circuit further local resistance.[8] Seven southern states fell under this ban.[9] They could escape only by proving that they had completely refrained from discriminatory practices in the preceding five years.[10]

This emphatic embrace of government by numbers generated strong objections, and not only from southerners. Throughout the 1960s, Congressman William McCulloch was a key Republican supporter of civil rights legislation. Nevertheless, he condemned the "numbers game" as "an arbitrary device," rejecting the notion "that a contrived mathematical formula" could reliably identify "those States that discriminate" without requiring "a judicial proceeding or a hearing of any kind."[11]

McCulloch's objections were overwhelmed by the popular demand for decisive action. Liberal Republican senator Jacob Javits, for example, emphasized that the triggering mechanisms raised "a basic question of principle," serving as the cornerstone of a system of administrative constitutionalism in which bureaucratic activity played the central role in breaking down institutional resistance.[12]

With images of the first Reconstruction burning bright, congressional debate focused on the dangers and rewards of direct federal intervention in the South. Nonetheless, like any good regulatory statute, the VRA looked beyond the present to provide the Justice Department with tools for overcoming new forms of institutional resistance as they emerged over time. Section 5 barred targeted states and localities from changing their electoral systems without first gaining the approval of the Justice Department or a special three-judge federal court sitting in the District of Columbia.

This was a revolutionary step. Senator Sam Ervin was right to emphasize its unprecedented "reversal of the fundamental principle of our law that every act of a State legislature is presumed to be Constitutional until it is clearly shown otherwise."[13] Key congressional Republicans shared these concerns. William McCulloch repeatedly grilled witnesses on the constitutionality of Section 5, and eliminated any such requirement from his proposed substitute.[14] But once again, McCulloch's objections were overwhelmed by the collective determination to put a decisive end to the seemingly endless cycles of southern resistance.

The result was a fundamental transformation in our constitutional law. Year after year, proud representatives of southern states such as Alabama and Mississippi would be traveling hat in hand to Washington to gain the consent of some underling of the attorney general. And if they were unhappy with the Justice Department's decision, they could not appeal to a panel of federal judges within their own circuit—judges who owed their jobs to southern senators who had endorsed their confirmation. They would have to apply to a federal panel in the District of Columbia, composed of judges who were generally more appreciative of national prerogatives.

JUDICIAL REINFORCEMENT

Like the Civil Rights Act before it, the VRA's revolutionary initiatives could not be secure without Supreme Court approval. We have already seen the Court moving quickly in the spring of 1966 to vindicate the VRA's positions on poll taxes *(Harper)* and literacy tests *(Morgan)*. But the statute's emphatic embrace of government by numbers and administrative interventionism was central to the entire effort, and the Court speedily moved to resolve doubts here as well. When South Carolina raised the inevitable challenge, the Justices refused to wait for lower courts to issue their own judgments on the merits. Instead, they exercised rarely used powers of original jurisdiction to enable the state to argue its case directly before the Supreme Court—permitting Earl Warren to hand down *South Carolina v. Katzenbach* at the same time the Court was vindicating other revolutionary features of the landmark statute.[15] *South Carolina* raised the same problem as *Morgan:* how to deal with the VRA's assault on established constitutional principles?

As we saw in Chapter 6, the problem was dramatized in *Morgan* by the VRA's determination to sweep away English-only literacy requirements despite the Court's unanimous 1959 decision upholding such barriers under the Equal Protection Clause.[16] Speaking for the Court, Justice Brennan responded with a pathbreaking opinion defining a new model of "coordinate constitutionalism" that emphasized Congress's independent authority to expand the scope of equal protection under the enforcement powers granted to it by the Fourteenth Amendment. Warren faced the same basic challenge in confronting the VRA's extraordinary grant of power to the federal government to suspend the operation of state laws.

He responded in precisely the same way. Like Brennan, he vindicated the statute by pointing to Congress's "enforcement" powers—except that it was those granted by the Fifteenth Amendment, not the Fourteenth, that served as the basis for a sweeping endorsement of the landmark's profound redefinition of federalism. In taking this course, Warren also followed Brennan in invoking John Marshall's famous words as authority: "Let the end be legitimate, let it be within the scope of the constitution, and all means which are appropriate, which are plainly adapted to that end, which are not prohibited, but consist with the letter and spirit of the constitution, are constitutional."[17]

But *was* the VRA's grant of extraordinary federal powers really "consist[ent]" with the spirit of the Constitution?

Not for Justice Black. If federalism meant anything, it meant "that the States have power to pass laws and amend their constitutions without first sending their officials hundreds of miles away to beg federal authorities to approve them." This amounted to dealing with states as "little more than conquered provinces."[18] Black was the Court's only Justice from the Deep South—and his emphatic recollections of the first period of Reconstruction had special meaning for him.

But not for his colleagues. On their view, there was simply no comparison between the ongoing military occupations of the 1860s and the bureaucratic interventions of the 1960s. The states' recurring ritual of submission to federal authorities in Washington, D.C., was perfectly consistent with the spirit of the Constitution—but only because Americans had fundamentally changed that spirit over the course of the twentieth century. Warren's confident reliance on Marshall's dictum was based upon the complex practices of "cooperative federalism" that had proliferated since the 1930s. While the VRA's centralizing bureaucratic initiatives represented a large step beyond then-existing forms of federal coordination, the Court was right to reject Black's view of them as alien to the developing constitutional tradition. By the 1960s, they were better seen as appropriate problem-solving responses to the grave injustices undermining the legitimacy of the entire New Deal–Civil Rights regime.

The VRA's extraordinary impositions on the South were temporary. The statute terminated them after five years if Congress didn't renew the provisions. This time limit helps account for the Court's speed in taking up South Carolina's complaint. If it had waited for cases to arrive on its appellate docket, much of the five years might have been lost in yet another round of southern resistance and Justice Department litigation. With the Court clearing the way, the federal effort went into high gear with remarkable results: between 1965 and 1968, the proportion of blacks on the voting rolls increased from 29 to 52 percent in the southern states targeted by the statutory formula, with Mississippi moving from 6.7 percent to an eye-popping 59.4 percent.[19]

Yet, inevitably, concrete enforcement actions generated another round of litigation, leading the Court to decide two more cases just as Richard Nixon and Congress began to consider renewing the VRA. These 1969 opinions emphasized the revolutionary character of the ongoing federal intervention. *Allen v. State Board of Elections* involved a Mississippi county's effort to maintain white political power despite the entry of black voters into the system.[20] When only whites had access to the ballot, each of the five members of the county Board of Supervisors was elected from a separate district. But once blacks began voting, their preferred candidates could win some of the districts. So the election board switched to an at-large system, permitting the countywide white majority to freeze out all minority representation. Speaking for the Court, Chief Justice Warren rejected this maneuver, expanding the concerns of the statute to include any change in the electoral laws even if they didn't directly limit access to the ballot box:

> The right to vote can be affected by a dilution of voting power as well as by an absolute prohibition on casting a ballot. See *Reynolds* v. *Sims,* 377 U.S. 533 (1964). Voters who are members of a racial minority might well be in the majority in one district, but in a decided minority in the county as a whole. This type of change could therefore nullify their ability to elect the candidate of their choice just as would prohibiting some of them from voting.[21]

Warren is moving far beyond the principle of "one person, one vote" famously announced in *Reynolds v. Sims.* Before the VRA, the Court was never prepared to strike down racial gerrymandering, except in the most egregious cases.[22] But under *Allen,* it upheld the VRA's commitment to a sweeping form of preemptive federal scrutiny that swept away any and all rules diluting black voting power.

The Court's second decision expanded the scope of the Second Reconstruction yet further. Even if a state or locality offended the statute's technocratic tests, it was not necessarily doomed to an extended period of federal control. Instead, the VRA allowed it to escape immediately if it could show that it had not used literacy tests or other exclusionary devices to exclude blacks on a discriminatory basis during the preceding five years.[23]

Gaston County, North Carolina, invoked this escape hatch and claimed the right to reinstate its literacy test—only to find the Justice Department raising a fundamental objection. The department submitted evidence that the county's segregated schools provided blacks with a systematically inferior education, leading them to fail the literacy test in vastly disproportionate numbers.

The county's reply: the VRA was concerned only with elections, not education, and so the status of its school system under *Brown* was irrelevant. So long as its voting registrars had administered its literacy test with scrupulous fairness, the county should be allowed to escape the statutory ban. It was the business of the Civil Rights Act, not the VRA, to provide tools for the courts and the Department of Health, Education, and Welfare to deal with school desegregation. Writing for the Court, Justice Harlan rejected this argument in an opinion that is especially significant in light of my larger thesis.[24]

I have been arguing that the Second Reconstruction followed *Brown*'s lead in taking a sphere-by-sphere approach to racial injustice. *Gaston County* stands as the only exception to this rule. Harlan refused to allow the county to escape the VRA's special provisions even if it could show that its registrars had acted impartially over the past five years. He insisted that the county's performance in the educational sphere was also relevant. Since its segregated schools had cheated blacks out of an equal education, the county could not disclaim responsibility for their relatively poor performance on literacy tests. This was enough to prevent the county from evading the continuing application of the ban imposed by the VRA.

Gaston County's break with the sphere-by-sphere approach is easy to understand. After all, the linkage between the spheres of education and elections was particularly intimate, with the county demanding literacy while simultaneously depriving many blacks of a fair chance to obtain it. Nevertheless, it serves as a counterexample to my general thesis—and if there were lots of others, I would have to reformulate a key element in this book's interpretation of the Second Reconstruction.

But as the following chapters show, there aren't lots of others.

CODIFICATION: THE VOTING RIGHTS ACT OF 1970

South Carolina, Allen, Gaston County: they added up to a shattering challenge to traditional principles of federalism, but would they last?

This was the big question when the statute came up for renewal in 1970. Sections 4 and 5 were the provisions authorizing extraordinary intervention, and came with a five-year sunset. This placed the burden on proponents to make the case for their enduring importance, but this time under vastly different political conditions. Richard Nixon, not Lyndon Johnson, was in the White House; Martin Luther King Jr. was dead, and his legacy was threatened by rising black nationalism and escalating ghetto riots. To put the point in terms of Part One, the higher lawmaking dynamic was now in its consolidation phase—when the polity takes a sober second look at recent innovations and decides whether they deserve to survive as foundational elements in our constitutional heritage.[25]

During his campaign, Nixon had explicitly affirmed the landmark status of the Voting Rights Act, and his initial proposal strengthened it further. While the original act had suspended literacy tests only in the seven states targeted by Sections 4 and 5, the administration's initiative also swept them away in the fourteen other states using such devices.[26] As Attorney General John Mitchell explained, "voting rights is not a regional issue" but "a national concern for every American which must be treated on a nationwide basis."[27] The Mitchell plan made similar nationalizing moves on other fronts.[28]

At the same time, however, the new administration eliminated the special regional provisions that had generated such bitterness amongst white southerners. Mitchell rejected the very idea that resistance to voting rights could be measured by mathematical formulae. He would have returned the system to a more familiar regime, in which the attorney general could go to court whenever he had "reason to believe" that electoral laws were being manipulated with the "purpose or effect" of abridging the right to vote. Federal prescreening would be eliminated, and it would be up to the Justice Department to complain in court after state laws had come into effect.[29]

This put the constitutional issue squarely before Congress. In Senator Hruska's words, "The administration's bill will return the thrust of enforcement back to the judicial process and away from the administrative procedures which now exist. This is important. . . . Administrative procedures, in place of judicial remedies, might be necessary under extraordinary conditions, but should not be extended once the basic conditions improve. . . . Registration and turnout of voters in the covered States has greatly increased. Let us now return to our courts of law."[30]

Hruska was from Nebraska, not South Carolina, and his remarks should have resonated with his colleagues. After all, senators and representatives win office by appealing to the distinctive values of their states and localities. They generally appreciate traditional values of federalism and support presidential calls for their reinvigoration.

Not this time. While Congress endorsed Nixon's nationalizing moves, it refused to retreat from technocratic targeting and bureaucratic prescreening in dealing with the worst abuses. For leading Republicans as well as for Democrats in Congress, government by numbers had become a fundamental safeguard of electoral integrity.

Consider the changing role of Congressman William McCulloch. In 1965, this key Republican leader strongly opposed government by numbers and federal prescreening. But listen to him just a few years later:

> When I voted for the Voting Rights Act of 1965, I hoped that 5 years would be ample time. But resistance to progress has been more subtle and more effective than I thought possible. Boundary lines have been gerrymandered, elections have been switched to an at-large basis, counties have been consolidated, elective officials have been abolished where blacks had a chance of winning, the appointment process has been substituted for the elective process, election officials have withheld the necessary information for voting or running for office, and both physical and economic intimidation have been employed. Section 5 was intended to prevent the use of most of these devices. But . . . the Federal Government was too timid in its enforcement. I hope that the case of Allen v. State Board of Elections . . . is the portent of change.[31]

Not only is McCulloch confessing error—something all too rare in politics—but he is endorsing *Allen* and urging Nixon's Justice Department to make the most of the VRA's revolutionary grant of authority.

The congressman's turnabout suggests a larger lesson. Americans were actually *learning* something from their initial experiment in transforming the federal system. In 1965, southern predictions of a disastrous rerun of the First Reconstruction could not be refuted by experience. But the Justice Department's success on the ground showed that southern fears were overblown. The vast increase in black turnout suggested that further centralized supervision was also essential in controlling the predictable efforts by the white establishment to maintain effective power.

Nixon had failed in his effort to eliminate intensive federal supervision in the South. His campaign had succeeded only in generating an especially self-conscious reaffirmation of the need for a revolutionary form of centralized supervision. No less paradoxically, it also encouraged Congress to expand the scope of federal control. The new VRA changed its mathematical formulae to target places such as Manhattan, Brooklyn, and the Bronx.[32] This was small consolation to the Deep South, which remained the main focus of federal oversight. Nevertheless, it represented a deep redefinition of the landmark's constitutional principles: national bureaucratic intervention was no longer an emergency response to a regional problem but a fundamental mechanism ensuring democratic integrity on a national basis.

There was one final stumbling block: Richard Nixon. Would he go along with this emphatic transformation of his initial proposal?

A veto had obvious attractions. By sending the bill back to Congress, he could show southern whites that it was now the Republicans, not the Democrats, who could be trusted to rein in the excesses of the Second Reconstruction. At the same time, Nixon could explain to northern moderates that he was perfectly happy to sign a nationally oriented initiative that respected traditional notions of federalism.[33]

A final feature of the bill also pushed in the veto direction. Under the leadership of Senator Mike Mansfield, Congress had taken a large step beyond the 1965 law by requiring states to open their polls to eighteen-year-olds.[34] Nixon knew that he would "lose votes if we sign"[35] a bill that enabled millions of teenagers to vote against his conduct of the Vietnam War in the next election.[36] Moreover, a veto message targeting the Mansfield provision would enable the president to take the high ground: Nixon could rely on leading liberals such as Dean Louis Pollak of the Yale Law School, who insisted that a constitutional amendment was required to compel the states to expand the suffrage to younger voters.[37] With key Nixon confidants including Mitchell and Bryce Harlow coming out strongly for a veto, the handwriting was on the wall—indeed, Mitchell even told Representative William Colmer of Mississippi, chairman of the House Rules Committee, that Nixon was going to veto the bill.[38]

But in the end, Nixon chose a different path. In an internal memo, "The Voting Rights Act—Sign or Veto?," the president's chief speechwriter, Ray Price, provides some insight into the larger political stakes. Price acknowledged "the political temptations to veto," since it would "(a) probably keep under-21s from voting in 1972, and (b) get credit in the (white) South for killing the voting rights act itself."[39] Nonetheless, it was important to "bear very closely in mind that whatever their views on other black claims—housing, jobs, schools, etc.—the right to vote is one thing that practically all Americans agree on. Therefore, if we *appear* to be aligning ourselves with the Thurmonds and the Eastlands on this one, we invite the label of blatant racism."[40] He concluded that a "veto, in today's circumstances, would be taken not as a failure to move forward, but as a deliberate, calculated move backward toward the old (and in this area, very real) patterns of repression and intimidation."[41]

Nixon was simply unwilling to take this "deliberate, calculated move backward." In approving the act, he embraced the VRA's past achievements as well as its future promise: "In the 5 years since its enactment, close to 1 million Negroes have been registered to vote for the first time and more than 400 Negro officials have been elected to local and State offices. These are more than election statistics; they are statistics of hope and dramatic evidence that the American system works. They stand as an answer to those who claim that there is no recourse except to the streets."[42] The president's signing statement portrays the VRA as giving a decisive "answer" to the riots and racial unrest of the 1960s. Federal intervention had provided "statistics of hope" that established that "the system works." The success of government by numbers was winning the VRA a special place in the living Constitution.

Nixon's law-and-order rhetoric should also be seen as challenging standard stereotypes. He is presently notorious for invoking racist code words to rally his "silent majority" against liberal notions of progress. This is true in some cases—most notably in his attack on the Warren Court's criminal justice revolution. But as the VRA story suggests, the imagery sometimes operated in the opposite fashion: to consolidate, not undermine, the emerging civil rights regime.[43]

In the case of the VRA, Nixon's commitment was for real. His Justice Department took aggressive steps to intensify its supervisory presence in states and localities that failed to meet the revised numerical threshold tests. During the preceding administration, the first priority of Johnson's Justice Department had been to get southern blacks registered to vote under the existing rules. This was so time-consuming that the department hadn't systematically used its powers to block evasive actions that minimized black political power by changing the rules. As a consequence, most southern jurisdictions followed their traditional practice of passing new electoral laws without seeking prior approval from Washington, D.C.

Now that the act had been reaffirmed, Nixon's Justice Department issued regulations providing the targeted states with clear administrative procedures for gaining preapproval—leading to an immediate fourfold increase in applications, from 255 in 1970 to more than 1,000 in 1971.[44] This increasing caseload, in turn, led the department to create operational standards for bureaucratic review, which also served to inform decisions by the courts in contested cases.[45]

After five years of practical experience, and a second round of political debate, constitutional consolidation was proceeding apace, with the presidency, Congress, and the Court actively legitimating a regime of technocratic ascendancy over the states.

By the People?

If this story doesn't jog traditionalists out of their dogmatic slumber, nothing will. Under the conventional view, the Court operates as the "forum of principle," while bureaucrats merely follow through at the implementation phase. In contrast, the administrative performance of the Justice Department in the South provided a crucial element in the larger process through which We the People came to a considered judgment on constitutional commitments. While *South Carolina, Allen,* and *Gaston County* crystallized basic issues, the true test of their enduring value was pragmatic: would the Justice Department deliver on the VRA's promise to achieve real-world gains in the South?

Congress and President Nixon were in a position to make a considered judgment only after the department demonstrated the effectiveness of bureaucratic intervention on the ground. "Administrative constitutionalism" was a fundamental element in the process by which the political branches transformed the VRA's revolutionary initiatives into three enduring elements of the emerging civil rights regime.[46]

The first element involved state sovereignty. Mississippi and the rest were no longer free to change voting rules that defined their very understanding of representative government. They had to go to Washington,

D.C., to gain prior approval—and when they got there, they were not even required to gain the consent of federal judges to their proposal. Instead, it was generally easier for them to take a second route provided by the statute and gain approval from specialists in the Justice Department. This amounted to a second shift in constitutional values in favor of the national administrative state.

Finally, when bureaucrats or courts reviewed the state's proposals, they did not simply ask themselves whether the new electoral rules undermined each citizen's effective exercise of the ballot. They went further to determine whether they diluted black voting power. This represented a large move beyond the individualistic "one person, one vote" standard established by *Baker v. Carr* to a straightforward embrace of group rights.

The suspension of state sovereignty, the affirmation of federal administrative authority, the assertion of group rights: none of this happened in a single moment, but developed through a three-step process of collective deliberation.

Step one: After winning his decisive electoral mandate in 1964, it was perfectly appropriate for President Johnson and Congress to respond to Martin Luther King Jr.'s call at Selma with the Voting Rights Act. With Americans demanding decisive change, the landmark statute was also right to move beyond the court-centered approaches of the past. These had notoriously failed to break the back of southern resistance, and the reassertion of this old model would only have generated cynicism about Washington's willingness to heed the popular mandate for change. Government by numbers wasn't generated by a top-down effort at bureaucratic self-aggrandizement. It was a response to the American people's demand for a decisive break with the constitutional past.

Step two: But would government by numbers deliver effective change? This was not a matter to be determined by the Supreme Court. It could only be established through real-world experience generated by the administrative process.

The lessons learned from this period of constitutional experimentation served as the basis for step three: sober reconsideration by a very different president who was finally persuaded to join with Congress and the Court to support government by numbers in the name of foundational constitutional values.

If this isn't government by the People, what is?

Separate Spheres?

The voting rights story may be enlightening, but it is only a story about a single sphere—voting rights. And we should beware premature generalization to other spheres.

Consider, for example, the very different tale we told about the public accommodations provisions (Title II) of the Civil Rights Act. Both stories began at the same place: systematic humiliation and exclusion.

A black man goes into a restaurant with the money he needs to buy a place at the table; his basic social competence is impugned when he is publicly denied service. A black woman goes into the voting registrar's office with the education she needs to pass the literacy test; her basic competence as a citizen is impugned when she is rejected with a sneer.

But the two landmarks respond differently to these abuses. The Civil Rights Act targets the individual owners of public accommodations and relies principally on individual blacks to go to court to enforce this obligation.[47] The Voting Rights Act takes a more bureaucratic and technocratic approach. Why the difference?

I provided a framework for an answer earlier, but it's time to dig deeper. Begin with public accommodations. Generally speaking, it's a lot easier for individual blacks to identify discrimination in this sphere—either they are denied service entirely or they are shunted to the back of the movie theater. So they are in a good position to threaten a lawsuit, and courts won't encounter serious evidentiary problems vindicating their rights.

The prospect of an effective judicial response has a benign feedback effect on business incentives. An individual restaurant integrates at the cost of losing all racist whites to its competitors. But once all restaurants are placed in legal peril, they can integrate simultaneously and racist whites won't have anywhere to go (except, maybe, private clubs).

The political sphere displays different characteristics. Begin with the identification problem: although a racist registrar might gain great personal satisfaction in humiliating a black while rejecting his application, he can readily achieve the same objective in less insulting ways—treating the black with respect, but asking questions harder than those he uses for whites. Unlike the neighborhood restaurant or movie theater, the voting registry is an opaque institution: if the VRA was to redeem popular demands for justice, it would have to take account of this fact, and devise more readily measurable output indicators to target suspect jurisdictions.

Institutional opacity posed only part of the problem. The second part involved the very different feedback loop prevailing in the political sphere. Instead of the positive dynamic in the marketplace, the admission of blacks to the voting rolls generated negative feedback—with white politicians manipulating other voting rules to dilute black voting power. As *Allen* suggested and Congress affirmed, the only effective remedy was federal pre-screening of all electoral changes to consider their real-world impact on the political power of blacks as a group, not merely blacks as individual voters.

Call this the problem of institutional resistance, and along with the opacity of voting registration, it accounts for the shift from anti-categorization norms in the sphere of public accommodations to the quantifiable-output approach endorsed by the Voting Rights Act. The shift from anti-categorization to group empowerment isn't a symptom of deep incoherence. It is a sign of remarkable sophistication in adapting the regulatory powers of the administrative state to the distinctive real-world problems posed by racism in two different spheres.

What is more, Congress turned out to be right in both cases. The classic court-oriented approach pursued by the Civil Rights Act did suffice, after some further pushing by black groups, to desegregate public accommodations in the South. But it was only the VRA's group-oriented and technocratic approach that finally broke the back of racist resistance in the political sphere.

Two spheres of life; two regimes of law; two successes in bringing the law to life.

It is easy to forget such triumphs and assume that "progress" was somehow inevitable. To the contrary, we should see these landmark provisions for what they are: proud achievements of the American people.

Were they repeated elsewhere?

CHAPTER 9

Technocracy in the Workplace

W E BEGAN EXPLORING GOVERNMENT by numbers in a re-markably clear-cut setting. The Voting Rights Act imposed an all-or-nothing test on suspect voting systems: if a jurisdiction failed to meet the statute's numerical targets, it was thrown into federal receiver-ship, and it would stay there for a very long time. The only thing that counted was results. The traditional principles of federalism were trumped by technocratic measures of performance.

This embrace of a sharp-edged output test was the product of bitter experience. The Justice Department had already been trying to overcome southern resistance through the use of traditional lawsuits, and it had very little to show for its efforts. Government by numbers served as the only credible response to the emphatic demand by ordinary Americans for a decisive breakthrough.

As we turn to the workplace, we will be telling a more complicated story. The Kennedy administration had never made employment discrimination a high priority. With President Johnson putting new energy into the ini-tiative, participants confronted basic questions of institutional design. For Democrats, the obvious model was the National Labor Relations Board, and they vigorously tried to create comparable powers for the EEOC. But for Republicans, the NLRB was a symbol of New Deal interventionism at its worst, and they fought for a classical court-centered approach.

The result was institutional creativity: Congress created the EEOC, but the agency engaged the courts in a distinctive fashion, generating a "third way" approach to government by numbers. In contrast to voting rights, there was no sharp break with traditional ideas of individual responsibil-ity. While notions of "intentional" discrimination remained important, they were reinterpreted to give large, but not decisive, importance to mi-nority headcounts. The result was *technocratic individualism*—not a pretty label, but it accurately describes the distinctive constitutional principles that ultimately emerged.

As with voting rights, we will be witnessing a three-act drama. Act One deals with the passage of Title VII in 1964. Act Two follows the EEOC and the courts over the next eight years as they developed the distinctive tools and concerns of technocratic individualism. This set the stage for Act Three—in which Congress and the president return to the key issues in 1972 and codify the distinctive mix of constitutional values that the EEOC had created in partnership with the courts.

ACT ONE: INITIAL BREAKTHROUGH

Title VII speaks in the grand language of principle: it will be an "unlawful employment practice" to "discriminate against any individual" on the basis of "race, color, religion, sex, or national origin."[1] This command applied to all significant employers in the private sector.[2] But it did not extend to any public employees. This limitation was important in practice and in theory. Practically, it exempted southern state bureaucracies even though they were notoriously segregated. But its theoretical implications are more important for twenty-first-century lawyers.

Reverse State Action?

By exempting public employers, Title VII established a "reverse state action" regime: placing private *but not state* actors under especially stringent egalitarian requirements.

Under typical conditions, this striking counterpattern would have provoked intensive scrutiny by the Supreme Court, once again forcing it to consider overruling the Civil Rights Cases. But, remarkably enough, the issue never came up. The reason, in four words, was *Heart of Atlanta Motel.* Once the Court had used the Commerce Clause to uphold Title II's ban on segregation in private restaurants and hotels, Title VII's exclusive focus on private firms no longer posed a problem. Once again, the Commerce Clause could come to the rescue, especially since the Court could rely on its famous New Deal decisions upholding the Wagner Act: if the Commerce Clause was good enough for a worker's right to join a union in 1937, it was good enough for a worker's right to fair treatment in 1964.[3] The point was so obvious that the Warren Court never bothered to write an opinion on the subject. It simply assumed that Title VII was constitutional without explaining why—any competent lawyer could fill in the blank.

Nevertheless, it's important to consider the road not taken. Suppose for a moment that the Court had upheld Title II on equal protection grounds, refuting state action objections in an opinion similar to my draft version of the Civil Rights Cases of 1964 in Chapter 7. Such a decision would have encouraged litigants to make Title VII's reverse state action doctrine into a cause célèbre, providing the Warren Court with another occasion to develop a *Brown*-style argument for moving equal protection law beyond the Civil Rights Cases of 1883. On this scenario, the *United States Reports* would have contained a second opinion explaining that private employment, like public accommodations, was a crucial sphere of social life in the modern world, that institutionalized humiliation predictably generated an enduring "feeling of inferiority as to [the black worker's] status in the community," and that the Civil Rights Cases of 1883 were wrong in dismissing these profound insults as unworthy of constitutional protection. I urge you to write up your own hypothetical opinion along these lines, since it is a great way to figure out where you stand on the distinctive pattern of *Brown*-style argumentation that I am offering up as a model for the future development of civil rights law. But I have said enough to make the key point: that the typical lawyer/judge of today doesn't give the question of reverse state action a moment's thought.

The villain, once again, is the exceptionally narrow character of the modern canon. Constitutional lawyers decode the meaning of the civil rights revolution exclusively by consulting the *United States Reports*. Since the Warren and Burger Courts didn't address the issue of reverse state action, we can ignore it. And that is that.

A big mistake. The Civil Rights Act was the most important egalitarian initiative since Reconstruction. Surely it has something to teach us about the meaning of constitutional equality. Isn't it time to give Title VII's decision to insist on the crucial significance of the sphere of private employment a new look?

The Dirksen-Mansfield Compromise

We should approach Title VII's operational standards in the same spirit. Congress understood its anti-discrimination principle in individualistic terms, rejecting "preferential treatment" for employees simply because their group was underrepresented in relation to their proportion of "the available work force."[4] It vindicated a worker's claim only if the firm had "intentionally" engaged in an "unlawful employment practice."[5]

These provisions were added at a crucial turning point: Everett Dirksen made them part of his compromise with Mike Mansfield that broke the Senate filibuster.[6] We should pause, then, to understand precisely what these provisions did, and didn't, require.

Quite plainly, the compromise rejected the hard-edged version of government by numbers endorsed the following year in the Voting Rights Act. It continued to speak in the traditional legal language of "intentional" discrimination, and made statistical "imbalance" insufficient, by itself, to justify such a finding. But these formulae did not imply a sweeping rejection of government by numbers. They established a basic framework within which the legal tradition revealed a remarkable capacity to introduce quantitative indicators into its interpretation of "intentionality" within the distinctive setting of the modern business enterprise.

To begin with the basics, the law has traditionally used an objective approach to matters of intentionality, presuming that people "intend" the "natural and probable" consequences of their acts. This general rule reintroduces numbers into the equation when applied to the special circumstances confronting personnel directors in modern firms. When our hypothetical director creates hiring and promotion policies for her firm, she *intentionally* discriminates if her policies *predictably* disadvantage blacks. There is only one way to escape this presumption. "It's true that my policies disproportionately hurt blacks," she may explain, "but they're necessary to ensure my goal: a qualified workforce." It's only in cases of business necessity that adverse impact would count as an unintended side effect of her decision, rather than one of its intended consequences.

Nothing in the legislative history challenges this understanding. Some have pointed to Hubert Humphrey's comment that the "express requirement of intent is designed to make it wholly clear that inadvertent or accidental discriminations will not violate the title."[7] But such remarks simply clarify a basic legal challenge raised by the Dirksen-Mansfield compromise: how to distinguish the "inadvertent or accidental" from the "natural and probable" in assessing each firm's employment policies.

In the modern world, there is only one responsible way to make that distinction, and that is to take advantage of statistical techniques in assessing probabilities. Only a Luddite would repudiate these modern methods, and Luddites were in short supply in Washington, D.C.

Congress created a new Equal Economic Opportunity Commission that was capable of engaging in the statistical heavy lifting. The statute authorized the agency to file an administrative complaint against any firm that it had "reasonable cause to believe" was engaged in discrimination.[8] This was no small task, since the act was designed to cover more than three hundred thousand firms and three-quarters of the entire workforce.[9] If the EEOC merely waited for complaints from individual workers, it would give a free pass to the most repressive employers, whose threats of reprisal would prevent workers from raising their voices. Statistical analysis of broad employment patterns provided the new agency with its best sense of the big picture, enabling it to target the worst offenders.

This much was obvious, and the statute gave the EEOC explicit authority to order firms "to maintain . . . records" needed for the agency to function effectively.[10] But lots of other matters were up for grabs. For liberal Democrats, it was not enough for the EEOC to investigate and target firms with discriminatory labor practices. They wanted to give the EEOC authority to follow up with legally enforceable cease-and-desist orders. Their model was the National Labor Relations Board. Just as the NLRB forced employers to deal with unions, the EEOC would force them to deal with prejudice. If employers didn't like the EEOC's commands, they could challenge them in federal court, but they would have the burden of showing that the agency had acted arbitrarily.

The Democrats' dream agency was the Republicans' nightmare. Senator Dirksen and many other Republicans had devoted their political lives to denouncing the NLRB for interfering with business prerogatives. They rebelled at the prospect of an NLRB clone issuing yet another stream of cease-and-desist orders. No surprise, then, that the Dirksen-Mansfield compromise stripped the EEOC of cease-and-desist power. Under their agreement, the new agency could function only as a conciliation service, prodding employers to respond to its complaints and those filed by individual workers. If the EEOC couldn't get the parties to solve the problem within sixty days, only affected workers—not the commission—could go to court to enforce their rights.[11]

All this added up to a distinctive form of agency-court collaboration. The landmark statute followed the New Deal script in creating an independent agency composed of five commissioners with power to investigate the labor market, target potential wrongdoers, and respond to individual complaints. But it relied on the courts, not the agency, to vindicate the complaints of workers at the enforcement stage.

Congress did temper its worker-centered approach by authorizing the Justice Department to sue anybody "engaged in a pattern or practice of resistance to the full enjoyment" of employee rights. Practically speaking, however, this was a narrow exception—the Civil Rights Division was an elite group with many large tasks, and it couldn't afford to engage in massive enforcement campaigns. The principal burden would rest on workers, with the help of the NAACP Legal Defense Fund and other groups with limited resources. To sum up, let's say that Title VII created a quasi–New Deal approach, mixing public and private actors in a distinctive pattern to realize its ambitious aims. Only one question remained: would it work?

The answer was mostly no. The act utterly failed to provide effective relief for individual complaints. But it was more successful in using statistical techniques to investigate the larger labor market, target its worst offenders, and expose pervasive discriminatory practices. These New Dealish successes were then confirmed by Congress in a 1972 consolidating statute. In short, our story parallels the three-phase development of the Voting Rights Acts of 1965 and 1970—but with important institutional variations.

Act Two: The Emergence of Technocratic Individualism

The 1964 law provided a one-year moratorium to give the EEOC a chance to tool up for business while employers reviewed their current practices. Yet the administration blew this opportunity—with one month to go, the commission had no commissioners, no staff, no offices. When Johnson finally landed a chairman, Franklin Delano Roosevelt Jr., this big name was more interested in running for New York's mayoralty than blazing a trail for his agency.[12] He didn't even bother to show up on Capitol Hill to make the case for his budget, and the EEOC obtained a pittance for its start-up year.[13]

At the same time, civil rights groups were organizing a campaign to overwhelm the infant agency with a flood of individual complaints. "The best way to get it [Title VII] amended is to show that it doesn't work," explained Jack Greenberg, head of the NAACP Legal Defense Fund.[14]

Over the middle run, Greenberg's strategy worked to convince Congress to enhance the agency's powers. But over the short run, it created havoc. A staffer recalled: "We were initially programmed for something like about 2,500 charges [for the first year]. We received 6,000. We've been dying ever since."[15] The agency managed to conciliate only 110 out of its first 15,000 cases—no surprise, since it hired only five conciliators to serve the entire country.[16] Things didn't get better: the commission received 15,000 more complaints in 1968, but conciliated just 513.[17]

Employees were free, after sixty days, to take their complaint to court. But this wasn't working either. Fewer than one hundred lawsuits were filed during 1968—and almost all failed. During the first four years, only four workers gained relief on their own (and in three of these, the Department of Justice had filed an amicus brief).[18] The 1964 compromise was a flop.

Government by Numbers

The infant agency could have sunk beneath this flood of complaints. Remarkably enough, it managed to find the energy to experiment with an alternative, and more promising, approach. This strategy began by requiring every firm in its regulatory universe to submit an annual Form EEO-1 reporting the racial profile of its employees in quantitative terms. The agency could then use the data to target the worst offenders without depending on the vagaries of individual complaints.

The spark plug behind this effort was law professor Alfred Blumrosen, an agency consultant during the start-up period. Even before the EEOC opened its doors, he urged it to take up a data-driven strategy: "I saw this as perhaps the most important tool in any program to eliminate employment discrimination. . . . Here at last was a basis for government-initiated programs which were not based on complaints and which could focus on possible potential discriminators effectively. . . . There was a perennial shortage of manpower and money in antidiscrimination programs. If government could focus, through the reporting system, on those employers where underutilization was sharpest, there was a possibility of successfully combating discrimination."[19]

Blumrosen quickly gained Roosevelt's support, but this wasn't enough to get the project off the ground. Given his role in creating the agency, Senator Dirksen might well have blocked the program by denouncing it as inconsistent with congressional intent. But when he was consulted, he quickly approved—providing further evidence that a bipartisan congressional majority fully expected the EEOC to make good on the New Deal promise of expertise.[20] The agency then pushed its proposal at a White House Conference on Equal Employment Opportunity in August 1965— the second month of its operation.

Where it encountered surprising resistance from civil rights groups. The NAACP's Clarence Mitchell argued that racial reporting would "open[] the door to discrimination and, if you say it isn't true, I regret to say that you haven't been exposed to all the problems in this country."[21] One would suppose that the opposition of civil rights leaders would be more than enough to kill the infant agency's brainchild.

But it wasn't, and for reasons that are central to my thesis. EEOC staffers emphatically argued that a racial reporting system was an essential means for targeting the worst offenders—and they were backed up by staffers from state fair employment agencies.[22] With repeated warnings that the agency's success was at stake, the administrative imperative carried the day. Support by the White House conference provided the agency with the momentum it needed for a national reporting program that began in early 1966.[23]

For some conservatives, the birth of racial reporting is evidence that civil rights activists had already captured the agency. But the opposition of leading civil rights groups at the White House conference makes this very implausible. What is more, a careful empirical study shows that EEOC personnel "ran the gamut" from conservative to liberal.[24] There is simply no evidence that policy making was dominated by "civil rights ideologues."[25]

Instead of indulging fashionable "capture" theories, we should view Form EEO-1 as a typical New Deal response to a standard regulatory problem: the agency would betray its claim to expertise if it failed to keep track of the complex and shifting patterns of discrimination prevailing in its vast regulatory universe. Without regular reporting, there was no hope of identifying the worst offenders in a sensible fashion; without successful targeting, there was little hope of bridging the gap between the law on the books and social reality—and that was what the Second Reconstruction was all about.[26]

Once firms began filling out their EEOC forms, the commission took the next logical step: beginning in 1967, it held a series of public "forums" targeting discrimination in a series of problem markets.[27] Here is Clifford Alexander Jr., the agency's new chairman, telling representatives of the pharmaceutical industry why he was calling them together:

> First, we want to show each of you, who is undoubtedly aware of minority employment patterns in your own company, the picture for the industry as a whole. We do not believe it is a picture of which you will be proud.
>
> Second, we want to describe the kind of effort that could help change that picture. *We want to attempt to avoid, in both your interest and ours, the time-consuming complaint process which could well be the inevitable alternative to the kind of voluntary action we seek to initiate today.*[28]

Alexander's concluding threat was mostly bluff: the agency's immense backlog could stall conciliation efforts for years—and employers had little to fear if they chose to resist, since aggrieved workers (or, in the rare case, the Justice Department) would be obliged to go to court for relief.

Nevertheless, the agency was setting the stage for a fundamental re-orientation in the operational meaning of racial discrimination. It was giving firms a choice: either keep on reporting bad racial numbers on their Form EEO-1 and run the risk of litigation, or report better numbers next year and get themselves off the hook.

Conservatives condemned this move as illegal, but there was nothing to this charge.[29] Although the statute banned the agency from "requir[ing]" quotas, the EEOC wasn't *requiring* anything, let alone hard-edged quotas. It was simply telling regulated firms how it intended to deploy its scarce investigative resources to fulfill its statutory mission—thus giving conscientious firms the information they needed to steer clear of potentially disruptive legal interventions. As Alexander suggested, this tried-and-true technique was in the best interests of all concerned.

Each firm had the right to call the agency's bluff and challenge workers or the Department of Justice to launch a serious lawsuit.[30] Nevertheless, the agency's decision to redeem the New Deal promise of expertise was returning the question of government by numbers to the political agenda: was this mode of "voluntary" negotiation on numerical targets—with a background threat of litigation—worthy of repudiation or reinforcement in the years ahead?

Nixon's answer was loud and clear: he gave it his emphatic support. The EEOC's budget more than doubled, and its staff quadrupled, from 359 in 1969 to 1,640 in 1972.[31] His new chairman, William Brown III, vigorously pursued Alexander's strategy, setting a breakthrough precedent in a 1970 settlement with AT&T. The agreement not only provided $15 million in back pay for aggrieved employees but also committed the telephone company to developing numerical goals in its future hiring of women and minorities. Brown proudly used this settlement to urge "companies to start to move on their own initiative to bring themselves into compliance with the law."[32] The administration was reinforcing this message on other bureaucratic fronts as well—most famously in the Philadelphia Plan, which aggressively required federal contractors in the construction industry to aim for numerical targets.[33]

All of this set the stage for a decisive congressional debate over the future of the EEOC in 1972. But before turning to this round of political reassessment, consider another agency development that posed the question of technocratic legitimacy in stark terms.

Standardized Testing

Government by numbers was part of a larger technocratic revolution in the organization of collective intelligence. American business was at the cutting edge: big employers were increasingly relying on standardized testing in making hiring decisions, and by the 1960s the testing business had become professionalized. Employment by numbers raised new questions about the meaning of equal employment opportunity. But it wasn't inevitable that Congress would confront these issues squarely in 1964. Nevertheless, it did so—thanks in large part to an accident of timing.

The media played a key role. Arthur Krock, a *New York Times* columnist, sounded the alarm in his report on a recent decision by the Illinois Fair Employment Practices Commission. The case involved Leon Myart, a twenty-eight-year-old black man who applied for a job as a quality control inspector with Motorola after serving a tour of duty in the army. The company rejected him, claiming that he failed a twenty-eight-question general aptitude test—though it never produced his exam results. Myart denied that he had failed, and in any event he passed the test when he was reexamined at the employment commission.

Illinois's hearing examiner did not focus on these suspicious facts. He issued a broad denunciation of standardized testing without even considering whether Myart's particular test was good at predicting his likely job performance.[34]

In Krock's view, *Myart* "furnished a graphic illustration" of "autocratic control" over "the hiring and firing policies of private business," which was now threatening the nation as a whole: "If Congress approves the pending measure, with Title Seven included, . . . the federal bureaucracy would be legislated into a senior partnership with private business," wielding "the power to dictate . . . standards . . . whenever the issue of 'discrimination' is raised."[35] With Krock propelling *Myart* before a national audience, the case became a cause célèbre for southerners trying to weaken the act.

Senator John Tower of Texas took the lead. His amendment would have created a safe harbor for any "professionally developed" test that was "designed to . . . predict" whether an employee was "suitable or trainable" for his job.[36] This was voted down by a margin of 49 to 38, with Senator Humphrey leading the opposition.[37] Two days later, however, Humphrey endorsed a narrower version of the Tower proposal making it clear that an employer couldn't use just any professionally prepared test. Under his amendment, the test would remain illegal if it was used to discriminate against minorities.[38] But how was the EEOC or the courts to determine whether the use was discriminatory?

Nobody in the Senate thought to ask, let alone answer, this key question. Once Humphrey's concerns had been satisfied, the amendment passed on a voice vote without further debate.[39] The Senate simply failed to provide clear guidance, either to the agency or to the courts, on when the use of tests should be prohibited.

The agency responded in New Deal fashion. Given the Tower-Humphrey emphasis on "professionally developed" tests, the agency's 1967 guidelines relied heavily on standards recently developed by the American Psychological Association.[40] Despite its crushing administrative burdens, Nixon's EEOC followed up with a more elaborate set of standards in 1970.

This classic New Deal effort generated criteria that fell well within the boundaries of conventional wisdom among professional psychologists. The agency emphasized that "[t]he ultimate standard . . . is not the test score but performance on the job," and it supported the use of tests only when they could be statistically verified as a "valid predictor" of minority "job performance."[41]

But would the judges agree? This was a key issue in *Griggs v. Duke Power,* handed down by the Supreme Court in 1971. The southern company had traditionally allowed blacks to work only as unskilled laborers. With the passage of the act, Duke Power recognized that times had changed, and announced that blacks could now gain promotion to other departments—but only if they could pass a standardized intelligence test (or obtain a high school diploma).

The company had made no statistical effort to establish that its test was a good predictor of job performance. Even though blacks were failing at higher rates than whites, Duke argued that its good intentions were enough under the Tower amendment, and it launched a broad assault on the commission's authority to assert otherwise.

The company recognized that it was fighting an uphill battle. Since the New Deal, the Supreme Court had granted administrative agencies lots of leeway in interpreting and applying their governing statutes. But the EEOC was different. Given the commission's humble role as investigator and conciliator, Duke Power urged the Court to cut the agency down to size and maintain judicial control over statutory interpretation.

Chief Justice Warren Burger rejected the invitation. Speaking for a unanimous Court, he insisted that the EEOC's statutory interpretations were entitled to the "great deference" generally accorded New Deal agencies, and used the agency's guidelines as a key element in evaluating the company's arguments.[42] In defending itself, Duke relied heavily on lower court findings acquitting its executives of racist motives in adopting their standardized test. But Burger rejected mind-reading as irrelevant and adopted the traditional view that an actor intended the predictable consequences of his actions. The company certainly intended to use the unverified test, and given the agency's guidelines on testing, Duke's decision condemned it under the statute. If a standardized test did not actually predict real-world performance, it was merely a technocratic way of blinding employers to each applicant's real-world qualifications; and if black applicants were failing the test at disproportionate rates, the company's technocratic methods amounted to a fancy form of job discrimination. The overarching aim of the act, Burger insisted, was individualistic and meritocratic—to force employers to assess candidates' qualifications for particular jobs, not their abstract test-taking ability. Within this framework, Title VII demanded more than good intentions from employers; it insisted on the eradication of all "practices that are fair in form but discriminatory in operation."[43]

Burger was reading the landmark statute to express the distinctive aspirations of the New Deal–Civil Rights regime—to bridge the gap between the egalitarian ideals expressed in the law books and the everyday realities of the job market. His point wasn't to banish technocracy in either government or business. It was to offer a new variation on the constitutional theme of checks and balances, with government technocrats checking business technocrats to ensure that testing was related to the statute's overriding aim—equal opportunity in the real world: "What is required by Congress is the removal of artificial, arbitrary, and unnecessary barriers to employment when the barriers operate invidiously to discriminate."[44]

Griggs's requirements are exigent but not unbounded. Burger is concerned only with equality opportunity within the workplace, not with more general forms of subordination. Given their segregated educations, for example, most blacks never had a fair chance to perform well on employment tests, even those tests that did in fact predict job success. But *Griggs* did not require firms to compensate for these deeper failures.

Call this principle "technocratic individualism": firms owe a duty to eliminate "unnecessary" barriers against qualified blacks, but not to fellow group members who never got a fair shot at gaining the skills required by tests that meet professional standards. In drawing this limit, *Griggs* is expressing the sphere-by-sphere approach characteristic of the Second Reconstruction. Rather than imposing a one-size-fits-all formula, the landmark statutes are seeking institution-specific solutions to real-world problems of injustice. In bringing this point home in *Griggs,* Burger's opinion offered a brilliant synthesis of the Civil Rights ideal of equality of opportunity and the New Deal ideal of expertise.

The Court would not have the last word on the matter. The very next year saw President Nixon and Congress rethinking Title VII from the ground up.

ACT THREE: CONSOLIDATION

We have been telling a surprising story. An infant agency is overwhelmed with individual complaints but somehow manages to develop a sophisticated structural approach to a daunting problem: how to identify the most serious abuses occurring in its enormous regulatory universe.

The EEOC responded with a two-part answer—one targeting the worst offenders; the other, suspect practices. On one hand, it initiated a technocratic strategy that used hard numbers to encourage lagging firms to set voluntary hiring goals. On the other, it mobilized professional expertise to focus on a key technique of modern personnel management, the standardized test.[45]

In both cases, the agency's success was greatly facilitated by an ongoing revolution in business practices. By the 1960s, major firms contained personnel departments devoted to managing "human resources" in technocratic fashion—using computer techniques to formulate data-driven policies on employment, promotion, standardized testing, and the like.[46] This new breed of professional greeted Form EEO-1 as a new opportunity to demonstrate their expertise, comparing recent minority hires with their firm's long-term track record. If the numbers didn't show "progress," they could alert top management of looming political dangers: wouldn't the company suffer a public relations disaster if it was targeted by the EEOC at a public hearing?

The official forms also gave these specialists more leverage in dealing with the firm's operating divisions. Like Burger in *Griggs,* the human resource professionals weren't aiming for some fixed quota of minority hires. They were pushing for a reexamination of practices that would unlock their employees' full potential by lifting artificial barriers that blocked minorities and women from the positions for which they were fully qualified.

This ongoing data-driven conversation—between the EEOC and top executives, between personnel departments and operating divisions— served as the institutional foundation for a remarkable transformation in legal language. Call it the *professionalization of intentionality.* Since personnel departments were in the business of analyzing statistical patterns, they would be acting unprofessionally if they ignored data on minority hiring they were compiling for the EEOC. Within the setting of the modern enterprise, discriminatory intentions had become a numbers-driven affair: only if bad-looking numbers had a good business justification could personnel offices discount them without demonstrating racial prejudice. The Court's unanimous opinion in *Griggs* was giving expression to these larger business realities, which helped frame the basic questions for political reconsideration in 1972.

As they set about rethinking Title VII, Nixon and Congress found themselves at a fork in the road. On one hand, the EEOC had a miserable track record of dealing with individual complaints. By 1972, the agency had a backlog of fifty-four thousand complaints, and it took eighteen months or more to move a case into conciliation.[47] Given this failure, the political leadership could have ordered a return to a traditional court-centered approach, eliminating the EEOC and placing the entire burden on workers to convince judges and juries that they had been wronged. Or they could focus on the agency's technocratic successes and build on the New Deal promise of their hybrid construction. Which would it be: a return to the classic court-only approach or the further elaboration of technocratic individualism?

The answer was astonishingly clear-cut. Nobody was inclined to clip the agency's wings; the debate was all about the best way to enhance the EEOC's powers.

The emerging consensus developed early in the Nixon years. When the Republicans regained the White House, they confronted a last-minute proposal by the Johnson team to kick-start political debate. In a parting gesture, the outgoing administration pointed to the EEOC's dismal record of handling individual complaints and called for the transformation of the EEOC into another NLRB, with full cease-and-desist powers.[48]

Given the traditional Republican distaste for the NLRB, it's surprising that the incoming Nixonians did not reject this proposal out of hand. In fact, Jerris Leonard, the new assistant attorney general for civil rights, argued that it was "on the whole satisfactory," and proposed its further refinement.[49] In the end, however, a more conservative group—including the young William Rehnquist and senior advisor Arthur Burns—emerged victorious. Nevertheless, they too recognized the need to beef up the EEOC. While they rejected cease-and-desist authority, they proposed to make the agency into the act's principal enforcer, giving it the power to go directly to court and hold violators legally accountable.[50]

When the administration went public with its initiative, traditional civil rights groups vigorously opposed it, insisting that the New Deal model provided the best way forward. The next three years were dominated by this debate—with the House or Senate endorsing one or another model but not joining together to enact a statute until 1972.[51] This ongoing disagreement shouldn't conceal how basic premises had shifted since the days of the Dirksen-Mansfield compromise. In contrast to 1964, mainline Republicans now agreed with liberal Democrats on the need for a powerful agency to redeem the real-world promise of Title VII. They simply disagreed about the best way to empower the agency.

This left southern conservatives politically isolated. They skillfully played a rear-guard game that bottled up final passage of the act for three years, but the handwriting was on the wall. What is more, the lengthy debate led to a deeper appreciation of the administration's reliance on the judiciary as the principal interpreter and enforcer of the law. Even the *New York Times*—no admirer of Nixon—ultimately concluded: "Even though civil rights organizations would have preferred to have the EEOC issue cease-and-desist orders on its own, we believe the court remedy is preferable to reliance on a politically appointed commission whose members change with each new President."[52] By the time Nixon's initiative became law, it was broadly recognized as a decisive advance.

No less important, the EEOC's earlier experience with government by numbers transformed Congress's understanding of the very meaning of the anti-discrimination effort. Consider Senator Harrison Williams's arguments as he opened the final Senate debate over the issue in January 1972. Speaking as the Democratic co-manager for the bill, he explained its principal rationale:

Title VII, quite frankly, has not been a notable success. In 1964, employment discrimination tended to be viewed as a series of isolated and distinguishable events, for the most part due to ill will on the part of some identifiable individual or organization. It was thought that a scheme that stressed conciliation rather than compulsory processes would be most appropriate for the resolution of this essentially human problem, and that litigation would be necessary only on an occasional basis in the event of determined recalcitrance. Unfortunately, this view has not been borne out by the experience of the last 7 years. . . . [D]uring each year of the Commission's existence, the number of charges filed per year has increased. In fiscal year 1970 alone, the Commission received 14,129 new charges; in fiscal year 1971, this number increased to 22,920; and the indications for the current year are that more than 32,000 charges will be filed with the Commission.

Compliance reviews and employment surveys [by the EEOC] continually reflect the same traditional situation. Minority workers—black, Spanish-surnamed, Oriental or Indian—are relegated to the lowest paying, least desirable jobs—if, indeed, they get hired at all. . . . The statistics are vivid, and I would like to recite just a few of the more significant results.[53]

The EEOC's compliance reviews were inviting Congress to redefine the very nature of the problem: discrimination was not an "isolated and distinguishable event . . . due to [the] ill will . . . of some identifiable individually"; it was a systemic feature of economic life, requiring systemic reorganization of the enforcement system. Just as the EEOC had used its reporting requirements to prod firms into action, government by numbers was now propelling Congress to rethink basic premises of administrative law.

Congress was also beating back efforts, led by Senator Ervin, to repudiate the EEOC's past settlements with companies such as AT&T, which had set numerical goals for minority hiring. Senator Ervin predictably condemned this embrace of "reverse discrimination," but his critique showed how much times had changed. In 1964, Ervin led the filibuster against any and all versions of Title VII, but eight years later, he appeared as the true defender of the 1964 act, protesting against its bureaucratic abuse by the Nixon administration: "[I] do not understand why the Federal Government orders employers to practice discrimination in employment while they are supposed to be preventing discrimination in employment."[54]

Tower's amendment would have barred any "officer" of the United States from ordering any sort of racial awareness in hiring, repudiating the very notion that a numerical goal was different from a hard-edged quota.[55] But the Senate rejected it by a two-to-one margin.[56]

Reading the handwriting on the wall, Senator Tower did not even try to challenge the Supreme Court's decision in *Griggs*. While he had championed standardized testing in Motorola's dispute with Myart in 1964, he refused to reopen the issue once Motorola's spokesman publicly accepted *Griggs* in testimony before Congress.[57] This turnaround symbolized the larger shift in public opinion—government by numbers had become a commitment of the Second Reconstruction.

Congress made the same point in affirming *Griggs*'s technocratic interpretation of the 1964 statute. To set the stage for its final passage, the leaders of the House-Senate conference prefaced their report with an explicit endorsement of "the present case law as developed by the courts," declaring that it should "continue to govern the . . . construction of Title VII."[58]

The 1972 act, in short, served as a culminating moment in a dynamic process of institutional experimentation and consolidation. During the preceding years, the EEOC had not only provided salient examples of technocracy in action. It had also generated the real-world experience that permitted Congress and the president to confront the key question—whether to build upon or repudiate the agency's efforts to realize the New Deal ideal of expert administration and enforcement.

The result was a distinctive variation on New Deal themes. In contrast to the NLRB model, the EEOC would not function as an expert arbiter of labor-management disputes, resolving disputes with cease-and-desist orders; it would function as an expert litigant, using its technocratic capacities to convince courts to interpret the statute in ways that did justice to the institutional realities of the workplace.

This change from arbitral mode to prosecutorial mode made sense, given the different role that courts had played during the New Deal and civil rights eras. When Congress passed the National Labor Relations Act in 1935, the conservative Four Horsemen on the Supreme Court were threatening to invalidate the entire initiative. Even if the statute managed to survive judicial review, Congress would have been foolish to depend on the justices to interpret its mandate sympathetically. Common sense pointed in a very different direction: design the system so that the NLRB could function as the act's principal expositor, and then insulate the board from intrusive review by the courts.

In contrast, the Warren and Burger Courts had been functioning as leading supporters of the civil rights revolution, and it was perfectly sensible to expect the judges to continue down this path. Within this context, the expert prosecutor model seemed the better bet, with the EEOC marshaling the numbers and the courts developing the law. Even if the prosecutorial ardor of the EEOC faded over time, the members of the Burger Court had life tenure, and it would take much longer for the president and the Senate to shift the course of the law.

Once the agency's powers had been enhanced, the EEOC immediately began to use them aggressively. With Nixon's support, it brought suit against 141 firms in 1972 and 1973, including many national leaders—leading to a series of high-profile consent decrees in which firms accepted numerical hiring and promotion targets.[59]

Previously, the EEOC had been mostly bluffing when it tried to convince major corporations to commit themselves to numerical hiring goals. But now that it could go to court, the balance of power shifted. *Griggs* had made it clear that businesses could not place "artificial, arbitrary, and unnecessary barriers" on their minority employees, and if the EEOC did its homework, it could expect courts to respond with respectful attention to its statistical evidence of disparate impact. Systemic enforcement, not case-by-case conciliation, had become the order of the day.

Nothing lasts forever. Perhaps a new generation of justices would refuse to sustain the mission established by the landmark statutes of 1964 and 1972—after all, the great achievements of the first Reconstruction suffered a similar fate over the longer haul. But in 1972, constitutional consolidation was as complete as it ever gets. Granted a new mandate by Congress and the president, the EEOC was redeeming the promise of government by numbers, and its new wave of settlements was providing leverage for personnel managers everywhere to translate the nation's constitutional commitments into workplace realities.[60]

Toward Synthesis

We can now move beyond our blow-by-blow account of employment law and integrate it into our previous studies of the law of public accommodations and voting rights.

To keep things simple, let's start with a comparison between employment and voting. These two stories share a three-part pattern of constitutional development: first, a landmark statute was passed at a peak moment of popular mobilization and national commitment; second, this provokes a period of administrative and judicial experimentation; third, the practical experience generated by bureaucrats and judges frames another round of political decisions during the Nixon years that led to the statutory consolidation and refinement of the breakthroughs of the 1960s. All in all, this pattern adds up to something special—a genuine exercise in collective learning and deliberation.

In 1964, only one thing was clear: the American people were giving their elected representatives a mandate for a new beginning in race relations. It was up to the president and Congress to translate this mandate into enduring legal structures. The landmark statutes of 1964 and 1965 necessarily engaged in lots of institutional experimentation. When Senators Dirksen and Mansfield announced their compromise on Title VII, nobody could say whether their quasi–New Deal solution would work. The same was true with the Voting Rights Act's sweeping endorsement of government by numbers: would its bureaucratic intrusions into the Deep South provoke a disastrous replay of the nineteenth-century Reconstruction or a constructive administrative engagement that would overcome massive resistance?

By the early 1970s, President Nixon and the Democratic Congress were in a better position to answer these questions—and they managed to consolidate both regimes on a bipartisan basis. Nixon's position differed in our two stories. In voting, he wanted to nationalize the act's concerns and eliminate the special measures targeting the South; in employment, he wanted to strengthen the EEOC but rejected the NLRB as an appropriate model. He lost in the first debate and won in the second, but there was a common feature in both—the political arguments on all sides were deeply informed by the administrative and judicial experience of the preceding period. If the Voting Rights Act had provoked a replay of the first Reconstruction, fierce local resistance would have forced anxious reappraisal of the landmark statute in Washington, D.C. But the 1965 act had visibly begun to work on the ground, and Congress refused to risk a return to the bad old days. With mainstream opinion weighing heavily on the side of Congress, Nixon accepted the need to continue the new technocratic system on an expanded basis that targeted a few areas in the North as well as large parts of the South. In 1965, government by numbers could be viewed as an emergency measure to secure basic voting rights; in 1970, it had become a basic building block of the New Deal–Civil Rights regime.

Title VII presented a different picture. While the statute's initial passage had encouraged lots of firms to comply voluntarily, it was clear by 1972 that its quasi–New Deal model of enforcement was a flat-out failure.[61] If permitted to continue, the existing system would allow hard-line offenders to escape sanctions, and encourage more cooperative firms to rethink their earlier egalitarian advances.

This time around, the Nixon administration did not even pause before finding the risk of backsliding unacceptable. It joined with Congress to build on the most promising aspects of the EEOC's experience and create a distinctive model of agency-court coordination that promised better results than the NLRB had managed to deliver.

In telling these stories, my aim isn't to say how well these promises panned out over the next generation. Rather, it is to reflect on how the living Constitution managed to translate the civil rights revolution into principled legal commitments. From this vantage, the system deserves high marks. To be sure, Johnson, Nixon, Dirksen, and Humphrey weren't engaged in a philosophy seminar as they constantly struggled for political advantage. But it is even more wrongheaded to view them as cynical practitioners of power politics.

This is the greater danger at present, given the current ascendancy of the so-called rational choice approach to politics in the American academy. Within this familiar framework, "rational" politicians are exclusively concerned with the pursuit of electoral advantage, choosing policies that maximize their chances of reelection (until they sell out as lobbyists at the end of their careers). Anything else is "irrational"—it happens sometimes but should be seen as aberrational.[62]

Here is where I get off the boat.[63] Of course politicians are interested in reelection, but they are also interested in making America a better place—that's what drives many of them into politics in the first place. Idealistic motives may fade, but then again, they may not: it is perfectly rational for politicians to believe that the pursuit of power is meaningless if it leads them to forget why they got into the business in the first place.

Richard Nixon is a case in point. The struggle for racial equality wasn't at the center of his political life, but from his days as vice president he was an important player in pushing a moderate civil rights agenda, and he wasn't about to join in a reactionary assault on its achievements. He was prepared to make many welcoming gestures to southern whites to break the Democratic monopoly on the region's politics, but there were limits. He was entirely aware that some of his actions to consolidate the civil rights revolution might not pay off politically. But he was sometimes willing to pay this price to make a constructive constitutional contribution to the Republic. By treating such decisions as aberrational, the rational choice school invites us to obliterate the rich tradition of political statesmanship that has been the lifeblood of American constitutional development.

TECHNOCRATIC INDIVIDUALISM?

We have been telling two success stories in popular sovereignty based on public deliberation—that's the common theme linking the spheres of working and voting into a common pattern.

Let's now explore the differences.

As Congresses and presidents and courts hammered out basic principles governing the two spheres, they came to very different conclusions. While the Voting Rights Act imposed hard-edged output tests on voting registrars, there is nothing comparable when dealing with employers—

firms did not face minority employment quotas, let alone intensive federal supervision if they failed to meet their numerical targets.

There is also a big difference in the substantive principles endorsed by the landmark statutes. The VRA moved beyond the individualistic ideal of "one person, one vote" and embraced a group-oriented effort to protect black political power. Title VII embarked on a more individualistic enterprise—using technocratic means to protect each worker's right to be judged on his or her merits.

To get a grip on the distinctive character of this ideal, I will be bringing a third sphere—public accommodations—into the equation. The Civil Rights Act responded to Jim Crow in this sphere without any significant technocratic apparatus. Title II principally relied on traditional lawsuits by traditional plaintiffs before traditional courts using traditional legal language to attack discrimination at restaurants, movie theaters, and the like.

Three different spheres, three different responses to the promise (or threat) of technocracy, three different substantive principles. What to make of this proliferation of legal-technocratic languages and ideals? Is it a symptom of deep moral confusion? Or does it express some deeper wisdom?

My answer elaborates on a central theme: the pluralism of argument patterns and organizational arrangements follows from the sophisticated pursuit of an overriding objective of the Second Reconstruction—to bridge the gap between law and life and actually achieve egalitarian advances in the real world.

I shall develop the argument by highlighting two institutional variables introduced in Chapter 8's preliminary contrast between public accommodations and voting. My first variable focused on the ease with which ordinary people could determine that they were the victims of discrimination; I called this the *identification* problem and suggested that customers found it easier than would-be voters to determine whether they were treated unfairly.

The second variable focused on the likelihood of *institutional resistance*. I emphasized how employers and voting registrars confronted very different feedback loops in dealing with egalitarian interventions: while economic competition gave firms incentives to comply with the new law, the threat of political competition provoked massive resistance from the white political establishment. Within this framework, I argued that both the court-centered approach in public accommodations law and the agency-centered approach in voting law represented judicious responses to the very different problems of identification and resistance arising in these distinctive spheres of life.

We are now in a position to extend the same framework to assess Title VII's choice of technocratic individualism as a "third way" between the group-oriented technocracy affirmed by the VRA and the classical individualism affirmed by the public accommodations provisions of the Civil Rights Act. I will argue that the embrace of this third way also represents a thoughtful response to the distinctive identification/resistance problems in the employment arena.

Begin with the identification problem, and the predictable difficulties an ordinary worker would confront in establishing that he or she has been wrongfully denied a job or promotion. In 1964, identification wasn't a big problem, especially in the South, since blacks were simply excluded from most high-skilled jobs. But as *Griggs* showed, they soon would be confronting more subtle barriers such as standardized testing, and they would have a tough job making out a case of discrimination without complex technocratic analysis.

From this perspective, the job seekers' problem broadly resembled that of a would-be voter confronting the challenges of a southern registrar's office once discrimination had moved beyond blatant exclusionary tactics. Suppose, for example, that the VRA hadn't banned literacy tests: registrars would have been free to provide a "standardized test" that was systematically more difficult for blacks to pass, leaving it to minority voters to establish its pervasive unfairness. Given the similar predicaments of would-be workers and voters, it's hardly surprising that neither Title VII nor the VRA relied on individuals to do the heavy lifting in bringing their problems to legal attention. Instead, the statutes assigned a big part of the job to expert agencies deploying technocratic tests to identify suspicious patterns of discriminatory activity.

In contrast, there was less need to pursue the technocratic path to real-world equality in the sphere of public accommodations. It isn't tough for a black couple to recognize that they've been denied a table at a restaurant or shunted to the back of the movie theater. In this area, the identification problem doesn't provide a powerful reason for moving beyond the traditional court-centered approach to righting wrongs—and Title II refuses to do so.

But when we turn to institutional resistance, the intersphere comparisons take on a very different valence. Employment no longer resembles voting, but it does begin to look like public accommodations. In both spheres, the logic of the marketplace supports an anti-discrimination initiative once it gets off the ground. But the opposite is true for elections. Once blacks start voting in large numbers, the white political establishment will make a bitter-end effort to gerrymander the voting system in other ways to dilute black political power. So it isn't surprising that Title VII doesn't adopt the drastic steps the VRA uses to counteract white backlash. While the EEOC emphasizes the technocratic identification of suspect employment patterns and practices, it doesn't follow through with the VRA's stringent quantitative tests or intensive federal supervision.

In Chapter 8's discussion of public accommodations, I described how it may be good business for individual firms to comply with anti-discrimination laws once they expect their competitors to do the same. But it's best to develop the argument further in the context of fair employment laws.

Meritocracy is a profit-maximizing proposition for a firm: if a black man is best for the job, it makes business sense to hire him. What is more, this point will be pressed by the professionals in each firm's personnel department, who will use it as a powerful weapon in their data-driven campaigns to pressure operational departments to give black workers a fairer shake.

These ongoing initiatives might well be deflected by racist resistance among the rank and file. But even this effect would diminish over time as middle management and workers learn that they can't escape the new regime by seeking employment elsewhere, since firms operating as racist havens will be especially targeted for Title VII sanctions.

The operation of these positive feedback loops doesn't imply that real-world gains in the workplace would be easy or straightforward. But it does mean that Title VII wasn't confronting a resistance problem on the same scale as the VRA was. Quite simply, the southern political system displayed the prospect of negative feedback, with the white political establishment responding to black voting by manipulating electoral rules to preserve white political power. If the VRA's initial victory was not to deteriorate into a meaningless gesture, the statute had little choice but to create a system of federal supervision that would guard against the dilution of black voting power. In contrast, there was no comparable need to move beyond technocratic individualism in the case of employment, since there was a decent chance that positive feedback loops would push the system toward real-world advances.

To sum up, the three styles of techno/traditional intervention exhibited in the spheres of work, elections, and public accommodations do not represent the arbitrary results of a political process dominated by narrowly self-interested politicians. They represent the product of "deliberation and choice," to recall Madison's phrase in the *Federalist No. 1*. We are witnessing the statecraft of serious statesmen concerned with the serious problem of redeeming basic constitutional commitments in the real world of social and political life.

Perhaps a simple chart can crystallize these points. It locates each of the three spheres by asking two questions: Is there a serious identification problem? Is there a resistance problem generated by negative feedback loops?

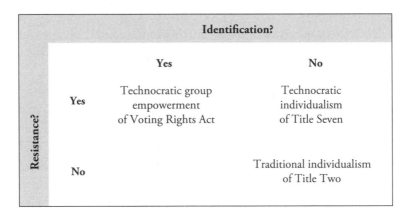

	Identification?	
	Yes	**No**
Yes	Technocratic group empowerment of Voting Rights Act	Technocratic individualism of Title Seven
No		Traditional individualism of Title Two

(Row label, left side: Resistance?)

Congress's choices will remain endlessly controversial, with partisans attacking its decision to place one or another sphere in one or another box. But like it or not, those choices do represent the solutions hammered out by the president and Congress, after a great deal of deliberation, in the name of the American people. And that is no small matter.

Most important, the landmark statutes raise a fundamental challenge to formalist interpretations of constitutional equality, which focus on the internal structure of legal doctrine without sustained analysis of their impact on social life. On this familiar view, the key question is whether a legal regime deploys "suspect categories" such as race in its administration; if so, the formalist almost invariably rejects the law on the ground that it lacks a "compelling" justification.[64]

This gets the landmark priorities of the civil rights revolution backward. For the Civil Rights Act and the Voting Rights Act, law is a tool for realizing real-world justice. If formal neutrality will deliver the goods (as in public accommodations), that's fine, but if it won't, the task is to design a system that will (as in employment and voting rights). Instead of searching for some elegant legal formula, the egalitarian challenge is more pragmatic: first, provide hardheaded analysis of the obstacles to the pursuit of real-world equality; second, devise legal-administrative tools that realistically promise to overcome these obstacles. This *constitutional pragmatism* requires a sphere-by-sphere approach, for the simple reason that different spheres differ in the ways they resist real-world egalitarian advances. Some spheres are dominated by opaque institutions whose decisions are mysterious to ordinary people, while others generate powerful feedback loops of institutional resistance.

These problems won't be going away soon. It is a serious mistake to suppose that administrative efforts to attack them are, at best, transitional devices on the path to the brave new world of formal equality. While the use of technocratic tools does generate tensions in our fundamental value commitments, the challenge is to minimize these tensions in a realistic fashion—without imagining that they will somehow magically disappear.[65]

Constitutional pragmatism was a key contribution of the landmark statutes of the Second Reconstruction, correcting a deep flaw in the constitutional amendments of the first period of Reconstruction. As Thaddeus Stevens and Charles Sumner saw, the Reconstruction Amendments were doomed from the start by their formalist approach to equality. Nineteenth-century America lacked a strong national administrative apparatus to make their promise into reality, and it was precisely this vacuum that forced the Radical Republicans to rely on military solutions to the problems posed by ongoing institutional resistance from southern whites.[66] When this militaristic approach alienated mainstream public opinion, it was only a matter of time before the entire effort collapsed.

It was precisely the development of activist national government that permitted the Second Reconstruction to blaze a more acceptable path to real-world equality, in which civilian officials took up the pragmatic challenges of overcoming institutional resistance. If we erase this aspect of the civil rights legacy, we risk a rerun of the tragedy of the earlier Reconstruction, when solemn constitutional commitments to racial equality disintegrated at the turn of the twentieth century.

CHAPTER 10

The Breakthrough of 1968

SPRING 1968: As Americans prepared for presidential elections, the civil rights agenda remained a central preoccupation in Washington, D.C., with all three branches taking up large questions they had previously avoided. In passing the Fair Housing Act in April 1968, the president and Congress resolved a hot-button issue they had repeatedly deferred in order to pursue more attainable goals—first in 1964, when fair housing issues threatened to sabotage the passage of the entire Civil Rights Act, and again in 1965, when Martin Luther King Jr.'s leadership at Selma pushed the Voting Rights Act to center stage. When President Johnson pressed for fair housing in 1966, his initiative died on the Senate floor, with Everett Dirksen denouncing it as unconstitutional.

But Dirksen withdrew his constitutional objections in 1968, joining with liberal Democrats to break the inevitable southern filibuster. Richard Nixon and Nelson Rockefeller, then competing for the presidential nomination, both intervened to drive the bill forward. After years of contention, the Fair Housing Act became law on a bipartisan basis—expanding the national commitment to a Second Reconstruction with a third landmark statute in four years.

During the same spring, the Supreme Court was providing new constitutional foundations for this achievement, moving decisively beyond its earlier decisions upholding the Civil Rights Act of 1964. As we saw, its opinion in *Heart of Atlanta Motel* concealed the revolutionary implications of the statute's sweeping imposition of egalitarian obligations on private business. Rather than using this breakthrough as an occasion for repudiating the restrictive teachings of the Civil Rights Cases of 1883, the Court manipulated the New Deal Commerce Clause to vindicate the landmark statute. But four years later, it was prepared to move beyond the New Deal to advance a radical reinterpretation of constitutional equality, putting to rest any serious challenge to the new Fair Housing Act.

As in *Heart of Atlanta,* the Court moved with extraordinary speed. While it upheld the Civil Rights Act within five months of its passage, the Court acted even more rapidly this time—two months after the Fair Housing Act became law, *Jones v. Mayer* propounded a revolutionary constitutional rationale that secured its constitutionality. In contrast to *Heart of Atlanta,* the Justices did not wait for a test case that directly challenged the new landmark statute; they used a fair housing case that was already on their docket as the vehicle for this fundamental reconstruction of our constitutional tradition.

This speedy resolution came at a price, depriving the Court of the opportunity to consider the distinctive constitutional arguments made by Dirksen and others in legitimating their legislative initiative. Since these claims never appear in the *United States Reports,* our judge-centered canon consigns them to oblivion. But if the Fair Housing Act is indeed a landmark achievement of We the People, we should retrieve these arguments from the margins of history. The challenge is to integrate the constitutional insights of *both* legislators and judges into a deeper understanding of the legacy of the Second Reconstruction.

This chapter has a second goal: I will be comparing the development of fair housing law with counterpart dynamics in the spheres of elections and employment. In both of these areas, the initial passage of a landmark statute opened a second stage of administrative experimentation that set up a final round of statutory consolidation during the Nixon administration. This three-phase pattern didn't repeat itself in housing. While the initial act did indeed catalyze a second stage of administrative experimentation, it did not lead to a culminating round of legislation that refined the initial breakthrough.

Why?

The Fair Housing Act

The initial dynamic propelling the Fair Housing Act forward looks like a variation on themes established in 1964 and 1965. Once again, presidential leadership and congressional bipartisanship provided the matrix for a breakthrough in the name of the American people.

The Decline and Rise of the Fair Housing Act

With the Voting Rights Act on the books, Lyndon Johnson made fair housing his next legislative priority—overruling politically-savvy supporters, such as Attorney General Ramsey Clark, who cautioned that an initiative "would be unwise, because it could not be passed; it would raise expectations; and it would manifest an unwillingness of the American people to really come all the way toward equal justice."[1] Key liberal senators, including Jacob Javits, expressed similar doubts, urging the president to issue an executive order forbidding banks to lend money to biased builders: "[T]he Administration is inviting a bitter civil rights fight when it could by a stroke of the pen extend antidiscrimination to 80 per cent of housing."[2] But Johnson was playing for bigger stakes: he was prepared to provoke a "bitter civil rights fight" to gain the broad and self-conscious support of the American people for another landmark statute. His special civil rights message in January 1966 put fair housing at the center of the congressional agenda.[3]

Only to redeem the gloomy predictions of the naysayers. The administration's initiative did pass the House, but in a grievously damaged condition. By a one-vote margin, representatives passed an amendment allowing real estate agents to continue discriminating against blacks so long as homeowners signed a written authorization. This effectively excluded 60 percent of the housing market from coverage; worse yet, it explicitly legitimated racism. Roy Wilkins, head of the NAACP and the Leadership Conference on Civil Rights, was right to fear that it would reinforce extremists who were "jeering at the legislative approach to civil rights" as well as "increase skepticism among more sober citizens."[4]

The worst was yet to come. When the bill reached the Senate, Everett Dirksen was once again in the driver's seat. But this time around, he refused to join forces with liberal Democrats to break the southern filibuster, denouncing the entire initiative as blatantly unconstitutional. He dismissed the notion that interstate commerce could be stretched to include the sale and rental of local real estate, and he refused to extend the Equal Protection Clause to cover private sales that didn't involve obvious forms of state action.[5]

He recognized that he had tolerated a dramatic expansion of federal power when throwing his support behind the Civil Rights Act in 1964. But enough was enough—and his determined opposition deprived Senate liberals of the two-thirds majority needed to close down the filibuster. At this point, it was Ramsey Clark, not his boss, Lyndon Johnson, who looked like the savvier politician—the campaign for a new landmark statute had shown only that "the American people [were unwilling] to really come all the way toward equal justice."

The future looked grim. Johnson's energies were increasingly diverted by the escalating war in Vietnam. The Watts riot was displacing the Selma march as the recurring image on the nation's television screens—casting blacks, not whites, as violent perpetrators of injustice. This shifting imagery was suggesting new and troubling questions: Perhaps it was time to give up on further landmark efforts at Reconstruction? Perhaps the time had come for decisive acts of repression that would halt the escalating wave of black violence?

Within this setting, the Fair Housing Act represents a remarkable show of determination by the American people to sustain the promise of the civil rights revolution. Johnson's political decline provoked civil rights groups and their liberal allies in Congress to take up the slack, pushing the initiative with renewed energy. The racial crisis also provoked serious second thoughts from Republican moderates. When a fair housing bill returned to the Senate floor in the spring of 1968, Everett Dirksen reversed himself and agreed to break the southern filibuster—negotiating a compromise with liberal Democrats just as he had in 1964 and 1965.

This required him to rethink his constitutional position. He never retracted the restrictive interpretations of the Commerce and Equal Protection Clauses that led him to support the 1966 filibuster. He based his turnaround on a different theory: "I have to remember that a citizen has a dual citizenship under the Constitution of the United States. [Section 1 of the Fourteenth Amendment] says, as plainly as print can make it, that he is a citizen of the United States and of the State where he resides. So we are dealing with the citizenship of the country. And my only hope is that he will be dealt with rather fairly, and that is the reason for the substitute proposal that is before the Senate today."[6]

Since the housing act would not have passed without Dirksen's turnaround, his expansive notion of the privileges of citizenship deserves serious attention. While it represented a radical expansion of traditional understandings, Dirksen had already made it plain in 1964 that he was prepared to use landmark legislation to express constitutional ideals "whose time ha[d] come."

A host of factors persuaded Dirksen that the time had come. On the micro level, newly elected Republican senators were largely racial liberals, and they shifted the party's balance of power in the fair housing direction.[7] No less important, presidential contenders Richard Nixon and Nelson Rockefeller made it clear that they wanted quick passage of the act.[8] Nixon's views were especially significant, since he had previously supported a go-slow approach that allowed local authorities to "advance at [their] own pace" and restricted national legislation to federally assisted housing.[9]

These shifts were expressive of a larger change in public opinion—exemplified by the general reception to the report of a presidential commission led by Illinois governor Otto Kerner.

Johnson's turn to Kerner had a hint of desperation about it. Most presidential commissions are soon forgotten, their reports sinking without a trace after a bit of contrived public relations hoopla. But this time was different. The Kerner Report was a runaway best seller, and its strong support for a fair housing law crystallized the larger public sentiment for a constructive response.[10] Its publication on March 1, 1968, came at a propitious moment: The bill's partisans had failed—for the third time—to gain the two-thirds majority needed to break the southern filibuster. Majority leader Mike Mansfield was seriously thinking about conceding defeat, but the late-breaking news of the Kerner Report convinced him to push for a fourth vote—and this time Everett Dirksen finally joined in to break the back of southern resistance.[11]

This micro-level fact made a macro-level point: the Kerner Commission both expressed and focused the broader public determination to stay the course in constructing a new regime of race relations. Mansfield and Dirksen were reflecting, not creating, this larger commitment by the American people. The Senate emphatically indicated its seriousness by rejecting a provision, like the one passed by the House in 1966, that would have enabled real estate brokers to continue to discriminate.[12]

The Senate bill then moved on to the House for a final test. Gerald Ford, the Republican minority leader, dug in his heels, calling on members to repeat their 1966 performance and cut the bill's coverage from 80 percent of the housing market to 40 percent.[13] But within days, the leadership was under intense pressure "from liberals and moderates within their own ranks" to accept the Senate bill. Ford's resistance began to crumble on March 21, after reports that Richard Nixon and Nelson Rockefeller had "called him to urge Republican support of legislation to ban racial discrimination in the sale or rental of housing."[14] With the number of House Republicans in favor of the bill rapidly increasing in early April, successful passage was ensured.[15]

I belabor these details because they refute the common view that King's assassination on April 4 was the principal cause of the bill's success. This is a mistake.[16] While the shocking news did propel a rapid House vote on April 10, all the hard work had been done beforehand. King's tragic death endowed the birth of the landmark statute with a terrible solemnity, but it should not be used to trivialize the commitment of the American people to a *constructive* response to the escalating violence. As the NAACP's Roy Wilkins put it, "We are not dependent upon the periodic slaughter of Negro leaders in order to get such laws passed."[17]

Spherical Justice, Reconsidered

The Fair Housing Act did more than maintain legislative momentum; it sustained the animating principles of the landmark statutes of 1964 and 1965. Here is Edward Brooke, the Republican co-manager of the bill, explaining its relationship to these previous efforts:

> There have been earnest attempts to alleviate the injustices which kept many Americans from the voting booth. There have been respectable achievements in opening public accommodations to all of our citizens.
>
> But in the critical areas of housing, education, and employment, change has been intolerably slow. It is in these realms that one finds the basic explanation for the malaise which disturbs America. It is in these realms that one finds discrimination still in the saddle and justice trampled underfoot. It is in these realms that our country must achieve its professed ambitions of equal justice under the law, or fail in the most noble aspects of the American experience. It is in these realms that the Senate must provide the leadership. . . . Without such leadership, without the voice of the Senate proclaiming the true and better spirit of the American citizenry, we must reckon with the danger that baser instincts will continue to prevail in too many sections of our country.[18]

Brooke was calling upon his colleagues to follow the sphere-by-sphere path blazed by earlier legislation. Only by ensuring real-world progress in housing, as well as the realms of employment and education, would the Senate be "proclaiming the true and better spirit of the American citizenry." Because Brooke was the first popularly elected black senator, his diagnosis of landmark principles has a special claim on our attention.

His co-manager of the bill, Democrat Walter Mondale, contributed a second fundamental theme. On his account, the bill was striking another blow against a pervasive evil: "Deeper than the material and physical deprivation is the humiliation and rejection and what this does to human beings."[19] Mondale had replaced Hubert Humphrey in the Senate when his fellow Minnesotan won the vice presidency in 1964. But he was delivering the very same message that Humphrey had emphasized as Democratic co-manager of the Civil Rights Act of 1964.[20]

The anti-humiliation theme resonated throughout the debate—with an important limitation.[21] As Mondale explained, the bill "would not overcome the economic problem of those who could not afford to purchase the house of their choice."[22] It simply guaranteed to "Negroes that they are free—*if they have the money and the desire*—to move where they will" (emphasis added).[23]

This proviso is characteristic of the sphere-by-sphere approach embraced by the landmark statutes. Although Congress provided activist legal tools for moving against assaults to the dignity of black people in one or another sphere, it didn't try to attack the cumulative impact of these injustices. Mondale and others were perfectly candid in recognizing that most blacks were condemned to low wages by systematically inferior educations and job prospects. But this did not lead them to do more than protect the "lucky ones"—as Edward Brooke described the black middle class from which he came.[24] While the statute required the Department of Housing and Urban Development to act "affirmatively" to further its objectives, it didn't expressly authorize HUD to force the white suburbs to open their doors to poor blacks. It was up to the suburbs themselves to decide whether they would accept federally subsidized housing projects.[25]

This is the same approach adopted by Congress in governing workplace justice: while Title VII targeted barriers to the employment of qualified blacks, it did not require firms to accept less-qualified minority applicants who had been handicapped by poor education in segregated schools. To put the general point in a single sentence: even an activist effort to achieve equal opportunity within crucial spheres did not add up to equal opportunity to get ahead in life as a whole, given the accumulated disadvantages of the past.

I shall return to this larger issue later, but for now I want to emphasize its key role in ensuring the passage of the Fair Housing Act—providing a convincing response to critics who denounced the initiative as an illegitimate cave-in before lawless black rioters. Here is Senator Joseph Tydings, a leading force behind the act, responding to this common charge:

> The true irony comes in when we consider just whom we would be punishing by the defeat of the fair housing amendment. Who would it be? Is it the small minority of Negroes who rioted?
>
> No. They are not very likely to be shopping for homes in the suburbs, even if they had the chance. The persons most directly damaged would be the responsible middle-class Negroes, with savings and steady jobs—those who do not see violence as the road to self-improvement, and who would be appalled by the suggestion. Those who would be punished most by the defeat of this amendment are the very ones who have heeded the stock lecture that every generation of Americans has been given: "Work hard, save your money, and you can improve the circumstances of your children by getting into a better neighborhood."[26]

We have seen this move before: the partisans of civil rights were portraying "law and order" as a friend, not an enemy—the landmark law would assure blacks, no less than whites, that they could share in the American dream and live in the suburbs if they worked hard and saved their money.[27]

In presenting this spherical defense, Tydings and many others were following up on Lyndon Johnson's message to Congress that framed the entire debate: "Every American who wishes to buy a home, *and can afford it,* should be free to do so" (emphasis added).[28]

Dynamics of Decision

When Senator Mondale introduced his housing bill, it provided HUD with sweeping powers of investigation and enforcement. Once the agency found evidence of wrongdoing, it would not need to wait for individual complaints to begin proceedings; it could even issue temporary restraining orders while holding administrative hearings. After establishing a violation, it could require wrongdoers to take affirmative action to ensure future compliance.[29]

Here is where Senator Dirksen replayed his historic role as Grand Compromiser. While he accepted a very broad definition of the act's coverage, he transformed HUD into a conciliation service without enforcement authority. When the agency received a complaint, it had thirty days to obtain a voluntary settlement of the problem. If it failed, the complainant could then go to court for serious relief. Even if he won, he'd have to pay his own attorney's fees unless the court found that he wasn't "financially able" to foot the bill. Dirksen also insisted on capping punitive damages at $1,000, putting an additional damper on litigation incentives.[30]

We have been here before. In 1964, Dirksen forced liberal Democrats to accept a similar deal on fair employment—granting the EEOC powers to investigate and to conciliate, but denying it any role in enforcing the law in individual cases. The new statute also tracked the employment provisions in authorizing the Justice Department to file suit against "patterns and practices" of discrimination.[31] But nobody believed that the department's elite Civil Rights Division could take up the slack.

Nevertheless, Dirksen's compromise wasn't chiseled in stone. As we saw in Chapter 9, the EEOC used its limited authority over the next few years (stage two) in ways that provided a basis for Nixon and Congress to enhance its enforcement powers in their consolidating statute of 1972 (stage three). We will soon be considering why this didn't happen in housing. But for now, it's best to conclude stage one with some words from Lyndon Johnson as he signed the bill into law on April 11, 1968:

> On an April afternoon in the year 1966, I asked a distinguished group of citizens who were interested in human rights to meet me in the Cabinet Room in the White House. In their presence that afternoon, I signed a message to the Congress. That message called for the enactment of "the first effective federal law against discrimination in the sale and rental of housing" in the United States of America.
>
> Few in the Nation—and the record will show that very few in that room that afternoon—believed that fair housing would—in our time—become the unchallenged law of this land.
>
> And indeed, this bill has had a long and stormy trip.
>
> We did not get it in 1966.
>
> We pleaded for it again in 1967. But the Congress took no action that year.
>
> We asked for it again this year.
>
> And now—at long last this afternoon—its day has come.

I do not exaggerate when I say that the proudest moments of my Presidency have been times such as this when I have signed into law the promises of a century.

I shall never forget that it was more than 100 years ago when Abraham Lincoln issued the Emancipation Proclamation—but it was a proclamation; it was not a fact.

In the Civil Rights Act of 1964, we affirmed through law that men equal under God are also equal when they seek a job, when they go to get a meal in a restaurant, or when they seek lodging for the night in any State in the Union.

Now the Negro families no longer suffer the humiliation of being turned away because of their race.

In the Civil Rights Act of 1965, we affirmed through law for every citizen in this land the most basic right of democracy—the right of a citizen to vote in an election in his country. In the five States where the Act had its greatest impact, Negro voter registration has already more than doubled.

Now, with this bill, the voice of justice speaks again.

It proclaims that fair housing for all—all human beings who live in this country—is now a part of the American way of life.[32]

Johnson is recalling some of the great themes of the civil rights revolution: anti-humiliation; government-by-numbers; in sphere after sphere, the Second Reconstruction was moving beyond abstract legal promises to attack the entrenched injustices of everyday life.

JONES V. MAYER

Two months later, the Supreme Court joined this effort at constitutional reconstruction in *Jones v. Mayer*.[33] Speaking for a seven-man majority, Potter Stewart's opinion contrasts sharply with the Court's earlier decision in *Heart of Atlanta Motel,* which confronted an analogous problem. Recall that the Civil Rights Act of 1964 broke through the "state action" barriers erected by the Civil Rights Cases of 1883 to impose sweeping obligations on private firms. While five justices were prepared to repudiate this legacy of the nineteenth century, Justice Clark's published opinion evaded the entire issue. His decision was motivated by sheer pragmatism: Justice Harlan, and perhaps others, was prepared to sign on to the decision upholding the statute only if it relied exclusively on the New Deal Commerce Clause. With bitter-end southerners threatening massive resistance, the Court wanted to present a united front in support of the statute's assault on Jim Crow.[34]

Things were different by 1968. The bipartisan passage of three landmark statutes in four years had effectively resolved the question of constitutionality in the public mind. Within this setting, a dissent by Justice Harlan (and Justice Byron White) no longer threatened to undermine the foundations of the Second Reconstruction. This time around, the seven-man majority could use *Jones* to express the obvious truth that the civil rights revolution was a *civil rights* revolution—requiring a break, once and for all, with limited notions of state responsibility inherited from the First Reconstruction.

It usually takes a couple of years before a constitutional challenge to new legislation can wend its way to the Supreme Court. But public interest lawyers had already placed *Jones* on the Court's docket, permitting the Justices to resolve the key constitutional issues raised by the Fair Housing Act within two months of its passage. Such speed, however, came at the cost of adequate deliberation. The *Jones* litigation began before fair housing had become a top priority on the national agenda. By the time it reached the Court, Dirksen, Mondale, and Johnson were struggling with similar constitutional issues that were confronting the Justices. Yet the Justices failed to consider how the Fair Housing Act's resolution of these issues might enrich their own confrontation with the parallel problems raised by *Jones*. This disjunction between the Court and the political branches frames our challenge here. We will be aiming to integrate the distinct judicial and legislative conversations into a larger constitutional whole. This will allow us to see how they add up to a remarkable effort, by all three branches, to rebuild the constitutional foundations of the Second Reconstruction in the springtime of 1968.

Jones v. Mayer was a typical test case of the time, calling upon the courts to deliver egalitarian breakthroughs that legislatures were unwilling to endorse. It began in 1965—a year before Lyndon Johnson made fair housing a central civil rights initiative. The lawsuit was the brainchild of Samuel H. Liberman II, the Harvard-educated, thirty-three-year-old lawyer-chairman of Greater St. Louis Freedom of Residence.[35] With fair housing legislation pushed to the sidelines in Washington, D.C., Liberman searched through the statute books and made a remarkable discovery: a century-old federal law had *already* banned housing discrimination!

There was only one problem: why hadn't anybody ever noticed?

To make his case, Liberman had to reinterpret old statutory language in a radically new way. In 1866, the Reconstruction Congress had enacted a statute granting all "citizens, of every race and color . . . the same right . . . to inherit, purchase, lease, sell, hold, and convey real and personal property . . . as is enjoyed by white citizens."[36] This grant of legal authority was a big deal when it was passed in the wake of the recently enacted Thirteenth Amendment. Until that time, slaves had been bought and sold as property; but now Congress was making it clear that the freedmen could buy and sell property in their own right. This was especially important at a time when the former Confederate states were passing Black Codes sharply restricting freedom of contract.

But a hundred years onward, the Second Reconstruction was aiming to move beyond formal freedom to real-world justice—and as a movement lawyer, Liberman wanted to pour new meaning into the old statute. Courts had traditionally construed the 1866 law in a straightforward way: blacks, like whites, now had the right to contract with sellers who were willing to accept their offers. Liberman wanted the words to carry a very different meaning. On his view, it gave blacks the right to compel *unwilling* sellers to deal with them on a nondiscriminatory basis.

No federal court had ever taken such a claim seriously—so, like a good lawyer, Liberman moved cautiously. At first, he didn't present a full-blown version of his revolutionary theory. He only asked the district court "to carve out a special exception" that required large-scale suburban developers to open up their subdivisions to blacks.[37] Even this claim was too radical for the district judge, who dismissed the case summarily in May 1966— when President Johnson was fighting and losing his first battle for a fair housing law.

With Washington at an impasse, Liberman gained the support of a formidable legal team to make the case for a full-scale reinterpretation to the Eighth Circuit. By a coincidence, the bench included future Supreme Court justice Harry Blackmun—who could barely contain his surprise that "the case comes close to raising nakedly the question whether, in the absence of federal and state open housing legislation, an owner of a home . . . may refuse to sell [it] to a willing purchaser merely because that purchaser is a Negro."[38] Writing for a unanimous panel, he explained why the traditional authorities precluded the court from tearing the 1866 statute away from its historical roots. Once he gave the Joneses the bad

news in June of 1967, their legal team immediately asked the Supreme
Court to review the decision.

The Justices said yes in the fall of 1967—almost the last moment they
could plausibly suppose that the future of fair housing depended on their
leadership. By that point, President Johnson was once again on the offensive on the fair housing front. But given the Senate's prior rejection, the
future of his initiative remained cloudy. Given the prevailing uncertainty,
the administration treated *Jones*'s arrival on the Court's docket as an insurance policy: if the fair housing bill once again failed to overcome Senator Dirksen's constitutional objections, perhaps the Court might transform the statute of 1866 into a fair housing law worthy of the Second
Reconstruction.

Solicitor General Erwin Griswold entered the arena as an amicus in
support of the Joneses—completing the transformation of a highly speculative test case in Missouri to an authoritative call by the administration
to rethink the foundations of Reconstruction. But things had changed
once again by early April, when the case came up for oral argument. At
that point, Dirksen had resolved his constitutional doubts by embracing a
revolutionary understanding of the Fourteenth Amendment's citizenship
clause. The fair housing bill was well on its way to final passage when the
Justices first discussed *Jones* at their April 5 conference.

Notes from their private meeting indicate that everybody wanted to
give the Joneses relief, but they disagreed on how to do it.[39] Once President Johnson signed the Fair Housing Act on April 11, the Court reconsidered the matter on April 18—with Justices Thurgood Marshall and Abe
Fortas urging their colleagues to avoid deciding the case, since the law of
1968, not the law of 1866, should now be central to the modern effort.
Brennan, Harlan, and White supported their request to call upon the parties for supplementary briefs on the new act's implications, with Fortas
"hop[ing] that a response will get the respondent to say that he will sell
the house so that we can avoid a decision."[40] But when the supplementary
briefs arrived, the Joneses still demanded relief. Harlan and White continued to insist on dismissing the case. As they later explained in their
published dissent, passage of the new law had so "diminishe[d] the public importance" of the 1866 act that it should be consigned to ancient
history.[41]

The dissenters' plea for restraint would have made sense if the majority
had been concerned only with the development of housing law. Stewart's

opinion made a hash of the history of the 1866 act.[42] As we shall see, it also distorted the future development of housing policy.

But the seven-man majority was after bigger game. Its revolutionary act of statutory interpretation was merely a preliminary to a profound redefinition of America's constitutional commitment to equality. Recall that Senator Dirksen was engaged in the very same project at the very same time on the other side of Capitol Hill. In 1966, he had based his steadfast opposition to Johnson's first fair housing initiative on constitutional grounds—defending the traditional view, expressed by the Civil Rights Cases of 1883, which insulated private market transactions from the Equal Protection Clause. But by the spring of 1968, Dirksen had led his fellow Republicans to embrace the initiative on the basis of a transformative reading of the constitutional "privileges" and "immunities" of "citizens of the United States."

This was a big moment in constitutional history. Until Dirksen spoke, the citizenship clause had been burdened by its nineteenth-century legacy. The Slaughterhouse Cases of 1873 had refused to read "privileges" and "immunities" as an open-ended grant for the elaboration of fundamental rights, and this body blow had consigned the citizenship clause to the constitutional periphery for almost a century. But suddenly Dirksen was giving it new life. He now proclaimed that Americans could claim fairness in the housing market as a privilege of national citizenship—which authorized Congress to protect this privilege against discrimination by private parties, not only state officials.

This transformational reading enabled Dirksen to construct a royal highway around the traditional limitations on the scope of the Fourteenth Amendment. Formally speaking, there was no need to launch a frontal assault on the state action doctrine announced in the Civil Rights Cases, since this applied only to the Equal Protection Clause, not the Citizenship Clause. But Dirksen's breakthrough made the old equal protection restrictions irrelevant, since the "new" Citizenship Clause would suffice for all practical purposes.

Dirksen wasn't just any ordinary senator. His turnaround was pivotal in the successful passage of the 1968 act, and it placed an entirely new perspective on the opinion filed by Stewart in *Jones.* To see my point, consider that Stewart found himself in the same position as Dirksen once he came to the remarkable conclusion that America's first fair housing act had been passed in 1866, not 1968. Like Dirksen, he was now obliged to explain why it was constitutional for Congress to impose an egalitarian regime on purely private transactions and not merely on the actions of state officials.

Stewart responded to this challenge in Dirksenian fashion. Like the senator, he did not directly challenge the state action doctrine under the Equal Protection Clause. He simply undermined its practical importance by transforming a different constitutional provision in order to get around the barriers posed by the state action restriction. Unlike Dirksen, he couldn't use the Citizenship Clause to accomplish this mission, since *Jones* involved a statute passed in 1866, two years before the Fourteenth Amendment. As a consequence, he had to rummage around his legal kit bag in search of a different doctrinal hook. The Thirteenth Amendment had been enacted in 1865, so it was the obvious choice.

The first step in Stewart's argument was uncontroversial. Everybody recognized that Thirteen, unlike Fourteen, swept away private as well as public forms of slavery and involuntary servitude. His transformative move came at the next step. Section 2 of the amendment granted Congress power to enforce these bans by appropriate legislation. But the Civil Rights Cases of 1883 seemed to block a broad use of this power, famously insisting that "[i]t would be running the slavery argument into the ground to make it apply to every act of discrimination which a person may see fit to make . . . as to the people he will take into his coach or cab or car, or admit to his concert or theatre, or deal with in other matters of intercourse or business."[43]

But like Dirksen, Stewart was determined to break free of the dead hand of the past. He dismissed the Civil Rights Cases in a single tendentious sentence buried in a footnote, and spoke to the issue in a twentieth-century voice: "At the very least, the freedom that Congress is empowered to secure under the Thirteenth Amendment includes the freedom to buy whatever a white man can buy, the right to live wherever a white man can live. If Congress cannot say that being a free man means at least this much, then the Thirteenth Amendment made a promise the Nation cannot keep."[44]

At the very least . . . : Stewart is not only creating a new rationale for an ancient statute whose meaning he had just revolutionized. His new foundation is broad enough to vindicate many of the landmark achievements of 1964 and 1968, whose precise aim was to give social reality to the meaning of "being a free man."

Stewart moves beyond Dirksen in one fundamental respect. The modern landmark statutes extended their protection to all residents of the United States, not only citizens. Stewart's rationale could accommodate this point without embarrassment, since his reconstruction of the Thirteenth Amendment applied to all "free m[e]n"; in contrast, Dirksen's appeal to the "privileges" of citizenship had trouble accommodating the Second Reconstruction's inclusionary thrust.

Stewart's argument also displays remarkable parallels with Lyndon Johnson's speech, upon signing the Fair Housing Act, that "it was more than 100 years ago when Abraham Lincoln issued the Emancipation Proclamation—but it was a proclamation; it was not a fact." Stewart was talking about the Emancipation Amendment, not the Proclamation, yet his message was the same: the 1960s were moving beyond the 1860s promise of formal freedom to demand true freedom from the "badges" of slavery in the real world.

———

It's time to turn a doctrinal corner. While Stewart's emphasis on the Thirteenth Amendment made it easier to accommodate certain aspects of the Second Reconstruction, Dirksen's emphasis on citizenship allowed for deeper insights on another important front. Given Stewart's Thirteenth Amendment framework, it was natural to condemn housing discrimination as a continuing "badge" and "incident" of slavery that continued to haunt modern America. But this formulation had limited resonance for the general public. For the ordinary man or woman, Stewart's invocation of slavery and emancipation conjured up a faraway time that they had last encountered in high school civics. Worse yet, his antiquarian vocabulary raised a very substantive question: was Stewart suggesting that the modern-day Emancipation Amendment could be invoked *only* against discriminatory practices that had their historical roots in slavery?

If so, he was opening up an endless debate about the extent to which more recent developments have displaced slavery in explaining the causes of the continuing disadvantage of blacks (and other oppressed groups) in the marketplace.

Political leaders such as Johnson and Mondale got to the heart of the matter. In defining the evil of housing discrimination, they emphasized the humiliation of exclusion and its consequences for the human spirit.

This was something that everybody could appreciate, and it did not depend on speculative historical arguments about the lingering impact of slavery. Whatever its historical causes, institutionalized humiliation undercuts the real-world experience of freedom, and this suffices to make it a constitutional wrong of the first magnitude.

Stewart and his colleagues could have learned something important from the nation's political leaders on this score. If they had been listening to the debate more attentively, they would have heard Lyndon Johnson making a more fundamental point upon signing the Fair Housing Act: "Now the Negro families no longer suffer the humiliation of being turned away because of their race."

Alas, the procedural posture of *Jones* did not invite this effort. The case involved not the Fair Housing Act of 1968 but a civil rights act of 1866—and so a sustained consideration of the views expressed by the political leaders of the Second Reconstruction didn't seem necessary.

Things might have been different if the majority had followed the advice of Harlan and White. Under this scenario, they would have dismissed *Jones* to await the appearance of a case directly challenging the constitutionality of the Fair Housing Act. Perhaps in 1970 or so the Justices would have had a better opportunity to confront the tensions we have been exploring—between the privileges of citizens and the rights of free people, and between the language of humiliation and the language of slavery. Perhaps, after hearing all the arguments, they would have delivered a better opinion—one that synthesized nineteenth- and twentieth-century themes into a compelling vindication of the constitutional achievements of the Second Reconstruction.

But no further opinion was forthcoming. With *Jones* on the books, there was no longer any need for the Court to take another case elaborating the constitutional foundations of the Fair Housing Act, since Stewart's reinterpretation of the Thirteenth Amendment sufficed to resolve any serious doubts.[45]

We are left, then, with two distinct patterns of constitutional reconstruction emerging from the high point of the civil rights revolution in 1968. One comes from the nation's judges and emphasizes the meaning of freedom and the need to reject the "badges" and "incidents" of slavery. The other comes from the nation's political leaders and emphasizes the meaning of citizenship and the evil of institutionalized humiliation. How to synthesize these two conversations into a larger whole?

This question of synthesis raises a central challenge as the twenty-first century confronts the task of interpreting the enduring legacy of the Second Reconstruction. Yet the existing professional framework doesn't even allow us to ask the question, let alone answer it. Under the conventional court-centered canon, we allow ourselves to view only half of the conversation—the half displayed on the pages of the *United States Reports*.

Worse yet, we trivialize *Jones*'s importance. Only a snippet of Stewart's opinion typically appears in student casebooks, and judges don't take its transformative significance seriously. They view it as creating a narrow Thirteenth Amendment exception to the mainline principles that limit the scope of America's egalitarian commitments. On the conventional view, these fundamental limits are determined by the Fourteenth Amendment, not the Thirteenth.

In turning to Fourteen, moreover, the conventional view entirely ignores Senator Dirksen's emphatic invocation of the privileges of American citizenship as the foundation for the Second Reconstruction. Since Dirksen made his turnaround in the Senate, the court-centered canon simply ignores it. Instead, it continues to focus on the Equal Protection Clause. Since the Civil Rights Cases have never been formally overruled, the legal community supposes that the state action doctrine they announced in 1883 continues to deserve a central place in the constitutional canon.

This is a mistake. *Jones* was more than just another case in the long line of legal precedents. It was part of the larger conversation through which the nation's political and judicial leaders joined together to define the constitutional principles of the New Deal–Civil Rights regime. We betray this achievement so long as we maintain the court-centered canon. Once we include the landmark statutes, we not only integrate the voices of Dirksen, Mondale, and Johnson into the legal legacy. We can deepen our appreciation of the strengths and limits of Stewart's analysis. By broadening the constitutional canon, we also enhance our understanding of the Court's contribution, just as we did in integrating the meaning of *Brown* into the larger constitutional conversation that yielded the landmark statutes of the 1960s.

I will return to this point in Chapter 14. But for now, it's more important to complete the fair housing story by considering its further development during the Nixon years.

RATIFICATION AND CONSOLIDATION?

The Fair Housing Act and *Jones v. Mayer* are remarkable achievements. Yet they don't amount to a "constitutional moment" when considered in splendid isolation. Their claim to enduring significance lies in their strategic location within a much longer narrative—beginning with *Brown's* decision to put civil rights at the center of the constitutional agenda (stage one, signaling), continuing through the decision by President Johnson and Congress to follow through with the enactment of the Civil Rights Act (stage two, proposing), and sustained by the self-conscious decision by the voters to repudiate Barry Goldwater and his constitutional critique of the act (stage three, triggering), thereby enabling Johnson and Congress to claim a popular mandate for further landmark statutes that culminated in the springtime breakthroughs on fair housing (stage four, elaborating).

The contributions of all three branches in 1968 set the stage for a further period of testing at the fall elections (stage five, ratifying), inviting Richard Nixon to hedge his commitments to the landmark statutes to undercut the appeal of George Wallace's candidacy.

Nixon did not back down. He reaffirmed his view that the Fair Housing Act was a "sound decision and one that I approve."[46] Putting such statements in the context of the larger campaign, the 1968 elections amounted to a popular ratification of the three landmark statutes that set the terms of the Second Reconstruction—or so I argued in Chapter 4.

Once Nixon won the White House, a distinctive problem emerged (stage 6, consolidation). In contrast to the spheres of voting (1970) and employment (1972), the political branches didn't pass a statute reaffirming and strengthening the Fair Housing Act during Nixon's first term. Does this failure call into question the depth of national commitment to the higher-law status of the 1968 housing initiative?

My answer is no. Legislative passivity was largely an unintended consequence of the Supreme Court's intervention in *Jones*. Quite simply, Justice Stewart's opinion gave civil rights groups much of what they could have hoped to win from Congress. As a consequence, they devoted their political energies to support more ambitious housing objectives—especially those advanced by Nixon's HUD secretary, George Romney. Romney was a strong liberal who wanted to move beyond the limited objectives of the 1968 act. While this landmark aimed to provide blacks with money the effective right to buy houses in middle-class white neighborhoods, Romney wanted to force the suburbs to open their doors to subsidized housing for poor people of all races. Economic, not merely racial, integration was his goal. He failed, and his failure has had enduring consequences to the present day.

But Romney's defeat does not imply the rejection of the narrower goal of the Fair Housing Act by the political branches or the American people. To the contrary, it only serves to reinforce a central theme: while the landmark statutes aimed for equal opportunity for blacks and other minorities within each sphere, they did not go further and seek to uproot deeper-seated forms of economic injustice.

I am getting ahead of myself. My first task is to show how *Jones* had the unintended consequence of diverting political energies away from a Nixon-era statute consolidating the Fair Housing Act. My claim is necessarily speculative—it's tough to explain why something did *not* happen. Nevertheless, I hope to make it plausible by contrasting the housing scenario with parallel developments in fair employment law that did indeed provoke a consolidating statute.

The comparative approach begins with the striking similarities in the political bargains that generated the original statute in 1964 (employment) and 1968 (housing). On both occasions, liberal Democrats initially wanted to attack the problem with a New Deal–style agency—granting the EEOC and HUD broad-ranging powers to find facts, promulgate regulations, and enforce the statutory mandate through cease-and-desist orders. In both cases, Senator Dirksen refused to go along. He insisted on compromises that stripped both agencies of all enforcement authority, transforming them into mediators. As we have seen, individuals complaining about employment or housing discrimination first had to ask EEOC or HUD to settle the problem informally before they could go to court. If the agency failed, it then dropped out of the picture. Although both statutes authorized the Justice Department to bring suits against "patterns and practices" of discrimination in the most egregious cases, it was generally up to private parties to enforce the law in court.

In both cases, the mediation model was a failure. Like the EEOC, HUD soon began to accumulate a big backlog.[47] Here is where our stories diverge. In the employment case, civil rights groups focused on this failure in their campaign for statutory reform. They even drummed up thousands of additional complaints to further overload the EEOC, generating one-third of the agency's entire docket.[48]

But *Jones* made a similar campaign less imperative when it came to housing. Now that Stewart had transformed the 1866 act into a fair housing statute, blacks could avoid the HUD logjam by going to court immediately. What is more, the new *Jones* remedy enabled them to litigate under more advantageous terms. As part of the Dirksen compromise, the 1968 act normally required litigants to pay their own attorney's fees—a serious obstacle for the middle-class blacks most likely to bring suit. But if plaintiffs sued and won under the 1866 law, they could readily obtain their attorney's fees from the losing party.[49] As a consequence, the 1866 statute became "the primary enforcement vehicle during the [next] generation"[50]—to the point where civil rights groups waited until 1978 before they began lobbying Congress to beef up HUD's enforcement powers.[51] In contrast, they pushed hard on the employment front, where only new legislation could undermine the Dirksen compromise.[52]

Instead of fine-tuning the Fair Housing Act, the legislative agenda during the Nixon years was shaped by a very different dynamic. The moving force was Nixon's new HUD secretary, George Romney, who declared, "We've got to put an end to the idea of moving to suburban areas and living only among people of the same economic and social class."[53] This represented a dramatic redefinition of the stakes. Only a year before, Johnson and Mondale had been fighting to establish the right of blacks to escape the ghetto if they could afford it. Now Romney was demanding that the suburbs open their doors to rich and poor alike.

Congress had already provided HUD with the funds for an ambitious program to subsidize 250,000 to 350,000 low- and moderate-income housing units annually. Under Romney's leadership, Operation Breakthrough pursued a "dispersal" policy that steered this new construction away from black ghettos to the white suburbs.

HUD's initiative first seemed to be in harmony with larger themes coming from the White House. Daniel Moynihan, Nixon's resident intellectual, kept up a steady drumbeat in favor of "dispersal," and in November 1969, a special presidential task force supported "a strong national policy" of "carrots and sticks" to shift subsidized housing to the suburbs.[54]

Appearances were deceiving: Nixon was personally opposed to the task force's vision of economic integration. Nevertheless, the White House did not take explicit steps to keep HUD in line.[55] In naming Romney to his cabinet, the president had known what he was getting: the emphatically liberal Michigan governor had challenged Nixon for the Republican nomination from the left. The Romney appointment was part of the president's effort to create an ideologically balanced cabinet that would generate an eclectic policy mix appealing to different elements in his disparate electoral coalition—racial liberals from the North no less than racial conservatives from the South. He was prepared to give each team member lots of leeway, intervening personally only when a particular initiative threatened to tear his coalition apart, forcing him to make hard choices.

Romney's moment of truth came as his housing initiative moved into high gear in 1970. The secretary went before congressional committees to propose the Open Communities Act, which went far beyond the Fair Housing Act to authorize a new offensive against "local legislative or administrative actions that discriminate against low- and moderate-income housing."[56] When HUD encountered "exclusionary zoning" or similar restrictive techniques, the statute would unleash a barrage of public and private lawsuits to support agency efforts to break down economic barriers to the suburbs.[57]

There was only one hitch: Romney made his bold proposal unilaterally—without working with civil rights groups or liberal White House insiders to prepare the ground for a coordinated political offensive.[58] When confronted with a fait accompli, the president acted with alarm, especially since his secretary was generating embarrassing headlines on a second front. As we have seen, the Housing Act contained a vague command that HUD "affirmatively" use its vast array of subsidy programs to further the statute's anti-discrimination objectives—and the secretary was pursuing this mandate with characteristic forcefulness.

The media made a lily-white suburb from Romney's home state into a test case for his initiative. The Detroit suburb of Warren, Michigan, was home to 179,000 people. Only 132 were black. When the city refused to pass a fair housing ordinance and rejected subsidized housing as part of its application for urban renewal money, HUD threatened to cut off all funds. The controversy reached new heights in May—the same month that the secretary was proposing Open Communities to Congress. At a highly publicized meeting with Warren's mayor, Ted Bates, Romney rejected the mayor's complaints about the funding cutoff: "Black people have as much right to equal opportunities as we do. . . . What is really at issue here is responsibility—moral responsibility." Bates left Washington fuming that his town had been marked out "as a guinea pig for integration experiments" and that the time had come for Detroit's suburbs "to fight this forced integration."[59] When Romney traveled to Warren to make his case in person, his car was mobbed by angry protesters. After months of polarizing debate, 57 percent of the city's voters rejected all urban renewal money rather than accept HUD's conditions.[60]

All this was more than enough to provoke Nixon's personal intervention and to stop Open Communities in Congress. After a series of ad hoc responses, the president issued an elaborate statement in June 1971. He emphasized the importance of distinguishing between "racial" and "economic" segregation: "It is important to remember . . . that the terms 'poor' and 'black' are not interchangeable. A higher percentage of blacks than of whites lives below the poverty line—but there are far more poor whites in America than there are poor blacks. . . . To equate 'poor' with 'black' does a disservice to the truth."[61]

This point led Nixon to insist on a sharply dichotomous response. On one hand, he refused "to impose economic integration upon an existing local jurisdiction." On the other hand, "racial discrimination in housing will not be tolerated." So far as race was concerned, "the Constitution and the laws are clear and unequivocal." Indeed, he presented a broad understanding of this national commitment: "[W]e will not countenance any use of economic measures as a subterfuge for racial discrimination. When such an action is called into question, we will study its effect. If the effect of the action is to exclude Americans from equal housing opportunity on the basis of their race, religion, or ethnic background, we will vigorously oppose it by whatever means are most appropriate—regardless of the rationale which may have cloaked the discriminatory act." Nixon is explicitly denying that racist motives are necessary for decisive action. To the contrary: "We will study its effect . . . regardless of the rationale which may have cloaked the discriminatory act."

Only three days later, the Justice Department put these words into action, seeking to invalidate a zoning ordinance passed in suburban Black Jack, Missouri, that effectively barred 85 percent of blacks living in the St. Louis metropolitan area.[62]

As Nixon expected, his statement was condemned from both the right and the left.[63] As he scribbled on his personal copy: "We shall lose on it politically—but the law and justice of the issue require it."[64] For our purposes, there is no need to address the merits of Nixon's position. Our concern is whether the president was calling into question the landmark status of the Fair Housing Act.

The obvious answer is no. Nixon's pronouncement was in perfect harmony with Senator Mondale's declaration that "the basic purpose of [the 1968 act] is to permit people who have the ability to do so to buy any house offered to the public *if they can afford to buy it*" (emphasis added).[65] Similarly, Nixon's entire position presupposed the constitutionality of federal intervention in private housing markets—Dirksen's turnaround and the Supreme Court's decision in *Jones* had dispatched all doubts raised by conventional understandings of the state action doctrine.

Political liberals such as myself will mourn Nixon's triumph over Romney. But as constitutionalists, we must recognize that it happened—just as conservatives should recognize that the landmark statutes of the 1960s went far beyond the first Reconstruction in defining modern America's egalitarian commitments.

Our common task is to interpret the legacy of the civil rights revolution—nothing more, but nothing less.

THEME AND VARIATIONS

Housing, employment, voting, public accommodations: we have been studying a theme and variations. We began at the point when the campaign for the relevant landmark statute moved into high gear on Capitol Hill. As the political protagonists hammered out a statutory solution, they confronted constitutional doctrines that sharply limited their capacity to express the rising popular demand for racial justice. These restrictive doctrines—state action is only the most notable—had deep roots in constitutional history, going back to the first Reconstruction. Yet the political leadership joined the civil rights movement to sweep these obstacles aside. In sphere after sphere, their landmark statutes intervened decisively in crucial areas that had been constitutionally reserved to the states and private businesses.

When faced with these breakthroughs, the Supreme Court could have used its established precedents to strike down these revolutionary redefinitions of the constitutional meaning of equality. Instead, the Justices upheld these landmarks of the Second Reconstruction through one doctrinal expedient or another. A half century later, thoughtful constitutionalists continue to study the resulting legal complexities with high seriousness.

Yet their continuing fascination with the details shouldn't excuse them from ignoring the main point: in dealing with employment, housing, public accommodations, and voting, it was the president and Congress—not the Warren Court—who were asserting constitutional leadership. While the Court had been in the lead during the first decade after *Brown,* it was now the president and Congress who were claiming a mandate from the people for a new commitment to the pursuit of racial justice.

Part One of this book argued that this claim to a popular mandate for fundamental change was constitutionally justified, and that it was right for the political branches to assume leadership during *Brown's* second decade. While Congress and the president were now in the lead, this part suggests that their vision was profoundly shaped by *Brown's* formulation of the constitutional problem. Like the Court in *Brown,* their landmark statutes took a sphere-by-sphere approach; like Warren in *Brown,* leaders such as Johnson, King, Humphrey, and Dirksen repeatedly committed the American people to the eradication of institutionalized humiliation—despite established constitutional doctrines, inherited from the original Reconstruction, that tolerated or entrenched their perpetuation.

This objective—however formidable it might have sometimes seemed—served only as a first step down the path toward a Second Reconstruction. The landmark statutes elaborated more ambitious egalitarian commitments, whose precise content varied from sphere to sphere—equal treatment in public accommodations, equal opportunity in the housing market, technocratic individualism in the workplace, minority group rights in the electoral process. These spherical versions of equality were not foisted on America by a few politicians and bureaucrats in Washington, D.C. To the contrary, they were the subject of endless debate in people's homes and workplaces as tens of millions responded to speeches and marches broadcast on TV and reported in the newspapers—sometimes engaging in protest or counterprotest themselves. What is more, the electoral system gave ordinary Americans clear opportunities to decide whether to support or repudiate these landmark initiatives. If they had voted in sufficient numbers for Barry Goldwater in 1964 or George Wallace in 1968, I would be telling a very different story—in which the landmark statutes might well have been repealed amid an escalating series of violent protests and counterprotests in the streets.

But instead, a broad and sustained majority consistently supported the efforts of the Humphreys and Johnsons, Dirksens and Nixons as they hammered out the terms of a bipartisan constitutional consensus. Modern lawyers have a high responsibility to take these principles seriously in coming to terms with the enduring legacy of the Second Reconstruction. They deserve a central place in the professional canon—indeed, we cannot even fully appreciate the great decisions of the Warren and Burger Courts without putting them in the larger context provided by these illustrious acts of constitutional politics.

This is, at least, the destination we have reached after traveling down the path marked out by Parts One and Two. While it has taken us far, there are many twists and turns ahead before we can glimpse the shape of the larger legacy left behind by the civil rights generation.

PART THREE

Dilemmas of
Judicial Leadership

CHAPTER 11

Brown's Fate

FOR AN ENTIRE DECADE, the Warren Court took on the full burden of institutional leadership. *Brown* had disrupted established party
alignments, and it would take lots of political struggle before Congress,
the president, and the American people were prepared to render final judgment on the questions of principle that the Court had placed on the constitutional agenda. During all that time, the Justices were proceeding at
deliberate speed, managing crises and hoping that the Civil Rights Acts of
1957 and 1960 were signs that political momentum would ultimately generate a decisive breakthrough.

The enactment of the landmark statutes transformed the Court's basic
situation. Its new challenge was to participate constructively in a joint
project with the political branches and executive agencies to redeem the
egalitarian objectives defined by the president and Congress in the name
of the American people. But on some large matters, this coordinating
strategy couldn't work, for the simple reason that the landmark statutes
did not address all of the big constitutional questions. This left the Court
in a position of continuing leadership on these matters—and the way the
Justices responded to their second-decade challenges has profoundly shaped
the conventional legal understanding of the civil rights legacy. This part
of the book urges a fundamental reassessment.

We shall be dealing with the Court's continuing engagement in two
spheres, each posing very different dilemmas for the Justices. The first involved public education. Here, the Court's continuing leadership resulted
from the political vindication of *Brown* by the Civil Rights Act of 1964.
While the president and Congress were sweeping aside the Supreme Court's
restrictive precedents in other spheres, there was no need for anything
similar when it came to *Brown*. In this area, the Court was not part of the
problem but part of the solution. The key question was how to force the

white South to respect the rule of law. Ten years after *Brown,* 98 percent of southern blacks children were still attending segregated schools. To break this impasse, the statute provided the judges with new and powerful enforcement tools. But it left it up to the Court to engage in an ongoing process of defining the ultimate constitutional objectives of the desegregation effort.

Supreme Court leadership was generated by a very different institutional logic in a second sphere: interracial marriage (and other forms of intimacy). The Court did not owe its preeminence in this area to pioneering decisions of the 1950s or landmark statutes of the 1960s. To the contrary: the Justices refused to strike down interracial marriage bans shortly after *Brown,* and so did the politicians a decade later as they hammered out new egalitarian principles for employment, housing, public accommodations, and voting. It was tough enough for Democrats and Republicans to agree on landmark statutes in these hotly contested areas without adding yet another hot-button issue to the mix. If anybody was going to strike down interracial marriage bans, it would be the Supreme Court—which (reluctantly) rose to the occasion and finally declared these laws unconstitutional in *Loving v. Virginia* in 1967. *Loving* provides a case study of judicial *leadership by default*—in contrast to *leadership by popular consent,* which propelled the Court forward in dealing with the public schools until the final Nixon years.

Despite its default character, *Loving* would prove of great importance. It not only permitted interracial couples to escape the institutionalized humiliations of the past but also serves as a leading precedent in the current campaign for gay marriage. As we will see, it provides a key marker in assessing the Supreme Court's recent decision striking down the Defense of Marriage Act.

Moving beyond its revolutionary implications in the sphere of intimate relations, *Loving* has also assumed a central place in the entire civil rights canon. When today's lawyers try to understand the civil rights legacy, their starting point is the doctrinal framework first articulated in *Loving* and its companion cases. This legalistic framework represents a great departure from the anti-humiliation principles set out by cases such as *Brown* and *Jones,* as well as the larger egalitarian commitments represented by the landmark statutes. I will argue that the rising centrality of *Loving*'s legalisms betrays the larger commitments of the Second Reconstruction to real-world equality—whose principles I shall summarize in Chapter 14.

We will be traveling a winding road before we reach this destination. Our first task is to follow the Court as it struggles to redeem *Brown*'s promise in the daily life of schoolchildren throughout the nation. While the Civil Rights Act left it to the Justices to define the ultimate aims of the enterprise, the new tools provided by the act reshaped the way the Court exercised this prerogative. Quite simply, the judges' new enforcement tools required the ongoing cooperation of the presidency. Whatever the Court might say about the Constitution, it would have to sound persuasive to Lyndon Johnson, Richard Nixon, and the cabinet officers in charge of the relevant executive agencies—otherwise they could readily sabotage the Court's interpretations of constitutional requirements.

This chapter focuses on the resulting judicial-executive dynamic in the struggle over southern segregation, which finally led a reluctant Richard Nixon to give his decisive support to the Court's campaign against Jim Crow. By the time Watergate forced Nixon's resignation, these executive decisions had transformed the old Confederacy into the most integrated region of the country.

The Court's desegregation campaign in the North came to a very different ending. As court-ordered busing moved northward, it provoked a massive white countermobilization. This grassroots movement led Nixon and Congress to the brink of an all-out assault on judicial independence. As the political branches squared off against the Court, the confrontation began to resemble the great crisis of 1937—but with changed political valence. During the New Deal, liberals in the presidency and Congress threatened to destroy the judicial independence of a conservative Court; this time around, conservatives in the presidency and Congress were threatening the independence of a liberal Court.

This political reversal made a big difference, but it should not blind us to a fundamental similarity: just as the Old Court responded to Roosevelt's threats with a "switch in time" that deflected the liberal attack, the Burger Court gained the same long-run advantage by making a similar switch in time in *Milliken v. Bradley* in 1974. By calling off its ambitious effort to integrate northern suburbs, the Court once again deflected the escalating political campaign to strip away its judicial independence.

At the same time, the Court's retreat marked the definitive end of the era of constitutional politics it had initiated in 1954. The popular mandate for *Brown,* so vividly demonstrated by the Civil Rights Act of 1964, was now a thing of the past. We the People were lapsing back into their more normal condition—with ordinary citizens sitting on the sidelines as liberal and conservative activists struggled to expand or contract the legacy of the Second Reconstruction.

I shall be dividing this high-stakes drama into two parts. The present chapter considers how the Civil Rights Act ultimately allowed the Justices to vindicate *Brown* in the South. Chapter 12 follows the Court as it moves northward and explores the sources—some self-inflicted—of its retreat in *Milliken*, and the ultimate constitutional significance of this latter-day switch in time. We then move on to the very different dynamics governing the Court's redefinition of interracial marriage.

REINFORCING THE COURTS

During its first decade, *Brown* was on life support, with the white South successfully resisting federal desegregation efforts. By 1964, only 2 percent of black students were attending white schools in the old Confederacy.[1]

Worse yet, the lower courts had diluted *Brown* in their desperate efforts to move forward with "deliberate speed." *Briggs v. Elliot*'s formulation was broadly influential: "Nothing . . . in the decision of the Supreme Court takes away from the people freedom to choose the schools they attend. The Constitution, in other words, does not require integration. It merely forbids discrimination."[2] On this view, *Brown* only gave black parents the right to send their children to white schools; it did not protect black children from the humiliations of separate schooling if their parents succumbed to white intimidation and failed to exercise this right.

It took a long time for the Warren Court to repudiate *Briggs*. With waves of massive resistance sweeping the South in the late 1950s, the Justices moved in the opposite direction, summarily approving lower court decisions that contemplated token integration.[3] The Court's only full-dress opinion was provoked by the Little Rock crisis, when the Justices famously asserted their constitutional "suprem[acy]" over rival institutions.[4] But this decision simply emphasized the need for others to bend their knee in compliance; it didn't elaborate on *Brown*'s constitutional vision.

The emphasis on compliance was perfectly sensible, since the Court couldn't take it for granted. Shortly before Little Rock, President Eisenhower told reporters, "I can't imagine any set of circumstances that would

ever induce me to send federal troops . . . into any area to enforce the orders of a federal court."[5] But at his moment of constitutional truth, he famously sent the 101st Airborne Division to Little Rock, and saved *Brown*
from destruction. While Eisenhower established a fragile sense of federal
supremacy in Arkansas, his intervention provoked memories of military
Reconstruction throughout the South, escalating white resistance further.[6]
Indeed, it was only in 1964 that the Court publicly expressed its dissatisfaction with "deliberate speed" and called for greater expedition (without
committing itself to a clear deadline).[7]

Within this context, it's no surprise that the Civil Rights Act also focused on implementation, taking decisive action to enable the courts to
break through the decade-long impasse.[8] Until this point, the NAACP
Legal Defense Fund bore the burden of litigation in the South, since the
Department of Justice lacked legal authority to bring its own lawsuits.
Given its limited resources, the Legal Defense Fund concentrated on five
hundred school districts in heavily populated urban areas, allowing the
region's two thousand rural school boards to pretend that *Brown* never
happened. By authorizing the Justice Department to bring its own lawsuits and to intervene in those brought by others, the act greatly increased
the court's capacity to transform *Brown* into a living reality.[9]

Especially when the prospect of a federal lawsuit was coupled with new
financial sanctions imposed by the Department of Health, Education and
Welfare. The key here was Title VI of the act, which authorized executive
agencies to cut off federal funds to "any program or activity" practicing
discrimination. Hubert Humphrey treated Title VI as if it were uncontroversial: "If anyone can be against [Title VI], he can be against Mother's
Day. How can one justify discrimination in the use of Federal funds?"[10]

Yet Title VI actually represented a big change.[11] During the previous
decade, Harlem congressman Adam Clayton Powell Jr. had fought a long
and fruitless battle to attach anti-discrimination requirements to funding
programs. Since Republicans opposed many of these spending measures,
they could pass only with votes from southern Democrats—who condi-
tioned their support on the defeat of anti-discrimination requirements.
As a consequence, even liberal icons such as Eleanor Roosevelt and
Adlai Stevenson refused to support Powell's initiative.[12] His victory in
1964 had dramatic implications for school desegregation, especially
when liberals followed up a few months later with the Elementary

and Secondary Education Act (ESEA). This statute doubled federal education funding in a single year, from $1 billion in 1964 to $2.1 billion in 1965.[13]

This big injection of funds was especially attractive in the South, the nation's poorest region. Yet all this money would be withheld under Title VI if school boards couldn't satisfy HEW's anti-discrimination demands.[14] Worse yet, turning down the money would trigger special attention from the Justice Department, which could now bring a lawsuit on its own initiative. Statutory sanctions were combining to revolutionize the compliance calculus: why not get all that money, and avoid costly litigation, by promising HEW to make a few token steps in *Brown's* direction?

Lyndon Johnson's landslide victory over Barry Goldwater served as a popular mandate for decisive action from the bureaucracy.[15] Francis Keppel, commissioner of education, transformed his agency into a powerful enforcement engine. He recruited a new team led by David Seeley, a recent Yale Law graduate, to redeem the commands of Title VI.

The clock was ticking, and Seeley only had weeks to tell southern schools how to comply and get all their federal money before the new school year began. After lots of chaos and confusion, his tiny staff came up with initial guidelines setting relatively modest goals. Districts should desegregate at least four school grades through freedom-of-choice plans, and eliminate all segregated bus routes immediately.[16] Even if school boards complied, the predictable result of freedom of choice would be token integration, since it required black parents to brave white hostility and take affirmative action to send their kids to white schools. Nevertheless, the guidelines marked a breakthrough.

Two thousand southern school boards had never submitted any desegregation plans to anybody. Even token compliance would signal an end to the era of massive resistance. HEW would also be providing school boards with priceless political protection if they moved forward. They could deflect white outrage by explaining that token integration was a small price to pay for heaps of federal money.

The strategy proved remarkably successful. After a few months of hard bargaining, only fifty school districts remained defiant.[17] This bureaucratic achievement was especially remarkable since the president did not formally sign the guidelines. This gave Johnson some running room if the HEW initiative generated too much political heat.[18] But it also reduced the guidelines to run-of-the-mill policy statements, since Title VI required explicit presidential approval before they could be legally binding.

Despite these legal and political ambiguities, Johnson's HEW stood firm behind the guidelines in the face of escalating southern protests. Within a few months, HEW's funding threat allowed it to make more progress than the entire judiciary had achieved over ten years—tripling the percentage of southern blacks attending white-majority schools from 2 percent to 6 percent between 1964 and 1965.[19]

HEW's breakthrough also generated a virtuous cycle. Once districts shifted from defiance to (grudging) compliance, they set themselves up for escalating agency demands. Many districts failed to show much progress when schools opened in 1965. In response, the Office of Education upped the ante: if 8 percent of a district's blacks had gone to white-majority schools, 16 percent would be required for the coming year; if 4 percent had done so, the next year it would need to be 12 percent; if near zero, "a very substantial start" would be required.[20]

By this point, government by numbers was no longer a novelty—the Voting Rights Act was already on the books, and the EEOC was beginning to demand numbers from private enterprise. But the new HEW guidelines generated the loudest opposition. It was one thing for school boards to make a gesture of compliance, quite another for the feds to measure real progress by hard-to-evade headcounts. Despite the storm of protest, the revised guidelines actually worked—black attendance in southern white schools rose from 6 percent in 1965 to 14 percent in 1967.[21]

But not without political backlash. Politicians from the South denounced the new commissioner of education, Harold Howe, in incendiary terms, and a congressman from North Carolina, L. H. Fountain, tried to cripple HEW's funding powers by requiring elaborate administrative hearings. Fountain tacked his amendment to the House education finance bill, but his maneuver proved counterproductive: the final version of the statute explicitly reaffirmed the agency's cut-off powers.[22] With HEW retaining congressional support, the agency's continuing efforts were paying off: black integration rates moved from 14 percent in 1967 to 23 percent in 1968.[23] The escalating momentum led the agency to ratchet up requirements once again, revising the guidelines to demand *complete* desegregation by 1969. Yet the fate of this new requirement was in the hands of the next president: Would he continue to stand behind the agency with Johnsonian determination?

THE REASSERTION OF JUDICIAL LEADERSHIP

Before Richard Nixon got a chance to confront this question, the courts reasserted their constitutional leadership. With school boards launching a series of challenges to government by numbers, the federal court of appeals for the Deep South responded in its *Jefferson County* decision of 1967. Writing for the entire Fifth Circuit, Judge John Minor Wisdom's opinion offered a landmark redefinition of the enterprise launched by *Brown*. It set the stage, in turn, for a Supreme Court effort to define the key issues as the country confronted the 1968 election.

Jefferson County

Wisdom's opinion challenged the premises of judicial leadership motivating the desegregation campaign since 1954.[24] He declared that *"[t]he courts acting alone have failed"* (in italics, just in case anyone might have missed the point).[25] But the Civil Rights Act had saved *Brown* by "bringing together Congress, the executive, and the judiciary" in a joint effort.

In Wisdom's view, Congress had worked a constitutional revolution in its creation of "an alternative to court-supervised desegregation."[26] Title VI "ma[de] administrative agencies effective instruments for supervising and enforcing desegregation of public schools."[27] He refused to treat the HEW guidelines as "run-of-the-mine agency pronouncements"— even though that was precisely their status under administrative law.[28] He endowed them instead with quasi-constitutional status, insisting that "our standards should not be lower than those of HEW." After all, they were "prepared by experts in education and school administration, and . . . intended by Congress and the executive to be part of a coordinated national program."[29]

Jefferson County heralded a new synthesis between New Deal administrative expertise and the egalitarian ideals of the civil rights revolution. Only this New Deal–Civil Rights synthesis, Wisdom insisted, could save *Brown v. Board of Education* from failure. To be sure, he cautioned that the "percentages referred to in the Guidelines and in this Court's decree are simply a rough rule of thumb."[30] Such caveats should not disguise the court's ringing endorsement of government by numbers.

Wisdom then moved beyond technocracy to ultimate constitutional values. He denied that *Brown* merely required school boards to offer freedom of choice. Though "the harm to individual Negro children" was very real, there was something of greater importance: "school segregation was an integral element in the southern state's general program to restrict Negroes as a class from participation in the life of the community, the affairs of the State, and the mainstream of American life: *Negroes must keep their place.*" (This time it's my italics, not the court's.)[31]

Wisdom is not only moving beyond "freedom of choice." He is moving beyond the anti-humiliation principle established by Warren in 1954. At that time, it was enough for *Brown* to condemn "feelings of inferiority" imposed on black children without demonstrating their role in a "general program" that "restrict[ed] Negroes as a class from . . . the mainstream of American life." By taking a sphere-by-sphere approach, Warren could strike down segregated schooling without overruling *Plessy* on transportation or similar segregationist decisions in other areas.

Now that landmark statutes and judicial decisions had revolutionized the law in an escalating series of spheres, Wisdom was in a position to emphasize the cumulative impact of the now-illegal forms of humiliation practiced throughout southern life. *Jefferson County* serves as a great statement of the anti-subordination principle, condemning systematic efforts to keep groups "in their place" *across* spheres, and not only *within* spheres.[32]

So the opinion is doubly revolutionary—rejecting *Brown*'s assertion of judicial leadership and Warren's anti-humiliation principle to celebrate the rise of coordinate constitutionalism and the triumph of the anti-subordination principle.

Would the Justices agree?

Green v. Brown

With the nation still reeling from the death of Martin Luther King Jr. in April, the Court announced its decision in *Green v. County School Board* on May 27, 1968.[33] If there ever was a moment for deep reflection on the civil rights revolution, this was it. The president had just pushed the Fair Housing Act through Congress, with Everett Dirksen announcing a new understanding of the Fourteenth Amendment. The Justices were at work on *Jones v. Mayer* and its revolutionary reinterpretation of the Thirteenth Amendment. Nevertheless, *Green* did not measure up to these high expectations: Justice Brennan's opinion bears no resemblance to Judge

Wisdom's effort in *Jefferson County* to reassess *Brown's* place within the emerging constitutional order opened up by the landmark statutes.

This glaring omission wasn't accidental. The archives reveal that Brennan did indeed confront fundamental issues in earlier drafts, and his vision of *Brown* gained the support of six Justices. When Black, Harlan, and White refused to go along, Brennan shifted into bargaining mode, dropping his discussion of first principles so that the three naysayers could join a unanimous opinion that begged the big questions.

To appreciate the stakes raised by *Green,* begin with some basic facts: Like most of the rural South, New Kent County, Virginia, had done nothing to comply with *Brown* until 1965. It was only then, Brennan explained, that the county submitted a freedom-of-choice plan "to remain eligible for federal financial aid."[34]

The county only had two schools—one for blacks, one for whites. Thanks to the HEW guidelines, the number of blacks going to the white school moved from 35 in 1965 to 111 in 1966 and 115 in 1967. But 85 percent of the county's black students remained in the all-black school, since no white parents had exercised their "free choice" to send their children there. Was this good enough?

Brennan's early drafts proceeded from first principles. He acknowledged that the lower courts had approved freedom of choice in their early efforts to wean the South away from its "long-established pattern" of strict segregation. During this phase, "[t]he principal focus was on obtaining for those Negro children courageous enough to break with tradition a place in the 'white' schools." But now that HEW had made a larger breakthrough possible, Brennan reinstated *Brown's* original rationale: "To separate [schoolchildren] from others of similar age and qualifications solely because of their race generates a feeling of inferiority as to their status in the community that may affect their hearts and minds in a way unlikely to be undone."

Given his emphatic reassertion of *Brown's* originating rationale, Brennan's remedy made perfect sense. New Kent County had to "convert promptly to a system without a 'white' school and a 'Negro' school, but just schools." Only then was there a realistic prospect of ending institutionalized humiliation: "So long as the racial identity ingrained . . . by years of discrimination remains in the system, the stigma of inferiority likewise remains."[35]

In taking this line, Brennan was traveling down a well-worn path: In contrast to Judge Wisdom, he was not urging his colleagues to move beyond Warren's originating rationale to embrace an anti-subordination doctrine. He was recommitting the Court to *Brown*'s anti-humiliation principle—and this relatively modest objective helps explain why he gained the support of Douglas, Fortas, Marshall, and Stewart.

But Harlan and White refused to go along unless Brennan left "notions of stigma 'implicit' in the opinion." They feared that the explicit reaffirmation of *Brown*'s originating rationale would further inflame southern resistance. Black went even further, threatening to write a dissent that repudiated all talk of stigma and insisted that freedom of choice was sufficient to satisfy *Brown*'s mandate.[36]

Though Warren was "firmly opposed to having anyone fooling around with the *Brown* decisions,"[37] he silently accepted Brennan's pragmatic choice to eliminate his discussion of "hearts and minds" to achieve the greater good of judicial unanimity.[38]

Brennan's pragmatism came at a heavy price. Not only did he cut out all references to *Brown*'s original rationale, but he put absolutely nothing in their place. The result was a formulaic opinion that replaced a discussion of fundamental values with the language of imperial command: the Court simply demanded that New Kent must "come forward with a plan that promises realistically to work, and promises realistically to work *now*" (italics in original).[39]

Green's treatment of constitutional objectives was equally peremptory. Brennan retained his slogan from previous drafts—"convert promptly to a system without a 'white' school and a 'Negro' school, but just schools." But he had stripped it of its justifying rationale.[40] This didn't cause an immediate problem, since New Kent had only two public schools. This meant that the county could comply by sending children of both races to one site for elementary school and to the other site for high school, reducing overall busing in the process.[41]

In larger school districts, however, the formula begged obvious questions. On its face, Brennan's insistence on "a system without a 'white' school and a 'Negro' school" was compatible with a rigid busing plan aiming for the same black-white ratio in every school. But the opinion recognized the need for greater flexibility, even allowing freedom of choice to operate as part of an effective plan. Yet it was tough for lower courts to define the necessary trade-offs since Brennan had eliminated mention of the overall goal: eliminating "the stigma of inferiority" that had been "ingrained" in all-black schools "by years of discrimination."[42] Once stripped of basic principle, all that remained in *Green* was a dramatic show of impatience, a broad approval of technocratic measures of compliance, and a caution that lower courts should temper desegregation demands with common sense.

Green v. Jones

At precisely the same moment the Justices were struggling with *Green,* they were also deciding *Jones v. Mayer.* The two cases display revealing parallels, which serve to emphasize the remarkable character of *Green's* evasions.

Both cases involve efforts by Harlan and White to block a liberal reinterpretation of a key Reconstruction text—the Thirteenth Amendment in *Jones,* the Fourteenth in *Green.*[43] In both cases, the majority was proposing to announce the same basic principle: just as Brennan focused on the "stigma of inferiority" that had been "ingrained" by generations of segregated education, Stewart denounced the "badges of slavery" imposed by generations of discrimination in the housing market. Both were seeking to reread the great texts of the first Reconstruction to provide suitable foundations for the Second Reconstruction's insistence that Americans must move beyond formal notions of equality and freedom to eradicate institutionalized humiliation in crucial spheres of social life.

Justices Harlan and White blocked the path to unanimity in both cases, but Brennan and Stewart reacted very differently. Stewart allowed Harlan and White to publish their dissent in *Jones,* and insisted on retaining his emphasis on "badges of servitude"; Brennan traded his principles for unanimity in *Green.* Why?

Not because Brennan's principles were more controversial than Stewart's—to the contrary, Brennan was simply reaffirming *Brown,* while Stewart was repudiating deeply rooted understandings of the Thirteenth Amendment. Not because the liberal majority in *Green* was less committed to its principles—to the contrary, Earl Warren was undoubtedly aggrieved by the Harlan-White effort to fool around with his epochal achievement in *Brown.* Under ordinary conditions, the other Justices might well have deferred to the Chief's sensibilities—especially as he was about to resign from the Court.

The difference between *Green* and *Jones* had nothing to do with principles or personalities and everything to do with the Court's relationship to the political branches. Stewart could be brave in *Jones* because Congress had just committed the American people to a revolutionary breakthrough in the sphere of housing; nothing that Harlan or White could say would refute this fundamental point.

But the fate of segregated schools depended on the continued presence of a loyal ally in the White House. A year after *Jefferson County*, Judge Wisdom's triumphant celebration of interbranch collaboration seemed distinctly premature. With George Wallace and Richard Nixon in the race for the presidency, the future of southern desegregation was up for grabs. Quite suddenly, the darker aspect of Wisdom's opinion came into plain view: *"[t]he courts acting alone [had] failed"* to redeem *Brown* during the decade before the Civil Rights Act. Was the Court facing another decade in the wilderness after Inauguration Day, 1969?

Brennan couldn't eliminate this risk, but *Green* did minimize it. By insisting that southern school boards implement desegregation plans that "realistically . . . work *now*," it dramatically raised the political cost of White House foot-dragging. With all nine Justices joining behind this command, the new president would be faced with a stark choice: was he really prepared to defy the Court and take the country back to the bad old days of Little Rock?

Brennan's effort to preempt presidential resistance raised a question of its own. Now that the Court had passed up a golden opportunity to reaffirm *Brown*'s original meaning, would it get another chance? Or would it win the battle to desegregate the South at the cost of burying the anti-humiliation principle?

NIXON'S MOMENT(S) OF TRUTH

Green put Richard Nixon in a tough spot. His candidacy returned the Republican Party to its mainstream traditions after the Goldwater disaster. Throughout the campaign, Nixon reaffirmed his support for the landmark statutes of 1964, 1965, and 1968, beating back a last-minute challenge from Ronald Reagan, who remained steadfast in his neo-Goldwater orthodoxy.[44] Nixon remained faithful to this commitment as he struggled to contain the electoral threat posed by George Wallace during the fall campaign. While he loudly denounced the Warren Court for its criminal justice revolution, he never allowed his defense of "law and order" to undermine his commitment to the landmark statutes—leading Wallace famously to lump him together with Humphrey as "unfit to be president."[45]

Similarly, his repeated promises to appoint "strict constitutionalists" to the Court were at odds with his performance on one of the headline issues of the day: Lyndon Johnson's lame-duck effort to replace the retiring Earl Warren with Abe Fortas as Chief Justice of the United States. When Strom Thurmond and other southerners launched a filibuster, Nixon refused to give it his public support, describing Fortas as "one of the ablest Justices on the Court"—as Wallace reminded his viewers in a nationally televised broadcast on election eve.[46]

At the same time, Nixon the politician was eager to make gestures to the rising Republican Party of the South. Despite his public position on Fortas, he may well have supported the filibuster behind the scenes in exchange for Thurmond's public support for his candidacy.[47] His position on school desegregation was also clouded in mystery. He coupled reaffirmations of *Brown* with warnings against aggressive busing orders that would make the South into "a whipping boy."[48] He also refused to take a clear stand on HEW's threat to withhold funds from schools that failed to meet the agency's 1969 integration deadline—allowing the rumor mill to assure white southerners that he had indeed promised a reprieve to Thurmond.[49]

The president continued to evade the tough questions upon entering the White House. Whatever the political temptations of a "southern strategy," he wasn't prepared to alienate millions of mainstream Republicans who remained moderate to liberal on civil rights. Instead, he created competing liberal and conservative power centers within his administration, enabling both teams to mount very different initiatives that appealed to different parts of his political coalition. The ongoing struggle between departments and advisors also provided Nixon with a broad range of options if and when politics absolutely required him to intervene with a high-visibility decision—allowing him to shift from liberal to conservative solutions, and back again, in an intricate balancing act.

The key operational issue was whether HEW and Justice would continue to back the Court through a combination of aggressive litigation and funding cutoffs. On this crucial matter, Nixon kept his distance from the fray, allowing the two departments to operate as rival power centers.

This gave Robert Finch, the new secretary of HEW, a first-mover advantage when it came to enforcing the existing HEW guidelines. Like George Romney at HUD, Finch was a strong liberal Republican. But unlike Romney, he was the president's personal friend, having served as Nixon's campaign manager in 1960—indeed, he almost gained Nixon's nod as his 1968 running mate before Spiro Agnew edged him out.[50]

During Finch's early weeks in office, he withheld funds from a few school districts despite cries of protest from the rising southern wing of the party. He then appointed Leon Panetta, an up-and-coming liberal Republican from California, to head his Office of Civil Rights. Panetta quickly committed HEW to the existing 1969 deadline, allowing a one-year deferral only for truly exceptional cases.[51]

All this energetic activity generated increasing alarm in John Mitchell's Justice Department. As Nixon's campaign manager in 1968, Mitchell was especially alive to the needs of southern Republicans. But he was no cynical apologist for segregation. He fully supported an ambitious litigation program proposed by Jerris Leonard, his new assistant attorney general for civil rights. But there was a big political difference between Justice Department lawsuits and HEW guidelines. When Leonard went into court, the judges were responsible for the final decisions. When Finch and Panetta enforced the guidelines, the Nixon administration had to take the heat.

Here is where Mitchell drew the line. He opposed HEW's fall deadline as politically unwise and pragmatically unrealistic.[52] Over the spring, he convinced Nixon that change was necessary, and the president ordered Finch and Mitchell to get together and hammer out a new policy.[53]

On July 3, the two department heads issued a joint public statement carefully crafted to mean different things to different people. It gestured to the south by suspending HEW's fast-approaching deadline, rejecting a "single arbitrary date" for all districts "regardless of the difficulties they face."[54] This symbolic softening of the deadline was headline news.

But its practical effect was far less congenial to southern interests. The statement emphasized that segregated districts would be "under a heavy factual burden" to show "bona fide educational and administrative problems."[55] HEW also won explicit recognition of funding cutoffs as a remedy of last resort.[56]

Given all this, Panetta felt perfectly free to continue his last-minute push to get southern school boards to "voluntarily" accept strong integration plans. For districts already under court order, HEW was also providing expert help to enable rapid compliance. All in all, the July 3 statement generated a mixed message—gesturing to the white South while reassuring mainstream Republicans that real progress would continue.

Then Nixon personally intervened to upset this balancing act. His motive had nothing to do with race and everything to do with his major preoccupation, which was foreign policy. The Finch-Mitchell statement came at a moment when the president was trying to push his anti-ballistic-missile initiative through Congress. John Stennis of Mississippi was in a strategic position as chairman of the Armed Services Committee, and he had already gained a "breathtaking, one-vote victory" to authorize the measure.[57] The battle lines were now forming for the necessary multibillion-dollar appropriation—and Stennis was determined to hold the bill hostage unless HEW backed off from its "ridiculous" demands to dismantle his state's notoriously segregated schools. Once Finch and Mitchell had officially lifted the strict deadline insisting on integration during the next school year, Nixon was in a position to strike a deal.[58]

It was going to be tough for the president to live up to his side of the bargain. Thirty-three Mississippi school districts were already under court order to produce desegregation plans by early August—and with the aid of HEW experts, they were preparing to put these plans into effect when schools opened. This meant that Nixon couldn't simply tell Finch to go easy on Mississippi. He would have to ask him to write an unprecedented letter to the Fifth Circuit telling the judges that the compliance plans were in fact inadequate (despite HEW's expert assistance) and that immediate implementation would "produce chaos, confusion, and a catastrophic educational setback to the 135,700 children, black and white alike."[59]

Finch's leading staffers told him that there was no basis for such representations. Nevertheless, the secretary played the good soldier and recruited a couple of regional staffers to testify in court on his behalf.[60]

With HEW undercutting its own plans, the Fifth Circuit withdrew its immediate desegregation order and gave the agency a few months to develop better plans for the next school year. Denouncing this betrayal, the NAACP Legal Defense Fund rushed to Justice Hugo Black, supervisor for the Fifth Circuit, who quickly referred its petition to the full Court for expedited treatment. With the Mississippi schools opening under their old and discredited freedom-of-choice plans, the parties raced to Washington for a final judgment.[61]

Nixon's deal with Stennis had exploded into a confrontation of historic significance. For the first time since *Brown,* the Justice Department was fighting the NAACP Legal Defense Fund in a school case. Dramatizing this remarkable turnaround, sixty-five of the seventy-five staff attorneys in the Civil Rights Division launched a public protest, denouncing Assistant Attorney General Leonard's refusal to heed the "clear legal mandates" laid down by *Green.*[62]

Confronting a mutiny in their own ranks, Mitchell and Leonard doubled down and reasserted their authority. Leonard even issued a direct challenge to the Justices at a September press conference, saying, "[I]f the Supreme Court were to order instant desegregation nothing would change. Somebody would have to enforce that order." In the words of the *New York Times,* the "Court could find itself . . . issuing a school desegregation order without full expectation that it could or would be enforced by the Justice Department."[63]

Shades of Little Rock, but worse—this time it wasn't a state governor but the executive branch itself threatening disobedience. Nixon's solicitor general added fuel to the flames. The solicitor general traditionally serves as a "tenth Justice," especially attentive to the Court's unique responsibilities. Mitchell had allowed Erwin Griswold, the former dean of the Harvard Law School, to stay in office as a holdover from the Johnson administration—making it headline news when Griswold refused to defend the administration and sat by silently while Leonard made his oral argument to the Justices.

Griswold's silence was more eloquent than Leonard's words. There was no mistaking the fundamental challenge to the Court's leadership—but the Justices were going to have a tough time framing a suitable response. The case from the Fifth Circuit, *Alexander v. Holmes County,* was argued on October 23. If the Justices reversed the lower court decision, they would have to grapple with Finch's August prediction of "chaos, confusion, and a catastrophic educational set-back." The reinstatement of the HEW busing orders would force Mississippi to disrupt ongoing classes and send 135,000 students to new schools and new teachers in the middle of the academic year—what a mess!

The Court was more impressed with the challenge to its authority. Within a week, it ordered the Mississippi schools to repudiate their freedom-of-choice system and *immediately* put HEW's desegregation plans into action.[64] This drastic decision was by no means required by *Green*—which was careful to say that school districts had to come up with plans that "realistically" promised "to work *now*."[65] "Now" was October, and the Justices could have readily ruled that a disruptive midyear transformation was unrealistic—especially since the Fifth Circuit was requiring the districts to work with HEW to develop strong plans for the next academic year.

But the Nixon administration's confrontation with the Court had spiraled far beyond the realm of prudential legalism. The threat to judicial authority was too obvious to ignore. To dramatize the point, Nixon's new Chief Justice, Warren Burger, joined the 9-to-0 rebuke to his sponsor.[66]

It's hard to believe that Nixon would have made his ABM deal with Stennis if he had recognized the danger of such a high-stakes constitutional confrontation. It was one thing for Jerris Leonard to invoke the shades of Little Rock, but quite another for Nixon to play the part of Orval Faubus. Now that the Court had called Leonard's bluff, Nixon folded his cards and called it quits. He immediately and publicly pledged to enforce the Court's remarkable command.[67] Federal judges responded by issuing orders for sweeping midyear school reorganizations in Mississippi and other bastions of intransigence.[68] As tens of thousands of students were bused to new schools to meet new classmates and teachers, they learned at least one lesson: *Brown v. Board of Education* was indeed the law of the land.

Nixon was seething with rage, condemning the Justices as "childish" and "irresponsible" in confidential meetings.[69] He was also going public with emphatic signs of disapproval. When the Senate rejected his nomination of southerner Clement Haynesworth to the Supreme Court, Nixon moved forward in late January to propose G. Harrold Carswell to fill the vacancy despite his public record of racist remarks; in February, he fired Leon Panetta from his frontline position as HEW's chief enforcer;[70] in March, he accepted Finch's resignation as HEW secretary;[71] and in April, he bitterly denounced the Senate when it rejected his Carswell nomination: "I have reluctantly concluded that it is not possible to get confirmation for the judge on the Supreme Court of any man who believes in the strict construction of the constitution as I do, if he happens to come from the South."[72]

He was also telling his three top advisors—John Ehrlichman, H. R. Haldeman, and Henry Kissinger—that he was now taking "personal responsibility" on school desegregation, since "it will be the major issue of controversy for the foreseeable future."[73]

This immediately provoked the usual White House competition between conservative and liberal advisors. Pat Buchanan developed an aggressive southern strategy, telling Nixon that "the second era of Reconstruction is over; the ship of integration is going down . . . and we ought not to be aboard. For the first time since 1954, the national civil rights community is going to sustain an up-and-down defeat."[74] He urged his boss to send Spiro Agnew down to Dixie to launch an all-out campaign against the Court, preparing a speech that would have had the vice president say, "For the life of me, I cannot see . . . any benefits to justify the terrible costs we are paying, and that we shall pay in the future, if we move toward racially unified schools throughout the country."

Nixon was already using Agnew as a megaphone for hotheaded attacks on antiwar demonstrators, and there were obvious political attractions in extending his brief. George Wallace posed a looming threat to Nixon's reelection in 1972: if southern anger at court-ordered busing kept rising, Wallace might become a formidable threat throughout the South, depriving Nixon of crucial electoral votes needed to beat his Democratic rival in another three-cornered race. If Nixon used Agnew to out-demagogue Wallace, he would be guarding his right flank. Buchanan's scheme began to gain momentum when Agnew publicly announced plans to address the matter in Atlanta.

Then Nixon called the whole thing off. He told Ehrlichman that there was "no good pol[itics] in P[at] B[uchanan]'s extreme view" because it was "bad law." For my purposes, it's profitless to speculate about the president's true motives. The key point is that Nixon was perfectly aware that he was confronting a moment of constitutional truth. If he had unleashed Agnew, the nation would have confronted a first-class crisis. With the Legal Defense Fund insisting on *Green* and *Alexander,* and Agnew stirring up white resistance, there was no telling whether or when the Court's effort to redeem *Brown* would gain final vindication in the real world.

In choosing (however reluctantly) to support the Court, Nixon not only opted for the rule of law. He also made a decision with big political consequences. He had acquired a powerful interest in preventing another round of resistance to the Court's desegregation decrees. Now that he had ceded the white backlash to Wallace, continued southern resistance would heighten his third-party challenge in 1972—undercutting Nixon's appeal in the South while exposing him to a strong civil rights Democrat in the North. If Nixon was to preempt this two-front threat to his reelection, it was imperative for him to resolve the issue before the 1972 campaign by supporting widespread southern compliance when the schools opened in 1970.[75]

Nixon's distinctive leadership style is best approached through contrasts with previous presidential turning points. Most obviously, he refused to follow the model of Lyndon Johnson's "We Shall Overcome" speech and get out ahead of the courts to insist on the moral imperative of an egalitarian breakthrough. His posture was closer to Eisenhower's at Little Rock—skeptical on the merits of the Court's initiative, annoyed at the judges for pushing him into a corner, yet finally resolved to uphold the rule of law.

But Nixon was following Eisenhower's lead at a very different stage in the higher lawmaking cycle. Thanks to the Civil Rights Act, HEW and Justice had already broken down school board resistance in the South and were collaborating with the courts in an escalating attack on Jim Crow. Within this context, an Eisenhower-style military intervention would have been counterproductive—further inflaming racist backlash, and endangering Nixon's reelection prospects. To avoid this result, Nixon continued his double-edged strategy in a way that paradoxically ensured the decisive elimination of old-style school segregation.

Begin with the legalistic dimension of Nixon's position. After publicly demonstrating his displeasure with the Court and HEW, Nixon tried to steer the Justices down a constitutional path that he would find acceptable. As a preliminary to this effort, the White House recruited Alexander Bickel of Yale to provide legal heft and James Coleman of Chicago to establish social science credibility.[76] Yet Nixon was not content to rely on these academics or his own staff to produce the final product. In a rare moment in the life of the modern presidency, he worked up his own elaborate eight-page document, which was published on March 24, 1970.[77]

Nixon recognized the Court as "the final arbiter of constitutional questions" and backed its demand that southern schools "terminate their dual systems at once." At the same time, he tried to preempt a dramatic expansion of this campaign to northern cities, where black schools were the by-product of racist housing patterns. He called de facto segregation "undesirable" but denied that it violated the Constitution and emphasized that the Court had not yet held to the contrary.

In contrast, the president made his opposition to busing in the South more conditional. While he rejected busing for purposes of "racial balance," he refused to support a statutory effort to restrict the court's powers to destroy the South's dual system: "I am advised," he said, that any legislative ban on busing "cannot constitutionally be applied to de jure segregation."

Paradox number one: Nixon's statement was committing him to a "southern strategy" diametrically opposed to the one for which he is now (in)famous. He was saying, in no uncertain terms, that he would be *tougher* on the South than the North.

Nixon backed up his words with deeds. On July 10, the Department of Justice announced fifty-two new lawsuits against southern school districts that were holding out. Even more remarkably, the Internal Revenue Service (IRS) joined in with an entirely new sanction: henceforth, it would deny tax exemptions to racist private academies that offered whites an escape route from integrated schools.[78] In undertaking this important initiative, the IRS was not taking unilateral action in the manner of Finch at HEW or Romney at HUD: Ron Ziegler, the president's spokesman, immediately endorsed the IRS ruling.[79] Indeed, Nixon himself gave it his personal approval, scribbling in the margin of the decision memo: "I believe we have to do what is right on this issue. But again let us be under no illusion that we are badly hurt politically."[80] Nixon's prophecy was rapidly redeemed by threats of electoral retribution from segregationists such as Strom Thurmond for his "arbitrary, vindictive, and anti-South[ern]" initiatives.[81]

Nixon's embrace of legalism allowed him to put the blame on the courts, but this was hardly sufficient to prevent another round of bitter-end southern resistance that might blow up in his face in the run-up to his reelection bid. Here is where a second, and more political, enforcement strategy came to the fore. The president created a Cabinet Committee on Education that organized a broad coalition of southern moderates to give their political backing to court-ordered desegregation. Under the effective leadership of labor secretary George Schultz, a strong racial liberal, administration teams went South to create biracial leadership committees in the seven states most affected by *Alexander*.[82] Their message: Like it or not, Nixon was *not* going to undercut court-ordered integration, and if the South succumbed to another round of violent resistance, it would only alienate big-time investors who would go elsewhere in search of business opportunities. As Nixon himself put the point: "Any community which permits the public school system to deteriorate condemns itself to economic and social stagnation."[83]

This no-nonsense approach proved remarkably effective in recruiting a key constituency to the statewide interracial committees. Many white business leaders remained personally committed to racist principles, but they stood up for the proposition that "New South" economics was no longer compatible with "Old South" segregation. At the same time, black leaders saw Schultz's initiative as their best hope for building a broad political coalition that could withstand demagogic race-baiting.

Paradox number two: Nixon's plea for political support from southern conservatives was greatly enhanced by his earlier shows of resistance to the Court in *Alexander,* his purge at HEW, and his defiant nomination of Carswell. These high-visibility gestures marked him out as the national politician most sympathetic to the southern white predicament. So his swing behind the Court's busing campaign served as political protection for local business elites to declare publicly that the time for good-faith compliance with *Brown* had come at last. Nixon's appeal for support was especially effective since it was framed in terms of the values of "law and order" and free market capitalism that resonated broadly in the southern business community.

The result was the domestic analogue to Nixon's China initiative. Just as his cold warrior image protected him against right-wing attacks on his rapprochement with Mao, his emphatic gestures to Dixie gained him credibility when he told the South that the time had come to accept defeat.

Creating credible state committees wasn't easy. It required Schultz's teams to work around strong opposition by leading senators and governors. When the time was ripe, Schultz brought each state delegation to the White House for a special meeting with the president to seal the deal. Here is how he described these visits:

> The first group to come to Washington was from Mississippi. We met in the Roosevelt Room of the White House, across the hall from the Oval Office. The discussion was civil, but deep divisions were evident. I let them argue for a while. Then, by prearrangement, I had John Mitchell . . . drop by. He was known in the South as a tough guy, and on the whole was regarded by whites as sympathetic to their cause. I asked Mitchell what he planned to do about the schools. "I am attorney general, and I will enforce the law," he growled in his gruff, pipe-smoking way. He offered no judgments about whether this

was good, bad or indifferent. "I will enforce the law," he repeated. With that, he left.

When lunchtime arrived, . . . I sat with the two people I wanted to lead the Mississippi advisory committee: Warren Hood, president of the Mississippi Manufacturers Association, and Dr. Gilbert Mason, a black physician and head of the Biloxi chapter of the N.A.A.C.P. I argued that if they would accept, the committee would have great credibility with whites and blacks.

I could see they were beginning to talk constructively to each other, so I left them alone. . . .

When the time was right, I let President Nixon know that we were ready for him. We walked across the hall into the Oval Office, where the president gathered his guests around his desk. . . . I remember him saying, "Just as decisions are made here in this office, decisions are made throughout the states and communities of our country. You are leaders in those communities and you have to step up to your responsibilities." They left the Oval Office inspired.[84]

Nixon was also helping out in more tangible ways. He announced a $1.5 billion federal initiative to manage the transition.[85]

The president's two-pronged strategy profoundly shaped developments on the ground. On one hand, he squarely placed the burden of constitutional leadership on the courts—putting them on notice that they would take the political heat if they used *Brown* as a springboard for a northern campaign against de facto segregation. On the other hand, he did all he could to create a political consensus for southern compliance, and offered fiscal help for a smooth transition to an integrated system.

As the Nixon-sponsored interracial committees came to life in the spring of 1970, they proved remarkably effective in providing an alternative to familiar forms of race-baiting. They worked on the ground to support school compliance and launched communications campaigns—featuring icons such as Billy Graham—to urge southerners to accept the inevitable. The overall effort was undoubtedly helped by the changing political realities wrought by the Voting Rights Act. Since Nixon had recently signed an extension into law, everybody recognized that a large black vote was here to stay, and that it was time to rethink old political tactics.

Lots of racial liberals were unimpressed by the Nixon-Schultz effort. The president's earlier public moves—his brinksmanship in *Alexander* as well as his (failed) effort to put a southern conservative on the Supreme Court—made it virtually impossible for them to concede that anything good could come from the Nixon White House.[86] Nevertheless, Nixon's strategy played a key role in gaining political support for another large advance in southern desegregation.

Numbers speak louder than words: When Lyndon Johnson left Washington in 1968, 23.4 percent of black students were attending majority white schools in the South; by 1970, it was 33.1 percent—making it the most integrated region in the nation.[87]

SWANN'S CONSOLIDATION

Holmes v. Alexander doesn't bulk large in the story American lawyers tell themselves about *Brown*'s fate—perhaps because the Court didn't publish a full opinion in the case. This isn't because the new Chief Justice, Warren Burger, didn't try. He initially treated the case for what it was—the greatest challenge to the Court's legitimacy since Little Rock. He wanted to follow the model established by *Cooper v. Aaron,* with each Justice signing his name individually to a unanimous opinion that he drafted as a rebuke to the Nixon administration. But the old-timers, led by Brennan, refused to cede intellectual leadership to the newcomer.[88]

As a consequence, the Justices settled for a five-paragraph order after a week of intensive give-and-take.[89] If Mississippi was going to attempt a midyear revolution of its school system, the Court couldn't indulge in the luxury of extended doctrinal debate before announcing its marching orders.

Despite *Alexander*'s unimposing presence on the pages of the *United States Reports*, Burger was right to endow the decision with decisive significance—or so our larger framework suggests. If *Brown* was the *signal* that placed desegregation on the constitutional agenda, the Civil Rights Act was an effort to *propose* New Deal–style administrative-legal sanctions to overcome southern resistance, and the landslide election of 1964 was a *trigger* for the Johnson administration's *elaboration* of these new sanctions into an effective strategy, then the *ratifying* election of 1968 opened the way for Nixon to *consolidate* these breakthroughs with a legal-political campaign in support of *Alexander*.

As the president reluctantly threw his support behind the Court, the Justices sealed their triumph in *Swann v. Charlotte-Mecklenburg.* The case was argued in October 1970, just as the remarkable progress in southern desegregation was becoming apparent.[90] It confronted problems vastly more complicated than those raised by the rural county involved in *Green.* Since this county only had two schools—one black, one white—it was pretty clear how to achieve "a system without a 'white' school and a 'Negro' school, but just schools."[91] As Justice Brennan suggested, the county could simply bus all children to one site for elementary school, and then use the other site for the upper grades.

In contrast, *Swann* arose in the major metropolitan area of Charlotte-Mecklenburg, North Carolina, where 29 percent of the region's eighty-four thousand students were black. But they were concentrated in the urban core. What did *Green*'s insistence on eliminating "white" and "black" schools mean here?

The federal district court took *Green* literally. It approved an aggressive desegregation plan that aimed for a ratio of 29 percent black students to 71 percent white students in each of the region's 108 schools, "so that there will be no basis for contending that one school is racially different from the others."[92] Speaking for a unanimous Court, Chief Justice Burger upheld this sweeping plan to bus students across city-suburban boundaries. But once again, he achieved unanimity at the cost of suppressing Warren's originating insights in *Brown*.

The loss may be measured by comparing Burger's published opinion to this draft from Brennan's files that never saw the light of day:[93]

> Separation of the races was found to be unconstitutional in *Brown* because it stigmatized members of the Negro race: that is, racial segregation involving state action was found to reflect a state policy or judgment that Negroes are inferior to whites. The Court found that as a result of this stigma (this label of officially determined inferiority), Negro school children suffered psychological harm and educational deprivation. However, the gist of the evil of segregation is not the psychological or educational disadvantages; even if there had been no evidence that segregation produces psychological or educational harm, segregation of the races would still have denied equal protection because it labeled one race as inferior. And that a State may not do under the Fourteenth Amendment.
>
> Since, in my view, the evil of segregation was stigma, the goal and purpose of desegregation is the elimination of stigma. A unitary school system is one whose pupil assignment, faculty assignment, school site location, facilities allocation, etc., do not stigmatize any race. A *de jure* segregated system is one whose policies have stigmatized and still stigmatize one race. . . .
>
> What is necessary to eliminate the stigmatizing effect of racial separation in a formerly *de jure* segregated school district? Clearly, the mere repeal of segregation laws is not enough if it leaves the situation of racial separation

substantially the same as it was before. The only way to remove the stigma of racial separation is to achieve substantial integration. This does not mean that every last Negro child must attend an integrated school; it does not even mean, necessarily, that there cannot constitutionally be an all-black school in a particular district. What it does mean is that there must be enough mixing of the races throughout the public school system that any remaining racial separation is fairly attributable not to state policy past or present, but to other factors such as *de facto* residential segregation, physical obstacles to larger school attendance zones, etc.

This text isolates three key elements of *Brown*'s originating logic, recapitulating themes that we first explored in Chapter 7. Brennan's first point distinguishes "stigma" from "psychological or educational disadvantages." The court's central task isn't to play psychologist or pedagogue but to interpret social meaning: "even if there had been no evidence that segregation produces psychological or educational harm, segregation of the races would still have denied equal protection because it labeled one race as inferior." To determine whether such labeling had occurred, the judge must rely on Karl Llewellyn, not Kenneth Clark, and use his "situation-sense" to grasp the dominant meanings of social practices.

The interpretive character of this exercise is emphasized by Brennan's second big point—"the only way" to eliminate the prevailing stigma is to create "enough mixing of the races throughout the public school system" to make it clear that the "remaining racial separation is not fairly attributable to state policy, past or present." A district judge can't make this determination without immersing himself in the life of the community to grasp the prevailing interpretation of one or another desegregation pattern.

After isolating the crucial significance of social meaning, Brennan's third big move is to reaffirm *Brown*'s one-sphere-at-a-time approach to the elimination of institutionalized humiliation. His text focuses exclusively on whether the actions *by the school system* were imposing a stigmatizing label on blacks. Brennan refuses to go beyond the sphere of education and insist that school boards take into account the impact of discrimination in other spheres.

None of these points survive in Chief Justice Burger's published opinion. His initial draft contained a passing mention of the "badge of inferiority" imposed by segregation, but he eliminated the reference to pacify Justice Black.[94] Recognizing the pragmatic imperative to close ranks, Brennan did not even circulate his "stigma" draft to his colleagues.[95] At the end of the day, *Swann* simply asserted that "[s]eparate educational facilities are inherently unequal," without explaining why.[96]

This led to predictable confusion in Burger's discussion of *Green's* insistence on the elimination of "black" and "white" schools. He explained that it did not mean that courts should require "every school in every community" to "reflect the racial composition of the school system as a whole." Indeed, there were "some circumstances [in which] certain schools may remain all or largely of one race."[97] All this would have made sense under Brennan's approach, which related the desegregation effort to the larger goal of eliminating stigma.

But now that Burger had expunged all references to *Brown's* originating rationale, he had trouble reconciling his statement of constitutional principle with the case before him—since the sweeping busing order in *Swann* did seem to aim for a black-white ratio of 29 percent to 71 percent in each school. If the Court were to reverse the lower court ruling, however, this would have halted the dynamic of compliance at a critical moment. Burger responded to his self-inflicted predicament by recharacterizing the lower court's use of government by numbers. Rather than operating as a "norm," he explained, the ratio was simply a "starting point" in the exercise of equitable discretion—and a legitimate one, given Charlotte-Mecklenburg's fifteen-year history of intransigence.

Green, Alexander, Swann—in each case, the Court spoke in the language of command, displaying a united front to the president and Congress, but at the cost of evading a discussion of basic principle. In each case, the strategy was successful. Once Burger upheld the sweeping desegregation of the Charlotte-Mecklenburg schools, Nixon followed through on his commitment to the "rule of law." While the Justice Department had previously opposed the district court's formulaic approach, it backed prompt enforcement of the Court's order. Charlotte-Mecklenburg's political leadership embraced the plan, transforming its metropolitan system into a living symbol of southern acceptance of *Brown's* legitimacy. With the Nixon administration helping to create congenial political coalitions throughout the South, *Swann* proved critical in bringing regional resistance to an end.

This episode serves as an immensely important exception to the general pattern we have been elaborating. In areas as disparate as employment, housing, public accommodations, and voting, it was the president and

Congress that pushed the law and its enforcement far beyond anything that the Court had previously envisioned. But in public education, the Supreme Court's leadership remained absolutely crucial. Even in this sphere, the Court wasn't able to break the back of southern resistance on its own. The new enforcement tools provided by the Civil Rights Act and the aggressive use of those tools by Johnson's HEW were essential in redeeming *Brown*'s promise. Nevertheless, it was up to Richard Nixon to make the final breakthrough, and he refused to go any further than the Court commanded.

By acting decisively in *Green, Alexander,* and *Swann,* the Court forced Nixon into a box. Both for political and principled reasons, he was unprepared to replay the role of Orval Faubus and catalyze yet another cycle of massive southern resistance. He was left with no other choice but to help build cross-racial coalitions across the South in order to transform the Court's orders into educational realities.

This triumph of judicial leadership was extraordinarily important. The legacy of the civil rights revolution would have been vastly different if Senator Stennis and his friends had preserved segregated public schooling in Mississippi and elsewhere. For all the backsliding during more recent decades, the fact remains that *Brown* was redeemed in the field of its original application: integration became the living law of the South, and that is no small matter.

CHAPTER 12

The Switch in Time

T HE COURT'S REMARKABLE victory generated new dilemmas as the struggle over desegregation moved north. While Nixon had contributed decisively to southern desegregation, he emphasized that the Court had not condemned de facto discrimination—putting the Justices on notice that they couldn't count on the president to shield them from the political backlash if they went further to condemn northern-style segregation. At best, the president might stand on the sidelines; at worst, he might throw his support behind a congressional assault on judicial independence.

While the political risks were obvious, the Court's southern victory also generated more subtle dangers to its doctrinal integrity. With the Justice Department threatening to disobey the Court's commands in *Alexander,* the Court deferred a potentially divisive discussion of *Brown's* future implications. Rather than battling over first principles, it was far more important to present a united front to compel Nixon to follow through on southern desegregation. But as the Justices looked northward, they could no longer defer a principled debate. As cases began to reach them from Denver and Detroit, they were not dealing any longer with schools that publicly separated blacks from the "master race." All schools were formally open to all races—but most blacks went to nearby ghetto schools that were surrounded by mostly white schools in the larger metropolitan area. If this pattern was unconstitutional, the Court would have to explain why.

Warren's original opinion in *Brown* provided one path forward: under this approach, the courts would explore the ways that ghetto schools systematically humiliated black children despite the absence of an expressly racist system of assignment. But it was also possible to leave *Brown's* originating principles behind and build a different framework for the distinctive problems that were now moving to center stage.

The rapid pace of litigation forced the Court to explore its options with blinding speed. The great debate began with *City of Emporia,* decided in June 1972. While this case came from the South, its special facts invited the Court to rise to the level of first principles. In a remarkable show of unanimity, the four Nixon appointees and the five Warren Court holdovers reaffirmed *Brown*'s anti-humiliation principle. But the Court abandoned Warren's approach the following year in its first direct confrontation with northern-style segregation in *Keyes v. Denver School District.*[1] While Justice Brennan cobbled together a majority to uphold a citywide busing order in Denver, he turned away from the anti-humiliation principle in favor of a more legalistic approach emphasizing the bad intentions of school officials.

Brennan's turn to legalism was not enough to deflect a rising political assault on the Court's leadership. Grassroots opposition to busing throughout the North started to gain serious attention on Capitol Hill. As the 1972 elections approached, Nixon called on Congress to pass restrictions on busing orders—legislation that gravely threatened judicial independence. Northern liberals were forced to a desperate Senate filibuster to stop the Nixon-inspired proposal. These dramatic scenes had high symbolic meaning. For the last generation, it had been southern die-hards, not northern liberals, who used the filibuster to prevent fundamental change; did the role reversal signify that the American people were changing sides and demanding an end to the Court's constitutional leadership?

After *Keyes* affirmed northern busing, this question returned to the constitutional stage with renewed intensity in 1974. With grassroots opposition rising to new heights, the political branches were threatening the Court's independence in ways similar to Roosevelt's famous 1937 assault on the Old Court—only this time around, it was a *conservative* Congress and president leading an assault on a *liberal* Court. This set the stage for the Justices' precipitous retreat on busing in their 1974 decision in *Milliken v. Bradley*—which, like the Old Court's retreat of 1937, marked a decisive turning point in constitutional history.

This story of rapid-fire shifts—from *Emporia*'s reaffirmation of *Brown*'s anti-humiliation principle (1972) to *Keyes*'s turn to legalism (1973) to *Milliken*'s switch in time (1974)—raises obvious questions: Could the Court have avoided the need for a high-stakes confrontation if *Keyes* had not departed from *Emporia*'s affirmation of *Brown*'s sociological jurisprudence? More generally, how is the 1974 switch similar to, and different from, the epochal switch of 1937?

Nixon Fills the Gap

I take up the story on March 24, 1970. The Court's forceful busing initiative in *Alexander* had pushed southern desegregation onto Richard Nixon's personal decision-making agenda. At the same time, northern judges were beginning to attract national attention with aggressive decisions of their own—most notably in Los Angeles, where a California district court had issued a sweeping decree aiming for racial balance in each of 561 schools within the 711-square-mile district. As whites mobilized to defend their suburban schools, busing was becoming a national problem.[2]

Nixon responded with an elaborate statement defining the way forward. We have already considered the way it shaped presidential policy in the South, but it also had a significant impact on the president's "northern strategy." In preparing for the White House initiative, liberal staffers Ray Price and Leonard Garment reached out to academic giants such as Alexander Bickel and James Coleman. These scholars were genuinely committed to civil rights but were already searching for innovative alternatives to busing.[3] Building on their work, Nixon developed a remarkably sophisticated position, containing a masterly survey of judicial decisions (Bickel), a thoughtful assessment of the social science data (Coleman), and a considered—though highly controversial—vision for the future.[4]

Nixon recognized that busing might be constitutionally required to destroy the Jim Crow systems of the South. But he argued that de facto segregation in the North raised entirely different issues: "[I]t is natural and right that we have Italian or Irish or Negro or Norwegian neighborhoods; it is natural and right that members of those communities feel a sense of group identity and group pride."[5] So long as the state didn't publicly brand blacks as inferior, Nixon contended, neighborhood homogeneity could be a source of pride, not humiliation. He also confronted the notion that "a predominantly black school is automatically inferior [even when it is] not a product of a dual system," and declared that such an idea "inescapably carries racist overtones."[6] Nixon did not explicitly invoke an "anti-humiliation" principle in distinguishing de facto from de jure segregation.[7] Nevertheless, his key claims were that ethnic or racial homogeneity by itself doesn't humiliate, and that it *is* humiliating to tell black children that they can't learn effectively without white role models.

Social science data, Nixon recognized, suggested that racial mixing might well have positive effects on educational outcomes. But he insisted that black schools generated poor results principally "because they serve poor children who often lack the home environment that encourages learning." In his view, it was class, not race, that lay at the heart of the problem—along with the failure to provide black schools with the money needed to provide an effective response to these class-based learning deficits. To fill this financial hole, he proposed a special $1.5 billion appropriation that would give priority funding to "districts that have 'the furthest to go to catch up educationally with the rest of the nation.'"[8] Nixon also called for a variety of innovative measures that would ameliorate racial isolation but fell short of "depriving the student of his own neighborhood school."[9] There is lots more to Nixon's statement.[10] But I have said enough to suggest that he was presenting a strong—if obviously controversial—case, arguing that once southern-style school systems had been dismantled, the courts shouldn't be emphasizing aggressive busing. While racial isolation was a bad thing, there were many innovative forms of cross-race engagement that did not deprive communities of their neighborhood schools.

Congress was getting to the same bottom line—but through a more confusing process. As public anxiety swept the country, the House was becoming a hotbed of anti-busing sentiment, and the annual appropriations bill for HEW became the occasion for attaching riders emphatically denouncing the threat of massive judicial intervention. Mississippi congressman Jamie Whitten took the lead in an annual campaign to bar HEW from using federal money to "force busing of students." Despite his transparent effort to shield Jim Crow systems, Whitten's initiatives regularly gained the support of House majorities starting in 1968. Nevertheless, his bark was bigger than his bite: the Senate and the joint House-Senate conference committee regularly added language to Whitten's riders that rendered them legally meaningless, and the House went along when the toothless version returned for final approval.[11]

But in 1970, Senator Stennis of Mississippi hit upon a clever expedient that didn't involve a busing ban. His proposal declared it national policy to treat all instances of segregation alike regardless of whether they arose from explicit racial assignment or residential housing patterns.[12] In arguing for a single national standard, Stennis was making a last-ditch effort to save his state's Jim Crow system from its impending demise. He was confident that once northern communities were endangered by court-ordered busing, the white backlash would be so formidable that it would force the courts to stop their southern campaign as well.

Stennis's transparently racist maneuver was transformed when super-liberal Connecticut senator Abraham Ribicoff joined as a cosponsor:

> The plain fact is that racism is rampant throughout the country. . . .
>
> Our problem is not only the dual system of education which exists sixteen years after the Supreme Court struck it down in 1954.
>
> The more fundamental problem is the dual society that exists in every metropolitan area—the black society of the central city and the white society of the suburbs.
>
> Massive segregation does not exist because we have segregated our schools but because we have segregated our neighborhoods.[13]

Ribicoff's claims split the civil rights coalition. Senator Peter Dominick of Colorado argued that Ribicoff's cure didn't match his diagnosis. If the problem was racism in the housing market, the right solution was rigorous enforcement of the Fair Housing Act, not aggressive busing between black and white areas.[14]

Dominick's rejoinder raised a fundamental issue. Ribicoff was indeed challenging the sphere-by-sphere logic initiated in *Brown* and continued in the landmark statutes. He was urging his colleagues to confront "the more fundamental problem" posed by "the dual society."[15] His amendment would have required a uniform approach to "conditions of segregation by race *whether de iure* [*sic*] *or de facto.*"[16] This would have left the courts to decide whether they should slow down busing in the South or proceed aggressively in the North. But in either event, it would bring to an end the "monumental hypocrisy" involved in pretending that northern segregation was fundamentally different from the Jim Crow variety.[17]

The Democratic and Republican leaders of the Senate were entirely unwilling to concede this point. For Mike Mansfield and Hugh Scott, there was a big difference between de jure and de facto—the Supreme Court had condemned the first but not the second. And until the Court spoke, it was wrongheaded for Congress to intervene. Their amendment authorized busing only to break down Jim Crow.

As debate reached a climax, both sides invoked Nixon in their support—with Stennis reciting occasions on which the president had explicitly opposed busing.[18] But the Mississippian put too much faith in the administration's "southern strategy." After a presidential meeting with Republican leaders, the White House endorsed a new version of Hugh Scott's amendment that continued to focus exclusively on the elimination of Jim Crow schools. With the Democratic leadership coming on board, the Scott-Mansfield amendment now had the support of the entire establishment.[19]

Nevertheless, it went down to a crushing defeat on February 18, 1970, when an odd coalition of southern racists and northern superliberals voted 56–36 in support of Stennis-Ribicoff.[20] For a moment Congress seemed to be taking constitutional leadership away from the Court, erasing the distinction between de jure and de facto segregation from American law.

The moment was short-lived. When the Senate bill emerged from the House-Senate conference committee, Stennis-Ribicoff had been replaced by Scott-Mansfield's narrower authorization of busing as a tool against southern-style segregation.[21] After predictable grumbling, both houses went along in early April 1970, giving the seal of congressional approval to the same principles that Nixon had developed in his statement the week before. Like the president, Congress respected the difference between de jure and de facto segregation—leaving it to the Supreme Court to take the heat if it rejected this distinction in its northern busing campaign.

The next move was the Court's—which proceeded to duck the big issues the following spring. In his unanimous opinion in *Swann,* Chief Justice Burger upheld a far-reaching busing order for Charlotte-Mecklenburg, North Carolina. But the Justices' overriding priority was to confront Richard Nixon and the South with a united front. They could not afford the luxury of a public debate over first principles that could be used to justify further stalling.[22] In demanding an immediate end to southern-style segregation, Chief Justice Burger focused narrowly on the task at hand—leaving to another day *Swann*'s potential implications for the North.

Swann also punted on a key remedial question. Charlotte happened to be an American city whose schools were part of a much larger metropolitan-area school district. But this was relatively exceptional. Most center cities confronted white suburbs that had their own elected school boards supervising their own school systems. This meant that *Swann* didn't consider when and whether federal courts should override traditions of local self-government by individual (white) suburbs by compelling them to accept minority students from the urban core.

Burger's unanimous opinion kept the pressure on Nixon, but its doctrinal evasions came at a price. Whether the Justices liked it or not, *Swann* was sure to escalate the national debate. The Court's question-begging affirmation of busing would predictably encourage northern judges to explore the terrain that *Swann* left open, developing aggressive readings of constitutional principle that would support busing campaigns in formally desegregated settings. This, in turn, would catalyze a broad anti-busing movement in defense of neighborhood schools during an election year.

Political Challenge and Judicial Response: Round Two

Swann marked a decisive turning point for Richard Nixon. He was no longer interested in alternatives to busing that promised to reduce racial isolation in northern ghettos.[23] He cut out White House liberals and their academic advisors, relying instead on hard-right staffers such as Charles Colson. Writing a month after *Swann,* Colson emphasized that, "unlike a lot of issues, [busing] is clearly voter motivational. It is one of those issues that is absolutely decisive in a voter's mind. He will put up with anything else if he feels that we not only are against busing, *but can and will do something about it.*"[24] Gallup polls were confirming the hard-liners, showing 76 percent of Americans against busing, only 18 percent in favor. Even blacks were sharply divided.[25]

Events took a dramatic turn when the liberal Michigan legislature prohibited funds for interdistrict busing, establishing a statewide policy in favor of neighborhood schools.[26] Michigan's defection from the liberal ranks was provoked by federal litigation in Detroit demanding massive interdistrict transfers of city blacks and suburban whites to achieve racial balance. In September 1971, federal district judge Stephen Roth began considering such a decree for the next school year,[27] generating "the largest and most sustained non-work-related protests in the city's history" in middle-class suburbs that had long been Democratic strongholds.[28]

Michigan's congressional delegation turned emphatically anti-busing overnight (with notable exceptions including Senator Philip Hart and Representatives John Conyers and Charles Diggs).[29] The political consequences became clear when the House turned to consider Richard Nixon's effort to provide national leadership on the issue. In his March statement on school desegregation, Nixon had called for the passage of an Emergency School Aid Act that provided $1.5 billion to help school districts cope with desegregation orders.[30] Fearing that it might become a massive "busing bill,"[31] many liberal Democrats backed an amendment offered by Michigan Republican William Broomfield suspending district court busing orders while they were under appeal—deferring the "moment of truth" for years, or forever, depending on the Supreme Court's resolution of the next round of cases.[32] The full House backed this initiative, as well as others that went beyond Whitten's earlier efforts to restrict HEW's support of busing.[33] Once again, these efforts were deflected in the Senate, although by voting margins that revealed weakening levels of liberal support.[34]

These maneuvers served as prologue to the further escalation of the debate. Representative Norman Lent of New York proposed a constitutional amendment providing that "[n]o public school student shall, because of his race, creed or color, be assigned or required to attend a particular school."[35] When Emanuel Celler used his prerogatives as chairman to bottle up Lent's proposal in his Judiciary Committee, House members circulated a discharge petition to force it onto the floor. As members flocked to sign up, the numbers rapidly moved toward the 51 percent required to oust the Judiciary Committee from control. When the signatories passed the 33 percent mark, Celler reluctantly agreed to hold hearings on this radical repudiation of the Supreme Court[36]—during which sixty-nine congressmen, from all regions of the country, lined up to denounce busing. Only three spoke in favor.[37]

The Judiciary Committee began its round of intensive hearings during the first two weeks of March. Nobody denied the obvious—that the overwhelming majority of Americans were firmly opposed to the courts' escalating busing campaign. The only serious question was whether a constitutional amendment was the right way to express the breadth of popular opposition. Most congressmen were willing to say yes, insisting that Article V was the only effective means for compelling the courts to heed the voice of the people.[38] The issue became more explosive on March 13, when George Wallace swept the Democratic presidential primary in Florida with 42 percent of the vote, carrying every county in the state over a strong field. (Hubert Humphrey finished a distant second with 19 percent.)[39]

With Wallace gaining popular momentum, Richard Nixon tried to preempt the threat in a television address on March 16.[40] The president had previously suggested that the amendment route might prove necessary.[41] He now maintained his position despite the surprising advice of right-wingers such as Spiro Agnew, who told him that it would "trivialize the constitution."[42] In his address to the nation, Nixon kept the amendment option alive but urged Congress to embrace his statutory proposals only because revision through Article V "takes too long."[43]

Nixon's two-step initiative began with the Student Transportation Moratorium Bill, which suspended all busing decrees through July 31, 1973. This would give Congress a chance to consider his more substantive measure: the Equal Education Opportunity Bill, imposing a strict set of limitations on courts seeking to remedy constitutional violations. The proposal would make busing a last resort for secondary schools, and barred it absolutely for elementary school students. In presenting his program, Nixon asserted that he was "aiding rather than challenging the courts, respecting the mandate of the 14th Amendment, and exercising the responsibility of the Congress to enforce that Amendment."[44]

This claim threw the constitutional community into an uproar. It fell to Yale's Robert Bork—soon to be appointed solicitor general—to turn the liberals' constitutional paradigm on its head. As we saw in Chapter 6, the Warren Court's decision in *Katzenbach v. Morgan* accorded Congress broad powers, under Section 5 of the Fourteenth Amendment, to revise equal protection doctrines devised by courts. In Bork's hands, *Morgan* turned into a two-edged sword—supporting conservative, no less than liberal, exercises in constitutional leadership by the political branches. According to Bork, Nixon's proposal didn't change substantive constitutional principles but only concerned itself with the status of busing as a remedy—and so fell within Section 5's explicit grant of power to enforce the Equal Protection Clause. To make his case, Bork quoted from the reigning guru on the subject, Professor Henry Hart of Harvard Law School: "The denial of *any* remedy is one thing. . . . But the denial of one remedy while another is left open, or the substitution of one remedy for another, is very different. It must be plain that Congress necessarily has a wide choice."[45] Since Nixon's bill specifically authorized courts to pursue alternative remedies for realizing *Brown,* and even permitted busing in some circumstances, what precisely was the constitutional problem?

Bork's display of legal virtuosity provoked spirited legal ripostes.[46] But it also stunned the larger academic audience into a state of confused perplexity. No fewer than 550 liberal law professors signed a letter prepared by the Harvard faculty opposing Nixon's initiative. But they based their position on policy grounds, refraining from sustained constitutional critique. On this crucial matter, the Harvard letter simply stated that "enactment by Congress under Section 5 . . . invokes a rarely exercised power whose limits are not at all clear. Strong doubts of constitutionality exist, with constitutional lawyers differing as to the outcome if the bills were to become law and their legality tested in the courts."[47]

Confusion also prevailed among Democratic contenders for the presidency. Despite Hubert Humphrey's great record on civil rights, he came out strongly against "forced busing." As the primary campaign moved to Michigan, whose politics had been inflamed by a court-ordered busing plan for Detroit and its suburbs, Humphrey declared: "Busing just hasn't worked. It hasn't helped the child, it hasn't brought about quality education, it hasn't solved our racial problems. That's why I am against forced busing to achieve racial balance."[48] Edmund Muskie also wobbled, if not so obviously, in his vain efforts to compete for white voters.[49] Only George McGovern squarely condemned Nixon's initiative as "a total surrender to Wallaceism."[50]

As the campaign heated up outside Washington, the president's program was running the gauntlet on Capitol Hill. The House gave it a mixed reception. Celler successfully killed Nixon's moratorium bill in committee. But the intensity of anti-busing sentiment forced him to allow the Equal Educational Opportunity Act onto the floor, where the majority embraced it with enthusiasm. Indeed, the full House out-Nixoned Nixon, adding amendments that prohibited busing for all schoolchildren, not only younger ones, as the president had proposed.[51]

The House bill arrived on the Senate floor in October, just as the presidential campaign was reaching its climax. Nixon had kicked off his fall campaign with a Labor Day speech condemning busing as symptomatic of a broader "welfare ethic" destroying America. He called on Congress, "as a matter of the highest priority, to approve, before it adjourns, the busing moratorium."[52] McGovern continued with his principled opposition: "There is no darker chapter in the Presidency of Richard Nixon than his exploitation of . . . emotion surrounding the issue of busing."[53] He condemned Nixon's initiative as a breach of fundamental principles: "[I]n a democracy which places law above men, even the President cannot place himself above the United States Supreme Court."[54]

McGovern's appeals to basic principles weren't very persuasive when the House bill came to the Senate floor in October. Senators knew what scholars have since confirmed: anti-busing sentiment was a significant force behind the tidal wave propelling Nixon to a landslide victory.[55] They were not about to dig their graves with a high-profile vote for busing only days before the election. There were no longer fifty-one votes to support the now traditional strategy of undercutting House initiatives on the Senate floor or in the conference committee.

Nevertheless, a significant minority were still willing to stand up against the juggernaut—because they weren't running in 1972, or had especially safe seats, or were fundamentally committed to judicial independence (or some combination of the three). This led the liberal rump to begin a filibuster on October 6, generating an ironic twist on themes that had been remorselessly repeated over the past half century. This time it was old-style southern segregationists denouncing the northern liberal minority's desperate attempt to deny the will of a mobilized national majority;[56] this time it was Richard Nixon, not Lyndon Johnson, jawboning senators to heed the voice of the people and put an end to the filibuster.[57] As newspapers and television reported on these bizarre role reversals, Senate majorities voted to end debate on three separate occasions—but they fell short of the two-thirds supermajority then required by Senate rules.[58] Nevertheless, there was no disguising liberal embarrassment: given their loud opposition to filibustering during the previous decades, how long could they sustain their enterprise in the face of constant mockery from their opponents?

We will never know. The liberals had the time clock on their side. Every day of delay brought senators facing reelection closer to their moment of truth in November. With the failure of the third cloture vote, the Senate adjourned to let incumbents do some last-minute campaigning.[59] The liberals' last-ditch battle had barely deflected the conservative juggernaut. But never fear, declared Richard Nixon—"if we don't get it now, we will go for it as a matter of the highest priority in the next Congress."[60]

This was no idle threat: While the composition of Congress didn't change much after the 1972 elections, the House and Senate were already primed to support decisive action.[61] And didn't Nixon's big victory on Election Day—crushing McGovern in the same way that Johnson had crushed Goldwater—enhance his authority to claim a mandate on busing from We the People?

THE JUDICIAL REASSERTION OF *BROWN*

While all this was going on, the Court was preparing to reenter the debate. On June 22, 1972, it broke its long silence on *Brown*'s enduring meaning in *Wright v. City of Emporia*.[62] The facts of the case suggested how far the Court had succeeded in overcoming southern resistance. *Emporia* no longer involved the legitimacy of extensive busing orders, but confronted last-ditch efforts by white enclaves to insulate themselves from the impending obliteration of Jim Crow education.

The problem: The city of Emporia had been sending its children into the larger system run by Greensville County, Virginia. When a federal judge issued a broad busing plan, Emporia tried to secede and establish its own school system for its disproportionately white residents.

The city denied that its motives were racist, and convinced the federal court of appeals that educational considerations were paramount. When faced with the prospect of Emporia's secession, the Supreme Court intervened and forced the city back into the countywide plan.

The vote in *Emporia* was 5 to 4. There was no longer a compelling need for the Justices to present a united front to the South. With the (reluctant but essential) aid of Richard Nixon, southern schools were now the most integrated in the country. This great achievement liberated the Court for a preliminary debate on fundamental questions it would once again confront as it began to grapple with the future of desegregation in the North.

Emporia not only split the Court but also set the five Warren Court holdovers against the four Nixonian newcomers. Writing for the five holdovers, Justice Stewart first considered the lower court's determination that the city's secession was not "merely a cover-up" for racism but that its "primary purpose" was "benign" and rooted in good-faith pursuit of educational excellence.[63] He responded by repudiating the lower court's basic premises. He not only found it "difficult or impossible" for judges to identify the dominant motives or purposes of multimember bodies. He condemned the entire inquiry, calling it "as irrelevant as it is fruitless":

> The mandate of *Brown II* was to desegregate schools, and we have said that "the measure of any desegregation plan is its effectiveness." Thus, we have focused upon the effect—not the purpose or motivation—of a school board's action in determining whether it is a permissible method of dismantling a dual system. The existence of a permissible purpose cannot sustain an action that has an impermissible effect.[64]

Instead of searching through official documents to determine "purpose or motivation," Stewart demanded an inquiry into the public meaning of Emporia's action:

While Emporia had long had the right under state law to establish a separate school system, its decision to do so came only upon the basis of—and, as the city officials conceded, in reaction to—a court order that prevented the county system from maintaining any longer the segregated system that had lingered for 15 years after *Brown I.* In the words of Judge Winter, dissenting in the Court of Appeals, "if the establishment of an Emporia school district is not enjoined, the black students in the county will watch as nearly one-half the total number of white students in the county abandon the county schools for a substantially whiter system." *The message of this action, coming when it did, cannot have escaped the Negro children in the county.* As we noted in *Brown I:* "To separate [Negro schoolchildren] from others of similar age and qualifications solely because of their race generates a feeling of inferiority as to their status in the community that may affect their hearts and minds in a way unlikely ever to be undone." We think that, under the circumstances, the District Court could rationally have concluded that the *same adverse psychological effect* was likely to result from Emporia's withdrawal of its children from the Greensville County system.[65] (Emphasis added)

Behold: *Brown*'s originating rationale returns to center stage after its repeated strategic suppression in *Green, Alexander,* and *Swann.* Government by numbers also finds a place, but it is distinctly secondary. Stewart isn't simply concerned that Emporia's secession will lead to the departure of almost half of the whites from county schools.[66] It's the social meaning of the numbers that is decisive: the city's exit, coming in response to the desegregation order, sends a "message . . . [that] cannot have escaped the Negro children," "generat[ing] a feeling of inferiority as to their status in the community."

No less important, the four Nixonian newcomers joined Stewart in affirming the enduring significance of Warren's great opinion. They dissented only when it came to the majority's application of Warren's principles to Emporia's case. Here is Chief Justice Burger's discussion:

In Brown I the Court emphasized that the legal policy of separating children in schools solely according to their race inevitably generates a sense of inferiority. These observations were supported *by common human experience* and *reinforced by psychological authority.* Here the Court seeks to make a similar judgment in a setting where no child is accorded differing treatment on the basis of race. This wholly speculative observation by the Court is supported neither by common experience nor by scientific authority.[67] (Emphasis added)

If anything, Burger was better than Stewart in crisply distinguishing between two distinct steps in *Brown*'s originating logic (see Chapter 7). He rightly gave pride of place to the test of "common human experience," where the judge provides a commonsense interpretation of a challenged practice to determine whether it systematically humiliates. In resolving this question, the judge was calling upon the common-law tradition, which emphasizes the centrality of community mores in legal interpretation. Only then did Burger follow Warren in appealing to the modern scientific tradition. On this second approach, the judge considered whether his commonsense judgment was "*reinforced* by psychological authority" (emphasis added). Burger's formulation rightly suggested that it is judicial commonsense that drives *Brown*-style decision, with social science serving as "reinforcement."

Emporia was 9 to 0, not 5 to 4, on these fundamental issues. Both newcomers and old-timers joined together in affirming the enduring significance of Warren's great opinion. Their 5-to-4 disagreement is no less enlightening.

Burger complained that there was no "scientific authority" that supported the majority's judgment, and Stewart seemed to concede this point—his opinion failed to cite any serious social science. He made his case entirely on the basis of common sense: "The message of this action, *coming when it did,* cannot have escaped the Negro children in the county" (italics added).

Stewart's emphasis on the city's timing was crucial. If Emporia had established its independent school system at some earlier moment, the racial meaning of its action might well have been "speculative"—to invoke Burger's term. But that's not how it happened. The city tried to secede immediately after the court's integration order. Could anybody with common sense ignore the obvious denigration of county black students expressed by a sudden effort to withdraw half the whites from their schools?

Stewart's sensitivity to contextual particularities makes his judgment compelling. In dismissing it as "speculative," Burger seemed to be lacking in "situation-sense," as Karl Llewellyn called this common-law capacity to root judicial judgment in the prevailing meaning of social practices.[68]

Whatever the merits of their particular dispute, one thing seemed clear: the Justices had joined together behind Warren's opinion to serve as a benchmark as they turned to the hot-button issue of northern school segregation.

Yet one year later, they were veering off in a very different direction.

BRENNAN'S TUNNEL VISION

The political challenge was clear as the Court settled down to decide its first northern busing case, *Keyes v. Denver School District*. Writing in the Sunday magazine of the *New York Times,* Harvard's Christopher Jencks, a leading liberal voice on educational policy, described the stakes to the general public:

> If the Supreme Court pushes ahead . . . , Congress may well pass a tough anti-busing bill that aims to nullify the Court's decisions. Worse yet, if the Court holds such legislation unconstitutional, Congress and 38 states may enact a constitutional amendment to stop busing, particularly with a President publicly committed against busing for racial balance. Such an amendment would be a political disaster of major proportions. Both blacks and whites would see it as a decisive defeat for the civil rights movement and triumph for segregationism.[69]

Nevertheless, he conceded that

> [o]pponents of a constitutional amendment may be able to find 13 states where there are so few blacks that the white majority is not worried about busing. Nonetheless for a strategy whose benefit seems so uncertain, busing entails considerable political risk.[70]

Jencks's essay is the only magazine article that Justice Brennan saved in his files on the *Keyes* case.[71] But the Justices didn't need Jencks to warn them of the political dangers: they began their deliberations just at the moment when Senate liberals were desperately filibustering against a direct assault on court-ordered busing.

Keyes was also legally difficult. *Swann* supported a sweeping busing order in a Jim Crow metropolis where the identity of "black" and "white" schools was deeply rooted in the public mind. Within this setting, metropolitan-wide busing was the only realistic way to eliminate the "black" identity of particular schools and the stigma experienced by black children attending them. But Denver had never maintained a Jim Crow system, and its school board insisted that student assignment was strictly governed by a neutral "neighborhood school" policy. On its view, the black majorities in ghetto schools were simply mirroring the racial composition of their neighborhoods. So long as it was acting neutrally in the sphere of education, it asserted, it should not be held responsible for de facto segregation generated by other factors.[72]

The trial court was unconvinced. Judge William Doyle first found that the school board's claim to neutrality was bogus—at least in its dealings with a racially transitional neighborhood called Park Hill. He found powerful evidence that the board was funneling the black children of Park Hill into racially concentrated schools through a host of low-visibility policy decisions—redrawing school attendance lines, selecting new school sites, and the like.

Doyle did not find similar evidence when he scrutinized the board's dealings with the main ghetto in the city's core. As a consequence, he developed a second ground for condemning these heavily minority schools. Reaching back to *Plessy v. Ferguson,* he denied they were providing "separate *but equal*" education to their students. To establish a sound basis for this holding, the Legal Defense Fund (as counsel for the plaintiffs) organized a formidable social scientific presentation comparing ghetto school opportunities with those afforded predominantly white students elsewhere in Denver. Putting his two holdings together—intentionality in Park Hill, inequality in the core ghetto—Doyle issued a wide-ranging busing order aiming to eliminate racial disparities in all of Denver's schools.

But the court of appeals approved only half of Doyle's rationale. It agreed that the board had intentionally segregated in Park Hill, but it rejected the inequality violation based on *Plessy.* As a consequence, it dramatically restricted Doyle's remedy to fit the limited scope of the violation: while Park Hill students could be bused to more integrated settings, the children in the central ghetto would be stuck in their existing schools.

Once *Emporia* came down, the appellate court's emphasis on bad official intentions immediately became problematic. As Potter Stewart emphasized, the judicial effort to figure out the motives of multimember bodies was not only "difficult or impossible" but legally "irrelevant." The right job for a court was, in Warren Burger's words, to use its common-sense understanding of "human experience . . . reinforced by psychological authority" to determine whether educational practices "generate[] a sense of inferiority." Yet an accident of timing made it tough for the litigants to reframe their arguments to take *Emporia* into account. The Legal Defense Fund persuaded the Court to take jurisdiction over *Keyes* on January 17, 1972—five months before *Emporia* was announced in June.[73] It then filed its brief on May 1, 1972—without an inkling of *Emporia*'s imminent reassertion of *Brown*'s anti-humiliation principle as the key for judging school cases.[74]

The Legal Defense Fund had a final opportunity to retrieve the situation in October, when James Nabrit presented *Keyes* before the Justices at oral argument. But Nabrit was not equal to the occasion: he failed to mention *Emporia* and continued to emphasize the bad intentions of the school board as if they were a key factor in the decision. His attention was further deflected by a new theme introduced by the Justices. Justice Powell pressed Nabrit on whether it made more sense to repudiate the entire distinction between de facto and de jure segregation. But Nabrit resisted: "I would say first that it is not necessary on the record to reach that issue . . . we viewed the case as a de jure case." When Justice Stewart pressed him further, Nabrit responded unenthusiastically, "Faced with that decision [to repudiate the distinction between de facto and de jure], I would still argue that we should win the case. I would be willing to follow it out to its logical conclusion if I had to."[75]

The Justices weren't bound by Nabrit's hesitations. Indeed, "[a]lmost from the beginning the Court was deeply divided on how to handle the case," according to a revealing play-by-play account prepared by Justice Brennan's law clerks for his confidential files.[76] Yet the Justices' debate did not focus on the implications of *Emporia*'s redefinition of de facto segregation. They concentrated instead on the very same issue that Senators Ribicoff and Stennis had pushed to the center of the public debate: "Justice Douglas and Justice Powell wanted to use the case to abolish the de facto–de jure distinction."[77]

Like Senator Ribicoff, Douglas's aim in taking this step was to impose sweeping busing orders throughout the North. Like Stennis, Powell wanted to deny that there was any real difference between southern-style and northern-style segregation and urge a more measured approach to busing on both sides of the Mason-Dixon line.[78]

Neither side could win a majority. According to Brennan, he and Marshall "were willing to go along with the abolition of the de facto–de jure distinction," but there was no chance of getting two more votes "since Justice White was out of the case and Justice Stewart was openly opposed to any evisceration of the de facto–de jure distinction." As a consequence, Brennan set out to write an opinion that "sought a more practical disposition of the case in order to avoid a 4–4 split."[79]

Here is where the Fund's failure to respond creatively to *Emporia* had a devastating effect. Brennan did indeed cobble together a majority to support citywide busing within the de jure framework.[80] But he did not use

Emporia as a springboard to reaffirm *Brown's* emphasis on the social meaning of educational practices. Instead, his opinion proceeded by noting that "petitioners [represented by the Fund] *apparently* concede *for the purposes of this case* that . . . plaintiffs must prove not only that segregated schooling exists but also that it was brought about or maintained by intentional state action" (italics added).[81]

Note the weasel words. Brennan was *not* affirmatively embracing the view that de jure segregation requires bad intentions. He was accepting this view "for purposes of this case" only because the Legal Defense Fund "apparently" endorsed it—a plausible interpretation, given Nabrit's performance at oral argument.

This concession was even more unfortunate, since the Legal Defense Fund's written brief contained lots of material that Brennan could have used if he had followed *Emporia*. Consider, for example, this passage from the brief that explained why the ghetto schools in the urban core violated the Equal Protection Clause even though their minority concentrations were not the product of intentional manipulations by the school board:

> Judge Doyle made findings about the . . . intangible factors which tend to label a school and reinforce [its] image as a segregated institution:
>
> "Since the students do not feel that the school is an effective aid in achieving their goal—acceptance and integration into the mainstream of American life—they are not motivated to learn. Furthermore, since the parents of these Negro students have similar feelings with respect to the segregated school, they do not attempt to motivate their children to learn. *Teachers assigned to these schools are generally dissatisfied and try to escape as soon as possible. Furthermore, teachers expect low achievement from students at segregated schools, and thus do little to stimulate higher performance.*" (Emphasis added)[82]

One might have expected Justice Brennan to be especially responsive to such findings. Even before *Emporia,* he had been trying (but failing) to convince his colleagues to proclaim their fidelity to Warren's anti-humiliation principle as they hammered out their opinions in *Green* (1969) and *Swann* (1971).[83]

But Brennan didn't make the effort.[84] As we shall see, this highly contingent and explicitly provisional decision would have fateful consequences when an escalating political assault on the Court led the Justices to make their switch in time only one year later in *Milliken.*

Before leaving *Keyes,* we should take note of another problematic aspect of Brennan's opinion, one that followed from his acceptance of the intentionality premise. Brennan's principal objective was to gain a majority for a citywide busing program, even though the lower courts had found that the school board had intentionally discriminated only in the isolated area of Park Hill. Here is where government by numbers came to the rescue. In remanding Denver's case for further proceedings, Brennan created a presumption in favor of citywide busing on the ground that "racially inspired school board actions" typically have an "impact beyond the particular schools" that are directly involved. He told the district court that the school board had the burden of proving that intentional discrimination in Park Hill didn't have an adverse impact on racial concentrations throughout the city.[85]

The next phase of the case, then, featured a technocratic display from the school board's statistical expert, which tried to meet Brennan's burden of proof. When the district judge rejected the school board's number-crunching exercise,[86] Brennan had achieved his goal: bad official intentions + technocracy = citywide busing.

This was the formula that allowed Brennan to treat Denver as the constitutional equivalent of Charlotte-Mecklenburg without squarely confronting the obvious difference between the two cases. On one hand, Charlotte had *publicly* identified particular schools as "black" or "white" for generations—this made comprehensive busing an absolute necessity in erasing the humiliating legacy of the past. On the other hand, busing's relationship to the concrete forms of humiliation in Denver—created by high teacher turnover and low institutional expectations—was a good deal more problematic. Changing the racial composition of schools might indeed be part of the solution. But other steps might well be more important in eliminating the "feelings of inferiority" imposed on minority children by the Denver schools. *Emporia*'s focus on stigmatizing social meanings, in short, required a complex recalibration of the remedial mix appropriate in northern settings.

In contrast, Brennan's "bad intentions + technocracy" formula promised a more clean-cut approach: first, search through school board files to find a smoking gun revealing malign intentions; second, bring in the number crunchers to devise the minority-majority ratio in each school that would eliminate significant traces of official misconduct. This approach could potentially propel comprehensive busing orders in those (many) northern cities where smoking guns remained hidden in school board files. However, it threatened to unhinge the entire effort from *Brown*'s more fundamental concerns, leading to a deep problem. As we surveyed legal developments in sphere after sphere of social life, we have been witnessing the relatively harmonious development of two distinctive logics of the Second Reconstruction: anti-humiliation, on one hand, and government by numbers, on the other. While the law embraced technocratic measures to ensure more ambitious notions of equality (as in the spheres of voting and employment), it did not lose sight of the special evils posed by institutionalized humiliation. But *Keyes* opened up precisely this prospect, making the technocratic pursuit of citywide busing formulas seem more important than the step-by-step remediation of concrete practices that humiliated black children.

There is no need to exaggerate. *Keyes* by no means precluded a more harmonious development of the social-meaning and technocratic strands in later school cases; indeed, the Court's opinion expressly insists on the provisional character of its embrace of the Legal Defense Fund's focus on bad official intentions as the trigger for a technocratic solution. Yet Brennan's gesture to the future was soon to be overtaken by events.

THE CRISIS OF 1974

The Court handed down *Keyes* on June 21, 1973, a moment when Congress was increasingly consumed by the escalating Watergate scandal. But as senators and representatives began looking forward to the 1974 elections, *Keyes* catapulted the busing issue back to center stage.

Now that the Supreme Court had decisively intervened in Denver, northern cities confronted an accelerating wave of busing orders—intensifying the local countermobilizations that had already demonstrated their power in national politics.[87] At the same time, the Court had taken another northern busing case, *Milliken v. Bradley,* that raised an even more explosive issue. *Keyes* involved busing within the city of Denver, without considering whether whites could escape racial mixing by fleeing to the suburbs. *Milliken* faced this issue head-on in Detroit, with the district court heading off white flight by ordering suburban school districts to participate in a metropolitan-area-wide busing effort.

Congressional anxieties crystallized when an educational funding bill reached the House floor in March 1974, shortly after the Supreme Court heard oral argument in *Milliken*.[88] As the Justices pondered their positions, it was painfully apparent that hard-line opponents of busing were now in total command. The House voted 293 to 117 to forbid courts from busing children any further than their next-closest school.[89]

Matters were looking grim as the bill moved to the Senate floor in May—especially since liberals could not, as in 1972, filibuster long enough to run out the clock before Congress adjourned for the November elections. With senators repeatedly citing Gallup polls reporting that more than 70 percent of Americans were opposed to busing, the Senate moved to a series of showdown votes.[90] As the main debate came to an end, liberals were dealt a stunning setback when, by a single vote,[91] the Senate refused to table an amendment for a total busing ban[92] offered by Michigan's (formerly liberal Republican) senator Robert Griffin.[93] Moving into panic mode, the majority and minority leaders, Mike Mansfield and Hugh Scott, modified Griffin's amendment to add provisos declaring that it was "not intended to modify or diminish the authority of the courts . . . to enforce fully the Fifth and Fourteenth amendments."[94] This last-minute defense of the judiciary won by a single vote—passing the problem on to the House-Senate conference committee, which somehow had to reconcile the House's hard anti-busing provision with the last-minute softening that had squeaked through the Senate.[95]

Civil rights advocates traditionally had an advantage at these conferences, since the delegations from each chamber were dominated by strong racial liberals with lots of seniority on their respective committees. During past sessions, conference members had used their advantage to water down extreme House proposals to the advantage of softer Senate measures. But this time around, liberals faced much greater resistance. As the conference proceeded over six long weeks, the full House passed three resolutions repeatedly instructing its delegation to reject any and all compromises on its hard-line assault on judicial independence.[96]

Nixon was adding to the pressure by threatening to veto any education bill that softened the House provisions.[97] While he had been gravely weakened by Watergate, he had recently selected House Speaker Gerald Ford to replace Spiro Agnew as vice president—and this vastly increased the credibility of his threat. Ford was from Michigan and had become a fierce opponent of busing as the Detroit controversy propelled the issue onto the national stage.[98] The Senate passed its measure on May 20, and the conference committee was soon consumed by "endless days and hours of debate" on the busing issue.[99]

During all this time, the Court was also struggling for closure on its Detroit busing case. The congressional conference committee and the Court resolved their disagreements almost simultaneously—the conference publishing its report on July 23, the Court handing down *Milliken v. Bradley* on July 25.[100]

The committee report was something of a surprise. While its new bill retained glancing references to the judiciary, the liberals had succeeded in deflecting the House's principal assault.[101] Though the bill retained each and every word of the House busing language, it added the Mansfield-Scott proviso declaring Congress's intention to "conform to the requirements of the Constitution."[102]

Yet this last-minute swerve was not nearly as surprising as the one announced in *Milliken* two days later.

The Court Retreats

With the anti-busing crusade reaching new heights on Capitol Hill, the Supreme Court was struggling with its second northern desegregation case. This came from Detroit, and differed from *Keyes* in one key respect: while two-thirds of Denver was white, two-thirds of Detroit was black. This meant that black-majority schools couldn't be eliminated by busing within city limits. So the district court included Detroit's overwhelmingly white suburbs within its decree, creating a plan in which the typical school was about 75 percent white and 25 percent black.[103] Remarkably enough, the court achieved this objective without requiring students to spend excessive time in school buses. To the contrary, the plan involved less busing time than those envisioning a city-only effort.[104] So it was both effective and efficient.

But if the Supreme Court upheld it, it would provoke a massive escalation of the current congressional assault on busing. The Justices would be asserting, in no uncertain terms, that whites could not escape integration by fleeing to the suburbs and protecting their neighborhood schools through local school boards.

Milliken was argued on February 27, 1974, just as the House was beginning debate on the education bill. When the Justices conferred on March 1, Chief Justice Burger won the support of a slim five-man majority to repudiate the metro busing strategy, but it took him three months to write a draft opinion explaining why. When he finally circulated his draft on May 31, it gained a cool reception from his conference supporters. This prompted the four dissenters, led by Thurgood Marshall, to urge their colleagues to postpone decision until the Supreme Court's next term. Given the high stakes, they said, a new round of argument and further reflection was required before defining the meaning of *Brown* for the next generation.[105]

Their suggestion gained a sympathetic hearing in Harry Blackmun's chambers. Blackmun had supported Burger at the conference. But he didn't like the Chief's draft opinion, and he asked his law clerk to clarify his options. The response: "[The case] touches almost every city in the country in a significant way. It is important therefore that the Court issue a single majority opinion that speaks for a majority of the Court. *Under normal circumstances it would seem advisable to hold this case over. The need to take this issue out of the political arena before the fall precludes this course I believe* and therefore I think it is important that the Chief's opinion be cleaned up" (emphasis added).[106]

As Blackmun was reading this memo, the House-Senate conference was beginning its six-week struggle over its anti-busing assault on the judiciary.[107] If the Court didn't preempt the threat, the House-Senate compromise would serve as a platform for another round of agitation during the November elections—opening the way for further escalation as an insecure new president, Gerald Ford, began searching for hot-button issues for his 1976 election campaign.[108] This is, at any rate, the logic behind the memo's conclusion that the "normal" need for further judicial deliberation should be trumped by the imperative "need to take this issue out of the political arena."

Blackmun was perfectly free, of course, to reject his clerk's appeal to realpolitik and insist on reargument. His views were decisive, since Burger could no longer write an "opinion of the Court" once Blackmun deprived him of the crucial fifth vote. But Blackmun didn't disagree. He joined in the hurried effort to "clean[] up" Burger's opinion—which underwent massive revisions in a series of drafts circulated on June 11, 21, and 22.

This rush to judgment was hardly conducive to a wide-ranging reconsideration of first principles. There was no inclination to interrogate Brennan's fateful decision, the year before in *Keyes*, to replace *Emporia*'s concern with real-world humiliation with a legalistic search for malign "intentions" by official decision makers. Since the Detroit school board had unquestionably used its discretion to concentrate blacks in ghetto schools, Burger's last-minute "opinion of the Court" simply followed *Keyes*— and silently supposed that massive busing was as appropriate in Detroit as it was in a southern city that had publicly humiliated blacks by shunting them all into separate schools.[109]

After accepting Brennan's master legalism, Burger tried to mitigate its political impact by adding more legalisms. While he endorsed systematic busing within Detroit, he stopped the enterprise at the city line, declaring that "[t]he constitutional right of the Negro respondents residing in Detroit is to attend a unitary school system *in that district.*"[110]

This was a jurisprudential shocker: the Fourteenth Amendment addresses each state and applies to *all* officials created by state law.[111] Under standard doctrine, the lowliest Detroit official is no different from the state's governor. If either discriminates intentionally, it is the state of Michigan that has violated the constitution. But Burger's opinion carved out an exception, insisting that Michigan's suburban officials could not be implicated in Detroit's problem so long as their intentions were innocent. While this distinction between "Michigan" and "Detroit" was a big surprise, Burger had five votes, and that was that.

He then propped up this doctrinal monstrosity with yet another legalism: "the nature of the violation determines the scope of the remedy."[112] Since only the Detroit school board had the requisite bad intentions, it followed—according to Burger—that traditional principles of equity limited relief to the Detroit school system, even though the district court had found that a metro-area remedy was the only way to provide effective relief.

These and other legalisms were persuasively contested by the four dissenters. No less important, the anti-humiliation principle made a belated return in their opinions[113]—most poignantly in the dissent penned by Thurgood Marshall:

Under a Detroit-only decree, Detroit's schools will clearly remain racially identifiable in comparison with neighboring schools in the metropolitan community. Schools with 65% and more Negro students will stand in *sharp and obvious* contrast to schools in neighboring districts with less than 2% Negro enrollment. Negro students will *continue to perceive* their schools as segregated educational facilities and *this perception* will only be increased when whites react to a Detroit-only decree by fleeing to the suburbs to avoid integration. School district lines, however innocently drawn, *will surely be perceived* as fences to separate the races when, under a Detroit-only decree, white parents withdraw their children from the Detroit city schools and move to the suburbs in order to continue them in all-white schools. *The message of this action will not escape the Negro children in the city of Detroit.* See Wright v. City of Emporia, 407 U.S., at 466. *It will be of scant significance to Negro children who have for years been confined by de jure acts of segregation to a growing core of all-Negro schools surrounded by a ring of all-white schools that the new dividing line between the races is the school district boundary.*[114] (Emphasis added)

In other circumstances, Marshall's citation to *Emporia* would have been utterly unremarkable—after all, it was only two years earlier that all nine Justices had joined in its ringing reaffirmation of *Brown*'s sociological jurisprudence. But now that Burger was barreling down the legalistic trail first blazed by Brennan, Marshall's appeal to *Emporia* represented a last-ditch call to reconsider the path not taken. In his view, the Court's emphasis on official intentions at the expense of social meaning "make[s] a solemn mockery of *Brown I*'s holding that separate educational facilities are inherently unequal."[115]

We can now glimpse the significance of the Court's politically motivated rush to judgment. If the Justices had deferred decision until the following term, they could have tried to do more than "clean up" Burger's draft. They could have taken the time to confront Marshall's call to return to the path marked out by Warren's opinion in *Brown*.

Under this scenario, Marshall's certainty that school district lines would "*surely* be perceived as fences" would serve as the start of a longer conversation with his colleagues. As in *Emporia,* Burger and his fellow conservatives could have offered up a very different interpretation of the social meaning of existing practices. Under their view, Marshall's poetic metaphor of the fence should be trumped by the raging dispute among social scientists about the impact of black-majority northern schools on student self-worth. In contrast to the apartheid systems of the South, it simply wasn't obvious that black-majority schools inexorably led to systematic humiliation. It was therefore open for the conservatives to insist that the spirit of *Brown* would best be served by remanding the case to the district court for a contextual investigation of whether and how the prevailing pattern of racial concentrations humiliated minority students. Only then would the court be in a position to define the role, if any, that busing might play in eliminating "feelings of inferiority" in black children.

After all, this was precisely the kind of argument that Burger had made in *Emporia*. Dissenting on behalf of four Justices, he had insisted that the Court should rely on "common human experience," especially when "reinforced by psychological authority," to assess the constitutionality of educational practices. The only difference between 1972 and 1974 was that Justice Stewart was now prepared to join the four dissenters and create a new majority for restraining busing. Yet it was Stewart who had written the majority opinion in *Emporia*. He would have had no difficulty in embedding its principles into constitutional bedrock for the next generation.

We are now in a position to appreciate the fateful significance of *Keyes*'s turn away from *Emporia*. If Brennan had followed *Emporia*'s path, the forces of doctrinal inertia would have propelled the *Milliken* majority in a very different direction. The starting point would have been Justice Stewart's rejection of inquiries into the motives of multimember bodies as "irrelevant" and "fruitless." Indeed, it is very likely that the *Milliken* majority would have returned to *Emporia* if it had heeded Justice Marshall's call for a new round of argument and deliberation on the Detroit case.

But the Court simply couldn't afford this luxury, given its imperative need to remove the issue from the political field.[116] As a consequence, the Burger majority transformed *Keyes*'s provisional embrace of intentionalism into a rigid formula that erased the spirit of *Brown* in the sphere of education, and replaced it with a toxic combination of ad hoc legalisms and government by numbers. The legalisms artificially confined the scope of the problem to center-city schools. Government by numbers focused attention on the ratio of blacks and whites in each city school, thereby making white flight to the suburbs legally irrelevant to the fate of urban systems that were increasingly dominated by blacks and other minorities.

Tragic.

THE MEANING OF *MILLIKEN*

Milliken is rightly recognized as a decisive turning point in American public education.[117] But its genesis has been misunderstood. The standard account puts full responsibility on Richard Nixon. Just do the math: the four Nixonian Justices, plus Potter Stewart, outvoted the four Warren Court holdovers. Nothing could be simpler: the Burger Court was simply following Nixon's lead in retreating from its all-out commitment to desegregation.

This story doesn't fit the facts. Led by its new Chief Justice, the Court refused to follow Richard Nixon's lead in *Alexander* and *Swann*. Instead, it boxed him into a position that led him to join the Court in finally forcing the South to accept *Brown* as the law of the land. The Court rejected Nixon again when *Keyes* endorsed an aggressive busing campaign in the North, with Stewart joining Brennan's opinion, and Burger concurring in the result. It pushed onward despite Congress's threat to join Nixon in an all-out assault on its judicial independence. Paradoxically, the Court retreated just as Nixon was leaving the White House in disgrace—but at a time when Senate liberals were no longer in a position to sustain a filibuster against further legislative assaults. Within this setting, the Court's switch in *Milliken* is better understood as an act of judicial statesmanship in the light of popular mobilization against its strong commitment to integration. The decision prevented an escalating confrontation with the political branches that might well have permanently damaged the Court's claim to judicial independence.

Consider the alternative, in which the *Milliken* majority had resolutely endorsed busing for the entire metropolitan area. On this scenario, Americans would have witnessed a constitutional drama that last had been on display in 1964. Just as Kennedy's assassination placed a burden on Lyndon Johnson to establish that he was more than an accidental president, Nixon's resignation put Gerald Ford in an identical position. In contrast to Johnson, he would not have made his mark by advancing a civil rights agenda that went far beyond the Warren Court. He would have tried to dominate the constitutional stage by calling on Congress to renew its attack on the Burger Court—first through a landmark statute, and if that failed to curb the Justices, then through a constitutional amendment.

Ford's campaign would have struck a chord throughout the country as grassroots movements in both the North and the South ratcheted up their already impassioned campaigns to defend neighborhood schools against integration across entire metropolitan areas. Nor would whites have been alone in mobilizing against the Court. Black public opinion was also deeply divided, and as black politicians gained power in center cities, they were often reluctant to cede control over their educational systems to courts and regional bodies. Even integrationist strongholds such as the NAACP were confronting challenges within its ranks.[118]

Within this setting, it is too quick to attribute *Milliken*'s retreat to Richard Nixon's success in packing the Court. To the contrary: if the Court had pushed in *Milliken,* it would have succeeded only in generating an even more powerful popular movement against judicial supremacy during the Ford years.

Taking the longer view, the Burger Court's problem was similar to the predicament facing the Hughes Court during the early New Deal. Both were confronting an escalating assault from the president and Congress. Both had to decide when, whether, and how to organize a retreat before sustained popular demands for a constitutional change overwhelmed its claim to authority.

There were differences, of course. First, in the early 1930s, the Hughes Court was trying to preserve traditional doctrine, and the president and Congress were the radical reformers; in the early 1970s, it was the Court leading the effort at revolutionary reform, and the president and Congress were defending tradition.

Second, during the New Deal, Roosevelt and his Congress were transforming constitutional understandings across a very broad front; during the Nixon years, the Court was seeking to transform long-standing practices in an important but circumscribed sphere. While Congress and the president were resisting aggressive busing, they were consolidating the landmark statutes of the 1960s in the spheres of voting and employment. Even in education, Nixon and Congress accepted busing as a tool to erase the public identification of "black" and "white" schools in the Jim Crow South. Opposition became overwhelming only when the courts expanded their campaign to northern schools that did not *publicly* stigmatize blacks.

This backlash might not have been contained if the Court had pushed onward in *Milliken.* At some point President Ford or his successor might have launched a broader assault on the statutory foundations of the Second Reconstruction. But *Milliken*'s switch in time preempted this possibility. While court-ordered busing remained a hot political issue, it never again catalyzed a frontal assault against the Court on the scale of 1972 and 1974. The potential danger, however, was acknowledged by Justice Marshall in the concluding lines of his powerful *Milliken* dissent: "Today's holding, I fear, is more a reflection of a perceived public mood that we have gone far enough in enforcing the Constitution's guarantee of equal justice than it is the product of neutral principles of law. In the short run, it may seem to be the easier course to allow our great metropolitan areas to be divided up each into two cities—one white, the other black—but it is a course, I predict, our people will ultimately regret. I dissent."[119]

I share Marshall's regret, but differ in my diagnosis. *Milliken*'s switch was the result of a self-inflicted wound: if the Court had remained true to *Brown*'s originating concerns with the "hearts and minds" of black children, it would have been in a much better position to weather the gathering storm. Under this alternative scenario, *Keyes* and *Milliken* would have followed up on *Emporia*'s recognition that, despite good intentions, northern school systems might still impose concrete patterns that humiliated black children, leading them to give up on their educations. The challenge, under this approach, was for district courts throughout the north to identify these stigmatizing practices, which would vary across different schools and school systems. Only then would they be in a position to tailor solutions to fit the facts of their particular case. Some busing might well ameliorate some problems, but judges would primarily understand themselves as prodding school officials to engage in a serious and sustained process of institutional experiment and reform that would yield measurable improvements in minority student performance over the long haul.

Just like the Warren Court of the 1950s, the Burger Court would have moved cautiously—with "deliberate speed"—to advance its anti-humiliation agenda in the 1970s, and for even more compelling reasons. The destruction of a Jim Crow system was a necessary, if not sufficient, step in uprooting institutionalized humiliation in the South. But it wasn't nearly so obvious how to deal with the northern pathologies that stigmatized blacks in less visible ways.[120] Consider, for example, the "school-to-prison pipeline": under this all too common scenario, school authorities treat relatively minor black student misbehavior with extreme measures, humiliating children in ways that can propel them further down the road to criminality.[121] This isn't a problem that can be fixed by the transfer of black students to whiter schools. But it *is* a pathology that goes to the core of *Brown*'s concerns—and courts could be effective only by engaging educators and school boards in a long-term institutional dialogue.

The parallel to the "deliberate speed" of the 1950s runs deeper. Warren's original opinion made an enormous contribution in putting the race question at the center of constitutional debate, though it was not nearly enough to win southern compliance. By allowing the district courts to move slowly, *Brown* II gave space for the national political leadership and the civil rights movement to engage in the enormous amount of political work required to pass a Civil Rights Act that finally provided Johnson and Nixon with the tools they needed to break the back of southern resistance.

As we have seen, legalists sometimes criticize the Warren Court for its slow pace during the 1950s. On this account, "deliberate speed" just gave the South time for endless foot-dragging, while "integration now" would have yielded southern compliance. This is sheer fantasy. *Brown* I generated an enormous backlash in the South, and it would take a decade before national politics could reorganize itself to generate a sustained response. It was one thing for Eisenhower to stand firm at Little Rock, but would he have persevered if there had been a chain reaction of such explosions provoked by a series of court orders insisting on immediate desegregation?

As the Burger Court looked northward, it was confronting an even greater political challenge. By the end of the Nixon administration, the American people were plainly disengaging from the intense struggle for black civil rights that had yielded such great breakthroughs in the 1960s: the issue was returning to the realm of normal politics, where civil rights advocates no longer could credibly claim that the mobilized majority of ordinary Americans were on their side.

It is beyond the power of any Court to prevent the inexorable decline of constitutional mobilization by ordinary Americans. As with *Brown* I and II, the most it could do was to keep the education question on the constitutional agenda for the next generation, pushing social movements and politicians to take the problem with high seriousness.

Constitutional moments come to an end. No great popular movement lasts forever—the people will inexorably return to more private concerns, and other public matters will begin to demand more exigent attention. This is not to say that further progress in race relations was impossible. The memory of the civil rights triumph profoundly shaped the politics of the next generation. Advocates could still win victories—and suffer defeats— through the more ordinary give-and-take of American law and politics. Perhaps a time would come when the Court's persistent focus on concrete patterns of institutional humiliation would catalyze a broad mobilization for a Third Reconstruction to complete the unfinished business of achieving racial justice in America.

But if such a time did arrive, it would take another generational effort. Liberals such as Brennan and Marshall had a hard time confronting this truth. They had been presiding over one of the greatest constitutional moments in American history, one in which the Court had played an unprecedented leadership role. It was tempting for the Justices to suppose that their moment of triumph would go on and on, and that they could continue to count on the grudging support of Congress and the president to their continuing constitutional leadership.

Given this premise, it may have made short-term sense for Brennan to cobble together a majority for citywide busing in *Keyes* even if this meant a turn away from *Brown*. After all, he assured us, this swerve was made only for the "purposes of this case": once the northern campaign was fairly under way, it would be time enough to return to the high road marked out by *Emporia*.

It only took a year for the political branches to explode these happy dreams—leaving us with the worst of both worlds. Many northern cities would escape judicial scrutiny entirely when litigators could find no evidence of bad intentions, even though their school systems systematically humiliated ghetto schoolchildren.

Worse yet, when courts could identify institutional wrongdoers, they often found themselves in situations like that of Detroit, where it was impossible to desegregate the schools because most whites had escaped to the suburbs. The result was a counterproductive form of government by numbers, equalizing black-white ratios without engaging school boards in the long-run effort required to attack entrenched patterns of humiliation prevailing in largely black schools.[122]

All this is ancient history. My aim is not to relitigate the past but to encourage the future to gain a deeper perspective on *Milliken*'s precipitous switch in time. We should recognize *Keyes*'s swerve away from *Brown* as a tragic mistake. Instead of endlessly repeating its intentionalist understanding of de jure discrimination, we should return to the deeper wisdom of *Emporia* and its unanimous reaffirmation of Warren's vision in *Brown* as an organizing principle of the Second Reconstruction.

CHAPTER 13

Spheres of Intimacy

THE COURT'S CONFRONTATION with public education was particularly complex, but its challenges were rooted in two fundamental factors. On one hand, the Justices' leadership in desegregating schools had been ratified by popular consent, as expressed by the Civil Rights Act of 1964. On the other, the Court could not redeem *Brown* in the real world without overcoming powerful resistance by state and local governments. If the Court was to succeed, then, it had to fulfill two conditions: first, convince presidents to use the new tools provided by the Civil Rights Act to overcome institutional resistance; second, convince the American people to stand by the commitments made in 1964.

Easier said than done. While the Court did manage to meet these conditions in the South, it could succeed in the North only by scaling back the ambitions of its busing program in *Milliken*. Given the escalating risks of statutory and popular repudiation, I do not challenge the wisdom of this switch in time. But I do mourn *Milliken*'s abandonment of Warren's great opinion as it beat a hasty retreat. The Justices could have sustained *Brown*'s anti-humiliation principle by proceeding with "deliberate speed"—cutting back on busing to focus more of its attention on the concrete practices that stigmatized minority children in ghetto schools. Yet the contingencies of litigation, and the need for rapid action, led it to stumble down a different path, one that emphasized the presence or absence of bad government intentions, not the humiliations suffered by ghetto children, as the decisive factor in limiting its northern busing campaign. This stumble, I suggest, should not blind us to the enduring significance of *Emporia*'s emphatic reaffirmation of Warren's opinion.

I will come to a similar conclusion, but from a different perspective, in assessing the Court's performance in revolutionizing the law of interracial marriage and sexual intimacy. When the Court finally struck down all miscegenation bans in 1967, its opinion in *Loving v. Virginia,* like *Milliken,* shifted legal attention away from the evil of institutionalized humiliation—in this case, the day-to-day humiliations suffered by interracial couples deprived of the right to marry. But *Loving*'s retreat from *Brown* was generated by a different institutional dynamic: *Loving*'s legalisms represent an ingenious solution to the problem of *leadership by default.*

My key point: Throughout the entire civil rights revolution, the president and Congress were completely unwilling to pass a federal statute banning state anti-miscegenation laws. If anybody was going to sweep these barriers away, it would be the Court. But the Justices were also very reluctant to intervene, fearing that a frontal attack on deeply entrenched taboos might generate backlash that would endanger their entire enterprise.

This became clear when a case challenging interracial marriage came to the Justices shortly after *Brown.* Virginia's Supreme Court had refused to apply *Brown* to condemn the state's marriage ban. But the Court declined to reverse, despite the compelling character of the appellants' case. Though leading legalists such as Herbert Wechsler condemned its action, Justice Felix Frankfurter convinced his colleagues to avoid the hailstorm of popular protest that would follow upon invalidation. At this vulnerable moment, the Court refused to do anything that would further endanger its efforts to desegregate southern schools at "deliberate speed."

The Justices continued to evade the issue until Congress passed the Civil Rights Act in 1964. In the great debate on this landmark statute, the miscegenation question never got serious consideration—it was hard enough to hammer out a settlement on issues such as public accommodations, education, and employment without throwing this hot-button issue into the mix.

Nevertheless, the Justices thought that the time was right to make a cautious entry into this area with *McLaughlin v. Florida.* Even then, the Court contented itself with a narrow opinion, waiting until 1967 to strike down interracial marriage bans in *Loving v. Virginia.* By this point, the landmark statutes of 1964 and 1965 were already generating real-world transformations on many other fronts, and it now seemed safer to enter into dangerous territory.

Once the time was ripe, the Justices could take advantage of a special feature of their problem to push ahead to a successful conclusion. In contrast to public education, the Court did not face a serious problem of institutional resistance: while some religious ministers and public authorities might refuse to participate in interracial marriages, it would be relatively easy to find others to fill this gap. So if the Court did decide to defy the intermarriage taboo, real-world results would follow.

Only one significant danger remained. While interracial couples might gain relief, the Court's decision might well inflame southern resistance to school desegregation, which was still very formidable in 1967. In writing his opinion for the Court, Earl Warren took steps to minimize this danger by avoiding an excessive reliance on *Brown*. Rather than basing his judgment squarely on school desegregation precedents, he reached back a quarter century to the Court's decisions upholding the detention of Japanese Americans during World War II and made those into foundational precedents for *Loving*.

Warren's choice might seem surprising at first. If you are writing an opinion that will sweep away the countless humiliations suffered by interracial couples barred from marriage, why resurrect wartime decisions that *upheld* the countless humiliations suffered by Japanese Americans in the detention camps?

The answer lies in the rhetorical gestures invoked by the wartime Court. Before reaching their notorious conclusions, the Justices took pains to emphasize that racial categories were "inherently suspect" and that they were upholding the detentions only because they were supported by an "overriding" interest in national security. These dicta provided Warren with the opening he needed to strike down Virginia's racial ban without emphasizing *Brown*. He explained that no similarly "overriding" interest was in play when it came to the ban on interracial marriage; to the contrary, it was "designed to maintain White Supremacy," and so was incompatible with the Equal Protection Clause.

By reframing the issue in terms inherited from the Second World War, Warren was deflecting the Court's underlying legitimation problem in a masterly way. No, he explained, the Court was *not* carrying on the civil rights revolution beyond the scope of the concerns endorsed by We the People. It was simply applying the law elaborated by We the Judges in resolving hard cases raised by the wartime struggle that had engaged *all* patriotic Americans, northerners and southerners alike. In enlisting wartime doctrine in the service of equal rights, Warren was remarkably successful in gaining acceptance for the Court's decision. Despite the continuing pervasive prejudice against interracial marriage, there was remarkably little opposition to *Loving*.

Warren's success in solving his legitimation dilemma came at a price. It shifted doctrinal attention away from *Brown*'s focus on the real-world humiliations of interracial couples to *Loving*'s focus on the suspect purposes of the legislators who imposed the marriage bans. While this might have seemed a worthwhile trade at the time, the shift from *Brown* to *Loving* has taken on more portentous meaning over succeeding decades. *Loving* is no longer understood as a virtuoso display of Warren Court leadership as it moved beyond the spheres of popular concern marked out by the landmark statutes. Instead, it threatens to displace *Brown* as the paradigmatic opinion of the civil rights era.

We return, at last, to the puzzle with which our doctrinal investigations began: while today's lawyers continue to recognize *Brown* as the greatest decision of the twentieth century, they fail to take Warren's words seriously as they reflect on the constitutional meaning of equality. This chapter gets to the roots of the problem by considering how *Loving* became *Brown*'s doctrinal competitor in the 1960s. In telling this story, I don't wish to minimize the importance of the Court's campaign against antimiscegenation laws. But I do deny that *Loving* deserves a central place in the civil rights canon. It simply represents an effort by We the Judges to fill in a gap left in the wake of an epochal set of decisions by We the People. We should view *Loving* as a supplement to, not a substitute for, the principles elaborated in *Brown, Emporia,* and the landmark statutes.

My "supplementation thesis" is best elaborated by following the winding path traveled by the Supreme Court as it readied itself to confront the widespread taboo against interracial marriage. This blow-by-blow account sets the stage for a deeper historical understanding of the Court's very recent decision in *United States v. Windsor,* striking down the Defense of Marriage Act. In requiring the federal government to recognize the legitimacy of same-sex marriages, Justice Kennedy's opinion for the Court provides a striking confirmation of my supplementation thesis. He treats *Loving*'s concern with suspect legislative purposes as a secondary issue, emphasizing instead the evils of institutionalized humiliation in vindicating the claims of same-sex couples. By making this breakthrough, Kennedy is inviting a new generation to restore the original understanding of *Brown* to its central place in the civil rights legacy.

From Deliberate Speed to Deliberate Evasion

Bans on mixed marriage were far more pervasive than other forms of legal discrimination. During the late 1940s, thirty states prohibited intermarriage, many barring white unions with Asians and Native Americans as well as blacks.[1] We are not dealing with a southern anomaly. The statutes expressed a nationwide taboo, with the Northeast and Midwest serving as exceptions to the racist rule.

The judiciary showed no inclination to challenge these bans. State supreme courts in Arizona, Colorado, Nebraska, Montana, and Oregon had recently affirmed their constitutionality, joining their brethren from more predictable places.[2] The legal foundation had been laid in the 1880s by the Supreme Court in *Pace v. Alabama,* where Justice Stephen Field upheld anti-miscegenation laws so long as the "punishment of each offending person, whether white or black, is the same."[3] *Pace* was unanimous—even John Marshall Harlan, who famously dissented in the Civil Rights Cases and *Plessy,* joined in the view that the Reconstruction Amendments did not extend to the sphere of sexual intimacy.

The judicial consensus was deeply rooted in popular sentiment. In his classic *American Dilemma,* Gunnar Myrdal moved beyond general reflections on prejudice to identify those racial bans that were of the greatest importance to blacks and whites. His extensive interviews with whites indicated that they overwhelmingly put their highest priority on maintaining "the bar against intermarriage and sexual intercourse involving white women," and that the second biggest menace was posed by interracial "dancing, bathing, eating, drinking." In contrast to this hard-line defense of racial purity, whites offered less resistance to concessions in more public spheres such as public education or politics. They were most open to black advances in gaining "jobs, or other means of earning a living."[4]

Black priorities were similar: jobs were number one, followed by advances in strategic spheres such as education and voting that could transform their economic and political situation. In contrast, they had a "distant and doubtful interest" in supporting intermarriage.[5]

Myrdal published in 1942, but the miscegenation taboo maintained its grip for a very long time. Throughout the 1950s, more than 90 percent of *non*-southern whites opposed interracial marriage, while it remained highly controversial among blacks.[6] Within this setting, the NAACP had better things to do with its time than launch a public attack on anti-miscegenation laws. While it gave quiet support to groups including the American Bar Association as they worked to repeal restrictive state laws in the late 1950s, it maintained a public silence on the marriage question.[7]

The NAACP Legal Defense Fund also refused to support test-case litigation: either lawsuits would fail and create bad precedents or they would succeed and heighten white resistance on issues of greater importance to the black community.[8] But the Legal Defense Fund couldn't prevent other public interest groups from taking up the slack. Most notably, the agenda of the American Civil Liberties Union (ACLU) emphasized individual rights, and it found the claims of interracial couples too compelling to ignore. Together with the Japanese American Citizens League, the ACLU scored its first victory in 1948, convincing the California Supreme Court to strike down its statute in *Perez v. Sharp*.[9] With the Legal Defense Fund firmly on the sidelines, the ACLU then spearheaded further litigation in the hope of bringing the matter before the Supreme Court.[10]

The result was *Naim v. Naim*, which reached Virginia's highest court in the immediate aftermath of *Brown*. Despite the vigorous advocacy of the ACLU, the court refused to extend Warren's logic to interracial marriage, insisting that the *Pace* decision of 1883 remained good law.[11] Its unanimous opinion declared that nothing "in the Fourteenth Amendment . . . denies the power of the State to regulate the marriage relation so that it shall not have a mongrel breed of citizens."[12]

The challenge raised by the state court's decision was plain. Throughout the South, opponents were denouncing *Brown* as the opening move in a liberal effort to "mongrelize" the white race.[13] Once boys and girls got to know each other in school, interracial sex and marriage were sure to follow. Was the Warren Court prepared to confirm these anxieties by squarely repudiating *Naim*'s proud declaration that "the preservation of racial integrity is the unquestioned policy of this State"?[14]

Normally the Justices can evade such politically explosive encounters by refusing to hear a particular dispute—which is precisely what they did in a similar case coming from Alabama.[15] But the ACLU closed off this escape hatch by framing its case in a way that put the Court under a statutory obligation to reach the merits.[16] To strengthen its position further, it reached out to potential allies to join in its appeal.

Only to encounter its first reality check. Its lawyers learned through the grapevine that Thurgood Marshall "was extremely unhappy about *Naim*," fearing its impact on school desegregation. The ACLU also got nowhere in its efforts to gain the support of the Justice Department, for the same reason.[17] But the law is the law, and like it or not, the Court couldn't evade its moment of truth.

Or could it? Justice Frankfurter took the lead in urging his colleagues to avoid a decision that would propel miscegenation into "the vortex of the present disquietude" and "very seriously . . . embarrass the carrying-out of the Court's decree of last May."[18] Frankfurter was referring to the Justices' recent decision in *Brown* II, which had endorsed a go-slow approach to desegregation. His fear was obvious: repudiating *Naim* would provoke such an uproar that "deliberate speed" would go nowhere at all. On his view, this large point should overcome the "technical" arguments for deciding *Naim* on the merits.[19]

Warren was "furious" at Frankfurter's maneuver, but the only other Justice he managed to enlist to his cause was Black.[20] On November 11, 1955, the Court issued a brief opinion sending the case back to the trial court for further clarification of the issues.[21]

The Virginia Supreme Court responded with outright defiance: it unanimously declared that the record was already clear enough to condemn the Naims' marriage, and refused to order the trial court to conduct further proceedings.[22] Within two months, the ACLU was back in Washington, D.C., insisting that the Court preserve the integrity of its mandate. But to no avail: the Court waved the white flag of surrender on March 12, 1956, dropping *Naim* permanently from its docket.[23]

In his Holmes Lectures of 1959, Herbert Wechsler condemned this cave-in as "wholly without basis in the law" and suggestive of a deeper incoherence in *Brown* itself.[24] His attack on Warren's decision as unprincipled generated one of the great debates of the twentieth century, with leading scholars trying to rewrite *Brown* in response to his critique.[25]

For present purposes, it's more important to emphasize that the Legal Defense Fund didn't join in this chorus. Instead, the Fund's Jack Greenberg restated its long-standing resistance to litigating the status of anti-miscegenation laws. He defended the Court's decision to avoid this "inflammatory subject" when "strident opposition was being voiced to less controversial desegregation" measures on the ground that they "allegedly lead[] to intermarriage."[26]

Greenberg's position anticipated the anti-Wechslerian themes voiced by Alexander Bickel three years later in his *Least Dangerous Branch*.[27] In this classic text, Bickel elaborated a vision of the Court as an engaged participant in a constitutional dialogue with the political branches and, ultimately, the American people. From this vantage, the Supreme Court was quite right to recognize that *Brown* was fighting for its very survival in 1956—and that it would take many years before the American people, acting through the political branches, could determine its fate. Rather than pretending otherwise, the Justices were wise to defer further brave pronouncements on *Brown*'s true meaning until the people had their say about the Court's first great intervention within the sphere of public education.

Since the 1960s, the scholarly struggle between Bickelians and Wechslerians has continued to the present day—and it won't be resolved anytime soon. Yet this great debate shouldn't blind us to the fact that the Bickelian vision won the day in *Naim,* with Felix Frankfurter triumphing over the legalistic insistence of Warren and Black by a vote of 7 to 2. What is more, the Justices sat resolutely on the sidelines while the legal academy loudly debated Wechsler's critique.[28] It was the dynamics of constitutional politics, not the controversies of constitutional lawyers, that finally brought an end to their decade-long silence.

THE CURIOUS CONSERVATISM OF THE WARREN COURT

On June 15, 1964, the Justices finally took a case raising the miscegenation question—just when Congress was passing the Civil Rights Act.[29] By the time it handed down *McLaughlin v. Florida* in December, Congress's ringing endorsement of *Brown* had been reaffirmed by Johnson's landslide victory.[30] Nevertheless, the Court handled the issues with extreme caution—taking such a small step that it had to return three years later to issue a sweeping condemnation of racist marriage laws in *Loving v. Virginia.* Even then, *Loving* adopted a very conservative doctrinal approach to the problem.

The Court's legalistic caution may seem puzzling. After all, the period between 1964's *McLaughlin* and 1967's *Loving* was a moment of great constitutional creativity in other spheres—recall *Harper*'s remarkable constitutional assault on poll taxes, for example.[31] Why the difference here?

Because the Court was operating against a very different institutional background. In cases such as *Harper,* it was presenting transformative interpretations of the Fourteenth Amendment in response to the express invitation of Congress, in the Voting Rights Act, to rethink basic principles.

In *McLaughlin* and *Loving,* by contrast, the Court wasn't elaborating on a decision made by We the People; it was *supplementing* these decisions by entering a sphere that remained too hot for the political branches to handle.

Before confronting the larger issues raised by this "supplementation thesis" it's best to follow the Justices, step by step, as they proceeded to repudiate *Naim* with all deliberate speed.

———◆———

Although it didn't command attention in Congress, the anti-miscegenation laws were gaining serious scrutiny elsewhere. Outside the South, legislatures were repealing their statutes, leading to a decline in the number of anti-miscegenation states from thirty in 1947 to seventeen in 1965.[32] These repeals tended to be low-visibility affairs, with bar associations and other law reform groups arguing that the statutes were no longer seriously enforced. But by the end of the 1950s, local NAACP chapters were joining civil liberties groups in the repeal effort.[33] The early sixties saw Roy Wilkins, executive director of the national organization, publicly denouncing anti-miscegenation laws.[34] Nevertheless, the issue remained on the periphery of the national agenda. When Americans were asked in December 1963 to identify "the main things . . . American Negroes are really trying to get" by engaging "the Civil Rights Movement," they emphasized equality in the workplace, education, public accommodations, and housing. Only 4 percent mentioned intermarriage.[35]

But the movement did not make a serious effort to change these public perceptions. Instead, the Legal Defense Fund threw its support behind the effort to convince the Supreme Court to strike down these prohibitions on its own authority. By the time *McLaughlin v. Florida* reached the Court in 1964, the Fund had fielded an all-star team led by William Coleman, an outstanding advocate, and Louis Pollak, dean of the Yale Law School. But alas, Pollak stumbled at oral argument in dealing with a difficulty in the case. His clients, Connie Hoffman and Dewey McLaughlin, had been convicted for interracial cohabitation, not interracial marriage. They were in fact married, but they were afraid to submit their marriage certificate at trial for a very simple reason: the penalty for interracial marriage was ten years in jail, while the penalty for cohabitation was "only" one year. As a consequence, it was safer for them to bring the marriage issue up indirectly, by arguing that they should be at least entitled to the status of common-law marriage that Florida extended to racially pure couples.

But Pollak failed to explain this point clearly when Earl Warren asked whether the couple was in fact married[36]—leaving an opening for Florida's assistant attorney general, James Mahorner, to tell the court that there "was much evidence which indicates that the defendants were not married . . . [and] not one iota of evidence that these parties were married to each other."[37]

When they retired to discuss the matter at their conference, Warren insisted that the absence of the marriage certificate was irrelevant: "I can't see any justification for denying common law marriage to those of different races and granting it to others."[38] But even Justice Douglas—not known for judicial restraint—disagreed, urging his colleagues to "dismiss [the case] as improvidently granted, because no marriage was involved and I thought there was when I voted to grant."[39] Black and Clark joined Douglas, but the majority finally settled on a compromise. They kept the case, but refrained from grand statements condemning interracial marriage.

Writing for the Court, Justice White focused his attention on *Pace v. Alabama,* which had upheld a similar cohabitation law in 1883. His opinion managed to overrule *Pace,* but at the price of rewriting the history of equal protection law:

> [W]e deal here with a classification based upon the race of the participants, which must be viewed in light of the historical fact that the central purpose of the Fourteenth Amendment was to eliminate racial discrimination emanating from official sources in the States. This strong policy renders racial classifications "constitutionally suspect," *Bolling* v. *Sharpe,* 347 U.S. 497, 499; and subject to the "most rigid scrutiny," *Korematsu* v. *United States,* 323 U.S. 214, 216; and "in most circumstances irrelevant" to any constitutionally acceptable legislative purpose, *Hirabayashi* v. *United States,* 320 U.S. 81, 100. Thus it is that racial classifications have been held invalid in a variety of contexts. See, [among other cases], *Brown* v. *Board of Education,* 349 U.S. 294 (segregation in public schools).[40]

White denies *Brown* a central place in the modern story. He merely places it on a list of precedents invalidating racial classifications "in a variety of contexts." While *Brown*'s companion case, *Bolling v. Sharpe,* is given greater prominence, *McLaughlin* gives pride of place to the Court's decisions dealing with the disgraceful treatment of Japanese Americans during World War II.

White finds inspiration in *Korematsu*'s insistence that racial classifications should trigger the "most rigid scrutiny," as well as *Hirabayashi*'s warning that "in most circumstances" this scrutiny will reveal that race-based categories are "irrelevant to any constitutionally acceptable legislative purpose." These brave words were belied by the Court's behavior: *Korematsu* upheld the mass detention of Japanese Americans during World War II, and *Hirabayashi* supported their conviction for violating a racially targeted military curfew. In giving these cases a central place, *McLaughlin* is emphasizing the vast gap that can separate the law on the books from the law in life. Little wonder that his opinion utterly fails to recognize the systematic humiliations imposed on racially mixed couples living under threat of criminal prosecution. Instead of emphasizing its stigmatizing impact on hearts and minds, White finds the Virginia law unconstitutional only because its racial categorizations fail the *Korematsu-Hirabayashi* test.

One obstacle remained: White had to explain why a unanimous Court was wrong in reaching just the opposite conclusion in 1883 when *Pace* denied that a similar law violated equal protection since the "punishment of each offending person, whether white or black, is the same."[41] *Brown* dealt with a similar problem raised in *Plessy* by moving beyond nineteenth-century constitutional understandings to confront the modern realities of social stigma. But *McLaughlin* takes a very different path. White bases his decision on "the historical fact" that the Fourteenth Amendment's "central purpose" was "to eliminate racial discrimination emanating from official sources in the States."[42] Why, then, did this "historical fact" elude all nine Justices of the Supreme Court in 1883?

White doesn't try to answer. There is no effort to confront the reluctance of the first Reconstruction to extend constitutional protection beyond "political" and "civil" rights to "social" spheres such as marriage. *McLaughlin* represents "lawyer's history" at its worst.

To summarize: White offers up a cartoon version of Reconstruction, together with dicta from the Japanese detention cases, as a suitable alternative to *Brown*'s real-world understanding of the meaning of equal protection.[43] What to make of this remarkable turn away from the sociological jurisprudence of the Second Reconstruction?

Such questions typically provoke abstract doctrinal debates between critics and defenders of the doctrine of "suspect classification." But my argument is concrete, not abstract, emphasizing the Court's distinctive predicament in moving into a sphere that was at the very core of white resistance to the civil rights revolution. By this point, popular opposition to intermarriage was softening—at least so far as criminalization was concerned. Gallup was reporting that 72 percent of southern whites continued to support state sanctions, but that northern whites had switched to opposition by a margin of 52 percent to 42 percent. There was still a nationwide majority of 48 percent to 46 percent in favor of these laws, even after nonwhites were included in the sample.[44] But Gallup was an uncertain guide on such sensitive questions, and the Court had every reason to tread carefully—especially since it was then particularly concerned with the threat of bitter-end southern resistance to the Civil Rights Act. Given the circumstances, it was only prudent to disarm critics by writing an opinion that disclaimed any special reliance on opinions, such as *Brown,* that were associated with "judicial activism."[45]

McLaughlin's embrace of prudential legalism was by no means exceptional. One week later, *Heart of Atlanta Motel* took a similar approach to the recently enacted Civil Rights Act. If the Court had upheld this landmark statute on equal protection grounds, its opinion would have broken decisively with traditional understandings that placed social rights beyond the scope of the Fourteenth Amendment. (Recall my alternative version of the Civil Rights Cases of 1964.)[46] But once again, it turned away from the anti-humiliation principles proclaimed by *Brown,* and reaffirmed by Hubert Humphrey and many others when passing the act, to adopt a less controversial rationale inherited from the Roosevelt era.

This time, the Court relied on its famous decisions of the early 1940s elaborating the New Deal vision of the Commerce Clause: *United States v. Darby* and *Wickard v. Filburn.* When viewed substantively, these cases announced doctrines very different from those of *Hirabayashi* and *Korematsu.* But when viewed pragmatically, they functioned in precisely the same way, cooling off the raging civil rights debate by appealing to legalistic formulae inherited from the Roosevelt Court.

With the passage of a half century, it is easy to lose sight of this prudentialist point. The modern generation treats the egalitarian advances represented by the Civil Rights Act and *McLaughlin* as self-evidently correct and in need of no New Deal legitimation. But that is not the way they appeared in 1964. When placed in historical context, *McLaughlin,* like *Heart of Atlanta,* appears as an entirely appropriate act of judicial states-manship, smoothing the way for broad popular acceptance by elaborating opinions that seemed constitutionally uncontroversial at the time.

The problem arises only when modern-day lawyers divorce *McLaughlin* from its historical context and offer the *Hirabayashi-Korematsu* frame-work as the key for understanding the entire civil legacy. This is a mistake. *McLaughlin* was simply an artful effort to legitimate a cautious judicial advance into a sphere left untouched by the Civil Rights Act. It shouldn't be mistaken for the principles animating this great legislative break-through. In passing this landmark statute, the president and Congress did not turn their back on *Brown's* call to abolish real-world forms of institu-tionalized humiliation. To the contrary, they propelled *Brown's* commit-ment into vast new spheres of social life. If we allow *McLaughlin* to di-vert attention from this great achievement, we are betraying the Second Reconstruction.

This, at any rate, is the essence of my "supplementation thesis."

LOVING

I have been linking the leading cases on interracial intimacy to larger pat-terns of constitutional development. *Naim* came down shortly after *Brown* II announced that school desegregation would proceed with "all deliber-ate speed." Both *Naim* and *Brown* II recognized, in different ways, that Warren's great opinion only opened a great constitutional debate about the modern meaning of equality, and that it was foolhardy to press for-ward at full speed unless and until the American people had made up their mind in a decisive fashion.

McLaughlin came at a different stage. The passage of the Civil Rights Act, followed by Lyndon Johnson's landslide victory, represented a turn-ing point in *Brown's* favor—but the shift was not yet irreversible. With bitter-end resistance continuing in the South, *McLaughlin* was wise to proceed with legalistic caution in moving into a new and highly charged sphere that Congress and the president had refused to touch.

Constitutional politics had accelerated yet further by the time the Court took its next step in June 1967, when *Loving v. Virginia* came down. By this point, the Voting Rights Act was on the books, reinforcing the popular commitment to a Second Reconstruction. These landmark statutes were beginning to show real results: southern blacks were registering in large numbers and Jim Crow was visibly crumbling in restaurants, movies, and hotels throughout the region. Yet the momentum was not irreversible. The fate of HEW's efforts to desegregate southern schools would ultimately be determined by the next president—and George Wallace was on the threshold of his presidential campaign.

The symbolic stakes involved in *Loving* still loomed large. Everybody recognized that southern resistance to desegregation was fueled by white anxieties over black-white sex. In striking down bans on interracial marriage, it was only prudent to avoid linking its decision too tightly to *Brown*'s emphatic condemnation of the dual school system.

Loving reflects these complex realities. Chief Justice Warren spoke for the Court, and he spoke with greater confidence than White.[47] But at a critical moment, he swerved away from a strong reaffirmation of *Brown*'s anti-humiliation principle.

Loving came from Virginia, on appeal from its supreme court's emphatic declaration that it would remain faithful to "our holding in the *Naim* case."[48] In defending Virginia's Racial Integrity Act, the state's attorney general built on *McLaughlin*'s emphasis on "the historical fact[s]" defining the Fourteenth Amendment's "central purpose." His brief emphasized the limits that Reconstruction Republicans placed on their transformative ambitions. To bring this point home, Virginia's brief quoted leading members of the Thirty-Ninth Congress repeatedly assuring their fellow Americans that state bans on interracial marriage would remain intact.[49]

Warren responded by abandoning *McLaughlin*'s appeal to the "historical fact[s]." Recalling *Brown* from the shadows, he quoted *Brown* I's rejection of originalism: "Although these historical sources 'cast some light' they are not sufficient to resolve the problem; '[at] best, they are inconclusive.'"[50] But if originalism was inconclusive, what tools should Warren use to resolve the problem?

The first half of the Lovings' brief confronts this issue head-on. After portraying Virginia's Racial Integrity Act as a historical remnant of slavery, it elaborates on its contemporary impact—relying on the work of social psychologists, and especially "the definitive treatise" by Gunnar Myrdal,[51] to make its case:

This history of illicit sex relationships conditions, psychologically and socio-logically, the entire pattern of American race relations. Nor can its impor-tance be overemphasized since "[t]o the ordinary white American the caste line between white and Negro is *based upon,* and *defended by,* the anti-amalgamation doctrine" . . . Myrdal, *An American Dilemma* 54 . . . cf. Brown v. Board of Education.[52] (Emphasis in the brief)

Yet Warren refused this invitation to use Brown's real-world focus as the basis for his opinion. Instead, he follows White's lead and retains *Hi-rabayashi* and *Korematsu* as the basis for his analysis. Why?

I asked Benno Schmidt, Warren's law clerk in charge of the case.[53] His answer: Virginia filed its own version of a "Brandeis Brief" full of citations to racist eugenics to support its marriage ban. These studies had long since been repudiated by the scientific community.[54] Nevertheless, the state's invocation of racist "science" put Warren in an awkward position of adju-dicating pseudo-scientific controversies. Rather than posing as a super-scientist, he chose to follow White's legalistic path instead.

Perhaps Warren was right to avoid a head-on confrontation with racist eugenics, but there was no need for scientific number crunching to dem-onstrate the stigmatizing impact of the law. Instead, Warren simply could have appealed to his fellow Americans' common sense, describing how the marriage ban forced interracial couples to present their relationship to the larger community as if it were diseased, disreputable, criminal. A commonsense discussion of the countless humiliations of everyday life would have yielded a far more compelling vindication of *Brown's* con-cerns with real-world stigma than an effort to refute pseudo-scientific findings.[55]

But Warren responded to Virginia's parody of a "Brandeis Brief" in a different way. Instead of vindicating *Brown's* enduring insights, he told his law clerk to prepare an opinion that followed in *McLaughlin's* foot-steps. The resulting draft contained an almost verbatim repetition of White's words emphasizing the need to impose "rigid scrutiny" on "suspect" racial classifications.

Despite these verbal repetitions, the *McLaughlin* formulae had a very different constitutional status when placed within Warren's larger argu-ment. When White first invoked *Hirabayashi* and *Korematsu,* they merely served as way stations en route to the "historical fact[s]" defining the "cen-tral purpose" of the Equal Protection Clause. But in the first phase of his argument, Warren had stripped *Hirabayashi* and *Korematsu* of their originalist pedigree. In continuing to use these cases as decisive precedents, he was doing something very different: treating major decisions of the Roosevelt Court as the basis for moving constitutional law forward in the next generation.

This was a standard move in Warren Court jurisprudence. Nevertheless, it raised an obvious problem in this particular case: when *Heart of Atlanta* made a similar appeal to the New Deal interpretations of the Commerce Clause, it was invoking Roosevelt Court decisions that culminated a decade of successful constitutional politics. But in relying on *Hirabayashi* and *Korematsu,* the Chief Justice was seeking guidance from opinions arising at one of the darkest moments of our entire judicial history.

Warren was the first to appreciate the ironies of the situation. As California's attorney general during the Second World War, he had been a strong and very visible supporter of the Japanese American internments. In working on *Loving* with his law clerk, he was highly aware of the controversial character of these wartime decisions but continued to defend them on their merits.[56] The Warren psychodrama was complicated yet further by a final factor: in pushing forward with *Hirabayashi* and *Korematsu,* he was not only putting a spotlight on a problematic moment in his own past. He was also diverting the path of the law away from *Brown,* his greatest contribution to the constitutional tradition.

This puzzling swerve becomes less mysterious if we move beyond psychodrama to view Warren as a judicial statesman. Despite the personal complexities, the entire Warren Court was very much alive to the danger of tying *Loving* too closely to *Brown* and giving credibility to racist charges that their true aim in integrating the schools was to mongrelize the white race. By appealing to *Hirabayashi* and *Korematsu, Loving* was reframing the issue in terms that were far removed from the present struggles over civil rights—appealing to wartime memories that invited southerners to reconnect themselves to patriots throughout the country. From this vantage, the Chief's move away from *Brown,* despite his deep pride in the decision, represents a statesmanlike effort to do everything in his power to defuse the desegregation controversy.

All this has been forgotten today. Oblivious to its prudential origins, modern lawyers and judges have transformed the *Hirabayashi-Korematsu* framework into an elaborate doctrinal structure, endlessly debating the particular classifications that should be treated as "suspect" and how rigorously they should be scrutinized. Such inquiries have their place—but only as part of a larger examination of the law's powerful capacity to stigmatize vulnerable groups in social life.

This fundamental point has been reinforced by a recent Roberts Court decision dealing with gay marriage—the twenty-first-century equivalent of the interracial marriage question. In striking down the Defense of Marriage Act, *United States v. Windsor* decisively repudiated the *Hirabayashi-Korematsu* framework inherited from *Loving,* emphasizing instead a version of the anti-humiliation principle inherited from *Brown.*[57]

Before reflecting on this remarkable transformation, it is best to return to *Loving* one last time. We shall be following Chief Justice Warren as he revised early drafts of the opinion into a final text. While retaining its emphasis on *Hirabayashi* and *Korematsu,* he reshaped his opinion to invite future Courts to move beyond it and restore *Brown*'s anti-humiliation principle to a central role in defining marriage equality. A half century onward, Justice Kennedy has led the Roberts Court to transform Warren's gesture into a constitutional reality.

A GESTURE TO THE FUTURE

When Warren's law clerk submitted a draft for his personal review, the Chief Justice made two important revisions. He first took aim at the draft's description of the law's purpose. The proposed opinion accepted the state's assertion that it was a "measure[] designed solely to maintain racial purity" before condemning this aim as insufficiently compelling. Warren replaced this pseudo-scientific emphasis on eugenics with a sociological characterization. As it now appears in the *United States Reports,* Warren's opinion describes the law as "designed to maintain White Supremacy."[58] This now famous phrase gestures toward the stigmatizing forms of social life that the marriage ban sought to enforce—though it still speaks in the language of legislative purpose and does not explicitly assess the law's impact on interracial couples in everyday life.

Warren's second intervention expressed a similar dissatisfaction.[59] This time he added a new concluding section to the opinion:

> These statutes also deprive the Lovings of liberty without due process of law in violation of the Due Process Clause of the Fourteenth Amendment. The freedom to marry has long been recognized as one of the vital personal rights [of] free men.
>
> [It is] fundamental to our very existence and survival. Skinner v. Oklahoma . . . To deny this fundamental freedom on so unsupportable a basis as

the racial classifications embodied in these statutes, classifications so directly subversive of the principle of equality at the heart of the Fourteenth Amendment, is surely to deprive all the State's citizens of liberty without due process of law. The Fourteenth Amendment requires that the freedom of choice to marry not be restricted by invidious racial discriminations. Under our Constitution, the freedom to marry, or not marry, a person of another race resides with the individual and cannot be infringed by the State.[60]

I am quoting Warren's words from the *United States Reports,* but the text looked different when he circulated his draft. At that point, he buttressed his appeal to family values by invoking a case from the 1920s striking down state legislation motivated by the anti-German xenophobia that swept the country during World War I. Speaking for the Court in *Meyer v. Nebraska,* Justice James McReynolds invalidated a ban on teaching foreign languages in private schools as a violation of the Due Process Clause.

Warren's draft cited *Meyer* as authority for the fundamental character of the right "to marry, establish a home and bring up children."[61] But this reliance on McReynolds was utterly unacceptable to Hugo Black. For this New Dealer, McReynolds was a paradigmatic jurist from the bad old days when the Old Court had wrongfully resisted the New Deal Revolution. He urged the Chief to base his opinion only on *Loving*'s equal protection analysis and dispense with his call to reinvigorate substantive due process.[62]

Warren responded in pragmatic fashion. He made a personal plea for Black's support—and gained his assent once he eliminated the McReynolds opinion from the discussion.[63] With the Court's only southerner on board, the Chief could announce *Loving* without any dissents that might provoke an angry reaction from the many Americans who continued to maintain a strong prejudice against interracial marriage.[64] Warren's coalition-building efforts, combined with his swerve away from *Brown,* helps account for the remarkable absence of loud public protest over *Loving* when the decision was announced in the spring of 1967.[65]

Nevertheless, Warren's pragmatic response to Black was hardly enough to answer a fundamental question: was the old New Dealer right in suspecting that Warren was resurrecting McReynolds's discredited doctrine?

My answer is no. Substantive due process played very different roles in the 1920s and the 1960s. For McReynolds, it served as a platform for elaborating the Middle Republic's constitutional commitment to property and contract as the preeminent vehicles of individual freedom. In *Meyer*, for example, McReynolds protected only the contractual rights of parents to send their children to private schools teaching German. He did not extend his rationale further to protect German's place in the public school curriculum.[66]

Black was quite right to insist that McReynolds's contractualist vision had been thoroughly repudiated by the American people during the New Deal. But he was mistaken in believing that Warren was calling for a return to the discredited *Lochner* era. Instead, he was using substantive due process as a platform for further developing one of the great constitutional themes of the Second Reconstruction: its sphere-by-sphere approach to the realization of constitutional values. As we have seen, *Brown* rejected the civil/political/social trichotomy inherited from the first Reconstruction and began the process of carving up the social into more differentiated spheres. The landmark statutes propelled this spherical dynamic further, marking out public accommodations, employment, and housing for special concern. Within this larger setting, Warren's closing paragraphs represent another step in the elaboration of a spherical approach, breaking down the doctrinal barriers separating equal protection from due process and thereby inviting us to consider the distinctive sphere of marriage as it is lived in the real world before crafting appropriate doctrinal responses. From this vantage, there is no sharp break between the Warren of *Brown* and the Warren of *Loving*—both express the sphere-by-sphere approach to social life that represents one of the principal legacies of the Second Reconstruction.

This spherical breakthrough, I hasten to add, was suggested only by Warren's closing lines. Future courts were free to focus on *Loving*'s lengthier discussion of equal protection while dismissing its appeal to substantive due process as merely an afterthought. Similarly, Warren's equality discussion was open to different readings. A narrow interpretation emphasizes the core doctrines of *Hirabayashi* and *Korematsu*, which deflect constitutional attention from the humiliations of real life to the purposes of lawmakers in enacting suspect classifications into law. A broad interpretation uses Warren's condemnation of laws "designed to maintain White Supremacy" as a springboard for reviving an approach to equal protection that emphasizes the real-world dynamics of stigmatization.

How, then, should *Loving* be remembered today? Should we be reading it narrowly or broadly? And if broadly, how broadly?

From *Loving* to *Windsor*

Justice Kennedy went a long way toward answering these questions in his opinion for the Court striking down the federal Defense of Marriage Act (DOMA). *United States v. Windsor* confronted DOMA's narrow definition of marriage as a relationship that can only involve a man and a woman. On first impression, Kennedy's opinion looks like a halfway measure—declaring DOMA unconstitutional, but refusing to extend this condemnation to the many state laws that maintain a traditional view of marriage. But when viewed from a deeper historical perspective, his opinion represents a fundamental turning point.

In Justice Kennedy's view, DOMA's particular problem involved its treatment of single-sex couples in states that had already legalized gay marriage. DOMA put these couples in a special predicament—legally married under state law, they confronted a federal government that refused to recognize their marital status. In declaring this disjunction unconstitutional, Kennedy could have adapted the *Hirabayashi-Korematsu* framework inherited from *Loving*. Under this approach, he would have found that DOMA had created a suspect distinction between gay and straight couples requiring rigorous scrutiny, and that Congress's purposes in enacting the provision failed to satisfy this test.

But writing for a narrow majority of five Justices, Kennedy blazed a very different path to his conclusion:

> By creating two contradictory marriage regimes within the same State, DOMA forces same-sex couples to live as married for the purpose of state law but unmarried for the purpose of federal law, thus diminishing the stability and predictability of basic personal relations the State has found it proper to acknowledge and protect. By this dynamic DOMA undermines both the public and private significance of state-sanctioned same-sex marriages; for it tells those couples, *and all the world,* that their otherwise valid marriages are unworthy of federal recognition. This places same-sex couples in an unstable position of being in a second-tier marriage. *The differentiation demeans the couple,* whose moral and sexual choices the Constitution protects, see Lawrence v. Texas, and whose relationship the State has sought to dignify. *And it humiliates tens of thousands of children now being raised by same-sex couples. The law in question makes it even more difficult for the children to understand the integrity and closeness of their own family and its concord with other families in their community and in their daily lives.*[67] (Emphasis added)

"The differentiation demeans the couple"—this is a claim about the *social meaning* of Congress's action. Second-class treatment would continue even if, as the dissenters suggest, lawmakers had plausible reasons for insisting on a uniform federal approach to marriage as state definitions diverged from one another.[68]

In moving beyond the law world to the lifeworld, Justice Kennedy treated his earlier decision in *Lawrence v. Texas* as a decisive precedent. In that case, he had led the Court to strike down traditional criminal laws against "sodomy" since their enforcement "demean[ed]" same-sex couples.[69] But his reliance on this relatively recent decision ignored *Windsor*'s deeper roots.

Justice Kennedy's opinion was simply a restatement of *Brown*'s anti-humiliation principle. The parallelisms became particularly pronounced when Kennedy emphasized the "humiliat[ions]" DOMA imposed on "tens of thousands of children now being raised by same-sex couples . . . mak[ing] it even more difficult for the children to understand the integrity and closeness of their own family and its concord with other families in their community and in their daily lives." This is a virtual paraphrase of Warren's denunciation of school segregation on the ground that it gives children "a feeling of inferiority as to their status in the community that may affect their hearts and minds in a way unlikely ever to be undone."[70]

Kennedy failed to follow *Brown* on one key point. Recall that Warren tried to buttress his commonsense claims about humiliation with an appeal to social science.[71] Kennedy made no similar move; perhaps a visitor from Mars might require a social science study to appreciate DOMA's stigmatizing impact, but Kennedy wrote as if his point was perfectly obvious to any American living in the early twenty-first century.

Justice Scalia was entirely unpersuaded. He denounced Kennedy's anti-humiliation language as meaningless "argle-bargle"[72]—and dangerous too. In Scalia's view, Kennedy was simply creating a rhetorical battering ram that would enable the Court to impose gay marriage by fiat on all fifty states of the Union.[73]

Justice Scalia's passionate denunciation doesn't invite a cool response by the reader. But once we put the "argle-bargle" to one side, it's clear that he was making a powerful analytic point. Now that Kennedy has called up the spirit of *Brown*, it will be tough for him to limit the anti-humiliation principle to cases, such as DOMA, that only involve the federal government. After all, *Brown* itself committed Scalia's original sin—requiring the states, as well as the federal government, to eliminate institutionalized humiliation from their school systems. If *Brown* was right to impose a far-reaching ban against humiliation on the basis of race, why isn't it also right to strike down state marriage laws that humiliate on the basis of sex? At the very least, there is a heavy burden on Justice Kennedy, and lower courts bound by *Windsor,* to provide a principled answer to this fundamental question.

Over the course of this book, I have tried to lay bare the constitutional legacy Americans have inherited from the civil rights era. But it is time to start asking a different question: after the passage of half a century, to what extent does the Second Reconstruction remain a vital force in the living Constitution?

I will reserve a serious answer for the next volume, but *Windsor* definitely deserves an important place in this more general reckoning. As we have seen, Chief Justice Warren's opinion in *Brown* introduced one of the central themes of the Second Reconstruction, which the president and Congress reaffirmed and extended to many other spheres of social life. But when it came to interracial marriage, President Johnson and Congress came to a screeching halt, refraining from a serious effort to ban state anti-miscegenation laws. While the Warren Court cautiously intervened to fill this gap, it steered clear of *Brown*'s anti-humiliation rationale. In contrast, Justice Kennedy has led the Roberts Court down the path that even the Warren Court refused to travel.

This single fact is deeply significant. In handing down *Windsor,* not only did the Roberts Court reaffirm the anti-humiliation principle, but it went far beyond the zone of its original application to address a high-stakes controversy of the twenty-first century. Kennedy's success in revitalizing Warren's master insight attests to the enduring importance of this aspect of the civil rights legacy.

But it is a mistake to rely too heavily on a single 5-to-4 decision in coming to a broader assessment of the current vitality of the civil rights legacy—especially when a different 5-to-4 majority recently pushed the law in a very different direction. A day before announcing *Windsor,* the Roberts Court handed down another major decision redefining the Court's relationship to the Second Reconstruction. *Shelby County v.*

Holder launched an unprecedented attack on a key provision of the Voting Rights Act, asserting that it can no longer serve as a legitimate foundation for constitutional life in the twenty-first century.

Chapter 14 confronts this remarkable decision, placing it against the background established by the book's larger argument.

Betrayal?

T HERE WERE GIANTS on the earth during the Founding and Reconstruction—men who spoke for the American people in an enduring fashion. But the twentieth century was an age of political pygmies who never gained comparable authority—no constitutional amendments defining the nature and limits of activist national government, none codifying the central achievements of the civil rights revolution. We the People have made no big decisions for almost a century.

Or so the lawyers say.

Americans deserve better. They should learn how their parents and grandparents contributed greatly to the tradition of popular sovereignty, creating twentieth-century foundations for the constitutional pursuit of economic and racial justice. In gaining the authority to speak for the People during the New Deal and the civil rights revolution, political leaders didn't use the Founders' system of constitutional amendment. But there were good reasons for their departure from these eighteenth-century formalisms.

When the Founders designed Article V, Americans understood their Union as a weak federation of sovereign states, with the Articles of Confederation requiring unanimous state consent to any formal amendment. The Philadelphia Convention repudiated this explicit requirement, asserting that three-quarters of the states would suffice. This pushed the system of revision in the Union's direction, but anything more centralized would have been unacceptable to most citizens of Virginia or Massachusetts.[1] Their state-centered vision of the federation was shattered by the Civil War and Reconstruction, and politics became increasingly national over the twentieth century. While states remained important, their absolute veto on fundamental change seemed increasingly at odds with American political identity.

As Franklin Roosevelt explained during the court-packing crisis, "Thirteen States which contain only five percent of the voting population can block ratification even though the thirty-five States with ninety-five percent of the population are in favor of it." He claimed that the Democrats' nationwide landslide of 1936 had earned the New Deal a "mandate of the people" to consolidate the activist welfare state into the country's constitutional foundations.[2]

The real question was whether, once liberated from Article V, governing elites could claim "mandates" to revise the constitution without winning the mobilized support of ordinary Americans, or whether our institutions could adapt to provide citizens with the tools they needed to intervene decisively in shaping the nation's constitutional future.

This is why the New Deal provides a central precedent. Roosevelt and the Democratic Congress had *to earn* their mandate—first by sustaining popular support for the New Deal against the withering critique of the Supreme Court and the Republican opposition; next, by winning a decisive national landslide in 1936; next, by sustaining control over the presidency and Congress long enough to create a New Deal Court that entrenched the new settlement into the living Constitution by the early 1940s. It was only through this extended process—in which all three branches engaged in a decade of mobilized constitutional debate, repeated electoral decision, and sustained judicial reflection—that gave broad credibility to Roosevelt's claims to a "mandate of the people."

American lawyers make a grievous error in trivializing this achievement. While it didn't conform to the federalist rules of Article V, it did succeed in adapting the separation-of-powers tradition to vindicate popular sovereignty in an America that had become a nation. At a time when the great democracies of Europe were staggering under the Great Depression, Americans were responding by adapting their institutions to redeem their faith in government "of the People, by the People, and for the People." This is no small thing.

Little wonder that the civil rights generation repeatedly used New Deal precedents to guide their own struggles over constitutional reform. They had lived through the New Deal drama as young men and women. They did not need history books to appreciate why Lyndon Johnson used the Roosevelt-Landon landslide to measure his own mandate in 1964, or why the Warren Court was anxious to avoid another disastrous "switch in time."

Yet history never repeats itself—and the civil rights path toward popular sovereignty differed from the New Deal in key respects. The most important involved the Supreme Court. From the days of Jefferson to the days of Roosevelt, the president and Congress had played the central role in pushing new issues onto the constitutional agenda, with the Supreme Court doing all in its power to resist each rising movement for fundamental change.

Not this time. If left to their own devices, President Eisenhower and Congress would have allowed the race question to remain in the shadows. Only *Brown* forced them to take the issue seriously. Given the Justices' decisive act of constitutional leadership, it's perfectly appropriate for lawyers to begin their study of the Second Reconstruction with the Warren Court opinions of the 1950s.

But it is a mistake to continue this practice as we reflect on *Brown*'s second decade. With Lyndon Johnson's ascent to the presidency, the era of congressional compromises and presidential half steps came to an end. Henceforth, the Justices would be sharing leadership with the political branches—often taking a backseat as the president and Congress claimed a mandate from the people for fundamental change.

The passage of the Civil Rights Act of 1964 and Johnson's landslide victory over Goldwater brought into play a variation on the New Deal model of popular sovereignty. Once again, a president was claiming a mandate from the people; once again, Congress was reinforcing this claim with landmark statutes; once again, the presidency, Congress, and the Courts continued to consolidate and refine the preceding breakthroughs after the next presidential election—with Richard Nixon and the Burger Court emphasizing the bipartisan character of their central achievements.

The Second Reconstruction proved more enduring than its nineteenth-century predecessor. Fifty years after the Reconstruction Amendments, blacks were barred from polling places throughout the South, and the Supreme Court had reinterpreted these constitutional texts to emphasize the protection of property rights, not minority rights. Fifty years after the Second Reconstruction, blacks remain a powerful political force, and their civil rights victories serve as the great precedents invoked by other oppressed groups in their own struggles for equal protection.

Yet lawyers and judges continue to look upon the First Reconstruction as the American people's last word on constitutional equality, treating the Second Reconstruction's landmark statutes and judicial superprecedents as a jumble of add-ons to the great work of the ancient lawgivers. In trivializing the civil rights revolution, the legal community is betraying the American experiment in popular sovereignty. We should quit worshipping at the shrine of the nineteenth century and ask ourselves a different question: how do the principles of the Second Reconstruction differ from those of the First?

This book provides only the beginning of an answer. Most obviously, it is narrowly focused on the struggle for black equality. I fail to do justice to social justice movements for other minorities, for women, and for poor people. It is also a Washington-centered book, failing to integrate the voices of movement activists, local political leaders, and ordinary Americans into the story. My ultimate excuse: "I have but one life to give to my country." So I have concentrated on the things I do best, and on the main point: that a bipartisan political coalition did indeed manage to harness the energy of the civil rights movement to build a new foundation for race relations in the name of the American people. Since this single claim requires a large shift in lawyerly discussion, it deserved a book-length effort.

If my basic thesis gains headway, it will naturally provoke wide-ranging efforts to move beyond the book's more obvious limitations. If the profession does expand its constitutional canon to include lots of new material from the legislative and executive branches, different lawyers, judges, and scholars will begin to read the material in lots of different ways. Who knows how many of my particular interpretations will stand the test of time?

The dynamics of debate will also redefine the terms of interdisciplinary dialogue. So long as lawyers tell a court-centered story, they isolate themselves from many leading currents in history and political science. But once they put the higher lawmaking process at the center of their project, they invite a wide range of interdisciplinary contributions. Political scientists of various stripes will enter into the debate on the constitutional significance of triggering and ratifying elections. Social historians will explore the complex ways their bottom-up accounts of the civil rights movement shaped and reshaped the terms of the Washington-centered story presented here. And so forth.[3]

The best way to contribute to these debates is to provide a summary statement of the civil rights legacy that emerges from my initial exploration.

Unraveling the New Deal Paradox

The Warren Court passed up a great opportunity to elaborate on the meaning of the Second Reconstruction when it responded to cases challenging the Civil Rights Act. The time was December 1964; the cases were *Heart of Atlanta* and *McClung;* the issue was the constitutionality of a federal ban on discrimination in public accommodations. In taking this step, the president and Congress had moved far beyond the Warren Court—which had refused, in *Bell v. Maryland,* to repudiate long-standing case law granting owners of private property the right to discriminate against blacks and other minorities.

This restrictive interpretation of the Equal Protection Clause was rooted firmly in the Civil Rights Cases of 1883. It also had served as a reference point for Barry Goldwater's opposition to the Civil Rights Act—both on the floor of the Senate and in his subsequent presidential campaign. But Goldwater's constitutional critique was crushed by his landslide defeat in November, setting the stage for Johnson and Congress to claim a mandate from the people for further civil rights breakthroughs. Since the Court decided *Heart of Atlanta* one month after Goldwater's defeat, the decision represented a precious opportunity: would the Justices follow up on Johnson's decisive popular mandate by making *Heart of Atlanta* into the *Brown v. Board* of the 1960s, profoundly reshaping the meaning of equal protection for generations to come?

The answer was no. For all its reputed activism, the Warren Court refused to make this effort. (Recall my sketch of an alternative version of *Heart of Atlanta* in Chapter 7.) It did not even treat the Civil Rights Act as a *civil rights act.* Instead, it upheld this great egalitarian breakthrough as if it were a garden-variety New Deal regulation of interstate commerce, treating its moral significance almost as an embarrassment.

This doctrinal swerve was a tribute to the legitimating power of 1930s precedents for the civil rights generation. Just as the New Deal model of presidential leadership was the central reference point for Lyndon Johnson, the New Deal expansion of the Commerce Clause had become an unchallengeable foundation for the Supreme Court—serving as common ground for the conservative Justice Harlan and the liberal Justice Douglas as a legitimate basis for upholding the act.

The New Deal consensus allowed the Court to speak with one voice in upholding the Civil Rights Act on Commerce Clause grounds. If the liberal majority had pushed forward with a pathbreaking opinion on equal protection, Harlan (and perhaps others) would have dissented, permitting southern die-hards to use his separate opinion to support their last-ditch defense of Jim Crow. Given the fraught political context, the Warren majority sensibly chose to present a united front—even at the cost of depriving posterity of an eloquent statement of the Second Reconstruction's expansive vision of the meaning of equal protection.

This tactical decision generates a "New Deal paradox" for later generations. On one hand, the Court's unanimous decision gave Johnson and Congress maximum credibility in claiming a Roosevelt-style mandate from the people for further breakthroughs in race relations. On the other hand, the quest for unanimity made it impossible for the Court to elaborate the Civil Rights Act's decisive transformation of the meaning of equal protection. If future generations are to fill this gap, they must lift their eyes beyond the *United States Reports* to hear spokesmen for the people such as Lyndon Johnson and Martin Luther King Jr., Hubert Humphrey and Everett Dirksen, explain the constitutional significance of their decisive achievement.

If we hope to sustain the tradition of popular sovereignty into a new century, we cannot afford to cast these leaders as tired epigones living off the constitutional heritage left by the giants of an ever-receding past. We should be reflecting on their achievements—both in adapting New Deal models to speak for the People and in moving beyond the First Reconstruction to establish new egalitarian principles for the modern age.

THE *BROWN* PARADOX

In calling on the profession to integrate the courts into a larger story of popular sovereignty, I hardly wish to push the Justices off center stage. To the contrary: in some respects, a redefinition of the constitutional canon serves to emphasize the crucial character of the judicial contribution.

Most important, *Brown*'s emphasis on "hearts and minds" provided a constitutional framework for the public justification of the landmark statutes. When King, Johnson, and other leaders repeatedly emphasized the evil of systematic humiliation in campaigning for their statutory breakthroughs, they were continuing a constitutional conversation that *Brown* had already brought to the center of the political stage. When these struggles culminated in the passage of landmark legislation, these statutes were rightly understood as a public vindication of Warren's act of leadership in *Brown*.

The existing court-centered canon ignores this crucial point. It does not use Warren's opinion as a key to unlock the distinctive character of solemn commitments endorsed by the American people in the landmark statutes. It merely sees *Brown* as the beginning of a long conversation between judges, and only judges, over the meaning of equality. The account it gives resembles a standard story of common-law development; on this view, it was perfectly acceptable for latter-day Justices to detach *Brown*'s holding from Warren's dicta, gradually displacing his emphasis on humiliation with other doctrines they found more compelling. Yet fifty years onward, this judge-made tradition has put the legal community in a paradoxical position: we are taught to revere *Brown* as a decisive turning point, but we no longer take Warren's opinion seriously.

Once we redefine the canon to include the landmark statutes, benign neglect seems indefensible. *We the Judges do not have the constitutional authority to erase the considered judgments of We the People.* Beginning with the Civil Rights Act of 1964, Americans began to resolve the decade of debate provoked by *Brown* by giving their sustained support to landmark legislation that repeatedly reaffirmed Warren's principles. In this key instance, the effort to redefine the constitutional canon to include landmark statutes has the paradoxical consequence of requiring lawyers to take the Supreme Court *more* seriously and treat *Brown* for what it was: the greatest judicial opinion of the twentieth century.

JUDICIAL ACTIVISM OR LANDMARK REINFORCEMENT?

More generally, the new canon permits us to move beyond the tired debate over the "judicial activism" of the Warren and Burger Courts. Instead of asking whether particular decisions were "activist" or "restrained," we should place them against the background provided by the higher lawmaking activity of the president, Congress, and the American people. This leads us to ask very different questions: Was the Court operating in a sphere in which the landmark statutes revolutionized egalitarian doctrine? Or did the political branches permit it to retain constitutional leadership during *Brown*'s second decade?

Part Two dealt with spheres in which the political branches assumed constitutional leadership: employment, housing, public accommodations, and voting. Part Three dealt with those in which the Court retained control: public schools and interracial marriage. Within the first domain, we showed that the Supreme Court tried to reinforce the constitutional legitimacy of the statutory initiatives of the political branches. But the Court acted very differently in the second domain. Rather than engaging in landmark reinforcement, it responded with legalistic caution in extending egalitarian principles onto problematic terrain.

This contrast between *landmark reinforcement* and *legalistic legitimation* generates deeper insights into the Court's opinions. If you have been persuaded, we have reached a second paradoxical-sounding conclusion: by bringing the landmark statutes into the canon, we gain more penetrating insights into the judicial opinions upon which the traditional canon lavishes its attention.

To elaborate this point, begin once more with *Heart of Atlanta*. Was the Court activist or restrained in making its Commerce Clause swerve?

The right answer is neither. The Court's New Deal gesture was an effort to reinforce the Civil Rights Act. Given the Justices' lived experience of the 1930s, they viewed the expansive Commerce Clause as an uncontroversial feature of the modern Constitution. By invoking it, they made it clear to Americans that there was absolutely no danger of repeating the confrontation scenario between the Old Court and the New Deal and thereby grievously undermine the credibility of Lyndon Johnson's civil rights mandate.

Once this bedrock issue had been resolved, the Warren Court reinforced later statutory initiatives with opinions that confronted their egalitarian ambitions more explicitly. *Jones v. Mayer* provides a telling example. When the case came before the Court in 1968, Congress was debating the last great landmark statute of the period, the Fair Housing Act. At this stage, the earlier landmarks were already changing realities on the ground—not only were blacks voting in large numbers, but they could increasingly walk into restaurants and obtain service without humiliation. With increasing public acceptance of breakthrough initiatives, judicial unanimity was no longer so imperative. So a strong majority endorsed an opinion by Justice Stewart that revolutionized the Court's traditional interpretation of the Thirteenth Amendment. Repudiating the restrictive reading endorsed by the Civil Rights Cases of 1883, Stewart deepened the Second Reconstruction's commitment to the real-world eradication of the "badges and incidents" of slavery that remained pervasive in the twentieth century—extending *Brown*'s anti-humiliation principle to new constitutional terrain.

This dramatic doctrinal expansion is sometimes condemned as an activist effort to repudiate the original understanding of the Thirteenth Amendment. But Stewart's opinion is better understood as a variation on *Heart of Atlanta*'s theme of landmark reinforcement. While *Heart of Atlanta* swerved to commerce to reinforce the Civil Rights Act, *Jones* swerved to the Thirteenth Amendment to reinforce the Housing Act's radical condemnation of racial discrimination in private as well as public housing.

Egalitarian elaboration was also on display in the Court's treatment of the Voting Rights Act. Voting is an act of citizenship, not an act of commerce—even in its expansive New Deal sense. So when this landmark statute swept away restrictive Supreme Court opinions limiting the constitutional protection of voting rights, the Justices could not credibly evade Congress's frontal assault on its doctrinal authority by indulging in a Commerce Clause swerve. As a consequence, Justice Brennan led the Court to confront the congressional claim to constitutional leadership head-on in *Katzenbach v. Morgan*. Once again, the traditional framework has difficulty appraising Brennan's canonical opinion of 1966: was *Morgan* activist or restrained?

If forced to choose, I guess the winner is restrained. After all, the essence of restraint is judicial deference to the political branches. And the Brennan majority was *extremely* deferential in authorizing the president and Congress to ignore restrictive Supreme Court decisions when the president and Congress found them unacceptable roadblocks to the proper enforcement of the Equal Protection Clause.

But why call this "restraint"? *Morgan*'s real importance lies in its novel rationale for reinforcing the legitimacy of the Voting Rights Act. The Supreme Court normally reinforces statutes by upholding them on their constitutional merits, overruling its prior decisions when appropriate. But this time the Court refused to overrule its inconsistent case law and yet upheld the statute—recognizing that the political branches may, on occasion, *appropriately* assume constitutional leadership.

Yet *Morgan* did not go all the way. It expressly supported congressional leadership when it came to enforcing the Equal Protection Clause. But the Voting Rights Act actually went further than this. It also designed a new form of collaboration with the Court in an interbranch effort to create new substantive rights—most notably, the right to vote free of any and all poll taxes. When, if ever, should the Justices collaborate with the political branches when they undertake this more ambitious project of redefining fundamental substantive rights in the name of We the People?

This large question was before the Court in yet another canonical case from 1966: *Harper v. Board of Elections*. Fifty years onward, Justice Douglas's *Harper* opinion is seen as a paradigm example of unbridled activism—proudly declaring that the Court can repudiate its earlier decisions whenever it decides that they are inconsistent with the reigning constitutional zeitgeist. But it was sheer accident that prevented Arthur Goldberg from leading the Court in a very different direction—toward an explicit recognition that landmark statutes could legitimately substitute for formal constitutional amendments in redefining fundamental constitutional rights. If Goldberg had remained on the Court, *Harper* would have moved beyond *Morgan* in recognizing that Congress and the president could appropriately challenge existing Court precedents on matters of substance, not only remedy. But alas, Goldberg chose to sacrifice his judicial career to work for a peaceful solution to the Vietnam War at the United Nations, leaving his draft opinion behind.

Douglas's last-minute substitution for Goldberg should not, however, conceal the remarkable effort by the political branches to design a method for redefining constitutional rights outside of Article V. As we have seen, the design of this new model was absolutely central to the successful passage of the entire Voting Rights Act. Though Douglas's activist opinion erases all traces of this fact, the new model of "coordinate constitutionalism" is on full display once we lift our eyes beyond the *United States Reports* and confront the *Congressional Record* and newspaper accounts of the period. These sources reveal that Lyndon Johnson, Martin Luther King Jr., Everett Dirksen, and Emmanuel Celler hammered out special provisions to make it clear to the Court that We the People would settle for nothing less than the destruction of all significant economic and racial restrictions on the right to vote. While these provisions, codified in Section 10 of the Voting Rights Act, have dropped from sight, they deserve a central place in the constitutional canon, serving as a decisive precedent for further acts of cooperative constitutionalism in the future.

Heart of Atlanta, Jones, Morgan, and *Harper*: these cases represent increasingly complex efforts at landmark reinforcement. The challenge is to use them as a source for deepening reflection on the complex process through which the Court, Congress, and the presidency worked with one another to express commitment by ordinary Americans to move the Second Reconstruction far beyond the constitutional principles of the nineteenth century.

JUDICIAL RESTRAINT OR LEGALISTIC LEGITIMATION?

As I write these words, the legal profession isn't particularly interested in a sustained effort to reassert the popular foundations of the Second Reconstruction. Courts and commentators are largely concerned with a different aspect of the Warren Court's egalitarian legacy. In *Loving v. Virginia,* the Court famously proclaimed that legal classifications on racial lines were inherently suspect, requiring a compelling justification if they were to survive strict scrutiny. Fifty years later, *Loving* has become the basis for an ever more complex conversation, with advocates endlessly debating whether all suspect classifications are equally suspicious. For example, are laws singling out women as pernicious as those targeting blacks? And if not, how should the courts define the level of intermediate scrutiny appropriate in such cases?

Questions like these have their genesis in *Loving*. While they are important, it is a mistake to put them at the center of doctrinal discussion. A collective fixation on their resolution seems misguided once we recognize that the Second Reconstruction was largely the creation of We the People, not We the Judges. Within the new canon, *Loving* enters the story only as a judicial mop-up operation, not as the great summation of the Warren Court's legacy. We cannot allow *Loving*'s legalistic legitimations to blot out the great principles motivating the landmark statutes.

Even at the height of the civil rights revolution, no serious political leader proposed landmark legislation attacking widespread state prohibitions on interracial marriage. Only when Congress began passing landmark statutes in other spheres did the Court cautiously confront sexual intimacy in *McLaughlin,* preparing the groundwork for its final assault three years later in *Loving*. Given all this caution, it is no surprise that *McLaughlin* and *Loving* refused to emphasize *Brown,* even though the real-world humiliations of interracial couples were obvious. If the *Loving* Court had created such an explicit linkage, it would have reinforced southern fears that the Warren's Court ultimate aim in *Brown* was the "mongrelization of the race"—provoking further resistance to school desegregation.

Within this context, the Court's cautious legalisms were perfectly understandable, if not precisely admirable—since they required Warren to give the notorious World War II Japanese detention cases a new prominence in modern equal protection law. Whatever the short-term merits of Warren's strategy, my concern is long-term understanding: what role should *McLaughlin* and *Loving* play in a twenty-first-century assessment of the civil rights legacy?

It all depends on your definition of the canon. Within the established court-centered framework, these cases can't help but appear critically important. After all, they were rendered at the Warren Court's triumphant moment—when its great effort of constitutional leadership in *Brown* was finally winning the broad support of the general public. So long as the *United States Reports* serves as the preeminent site for remembering the Second Reconstruction, Warren's opinion in *Loving* might well supplant his earlier opinion in *Brown* as the key to modern equal protection law.

But if the Second Reconstruction was preeminently the work of We the People, not We the Judges, *Loving* can only have a secondary place in the constitutional canon. When looking at the work of the late Warren Court, cases such as *Heart of Atlanta, Jones, Morgan,* and *Harper* are far more important. These cases represent an increasingly sophisticated judicial effort to legitimate the claim by the political branches to speak in the name of We the People. If we hope to understand them adequately, we must look beyond the *United States Reports* and understand the Justices' doctrinal efforts as part of a larger pattern of interbranch cooperation in building solid constitutional foundations for the Second Reconstruction.

It is this effort that should be our main concern, not spinning our wheels over *Loving*'s doctrinal legacy. The Court's recent decision in *Windsor* provides a splendid opportunity for this larger reappraisal. In striking down DOMA, *Windsor* decisively moved beyond *Loving*'s framework to reaffirm the centrality of *Brown*'s anti-humiliation principle, inviting the profession to engage in a larger reassessment of its constitutional inheritance.

The two canons also diverge in assessing *Brown*'s fate in its home sphere: public education. Here too Congress and the president deferred to judicial leadership—but for very different reasons. In *Loving,* the Court retained its centrality by default—the politicians had no interest in challenging sexual taboos. But in public education, the Justices' continuing leadership was based on the self-conscious consent of the American people and their representatives in Washington—generating very different dilemmas.

The Civil Rights Act was a ringing affirmation of *Brown,* providing the courts with crucial enforcement tools that finally broke the back of southern resistance during the Johnson and Nixon administrations. But the landmark statutes did not go further to revolutionize substantive doctrine, as they did in the spheres of employment, housing, public accommodations, and voting. Given the Court's success in inspiring the country to face up to Jim Crow in public education, the political branches continued to defer to the Justices when it came to defining the path forward.

Once again, the Court responded with a large dose of legalism. As the Justices confronted the South in 1968 and 1969, they refused to indulge in a grand jurisprudential debate on the meaning of equal protection. Although their 9-to-0 opinions in *Green* and *Alexander* begged the big questions, their legalistic demands for sweeping desegregation put maximum pressure on the Nixon administration, which reluctantly backed the requirements of the "rule of law."

By the end of Nixon's first term, the Justices' legalistic acts of leadership had finally been redeemed by the facts on the ground: southern schools were fast becoming the most integrated in the country. Only then did the Court confront the enduring meaning of *Brown*. At its moment of triumph, the Burger Court reached a principled consensus that had eluded its Warren Court predecessor. In its June 1972 decision in *City of Emporia,* all four Nixon appointees joined with the five remaining old-timers in a ringing reaffirmation of *Brown*'s anti-humiliation principle.

But accidents of timing conspired to prevent civil rights litigators from making the most of *Emporia* as they took up the problem of northern segregation in *Keyes v. City of Denver.* Although *Keyes* was decided only a year later, it barely mentions *Emporia.* Justice Brennan instead led the Court on a legalistic swerve away from *Brown* in dealing with segregation in Denver's schools. While Brennan cobbled together a majority for a broad busing order that aimed for citywide integration, his clever legalisms did not deflect Congress and the president from a full-scale assault on the Court's judicial independence. This threat led the Justices to a helter-skelter retreat the following year in *Milliken v. Bradley.*

Milliken's switch in time did succeed in defusing the escalating political assault. But it prevented the Court from taking the time it needed to reconsider a key question: should it base its retreat on *Brown*'s anti-humiliation principle, or should it justify its switch by manipulating the same legalistic framework that *Keyes* had used to launch the northern busing campaign the year before?

The *Milliken* majority took the second course. A half century onward, the profession should rethink this fateful decision. We should extricate ourselves from the jurisprudential wreckage of the Court's failed busing enterprise in the North and return to *Emporia*'s reflections at the end of the Justices' successful southern campaign. Eighteen years after *Brown,* the Court had finally gained the political support required to destroy Jim Crow in southern schools—and it crowned its victory with *Emporia*'s reaffirmation of *Brown*'s originating insights. On this crucial matter, the Burger Court was at one with the Warren Court. The Justices all joined together in giving the same constitutional meaning to their greatest success in judicial leadership.

We should never allow ourselves to forget this moment. Remember *Emporia;* remember *Brown;* remember the anti-humiliation principle.

Landmark Principles

The landmark statutes went beyond *Brown* in four fundamental respects. They moved beyond spheres of direct state involvement to impose egalitarian obligations on private property owners. They moved beyond a ban on humiliation to impose more stringent requirements of equal treatment. They moved beyond traditional legal language to endorse technocratic forms of government by numbers. They adapted New Deal forms of public administration in ways that revolutionized traditional notions of states' rights.

Begin with the political extension of *Brown*'s spherical logic to nonstate actors. As Congress and the president were struggling to reach agreement on the Civil Rights Act of 1964, the Court was also rethinking its traditional state action doctrine in *Bell v. Maryland.* When Justice Clark wrote a majority opinion effectively undermining state action restrictions inherited from the Civil Rights Cases of 1883, Justice Brennan had second thoughts. He worried that a decision in *Bell* requiring restaurants to open their doors would sabotage the campaign for decisive action on Capitol Hill: why pass the public accommodation provisions of the Civil Rights Act, congressional fence-sitters would ask, when the Court had already done the job for them? After some last-minute pulling and hauling, Brennan persuaded his colleagues to replace Clark's pathbreaking statement with an opinion that ducked the key issues.

Brennan's strategy was rewarded by Congress's decision to push ahead with sweeping egalitarian obligations on private providers of public accommodations, as well as employment and (in 1968) housing. *Brown*'s concern with stigma played a prominent role in the constitutional debate: humiliation was no less humiliating and no less public when it involved institutionalized rejection of black people at a privately owned lunch counter or workplace. This point was made repeatedly in response to Barry Goldwater's libertarian critique in 1964 and George Wallace's populist attack in 1968—with a broad bipartisan coalition, including Humphrey, Dirksen, Johnson, and Richard Nixon, supporting King's call for human dignity.

The landmark statutes, and their further codification during the Nixon years, express this mobilized constitutional consensus in the name of We the People. And yet today's lawyers treat the state action doctrines of the Civil Rights Cases of 1883 as if they were untouched by the Second Reconstruction. This is a mistake.

The landmark statutes also moved beyond *Brown* to embrace more ambitious egalitarian objectives. Humiliation involves an insult in the here and now—a face-to-face challenge to your basic competence as a social actor. But it is perfectly possible for employers and workers to treat their black colleagues respectfully in day-to-day relationships and yet deny them an equal chance when it came to promoting them to better positions—say, by using unconscious racial stereotypes in evaluating their performance. Similarly, election officials might allow blacks to vote on the same terms as whites but minimize their political effectiveness by gerrymandering election districts.

The landmark statutes attacked these abuses, insisting on equal opportunity measured in real-world terms. In the field of employment, this meant using technocratic techniques to assess the fairness of hiring and promotion procedures; in the field of politics, it meant assessing the impact of election rule changes on the political power of blacks as a voting bloc. Since different spheres posed different regulatory problems, the landmark statutes displayed a distinctly pragmatic form of constitutionalism, deploying different operational principles to achieve the same objective: *genuinely* equal opportunity within each sphere.

"Within each sphere": the proviso is significant. The statutes did not take account of the cumulative impact of inequalities across spheres. A worker who had been denied an equal chance at a good education could not expect his employer to grant him a compensating advantage in a promotion decision, or a private restaurant to give him a compensating discount on the bill, or a homeowner to sell him a house at a discount. He could only insist that he be treated the same as others with equal skills or wealth. There was one important exception: in 1969, the Supreme Court held that states couldn't impose literacy tests on voting, given the unequal educations that had been systematically provided black citizens. But in other areas, the law refused to recognize interspherical impacts.

This meant that poor blacks benefited less than their middle-class counterparts from the landmark statutes—when they entered each sphere as adults, they could not enjoy the latter's education, money, or respectability. While poor blacks lagged behind, the spherical framework made it easier for other groups to gain enhanced protection. For example, if an upper-class woman was humiliated by sexual harassment in the workplace, this was enough to invoke the guarantees of Title VII. She did not need to show that she also suffered systematic disadvantages in other spheres of life, let alone that they were comparable to those imposed on blacks in the Jim Crow South.

I do not minimize the dignitarian advances that all stigmatized groups—poor and rich alike—gained from the landmark statutes. But we shall shortly return to the larger problem raised by the class distribution of these gains.

———————

We have been dealing with two statutory movements beyond *Brown*—one that expanded the sphere of constitutional concern to the private marketplace, and another that moved beyond the ban on institutionalized humiliation to guarantee blacks and other protected groups spherical equality of opportunity in the real world.

These ambitious aims led the president and Congress to endorse a constitutional revolution in the structure of government. To bridge the gap between law and life, the statutes deployed the rising technocratic capacities of the modern administrative state to achieve decisive breakthroughs—most notably in the spheres of education, employment, and voting.

The transformation occurred on two levels. The statutory regimes increasingly defined substantive obligations in quantitative terms, displacing the qualitative standards familiar in the American legal tradition. While New Deal economic regulation had already emphasized numerical indicators, the extension of government by numbers to civil rights is one of the hallmarks of the Second Reconstruction.

The embrace of technocracy propelled a new generation of administrative agencies to the fore. The numerical guidelines issued by the EEOC and the Office of Education in HEW played critical roles in the spheres of employment and public education. These agencies differed significantly from their New Deal prototypes. The National Labor Relations Board and the Securities and Exchange Commission employed plenary rule-making power, with the courts exercising relatively restrained powers of judicial review. This arrangement made sense in an era in which the Old Court had been the principal obstacle to activist government. Since the courts were hostile, the New Deal tried to narrow their effective power to subvert its regulatory aims. In contrast, the Warren Court was broadly supportive, so the civil rights statutes envisioned a more collaborative relationship between bureaucrats and judges, with expert agencies relying on the courts to elaborate the principles of the landmark statutes on the basis of their technocratic presentations.

Federal-state relations also underwent a transformation. The New Deal used carrots, not sticks, to entice the states into patterns of "cooperative federalism" that effectively subordinated them to federal oversight. It was very tough for state politicians to reject administrative guidelines when constituents were clamoring for huge sums of federal money.

The power of the federal carrot was on display in the struggle for southern school integration. It was only when HEW threatened to withhold funds that most school boards began to take desegregation seriously. But the push for real-world gains sometimes propelled the landmark statutes to move beyond New Deal paradigms. Most notably, the Voting Rights Act used federal sticks, not carrots, to break the back of discrimination against black voters. Under the 1965 and 1970 statutes, states and localities with racist histories could not change their electoral rules without obtaining prior permission from the Justice Department or the federal courts.

This potent combination of preemptive administrative and judicial power represented the greatest transformation of federal-state relations since the military occupation of the South during the first Reconstruction. But the nineteenth-century disruption was only temporary, while the twentieth-century transformation contemplated the ongoing subordination of the states to federal supervision—even on electoral matters that were at the very core of traditional notions of state "sovereignty."

———————— ◆ ————————

Private actors, not only state authorities, must recognize constitutional rights; these rights include equal opportunity as well as respectful treatment within each sphere of constitutional concern. The federal government will insist on the real-world realization of these rights through the collaborative efforts of expert agencies and courts, even at the cost of revolutionizing traditional notions of "states' rights." These four transformations add up to an enormous expansion of national constitutional authority over both private firms and the states, as well as an enormous expansion in the effective protection of the real-world rights of blacks and other protected groups.

The question is whether the legal community will sustain these achievements into the twenty-first century. This is by no means a certainty. The fate of the First Reconstruction serves as a cautionary tale. Within fifty years, the Fifteenth Amendment had become a dead letter; the Fourteenth, a charter for big business; the Thirteenth, a pale shadow of itself. The Reconstruction Republicans had canonized these egalitarian breakthroughs by means of Article Five amendments. But this wasn't nearly enough to prevent the legal profession from betraying these commitments, allowing them to fade from collective memory. Does a similar fate await the Second Reconstruction?

VARIETIES OF ERASURE

The threat is very real. The brand of textualism championed by Justices Antonin Scalia and Clarence Thomas insists that it is *only* the First Reconstruction that really counts in constitutional interpretation. Never mind that *Brown* explicitly denied that its constitutional principles were rooted in the original understanding of the Fourteenth Amendment; never mind that the civil rights movement, working with a broad bipartisan coalition, hammered out landmark statutes that went far beyond *Brown;* never mind that these landmark principles were repeatedly affirmed by

Richard Nixon, as well as Lyndon Johnson, with the broad and self-conscious support of the American people. According to these jurists, we should ignore the great constitutional achievements of the twentieth century because they did not conform to the rules laid out in Article V.

There is a bitter irony here. Article V formalisms did not save the First Reconstruction's egalitarian breakthroughs from obliteration within the short space of half a century. The leaders of the Second Reconstruction were on solid ground in refusing to make the same mistake by depending on Article V to propel their hard-won gains into the future. Given the New Deal's great success in deploying the separation-of-powers model to entrench its constitutional principles, it was only common sense for the civil rights leadership to adapt this model on behalf of the Second Reconstruction. Yet a half century later, Scalia and Thomas insist that these twentieth-century acts of popular sovereignty can be safely ignored since their leaders failed to amend the Constitution appropriately during the civil rights revolution—even though Article V formalisms failed the first time around, and even though Martin Luther King Jr. and a bipartisan political leadership self-consciously designed alternative methods for constitutional revision.

In taking this stand, Scalia and Thomas call themselves "originalists"—but they are wrong in doing so. I am the originalist, not they: this book has been dedicated to the elaboration of the *original understanding of We the People at one of the greatest constitutional moments in American history.*

Our disagreement lies elsewhere. Scalia and Thomas suppose that Article V provides the *only* way that We the People can speak, and I reject their hyperformalism as historically unjustified. As previous volumes show, their exclusivist interpretation of Article V cannot withstand an encounter with the facts surrounding the Founding or Reconstruction. On both occasions, America's leaders gained the authority to revise the forms of higher lawmaking to express new constitutional commitments in the name of the People. These early exercises in popular sovereignty provide precedents of constitutional adaptation that twentieth-century Americans developed further in speaking for the people during the New Deal and Second Reconstruction.[4] In ignoring this rich historical tradition, these hyperformalists are betraying the very idea of government by the People that they claim to champion.

A question-begging originalism serves as the most notorious judicial battering ram for obliterating the achievements of the twentieth century.

Chief Justice Roberts's recent opinion in *Shelby County v. Holder* represents a more insidious form of erasure—and one with which this book is primarily concerned.[5] Writing for a sharply divided Court, he struck down a key provision of the Voting Rights Act, basing this decision on a principle he derived from past judicial opinions—without even noticing that the American people, during both the First and the Second Reconstruction, self-consciously repudiated the application of his asserted principle to voting rights. By relying on We the Judges instead of We the People to invalidate a major accomplishment of the civil rights revolution, he demonstrated how the use of a narrowly court-centered canon can destroy our constitutional legacy.

Shelby County confronted the Voting Rights Act's decision to single out mostly southern states and localities for preemptive federal scrutiny of any changes they make in their electoral systems. Roberts rightly insisted that this step transformed conventional notions of federalism, requiring states to "beseech the Federal Government for permission to implement laws that they would otherwise have the right to enact and execute on their own."[6]

But does this break with the past violate the Constitution?

The Chief Justice recognized that *South Carolina v. Katzenbach* upheld the measure in 1966 and that later Courts approved subsequent extensions of the VRA. Nevertheless, he viewed the act's targeting provision (Section 4) with grave suspicion. Rather than giving it the deference normally accorded to statutes, he insisted that a "fundamental principle of *equal* sovereignty among the States" requires searching scrutiny—and that the provision failed this test.[7] But what is the constitutional basis for Roberts's asserted principle?

The Chief Justice did not root it in the Founding text or original understandings—for good reason, since the Founders notoriously refused to treat all states equally in their campaign for a new Constitution.[8] He relied exclusively on a handful of Supreme Court opinions, and even here his arguments were remarkably weak. But I leave my critique of his case law analysis to an endnote and focus on a more fundamental point.[9] In relying exclusively on a few judicial decisions, Roberts utterly failed to confront the fact that We the People have repeatedly and authoritatively repudiated the application of his asserted principle to the sphere of voting rights.

Begin with the Fourteenth Amendment. Its first section famously grants citizenship to the freedmen, but its second section is more relevant here. This provision expressly addresses the danger that some states will

deprive their new black citizens of voting rights, and targets such jurisdictions for a punitive response. It provides that states creating barriers
against black voters will suffer a proportionate reduction in the number of
representatives they can send to the House: if State X's population would
otherwise entitle it to ten members, but 40 percent of its citizens were
black, it could only elect six representatives if it abridged black voting
rights.[10] This constitutional command is flatly inconsistent with Roberts's
principle: it *explicitly* treats such states as second-class members of the
Union, and in the most fundamental way possible. While the VRA merely
requires targeted jurisdictions to submit changes in their election law for
prior federal approval, this sanction is mild compared to a reduction in
a state's representation in the House (and in presidential contests as
well, since a state's Electoral College vote depends on the number of its
representatives).

It is true, of course, that neither Congress nor the Court enforced this
constitutional requirement during the first two-thirds of the twentieth
century, allowing the white South to retain its full share of House members despite blatant acts of black disenfranchisement.[11] But this shameful
fact hardly excuses Roberts's failure to mention Section 2 at any point in
his opinion. To the contrary, his cavalier omission only dramatized his
judicial hubris in imposing a principle of "equal state sovereignty" in the
face of its explicit rejection by the Fourteenth Amendment.

Roberts followed up by erasing the Second Reconstruction. While he
made passing references to the civil rights movement's role in propelling
the VRA into law in 1965, he provided no analysis of the fierce constitutional debates provoked by this initiative. Congress and the states had recently taken the position that a formal Article V amendment was required to impose a relatively modest prohibition on state poll taxes, banning
them only in federal elections. This limited ban was finally ratified as the
Twenty-Fourth Amendment in 1964. Yet only one year later President
Johnson was proposing to take a detour around Article V and impose far
more sweeping incursions on states' rights under the VRA. Given the cautious steps approved by Twenty-Four, how in the world could Johnson's
initiative pass constitutional muster?

This question was taken with high seriousness by the Justice Department and congressional leaders of both parties. Recall that the NAACP
and other civil rights groups had *opposed* the proposal of the Twenty-
Fourth Amendment precisely because it would establish a precedent that

would block the far-reaching statutory interventions necessary to make black voting rights a reality in the South.

When Lyndon Johnson went before Congress to propose the VRA in his great "We Shall Overcome" speech, he was not only joining rhetorical forces with the civil rights movement. He was speaking a literal truth: it would indeed be necessary to overcome *very* formidable constitutional objections before the VRA could become law. The Justice Department and the congressional leadership rose to this challenge with great creativity, rejecting the claim that Article V provided the exclusive means of revising the Constitution in the name of the American people. This claim generated a very serious and highly visible debate—but it finally succeeded in gaining decisive congressional support, thanks to the last-minute intervention of Martin Luther King Jr.

In *Shelby County,* the Chief Justice consigned all this to the shadows. He applied his judge-made principle of "equal state sovereignty" without noticing how King, Johnson, Dirksen, Nicholas Katzenbach, and Mike Mansfield successfully redefined the relationship between landmark statutes and formal constitutional amendments, putting the VRA on the same level as the Twenty-Fourth Amendment. (For more, return to Chapter 5.)

But the VRA was not propelled into our higher law at a single moment in 1965. As the Chief Justice noted, "given the unprecedented nature of these measures,"[12] its experiment in preemptive federal supervision was scheduled to expire in five years, requiring a sober reconsideration of its enduring value. Once again, however, Roberts failed to give *any* consideration to the debate provoked by the renewal question. By this point, initial federal interventions under the VRA had already yielded large gains in the South, with a million new black voters and four hundred black elected officials already making their voices heard.[13]

By 1970, conservatives were arguing strongly that the time had come to return to traditional federalist principles. But after a long and highly visible discussion, President Nixon and Congress decided that the regime of preemptive federal supervision should continue. What is more, the ongoing debate expressed an emphatic concern with the danger that second-generation forms of voter disempowerment such as racial gerrymandering would undermine recent gains. It was this threat that led leading Republicans to endorse the need for continuing preemptive federal oversight.[14]

Since he turned his back on this reenactment history, Chief Justice Roberts failed to recognize the significance of second-generation voter discrimination as a basic motivation for the VRA's transformation of federal-state relations.[15] More fundamentally, he failed to appreciate how the second round of deliberation in 1970 greatly enhanced the legitimacy of the entire higher lawmaking process, permitting the participants to reflect on the lessons of five years of experience before giving their considered approval to continued federal intervention in states with histories of discrimination. (For more, return to Chapter 8.)

At three critical moments in 1868, 1965, and 1970, America's political leaders made solemn constitutional commitments, in the name of the American people, to target states that posed a special danger to minority voting rights. It is only by consigning these moments to oblivion that Chief Justice Roberts could view the VRA as a constitutional anomaly, requiring specially compelling justification to pass muster under his judge-made principle of "equal state sovereignty." This entire book is one long argument against such acts of erasure from the constitutional canon.

Once deprived of his master principle, Roberts's case against the VRA would collapse, as his only objection to the statute depends on the validity of the Constitution's purported commitment to equal sovereignty. Roberts's critique focused on the formula used by Section 4 to identify the states and localities requiring preemptive federal oversight. When President Nixon and Congress reapproved the new regime, they once again wrote a five-year sunset into the law, requiring reconsideration in 1975. At that point, President Ford and Congress reinvigorated the law for a seven-year term, updating Section 4's targeting formula by making low voter participation in 1972, the most recent presidential election year, the decisive trigger for Justice Department oversight.

In 1982, President Reagan and Congress took a different approach. On one hand, they cemented federal intervention into the living Constitution by renewing it for a quarter of a century. On the other hand, they didn't update the formula, retaining 1972 voter turnout as the trigger for federal intervention. In 2006, President George W. Bush and Congress followed down the same track, renewing the provisions for another quarter-century but leaving the 1972 trigger intact.

This was not good enough for the Chief Justice. He insisted that, before the act could pass constitutional muster, Congress must update its triggering formula to take recent conditions explicitly into account. In making this demand, Roberts recognized that Congress's decision to retain the old formula was very deliberate. As Justice Ruth Bader Ginsburg explained in her opinion for the four dissenters, the House and Senate held repeated hearings and compiled a fifteen-thousand-page record exploring all sides of the issue. She showed that Congress had lots of evidence to support the 1972 formula's continued utility in identifying states that posed a relatively great threat to minority voting rights. If judged by ordinary standards, there can be no question that Congress's elaborate evidentiary record more than satisfied constitutional requirements.[16]

Only the Chief Justice's commitment to "equal state sovereignty" led him to impose a far more rigorous standard of proof—one that he claimed could not be satisfied without an explicit update of the formula. But this conclusion cannot be any better than its premises, and we have seen that Roberts's purported principle was expressly repudiated during both the First and Second Reconstructions. Once these self-conscious constitutional decisions are exposed to view, the Roberts opinion appears as a shattering judicial betrayal of We the People.

Shelby County represents a tragic role reversal in standard institutional relationships. Generally speaking, the political branches emphasize current realities, while the courts take constitutional history seriously. But a very different scenario is at work here: Chief Justice Roberts imposed his view of present realities on the decision by President Bush and his Congress to honor the constitutional achievements of the past.

Recall the condition of the country in 2005 and 2006, when the VRA was last up for political review: Americans were still reeling from the shock of September 11, battling in Afghanistan and Iraq, and confronting the grim prospect of a global "war on terror." The center of constitutional politics had shifted accordingly, with passionate debates over the scope of presidential power and the proper balance between national commitments to liberty and security. With headlines dominated by these concerns, the debate over the VRA's renewal competed for public attention with a host of other issues on the second-order political agenda. Within this context, the entire effort at VRA renewal could well have ended in complete failure—especially given southern politicians' desire to liberate themselves from intrusive federal oversight. But this didn't happen. President Bush and Congress were determined to honor the past, and they did so with overwhelming majorities in their aptly named Fannie Lou Hamer, Rosa Parks, and Coretta Scott King Voting Rights Act.

Undoubtedly, Chief Justice Roberts was right in thinking that these statesmen—to call them by their proper name—could have written a better statute if they had spent even more time and energy hammering out a new technocratic formula. But this was far too much to expect at a time when the mass mobilizations and wide-ranging debates of the 1960s and 1970s had long since faded into the past. Now that VRA renewal is treated as a matter of "normal politics," the crucial question is whether the rising generation of Americans will remain faithful to the higher lawmaking achievements of their parents and grandparents. President Bush and Congress deserve praise, not censure, for answering that question with a resounding yes.

The Roberts Court was profoundly mistaken in forcing this question back onto the political agenda, especially when mere congressional inaction will suffice to erase a central act of higher lawmaking by We the People in the twentieth century.

———————◆———————

I am not in the business of predicting the future. Perhaps the next few years will see the rise of a coalition of Democrats and Republicans who are determined to reaffirm the Voting Rights Act; perhaps not. Only one thing is clear: it is not enough to undo the damage done by the Roberts Court in *Shelby County*. A much broader effort is required to sustain the commitments of the Second Reconstruction.

Consider the stakes involved in restoring *Brown* to its rightful place at the center of the constitutional canon. If taken seriously, the principles announced in Earl Warren's great opinion have a broad reach: blacks and women, Muslim and Hispanic Americans, the mentally and physically disabled, gays, lesbians, and the transgendered—all these people often find themselves in conditions of institutionalized humiliation. They are all entitled to constitutional protection under *Brown*'s understanding of the Equal Protection Clause, affirmed by the People during the Second Reconstruction.

But one pathology looms especially large. If we look squarely at social reality, as *Brown* demands, no thoughtful American can ignore the daily humiliations heaped upon the eleven million undocumented immigrants who live among us. These men, women, and children are now part of America. They will not be going away. The only serious question is whether the Constitution allows today's Americans to treat them in the same demeaning fashion in which southerners treated blacks before the civil rights revolution.

If the spirit of *Brown* survives in the living Constitution, the answer must be no. It is the solemn duty of our standing institutions to signal the need to confront the reality of their pervasive institutionalized humiliation, and to remedy the ongoing denial of equal protection "with all deliberate speed."

As *Windsor* suggests, even the very conservative Roberts Court will sometimes strike a blow against institutionalized humiliation. But there is zero chance that it will exercise constitutional leadership on this key issue. It is up to the president and Congress to take on this challenge, at least in the short run. Over the next decade, the role of the Supreme Court will depend on the political contingencies prevailing when vacancies open up. Will future presidents nominate, and Senates confirm, more Justices who are at war with the twentieth century? Or will the future belong to jurists who are willing to give full recognition to the century's greatest achievements?

Suppose the escalating betrayal of the Second Reconstruction by the Roberts Court provokes a strong political reaction and the subsequent appointment of justices who take the twentieth century seriously. Even then, the legal community confronts formidable challenges. The Constitution is a work of many generations. While the Second Reconstruction made important contributions, it by no means transformed all that went before; many traditional understandings survive, and many others may be thoughtfully adapted to accommodate the civil rights revolution. This is the challenge of *intergenerational synthesis,* and I have sketched its distinctive features in an earlier volume.[17] The final book in this series will make a more sustained effort to integrate the contributions of each constitutional moment into a larger doctrinal synthesis. But I encourage each of you to take up this task in your own efforts to make sense of the Constitution. Almost every important problem requires an interpreter to integrate principles inherited from at least two turning points of constitutional history. It will take lots of work, and many different workers, to gain an informed sense of the ways in which the contributions of different generations should be brought to bear in a wide variety of concrete issues. Indeed, recent writers are already contributing valuable insights to this project.[18]

We could simplify our interpretive problem by privileging the efforts of one or two generations, in the manner of Justices Scalia and Thomas. Or we could simply ignore the higher lawmaking tradition altogether, in the manner of Chief Justice Roberts. But the aim of constitutional interpretation isn't to simplify the lives of lawyers. The great task is to redeem the proud boast that We the People *do* have the last say in America—by giving due recognition to *each* generation's achievements in shaping and reshaping the country's constitutional commitments over the course of the centuries.

A THIRD RECONSTRUCTION?

Both political determination and legal insight will be required if America is to sustain its commitment to the Second Reconstruction over the coming decades. The struggle to preserve the civil rights legacy, however, should not blind us to its very serious limitations.

Consider Lyndon Johnson's remarks in his famous address to the graduating class of Howard University in 1965. With the Civil Rights Act on the books, and the Voting Rights Act speeding its way to enactment, Johnson provided this sobering overview:

> The voting rights bill will be the latest, and among the most important, in a long series of victories. But this victory—as Winston Churchill said of another triumph for freedom—"is not the end. It is not even the beginning of the end. But it is, perhaps, the end of the beginning."
>
> That beginning is freedom; and the barriers to that freedom are tumbling down. Freedom is the right to share, share fully and equally, in American society—to vote, to hold a job, to enter a public place, to go to school. It is the right to be treated in every part of our national life as a person equal in dignity and promise to all others.
>
> But freedom is not enough. . . . You do not take a person who, for years, has been hobbled by chains and liberate him, bring him up to the starting line of a race and then say, "you are free to compete with all the others," and still justly believe that you have been completely fair.
>
> Thus it is not enough just to open the gates of opportunity. All our citizens must have the ability to walk through those gates.
>
> This is the next and the more profound stage of the battle for civil rights. We seek not just freedom but opportunity. We seek not just legal equity but human ability, not just equality as a right and a theory but equality as a fact and equality as a result. . . .

To this end equal opportunity is essential, but not enough, not enough. Men and women of all races are born with the same range of abilities. But ability is not just the product of birth. Ability is stretched or stunted by the family that you live with, and the neighborhood you live in—by the school you go to and the poverty or the richness of your surroundings. It is the product of a hundred unseen forces playing upon the little infant, the child, and finally the man.

This graduating class at Howard University is witness to the indomitable determination of the Negro American to win his way in American life. . . .

These are proud and impressive achievements. But they tell only the story of a growing middle class minority, steadily narrowing the gap between them and their white counterparts.

But for the great majority of Negro Americans—the poor, the unemployed, the uprooted, and the dispossessed—there is a much grimmer story. They still . . . are another nation. Despite the court orders and the laws, despite the legislative victories and the speeches, for them the walls are rising and the gulf is widening.[19]

The president was continuing the great jurisprudential theme announced in *Brown* and carried forward by the landmark statutes. He insisted that the nation's commitment to equality extends beyond legal theory to the facts of social life. Yet his main point was to emphasize the limited spheres in which the landmark statutes will operate: guaranteeing the right "to vote, to hold a job, to enter a public place, to go to school." Johnson called this "freedom"; I have been calling it "spherical equality of opportunity." But whatever you call it, the president said that it represents only a first step.

His ultimate objective has often been misinterpreted. In using the phrase "equality as a fact and equality as a result," Johnson did not mean that everyone should get the same results regardless of his or her efforts and achievements. He was saying that *real* equality of opportunity required a new series of landmark statutes aimed at eliminating the unequal conditions endured by the "great majority of Negro Americans—the poor, the unemployed, the uprooted and the dispossessed."

In the rest of his speech, Johnson announced his program for a "Great Society" that would target "the root causes of . . . poverty" and the special burdens of "hatred and hopelessness" imposed by the nation's history of slavery and racism. He insisted that "we will accelerate, and we will broaden [our] attack [on these conditions] in years to come until this most enduring of foes finally yields to our unyielding will."

But it was one thing for Johnson to gain the applause of the graduates of Howard, and quite another for him to win the consent of We the People. While Congress did pass a first round of anti-poverty legislation, and Martin Luther King Jr. moved to expand these initiatives until an assassin's bullet cut him down, this wasn't nearly enough to win landmark status for the Great Society. Before they could earn a constitutional mandate for a radical expansion of the aims of the Second Reconstruction, the political leadership and its movement base would have had to sustain broad popular support in election after election, and this simply didn't happen. To the contrary, Richard Nixon's landslide victory over George McGovern represented a popular repudiation of Johnson's and King's efforts to lead the nation to another decisive breakthrough.

Hundreds of books have been written to explain the causes of this failure. This isn't one of them. I want to interpret the constitutional meaning of the Great Society's failure, not the causes. From this perspective, a parallel with Radical Reconstruction of the 1860s is most instructive.

Recall Thaddeus Stevens's great speech, reprinted at greater length in Chapter 8, in which he presented a vision of a "purified Republic" that would be "freed . . . from every vestige of human oppression, of inequality of rights, of the recognized degradation of the poor, and the superior caste of the rich." He delivered his speech just before the House approved the Fourteenth Amendment, but he did not rise to the floor to celebrate this great turning point in constitutional history. To the contrary, he viewed it as an act of betrayal: "I find that we shall be obliged to be content with patching up the worst portions of the ancient edifice, and leaving it, in many of its parts, to be swept through by the tempests, the frosts, and the storms of despotism."[20]

For Stevens and other Radicals, the Fourteenth Amendment represented the decisive failure of their campaign to provide blacks with the crucial resources they needed to win *real* equality of opportunity in the New South—including "forty acres and a mule" and a free public education. Without these resources, the freedmen would be unable to defend their interests against white oppression.[21]

He was right. So was Lyndon Johnson when he warned that "the gulf is widening" between the college-educated elite and "the poor, the unemployed, the uprooted, and the dispossessed." A half century later, we are living in a new Gilded Age, with economic inequality reaching new heights.

How will Americans of the twenty-first century respond to this challenge? Will they fulfill the hopes of Stevens and Johnson and take wide-ranging action against "the root causes of . . . poverty" and the burdens of "hatred and hopelessness"? If they fall short, will they make large if limited commitments to equality comparable to those endorsed by We the People at the Founding, during the First Reconstruction, in the New Deal, and in the Second Reconstruction?

Or will the very memory of these commitments be lost in a fog of ancestor worship?

NOTES

INDEX

NOTES

Abbreviations

CR	*Congressional Record*
FFF	Bruce Ackerman, *The Failure of the Founding Fathers* (2005)
LAT	*Los Angeles Times*
NYT	*New York Times*
WP	*Washington Post*
WP: F	Bruce Ackerman, *We the People, Volume 1: Foundations* (1991)
WP: T	Bruce Ackerman, *We the People, Volume 2: Transformations* (1998)
WSJ	*Wall Street Journal*

Introduction

1. See Ernest Renan, *What Is a Nation?* (W. R. Taylor trans. [1996]), on the importance of remembering and forgetting in the construction of a national ethos.
2. See *WP: T* 437–39, nn. 34, 38.
3. See *WP: T* 99–278.
4. See generally *FFF*.

1. Are We a Nation?

1. See generally Akhil Amar, "Intertextualism," 112 *Harv. L. Rev.* 747 (1999).
2. See Sanford Levinson, "Authorizing Constitutional Text: On the Purported Twenty-Seventh Amendment," 11 *Const. Comment.* 101, 101–08 (1994).
3. The opinion filed by the four dissenters was especially emphatic; see Nat'l Fed'n of Indep. Bus. v. Sebelius, 183 *L. Ed. 2d* 450, 536 (2012), but Chief Justice Roberts's separate opinion also advanced a remarkably restrictive approach to Congress's power under the Necessary and Proper Clause to regulate interstate commerce. See id. at 473–80.
4. Alfarabi, by the way, was a great Islamic thinker who spent most of his life in tenth-century Baghdad. His main project was the integration of Greek philosophy

343

into Islamic thought, but he was also an important music theorist and performer. See Philippe Vallat, *Farabi et l'École d'Alexandrie: Des prémisses de la connaissance à la philosophie politique* (2004). Any similarity between the historical Alfarabi and my imaginary character is strictly coincidental.

This isn't true when it comes to the not-so-subtle reference to my friend Akhil Amar—though his views on the latter-day amendments are far from those I attribute to Alfarabi. See generally Amar, *America's Unwritten Constitution* (2011).

5. For a fuller account, see *WP: T* 32–95.

6. See *WP: T* 57–63.

7. McCulloch v. Maryland, 17 U.S. (4 Wheat.) 316, 403 (1819).

8. I describe the pervasive constitutional problems in *WP: T* at 99–252.

9. See generally Charles Fairman, *History of the Supreme Court of the United States: Five Justices and the Electoral Commission of 1877* (1988).

10. Slaughterhouse cases, 83 U.S. 36 (1873).

11. Professor Robert Wiebe, who devoted much of his life to the subject, remarks: "Contrary to later myths, the Civil War strengthened regional far more than comprehensive loyalties. Union referred to a constitutional doctrine, to the winning side in the war, not the whole United States." Wiebe, *Who We Are: A History of Popular Nationalism* 92 (2002).

12. For a good account of the rise of the Guarantee Clause during the first century and its precipitous decline after Reconstruction, see William Wiecek, *The Guarantee Clause of the U.S. Constitution* (1972).

13. For a notable exception, see Michael Gerhardt, "Super Precedent," 90 *Minn. L. Rev.* 1204 (2006).

14. Abraham Lincoln, Speech at Peoria, Illinois (Oct. 16, 1854), in Roy P. Basler ed., 2 *Collected Works of Abraham Lincoln* 247, 251–52 (1953).

15. Harlan Fiske Stone, "The Common Law in the United States," 50 *Harv. L. Rev.* 4, 13 (1936).

16. William Eskridge & John Ferejohn, *A Republic of Statutes* (2010).

17. Cass Sunstein, *The Second Bill of Rights* 62 (2004).

18. Although my view of landmark statutes is innovative in the American context, it is already an established part of contemporary French constitutional practice. See Champeil-Desplats, *Les principes fondamentaux reconnus par les lois de la république* 69–107 (2001).

19. Jed Rubenfeld's fine work on the nature of constitutional commitment is particularly relevant. See Rubenfeld, *Freedom and Time* 91–103 (2001); Rubenfeld, *Revolution by Judiciary* 71–141 (2005).

20. Compare Ronald Dworkin, *Freedom's Law* 1–38 (1996), with Antonin Scalia, *Common-Law Courts in a Civil-Law System,* in Amy Gutmann ed., *A Matter of Interpretation* 3 (1997). There is a very wide distance between Justice Scalia and Professor Dworkin, with space for many different views—mine is only one among them.

21. For two notable, but very different, recent contributions to this line, see Jack Balkin, *Living Originalism* (2011) and David Strauss, *The Living Constitution* (2010).

22. Justice Scalia has famously described himself as a "faint-hearted originalist," Scalia, "Originalism: The Lesser Evil," 57 *U. Cin. L. Rev.* 849, 861–64 (1989) who deploys *stare decisis* as a pragmatic device to restrain an all-out assault on the twentieth century.

23. For some preliminary reflections, see *WP: F* at 86–99.

24. My dictum is a variation on Holmes's famous pronouncement, which categorically devalues logic in a way that I reject. See Oliver Wendell Holmes, *The Common Law* 1 (1881).

2. The Living Constitution

1. Compare Sacvan Bercovitch, *The American Jeremiad* (1978) with Hannah Arendt, *On Revolution* (1963). See *WP: F* 203–21.

2. See *FFF*, 249–50.

3. See Gordon Wood, *The Creation of the American Republic* 162–67 (1969).

4. See James Ceaser, *Presidential Selection* 41–87 (1979).

5. See *FFF* 16–35, 77–93.

6. See *FFF* 203–06.

7. In speaking of the normalization of movement politics, I adapt a familiar Weberian notion—the "bureaucratization of charisma"—to American political life.

8. Though it does not use the term, the best book in political science on presidential plebiscitarianism is by Stephen Skowronek, *The Politics Presidents Make* (1993).

9. See Joseph Schumpeter, *Capitalism, Socialism and Democracy* (1942). Schumpeter's theme is elaborated in countless variations by modern political scientists, most notably by William Riker, *Liberalism Against Populism* (1982).

3. The Assassin's Bullet

1. See Ira Katznelson & Quinn Mulroy, "Was the South Pivotal?," 74 *J. Pol.* 604 (2012); and generally Ira Katznelson, *Fear Itself* (2013).

2. See Jacquelyn Hall, "The Long Civil Rights Movement and the Political Uses of the Past," 91 *J. Amer. Hist.* 1233 (2005). Some notable recent contributions include Mark Brilliant, *The Color of America Has Changed* (2010), Tomiko Brown-Nagin, *Courage to Dissent* (2011), Glenda Gilmour, *Defying Dixie* (2008), and Thomas Sugrue, *Sweet Land of Liberty* (2008).

3. The Dixiecrat revolt at the 1948 Democratic National Convention gave Truman the political space he needed to issue his executive order desegregating the military. Since Strom Thurmond's Dixiecrat candidacy would predictably deprive Truman of some electoral votes from the Deep South, it made sense to appeal to northern liberals who might otherwise be attracted to the left-wing candidacy of

Henry Wallace. But in fact Truman avoided taking a strong position on other civil right issues during the campaign. See Gary Donaldson, *Truman Defeats Dewey* 188–89 (1999).

    Once elected, Cold War imperatives encouraged the Truman administration to make other gestures, including an amicus brief in *Brown* urging the Court to overrule *Plessy*. See Mary Dudziak, "*Brown* as a Cold War Case," 91 *J. Amer. Hist.* 32 (June 2004). But when the Justices deferred decision until the following year, the Eisenhower administration filed a supplemental brief that failed to reaffirm this position. Since Assistant Attorney General J. Lee Rankin expected to be pressed on the issue at oral argument, he "got his instructions from [Attorney General] Brownell, who presumably had cleared them with Eisenhower. The instructions were: "Don't volunteer . . . However if you're asked, and only if you're asked, then you say, 'We adhere to the position previously taken by the United States.'" Rankin followed these instructions to the letter. See Norman Silber, *With All Deliberate Speed: The Life of Philip Elman* 212 (2004) (quotation from Elman, an assistant solicitor general, who helped prepare Rankin for the oral argument).

4. See Barbara Sinclair, *The Transformation of the U.S. Senate* 53 (1990).
5. The legalists are legion. The classic political science account is by Gerald N. Rosenberg, *The Hollow Hope* 42–169 (1991), who rightly emphasizes the crucial role of politics in ratifying *Brown* in the 1960s but downplays the Court's constructive role in forcing the political establishment, and Americans more generally, to confront the constitutional issue during the 1950s.
6. See Michael Klarman, *From Jim Crow to Civil Rights* 364–66 (2004).
7. This key point is trivialized by legal scholars who try to vindicate *Brown* by pointing to public opinion polls and other evidence suggesting that a narrow national majority supported *Brown* in 1954. See Barry Friedman, *The Will of the People* 244–45 (2009); Jeffrey Rosen, *The Most Democratic Branch* 63–64 (2006). But the *Brown* Court could not know whether this weak majority would collapse under the pressure of backlash or whether it would yield a mobilized movement for civil rights. For a penetrating critique, see Justin Driver, "The Consensus Constitution," 89 *Tex. L. Rev.* 755 (2011). For thoughtful reflections on the regime-shattering implications of the rise of civil rights, see Paul Frymer, *Black and Blue* (2008).
8. Edward Carmines & James Stimson, *Issue Evolution* 111–12 (Figs. 4.7, 4.8) (1989).
9. Id. at 35–37, 56 (Fig. 2.3). Apart from his public stands, Stevenson's private conversation with Arthur Schlesinger in 1956 is revealing:

> On civil rights, he kept saying that . . . it was raising false hopes to suggest that people's minds and hearts could be changed by coercion; that the Negro leaders were defeating their own purposes when they put on pressure; that the only Negro hope was to reduce tension and let the moderate-minded southerners assume local leadership and work out the problems of adjustment in a gradualist way.

> I pointed out . . . that the Negroes had never gotten anywhere except through putting on pressure, and they knew it. . . . I said that he expected the Negroes to be more reasonable than he expected the southerners to be, and that this seemed to me unfair. He replied that of course it was unfair . . . but life was unfair.

Arthur Schlesinger, *Journals: 1952–2000,* 41–42 (Andrew and Stephen Schlesinger eds., 2007).

10. See Nick Bryant, *The Bystander* 58 (2006),

11. See Herbert Brownell with John Burke, *Advising Ike* 163–230 (1993).

12. See Robert Burk, *The Eisenhower Administration and Black Civil Rights* 204–27 (1984). Daniel Rodriguez and Barry Weingast fail to appreciate this point in their influential study "The Positive Political Theory of Legislative History: New Perspectives on the Civil Rights Act of 1964 and its Interpretation," 151 *U. Penn. L. Rev.* 1417, 1458 (2003): "[A]lthough it is true that, since President Lincoln, the Republicans had been the party supporting the rights of African Americans, this historical association changed to a degree with Franklin Roosevelt and the New Deal. This shift continued into the 1950s, by which time President Eisenhower was a reluctant supporter of civil rights." To the contrary, Americans continued to identify Republicans as the racially liberal party through the late 1950s and early 1960s, and Eisenhower's success in carrying 40 percent of the black vote in 1956 made it seem realistic to believe that most blacks might well return to the party of Lincoln. While Eisenhower was personally "reluctant" to endorse *Brown,* Adlai Stevenson was even more so. See Carmines & Stimson, supra n. 8, at 35–37, 56 (Fig. 2.3), 111–12 (Figs. 4.7, 4.8), and Schlesinger, supra n. 9.

13. See 103 *CR 1,* 178–79 (1957).

14. See Robert Caro, *The Years of Lyndon Johnson: Master of the Senate* 857–58 (2002).

15. During his first decade in the House, from 1938 to 1948, Johnson voted in stereotypical southern fashion against every civil rights initiative. See Mark Stern, *Calculating Visions: Kennedy, Johnson, and Civil Rights* 120 (1992). Johnson followed a similar temporizing strategy in dealing with the Civil Rights Act of 1960, once again drastically weakening the bill to avoid a southern filibuster. See Robert Mann, *The Walls of Jericho* 198–99, 252–60 (1996); Jonathan Rosenberg & Zachary Karabell, *Kennedy, Johnson, and the Quest for Justice* 23–25 (2003).

16. See Nick Kotz, *Judgment Days* 76 (2005). Once again, Daniel Rodriguez and Barry Weingast, supra n. 12, fail to appreciate these complexities in asserting that "it was the Democrats who pushed [civil rights] legislation in 1957 and 1960." Id. at 1458. While my discussion in the text highlights the 1957 act, the dynamics of the 1960 act were similarly complex, with Republican William McCulloch playing a central role in propelling the act through the House while Lyndon Johnson diluted key provisions in the Senate. See sources cited at n. 15.

17. Michael Klarman brilliantly describes the radicalization of southern politics provoked by *Brown* in *From Jim Crow, supra* n. 6, at 385–408 (2004).

18. Dan Carter, *The Politics of Rage* 96 (1995).

19. See Gayle v. Browder, 352 U.S. 903 (1956).

20. See Taylor Branch, *Parting the Waters: America in the King Years, 1954–63*, 206–71 (1988).

21. See generally Klarman, *supra* n. 6.

22. With the help of his running mate, Lyndon Johnson, Kennedy carried most of the South, winning electoral votes from white supremacist Alabama (5 votes), Arkansas (8 votes), Georgia (12), South Carolina (8), Louisiana (10), as well as somewhat more moderate North Carolina (14), Missouri (13), and Texas (24). Since Kennedy won only 303 electoral votes, he needed those of four of the first five racist states to put him over the 270-vote majority required for victory. See David Leip, "United States Presidential Election Results," *Dave Leip's Atlas of U.S. Presidential Elections* (2012), http://uselectionatlas.org/RESULTS/index.html.

23. See generally Karen Orren, *Belated Feudalism* (1991).

24. See Irving Bernstein, *Turbulent Years* 37–125 (1970).

25. A generally admiring Arthur Schlesinger summarizes Kennedy's civil rights program during his first two years as "piecemeal improvements in existing voting legislation, technical assistance to school districts voluntarily seeking to desegregate, an extension of the life of the Civil Rights Commission." Schlesinger, *A Thousand Days: John F. Kennedy in the White House* 951 (1965). For two more detailed views, compare Carl Brauer's sympathetic account, *John F. Kennedy and the Second Reconstruction* (1977), with the more critical interpretation offered by Bryant, *supra* n. 10, at 225–427.

26. Drew Hansen, *The Dream* 77–78 (2003). I have added the five-point enumeration for ease of exposition.

27. King's emphasis on police brutality is not addressed by the landmark statutes—though it is one of the great themes of the Warren Court. The relationship between the Court and the movement is particularly complicated in this area, and I shall take it up in volume 4 of this series.

28. See Kotz, *supra* n. 16, at 62 (2005) ("As it became clear that Senator Barry Goldwater . . . probably would be the Republican presidential nominee, King sensed that Kennedy was less inclined to push for civil rights"); Robert Caro, *The Years of Lyndon Johnson: The Passage of Power* 347 (2012) ("In his final news conference . . . Kennedy, instead of repeating his demands for speedy passage . . . , had spoken of an 'eighteen-month delivery' which would mean that the . . . civil rights bill [would pass] by the end of [1965]").

29. See Branch, *supra* n. 20, at 922 (internal quotation marks omitted). Establishment insiders voiced similar sentiments. Harvard Law School dean Erwin Griswold, a member of the Civil Rights Commission from 1961 through 1967, remarked, "Much more was accomplished under Johnson than would have happened if Kennedy had stayed [alive]. Of course, the times were different, but it

wasn't just the assassination. Kennedy did not have his feet on the ground in civil rights." Interview, Oct. 29, 1975, on file with the Kennedy Library, Boston, Massachusetts, Scott Rafferty Papers, Box 1.

30. See Mann, supra n. 15, at 252–60.

31. See Hansen, supra n. 26, at 79–80.

32. I explore this Founding mistake, as well as the failure of the Twelfth Amendment to remedy it, in *FFF* 203–06.

33. See generally *WP: T* 169–78.

34. Lincoln repeatedly stated that he wanted to get Dred Scott "reversed if we can, and a new judicial rule established upon this subject." Abraham Lincoln, Sixth Debate with Stephen A. Douglas, Oct. 13, 1858, in Roy P. Basler ed., 3 *Collected Works of Abraham Lincoln* 245, 255; Abraham Lincoln, Speech at Columbus, Ohio, Sept. 16, 1859, in 2 *Collected Works*, at 400, 401.

35. I tell this story at length in *WP: T* 137–234.

36. See Lyndon Johnson, *The Vantage Point* 91 (1971) (reporting Kennedy's effort to persuade him to accept the vice presidential nomination because it would "assure support in the Southern states").

37. See generally Kotz, supra n. 16, at 250–77 (elaborating the complex relationship between King and Johnson).

38. Johnson's previous civil rights record in Congress was mixed at best. See n. 15 supra. Once he became vice president, he also pursued a cautious approach as chairman of the Committee on Equal Employment Opportunity. See Robert Dallek, *Flawed Giant* 23–30 (1988). When he began to play a more active role in early negotiations on civil rights legislation, the Kennedy administration cut his engagement short. See Caro, supra n. 28, at 263–64 (2012).

39. Dallek, supra n. 38, at 114 (alteration in original). See Caro, supra n. 28, at 348–49.

40. Woodrow Wilson was born and raised in the South, but he owed his national prominence to political success in New Jersey.

41. See Dallek, supra n. 38, at 182–83.

42. It's hard to prove a counterfactual, but my hypothesis is fortified by the masterful account provided by Taylor Branch, *At Canaan's Edge: America in the King Years, 1965–68* (2006).

43. See generally Michael Kammen, *A Machine That Would Go of Itself* (1986). I contest this view in *WP: F* 200–65.

4. The New Deal Transformed

1. Lyndon Johnson, *Public Papers of the Presidents of the United States, 1963–64* 8–10 (1965).

2. Johnson was perfectly aware of the fateful character of his decision to use the Kennedy legacy as a springboard for a civil rights breakthrough. Robert Caro describes the crucial meeting between Johnson and his closest advisors as they hashed out the crucial terms of the president's speech:

After dinner Fortas, Humphrey and several other Johnson allies worked on the speech at the dining room table. . . . [A] fierce debate then erupted—over the emphasis to be given in the speech to civil rights. "A great issue was whether he would recommend congressional action" on rights, Fortas was to recall, "and, if so, whether he should put that as a number one item." Several of the men at the table said that pressuring for passage of a civil rights bill would jeopardize the tax cut, and the appropriations bills, and would shatter Johnson's relationship with the southerners who had always been the base of his strength in Congress, and whose support he would need there now. The discussion had gone on, Fortas was to say, "for hours"—until about 2:30 in the morning—with Johnson sitting silently listening when . . . "[o]ne of the wise, practical people around the table" urged Johnson not to press for civil rights in his first speech, because there was no chance of passage, and a President shouldn't waste his power on lost causes—no matter how worthy the cause might be. "The presidency has only a certain amount of coinage to expend, and you oughtn't to expend it on this," he said.

"Well, what the hell's the presidency for?" Lyndon Johnson replied.

Robert Caro, *The Years of Lyndon Johnson: The Passage of Power* 428 (2012).

3. See Chapter 3, n. 15.

4. McCulloch was the ranking minority member of the Judiciary Committee throughout the period, and was the key Republican deal maker on civil rights legislation. See William Eskridge, *Dynamic Statutory Interpretation* 22 (1994).

5. Charles & Barbara Whalen, *The Longest Debate* 13 (1985); Nicholas Katzenbach, *Some of It Was Fun* 120–27 (2008).

6. See survey by Louis Harris & Associates, April 1964, retrieved February 15, 2007, from the iPOLL Databank, Roper Center for Public Opinion Research, University of Connecticut, at www.ropercenter.uconn.edu.ezp1.harvard.edu /ipoll.html.

7. 110 *CR* 13319 (1964). In emphasizing Dirksen's Lincolnian convictions, I part company from Daniel Rodriguez and Barry Weingast, who argue in their influential article, "The Positive Political Theory of Legislative History: New Perspectives on the Civil Rights Act of 1964 and its Interpretation," 151 *U. Penn. L. Rev.* 1417 (2003), that Dirksen's support for the landmark statute was partially motivated by a "larger project of weakening the Democratic Party's control of national politics." On their view, Dirksen was playing a Machiavellian game: by allowing Johnson to claim credit for the legislation, Dirksen would enable the Republicans to "dislodge the southern wing" of the Democratic Party, and thereby build a new Republican majority. Id. at 1478.

This is a bold conjecture, transforming Dirksen from a committed Lincolnian into one of the earliest architects of the "southern strategy" pursued in later decades. But the authors provide absolutely no evidence to support their extraordinary claim, as they obliquely recognize at n. 209: "We note that this argument does not require that Dirksen mastermind the Republican southern

strategy, but rather that he be sufficiently aware to take advantage of it." In indulging this premise, the authors suppose that, as early as 1963–1964, sensible
Republicans realized that they could not compete with Democrats for the vote
of blacks and strong racial liberals and therefore had nothing to lose by engaging in a southern strategy. This is simply false; see Chapter 3, nn. 12 and 16.
Dirksen was entirely reasonable in supposing that he could continue winning
elections in his home state, Illinois, by appealing to mainstream pro-business
voters who were also racial liberals or moderates—and that this was also a winning strategy in vast areas of the country, including the upper South. Moreover,
his public and private statements, along with his political actions, were entirely
consistent with those of many other mainstream Republicans, and completely
inconsistent with the Rodriguez-Weingast hypothesis. See generally Chapters
6–10.

8. See Nick Kotz, *Judgment Days* 141 (2005). Since I have emphasized my disagreements with Professors Rodriguez and Weingast, supra n. 7, I want to stress a key
point of agreement: I join them in rejecting the view, held by many writers,
suggesting that "civil rights legislation was all but certain by 1963." Id. at 1456–
57. To the contrary, without the many acts of statesmanship by Republicans
such as Dirksen and McCulloch, as well as Democrats including Humphrey
and Johnson, the legislative effort would have failed, making it impossible for
the Civil Rights Act to frame a fundamental constitutional choice for the American people as they considered the opposing views of the statute offered up by
Goldwater and Johnson in their presidential contest.

9. See Theodore White, *The Making of the President 1964*, 124 (1965).

10. See Charles Mohr, "Goldwater Says He'll Vote 'No' on the Rights Measure,"
NYT, June 19, 1964, at 1 (" 'If my vote is misconstrued, let it be, and let me suffer
its consequences,' the Arizona Senator said"). The *Times* reproduced the Republican front-runner's speech in full, id. at 18. Legal columnist Anthony Lewis
explained, on the same page, why Goldwater's opposition to the New Deal
Constitution was no longer accepted by the courts. See Anthony Lewis, "The
Courts Spurn Goldwater View," *NYT*, June 19, 1964, at 18.

11. See 110 *CR* 14,319 (June 18, 1964). Goldwater emphasized that his "basic objection" was to New Deal constitutional principles that authorized Congress to
pass the Civil Rights Act without a formal Article V amendment.

12. Lyndon Johnson, "Remarks on the River Front in Memphis," 2 *Public Papers of
the Presidents of the United States* 1408–09 (1965).

13. See generally, Ira Katznelson, *Fear Itself* (2013).

14. See Lyndon Johnson, *The Vantage Point* 103 (1971); see also Stephen Skowronek,
The Politics Presidents Make 336–41 (1997).

15. See Barry Goldwater, "The Conscience of a Conservative" 25–31, 65–67 (1960)
(attacking modern Republicanism); id. at 68–75 (attacking the welfare state as
socialistic).

16. For a classic statement of the skeptical case, see Robert Dahl, "Myth of the
Presidential Mandate," 105 *Pol. Sci. Q.* 355 (1990). Other important studies in

political science include Patricia Conley, *Presidential Mandates: How Elections Shape the National Agenda* (2001); George Edwards, *At the Margins: Presidential Leadership of Congress* (1989); George Edwards, *The Public Presidency: The Pursuit of Popular Support* (1983); Stanley Kelley, *Interpreting Elections* (1983).

17. See Denise Bostdorff, *The Presidency and the Rhetoric of Foreign Crisis* 57 (1994).

18. For a discussion of these conditions, see *WP: F* 266–94.

19. For some suggestions, see *WP: T* at 410–16; and Bruce Ackerman, "The New Separation of Powers," 113 *Harv. L. Rev.* 633, 666–68 (2000).

20. The "Great Society" came even later, on May 22, 1964. See Lyndon Baines Johnson, Remarks at the University of Michigan (May 22, 1964), available at www.lbjlib.utexas.edu/johnson/archives.hom/speeches.hom/640522.asp.

21. See White, supra n. 9, at 305 ("[D]iscussion of [civil rights] probably obsessed [private] American conversation in the summer and fall of 1964 more than any other [issue]").

22. On July 24, Goldwater and Johnson responded to a wave of black urban riots by agreeing informally to refrain from statements that could further inflame the volatile situation. But at a press conference before their meeting, Johnson made it clear that "he had no intention of taking the civil rights issue out of the campaign." Robert Dallek, *Flawed Giant* 134 (1988). Barry Goldwater's position on civil rights was long standing and well known. He repeated his familiar positions in a nationwide television address on October 22, and he blitzed the South during the closing weeks of the campaign with regionally televised speeches. See Gene Shalit & L. K. Grossman eds., *Somehow It Works: A Candid Portrait of the 1964 Presidential Election* 203 (1965).

23. Heart of Atlanta Motel v. United States, 379 U.S. 241 (1964); Katzenbach v. McClung, 379 U.S. 294 (1964).

24. At the Court's conference, Harlan unequivocally stated, "On the Fourteenth Amendment, I would stand by the Civil Rights Cases and hold [the Civil Rights Act of 1964] unconstitutional." Del Dickson ed., *The Supreme Court in Conference (1940–1985)* 727 (2001); Tinsley Yarbrough, *John Marshall Harlan* 253 (1992).

25. During the early 1950s, Chief Justice Warren could afford to take a lot of time to gain unanimity for Brown. See Richard Kluger, *Simple Justice* 678–99 (1976). But by 1964, the Court was no longer in control of events—once the voters had decisively rejected Goldwater, a lengthy delay by the Court would have generated widespread uncertainties about the act's constitutionality, thereby granting provisional legitimacy to bitter-end efforts to defend Jim Crow on the ground.

26. Technically speaking, Justice Clark's opinions for the Court in Heart of Atlanta Motel and McClung were not unanimous, since Justice Hugo Black filed a special concurrence. See Heart of Atlanta Motel, supra n. 23, at 268–78. But from the doctrinal point of view, Justice Black adopted the same Commerce Clause theories elaborated by Justice Clark. While Justices Douglas and Goldberg also endorsed the Commerce Clause, they filed concurrences that relied on

the Fourteenth Amendment as an alternative ground. Heart of Atlanta at 279 (Douglas, J., concurring); Heart of Atlanta 291 (Goldberg, J., concurring).

27. Id. at 257.

28. McClung, supra n. 23, 296–97 (1964).

29. Perhaps the most distinctive achievement of Roosevelt's second term was the Fair Labor Standards Act of 1938, which established a national minimum wage for the first time in American history, repudiating the Old Court's restrictive doctrine in Hammer v. Dagenhart. While this was an important breakthrough, it pales by comparison to the achievements of Roosevelt's first term.

30. See *WP: T* 368–75.

31. Perhaps the most noteworthy achievement of the Kennedy years was the president's support of Congress's decision to approve the Twenty-Fourth Amendment. But as Chapters 5 and 6 show, this "success" was full of bittersweet paradoxes.

32. See Robert Mason, *The Republican Party and American Politics from Hoover to Reagan* 79–95 (2011); Joseph Barnes, *Willkie* 125–210 (1952).

33. "[Reagan] opposes the 1964 and 1965 civil rights laws as fully as Nixon supports them." Stephen Hess & David Broder, "Durability in Drive for Power Is Demonstrated," *WP*, Dec. 1, 1967, at A18. See Theodore White, supra n. 9, 236–247 (1969).

34. See Chapter 10.

35. Wallace called for "modifications in the Civil Rights Bill," which was "not in the interests of any citizen of this country, regardless of their race." George Wallace, *Hear Me Out* 18 (1968). He also continued to preach segregation: "[I]f we amalgamate into the one unit as advocated by the Communist philosophy, then the enrichment of our lives, the freedom for our development is gone forever. We become, therefore, a mongrel unit." Id. at 118.

36. Nixon did oppose court-ordered busing, but this Warren Court initiative was not rooted in the requirements of the civil rights acts. See Chapter 11. Otherwise, he explicitly supported "a decade of revolution in which the legal structure needed to guarantee equal rights has been laid in place." Nixon-Agnew Campaign Committee, *Nixon Speaks Out* 59 (1968); see also his promise to "enforce Title VI of the Civil Rights act"—a key element in breaking the back of school segregation in the South. Nixon-Agnew Campaign Committee, *Nixon on the Issues* 98 (1968).

37. See White, supra n. 9, at 363. See also id. at 372.

38. Nixon won 31,783,783 (43.4 percent), Humphrey 31,271,839 (42.7 percent); the difference was 600,000 votes. Wallace won 9,901,000 votes—or 13.5 percent. See David Leip, "1968 Presidential General Election Results," *Dave Leip's Atlas of U.S. Presidential Elections* (2012), at http://uselectionatlas.org/RESULTS/national.php?year=1968.

39. See Eric Foner, *Reconstruction* 557–62 (1988); William Gillette, *Retreat from Reconstruction 1869–1879* 25–55, 166–86 (1979).

40. See my *FFF* for an account of the birth agony of the movement-party-presidency model during the electoral crisis of 1800.

41. As King explained in the *Saturday Review,* his aim in organizing nonviolent demonstrations at Selma was to provoke violence and force the nation to witness scenes of police brutality, thereby calling "Americans of conscience" to "demand federal intervention and legislation." See Martin Luther King Jr., "Behind the Selma March," *Sat. Rev.*, Apr. 3, 1965, at 16: see also Michael Klarman, *From Jim Crow to Civil Rights* 429 (2004).

42. See Klarman, supra n. 41, at 421–42.

5. The Turning Point

1. See Edward Carmines & James Stimson, *Issue Evolution: Race and the Transformation of American Politics* 73 (1989).

2. See 102 *CR* 4515–16 (1956).

3. "The Twenty-Fourth Amendment," 1962 *Cong. Q. Almanac* 405.

4. "NAACP Against Tax Amendment," *Pittsburgh Courier* 16, Mar. 31, 1962.

5. See Manfred Berg, *The Ticket to Freedom* 105 (2005).

6. See Jerome Mileur, "The 'Boss': Franklin Roosevelt, the Democratic Party, and the Reconstitution of American Politics," in Sidney M. Milkis & Jerome M. Mileur eds., *The New Deal and the Triumph of Liberalism* 121–24 (2002); Kevin McMahon, *Reconsidering Roosevelt on Race: How the Presidency Paved the Road to Brown* 17–18 (2004).

7. See William Leuchtenburg, *The White House Looks South* 91–98 (2005).

8. Steven Lawson, *Black Ballots: Voting Rights in the South, 1944–1969,* 57 (1976) (quoting letter from Franklin D. Roosevelt to Aubrey Williams, Mar. 28, 1938).

9. Frank Freidel, *F.D.R. and the South* 99 (1965); McMahon, supra n. 6, at 17, 120; Sidney Milkis, *The President and the Parties: The Transformation of the American Party System Since the New Deal* 77 (1993).

10. Lawson, supra n. 8, at 57. He also distanced himself from local efforts to abolish the tax, calling them "campaigns of state issues" in which he was not personally involved.

11. See McMahon, supra n. 6, at 157.

12. See Jerry Hough, *Changing Party Coalitions* 131–32 (2006).

13. See Michael Klarman, *From Jim Crow to Civil Rights* 31 (2004); Nicholas Katzenbach, "Toward a More Just America for All," in Thomas Cowger & Sherwin Markman eds., *Lyndon Johnson Remembered* 130 (2003).

14. See Allen Morris, *The Florida Handbook* 172 (1997).

15. In contrast to "obstructionist conservatives" who "generally opposed all that Franklin Roosevelt and the New Deal represented," Holland was a "new" conservative who accepted "an enlarged role for the state." John Malsberger, *From Obstruction to Moderation: The Transformation of Senate Conservatism* 12–13 (2000).

16. Breedlove v. Suttles, 302 U.S. 277 (1937).

17. Harper v. Va. Bd. of Elections, 383 U.S. 663, 670–80 (1966) (Black, J., dissenting).

18. See Virginia Foster Durr, *Outside the Magic Circle* 152 (1990).

19. Lawson, supra n. 8, at 61; Harvard Sitkoff, *A New Deal for Blacks* 133 (1978).

20. Although the committee included fifty different organizations, including the AFL, the CIO, and the American Civil Liberties Union, "[t]here was no question that the NAACP, as the largest and best-known African-American civil rights group, would play a prominent role." Berg, supra n. 5, at 105, 106. The organizational effort continued in a variety of forms until the successful enactment of Twenty-Four in 1962.

21. See Philip Klinkner & Rogers Smith, *The Unsteady March: The Rise and Decline of Racial Equality in America* 174 (2002).

22. Lawson, supra n. 8, at 63.

23. Id. at 76. Roosevelt was more discreet in dealing with his wife, who believed that "Franklin was in favor of" a poll tax ban, though she conceded that it "never became 'must' legislation." Eleanor Roosevelt, *Autobiography of Eleanor Roosevelt* 191 (1992).

24. Lawson, supra n. 8, at 76.

25. Frederic Ogden, *The Poll Tax in the South* 248 (1958).

26. See 108 *CR* 17,655 (1962) (Representative Celler, summarizing these efforts).

27. See Chandler Davidson & Bernard Grofman, *Quiet Revolution in the South: The Impact of the Voting Rights Act, 1965–1990*, 19–298 (1994).

28. Id. at 276.

29. Id. at 298–99.

30. Id.

31. Throughout the debates, Holland emphasized that his concern was wealth, not race, discrimination: "[T]he proposal does not come under the ordinary classification of the ordinary civil rights legislation. It applies to majorities, to minorities, and to every person of every color." 108 *CR* 2851, 4154 (1962). Eight southerners voted for the amendment; only one, Ralph W. Yarborough (Texas), was from a poll tax state. See "The Twenty-Fourth Amendment," supra n. 3, at 404.

32. 108 *CR* 2851, 17,670 (1962). Supporters included 132 Republicans and 163 Democrats. Fifteen Republicans and seventy-one Democrats voted nay—all but one from the South.

33. See Robert A. Caro, *Master of the Senate: The Years of Lyndon Johnson* 944–89 (2002).

34. See Richard Valelly, *The Two Reconstructions* 173–98 (2004).

35. Abolition of Poll Tax in Federal Elections: Hearings on H. J. Res. 404, 425, 44, 594, 601, 632, 655, 663, 670, S.J. Res. 29 Before the H. Comm. on the Judiciary, 87th Cong. 28 (1962) (statement of Clarence Mitchell).

36. According to Javits, "If the Senate would set the precedent that a matter of this character has to be done by constitutional amendment, the very same argument will be made" in future efforts to abolish the literacy test. 108 *CR* 4155 (1962). Another liberal Republican, John Lindsay, echoed these concerns in the House. 108 *CR* 8887 (1962).

37. See Anthony Lewis, "Senate Approves Ban on Poll Tax in Federal Votes; Amendment to Constitution Wins, 77–16, After Defeat of Objection by Russell," *NYT*, Mar. 28, 1962, at 1.

38. Abolition of Poll Tax in Federal Elections: Hearings on H.J. Res. 404, 425, 44, 594, 601, 632, 655, 663, 670, S.J. Res. 29 Before the H. Comm. on the Judiciary, 87th Cong. 2 (1962) (statement of Sen. Holland, quoting Nicholas Katzenbach).

39. During the 1965 debates on the Voting Rights Act, Holland joined his fellow Southerners in their lengthy filibuster. See n. 42, infra.

40. See "The Twenty-Fourth Amendment," supra n. 3, at 405.

41. Letter from Spessard L. Holland to E. H. Crowson, May 12, 1962, Spessard Holland Archives, University of Florida, Gainesville.

42. The prospect of a statutory ban prompted Senator Holland to plead with his colleagues to return to the path established by the Twenty-Fourth Amendment:

> I am still standing where I have been standing all these years; namely, for the elimination of the poll tax as a requirement for voting, but not by unconstitutional means and not by offering a gap in the armor of the Constitution through which temporary majorities of both Houses of Congress may find it desirable to vote many other suspensions of constitutional provisions, and in knocking out many other constitutional provisions.

> 111 *CR* 9943 (1965). Other southerners echoed Holland's line, 111 *CR* 10,028 (1965) (Eastland); 111 *CR* 10,045 (1965) (Stennis).

43. "Frontlash" was Johnson's neologism; see Nick Kotz, *Judgment Days* 198 (2005). I must confess I'm to blame for "legalistic backlash."

44. See Clayborne Carson, "The Crucible: How Bloody Sunday at the Edmund Pettus Bridge Changed Everything," in Dara Byrne ed., *The Unfinished Agenda of the Selma-Montgomery Voting Rights March* 27 (2005).

45. After he signed the Civil Rights Act of 1964, Johnson "immediately" announced his intention to pursue a voting rights law, though he was vague on the timetable. Garth Pauley, *LBJ's American Promise: The 1965 Voting Rights Address* 74 (2007). According to Eric Goldman, a presidential advisor, Johnson gave his instructions in "mid-1964" but "kept [it] out of the press," lest it help Goldwater in the South. See Eric F. Goldman, *The Tragedy of Lyndon Johnson* 318 (1969).

46. See Ronald Walters, *Freedom Is Not Enough* 15 (2005).

47. See Martin Luther King Jr., *The Autobiography of Martin Luther King, Jr.* 270–71 (1998).

48. Pauley, supra n. 45, at 76.

49. Here are the key provisions of the Justice draft:

> Section 1. The right of citizens of the United States to vote shall not be denied or abridged by the United States or by any State for any cause except (1) inability to meet residence requirements not exceeding sixty days or minimum age requirements, imposed by State law; (2) conviction of a felony for which no pardon or amnesty has been granted; (3) mental incompetency adjudi-

cated by a court of record; or (4) confinement pursuant to the judgment or warrant of a court of record at the time of registration or election.

Section 2. The Congress shall have power to enforce this Article by appropriate legislation.

Dept. of Justice Memorandum (unsigned), "Constitutional Amendment," Jan. 18, 1965, Lyndon B. Johnson Library Archives.

50. Memorandum from Nicholas Katzenbach to Lyndon Johnson, Dec. 28, 1964, Lyndon B. Johnson Library Archives, Lee White Files, Box 3.

51. Id.

52. Id.

53. Pauley, supra n. 45, at 76.

54. Garth Pauley, *The Modern Presidency and Civil Rights: Rhetoric on Race from Roosevelt to Nixon* 174 (2001).

55. Pauley, supra n. 45, at 77.

56. Transcript Recording: Telephone Conversation Between Lyndon B. Johnson and Martin Luther King, Jr., Jan. 15, 1965, Lyndon B. Johnson Library Archives No. 1803, WH6501.04.

57. See David Garrow, *Bearing the Cross: Martin Luther King, Jr., and the Southern Christian Leadership Conference* 388 (2004).

58. Pauley, supra n. 45, at 77.

59. See Lawson, supra n. 8, at 309; Denton Watson, *Lion in the Lobby: Clarence Mitchell, Jr.'s Struggle for the Passage of Civil Rights Laws* 662 (2002).

60. Memorandum (unsigned) to Lyndon B. Johnson, Reports on Legislation, Feb. 15, 1965 (on file with author); David Garrow, *Protest at Selma: Martin Luther King, Jr. and the Voting Rights Act of 1965* 60 (1978); Pauley, supra n. 45, at 78 (quoting Letter from Ramsey Clark, Att'y Gen., to Lawrence O'Brien, Postmaster Gen. (Feb. 15, 1965)).

61. See Brian Landsberg, *Free at Last to Vote* 158 (2007). By March 4, 1965, Lee White was writing a memo to Lyndon B. Johnson giving him "Notes for Meeting with Dr. King on March 5th," stating that "[t]here is general agreement that the Constitutional amendment approach would require too much time and thus we have concentrated on a statute." Memorandum from Lee C. White to Lyndon B. Johnson, Mar. 4, 1965, Lyndon Johnson Library Archives, LE/HU 2–7, F6155–18.

62. S. 1564, 111th Cong. (1965) (as submitted by Mr. Mansfield, March 18, 1965).

63. See Janus Adams, *Freedom Days: 365 Inspired Moments in Civil Rights History,* March 7 (1998); Garrow, supra n. 60, at 73–77.

64. Shortly after 9:00 p.m. on Bloody Sunday, ABC interrupted its evening movie, *Judgment at Nuremberg,* "for a long film report of the assault on Highway 80, a sequence which showed clearly the quiet column, the flailing clubs, the stampeding horses, the jeering crowd and the stricken, fleeing blacks." Garrow, supra n. 60, at 78. The story also ran on the front page of almost every major newspaper, accompanied by grisly photos. See Leon Daniel, "Tear Gas, Clubs

Halt 600 in Selma March," *WP*, Mar. 8, 1965, at A1; Roy Reed, "Alabama Police Use Gas and Clubs to Rout Negroes," *NYT*, Mar. 8, 1965, at A1.

65. On March 16, 1965, reporters asked the White House's George Reedy about the status of the Administration's voting rights proposal, only to be told: "That's still down the road a ways." Garrow, supra n. 60, at 82.

66. Pauley, supra n. 45, at 77.

67. Landsberg, supra n. 61, at 161 (noting the Department of Justice's continued tinkering).

68. See Lyndon B. Johnson, "Special Message to Congress: The American Promise," Mar. 15, 1965, at www.lbjlibrary.net/collections/selected-speeches/1965/03–15–1965.html.

69. See *WP: T* 131–33.

70. S. 1564, 89th Cong. §§ 3 (a) and (c) (1st Sess. 1965).

71. The bill authorized federal examiners to accept poll tax payments and required state authorities to recognize these receipts as qualifying the recipient for any election during the year of payment. S. 1564, § 5(e). See Voting Rights: Hearings on H.R. 6400 Before the H. Comm. on the Judiciary, 89th Cong. (1965).

72. Id. at 22 (1965).

73. Id.

74. See Hearings Before the S. Comm. on the Judiciary, 89th Cong. 148–49 (1965):

> KATZENBACH: "Because I have reservations that [a statutory ban relying on the poll tax's discriminatory effect] would be sound constitutionally, Senator. . . . I believe that figures derived as the Civil Rights Commission derived them could probably be successfully contested.

> See generally, U.S. Comm. on Civil Rights, *Freedom to the Free: Century of Emancipation, 1863–1963* (1963).

75. Senator Kennedy insisted that the statutory ban would "work quickly while [proposed substitutes would] work slowly. Ours clearly expresses the policy of Congress in this area while theirs leaves the making of policy to the courts." 111 *CR* 9913 (1965). Emanuel Celler, opening House debate, declared that the committee bill built a system that was "impervious to all legal trickery and evasion." "Voting Rights Act of 1965," 1965 *Cong. Q. Almanac* 540, 560. Representative Farber elaborated by declaring that the "constitutionality of section 10 [banning the poll tax] has been, and will again be, the victim of attacks from those among us who perpetually caution, 'Go slow, beware, hold back!' I think we have held back too long." 111 *CR* 15,717 (1965).

76. See Kotz, supra n. 43, at 328–29.

77. 111 *CR* 10,078 (1965).

78. See Landsberg, supra n. 61, at 185.

79. 111 *CR* 10,073, 10,866 (1965) (emphasis added).

80. The Justice Department did not cite any precedents, simply asserting that the provision represented the "safest, swiftest and most efficient course to eliminate

the poll tax." Memorandum from Atty. Gen. Nicholas Katzenbach to President Lyndon B. Johnson, "Reasons Why the Department of Justice Has Favored the Mansfield-Dirksen Approach to Elimination of the Poll Tax," May 21, 1965 (on file with author).

81. 111 CR 9926 (1965).

82. 111 CR 11,013 (1965) (Thurmond).

83. 111 CR 9939, 9943 (1965) (Holland).

84. 111 CR 9924 (1965).

85. 111 CR 9913 (1965).

86. "Voting Rights Act of 1965," supra n. 75, at 545 (1965); 111 CR 10,073, 11,018 (1965).

87. "Voting Rights Act of 1965," supra n. 75, at 559 (1965); 111 CR 16,038 (1965).

88. Transcript of Recording of Telephone Conversation Between Lyndon B. Johnson and Martin Luther King Jr., July 7, 1965, LBJ Library, Citation No. 8311, Tape WH6507.02, Recordings of Telephone Conversations—White House Series, Recordings and Transcripts of Conversations and Meetings.

89. Id.

90. Johnson: "So if we beat off McCulloch . . . we still have one bill in the Senate and one in the House, that's what the Southerners that are smart parliamentarians want us to do. They want your wife to go in one direction and you to go in the other. And the kids don't know which one to follow." Id.

91. Id.

92. 111 *CR* 16,230 (1965).

93. The conference began on Monday, July 12, but reached an impasse during the week of July 19. See Garrow, supra n. 60, at 130–31.

94. Robert C. Albright, "Conferees Bog Down on Poll Tax Ban," *WP*, July 28, 1965, at A2.

95. 111 *CR* 10,078 (1965).

96. Voting Rights Act § 10, 42 U.S.C. § 1973h(b) (2000).

97. See Garrow, supra n. 60, at 130–31. Katzenbach's key role is suggested by a memo from Mike Manatos—a White House aide—that reported: "Nick Katzenbach tells me that the conference will reach agreement tomorrow on Voting Rights. Apparently, the compromise language which Nick suggested on Poll Tax is acceptable to Dirksen and Celler. It is my understanding that these two individuals will meet off-the-record tomorrow at noon." See Memorandum from Larry O'Brien to Lyndon B. Johnson, April 26, 1965, LBJ Library, LE/HU 2-7, FG 11-8-1/O'Brien.

98. 111 *CR* 19,444 (1965).

99. King's intervention was particularly decisive for House conferees Peter Rodino and Harold Donohue. See Garrow, supra n. 60, at 435.

100. "Voting Rights Act of 1965," supra n. 75, at 563; 111 *CR* 19,200 (1965).

101. 111 *CR* 19,195 (1965).

102. "Voting Rights Act of 1965," supra n. 75, at 563.

103. In keeping it secret, Celler was keeping faith with Katzenbach, whose letter concluded:

Dr. King further assured me that he would make this statement publicly at an appropriate time. While you are free to show this letter privately to whomsoever you wish I would appreciate it if you did not use it publicly without informing me so that I, in turn, may discuss it with Dr. King.

111 *CR* 19,444 (1965).

104. Richard Lyons, "Voting Rights Bill Passed by House After GOP Attack," *WP* Aug. 4, 1965, at 1.

105. The letter appeared on August 4, the same day as the *Washington Post* story. 111 *CR* 19,444 (1965).

106. President Lyndon B. Johnson, "Remarks in the Capitol Rotunda at the Signing of the Voting Rights Act," August 6, 1965, at www.lbjlibrary.net/collections /selected-speeches/1965/08-06-1965.html.

6. Erasure by Judiciary?

1. See *WP: T* 290–382.

2. Voting Rights Act § 10, 42 U.S.C. § 1973h(a)(2000).

3. See Jurisdictional Statement of Appellants, Harper v. Va. Bd. of Elections, 380 U.S. 930 (1964), in Philip Kurland & Gerhard Casper eds., *Landmark Briefs and Arguments of the Supreme Court of the United States: Constitutional Law* 835–51 (1975).

4. See Bernard Schwartz, "More Unpublished Warren Court Opinions," 1986 *Sup. Ct. Rev.* 317, 321–22.

5. I am indebted to the late Professor Bernard Schwartz, who discovered and published this opinion a quarter century ago—see Schwartz, supra n. 4, at 324–27—though its significance hasn't been adequately appreciated.

6. Id. at 321.

7. Harper v. Va. Bd. of Elections, 380 U.S. 930 (1965) (noting probable jurisdiction).

8. See, e.g., United States v. Texas, 252 F. Supp. 234 (February 9, 1966); United States v. Alabama, 252 F. Supp. 95 (March 3, 1966).

9. Ralph Spritzer, the principal deputy assistant to the solicitor general, also signed the brief, but when I talked to him about the case in the late 1960s, he told me that Richard Posner wrote it. In response to a recent query, Judge Posner wrote: "Unfortunately, I have zero recollection of having worked on the Harper case. If I signed it, that would mean I wrote it." Email, May 17, 2007.

10. Brief for the United States as Amici Curiae, Harper v. Va. Bd. of Elections, 383 U.S. 663 (1965) (No. 48 25–26).

11. Id. at 27 (emphasis added).

12. During the 1960s, transcripts didn't identify particular justices, but I'd guess the speaker was Justice Harlan, since he made similar claims in his dissent in *Harper*.

13. See Philip Kurland & Gerhard Casper eds., *Landmark Briefs and Arguments of the Supreme Court of the United States: Constitutional Law* 1023–87, Transcript of Oral Argument 28 (1975).

14. Id. at 1027.

15. Id.

16. Harper, supra n. 10, at 669–70 (1966) (citations omitted).

17. Id. at 668.

18. Voting Rights Act of 1965, Pub. L. No. 89–110, § 4, 79 Stat. 437, 442 (codified as amended at 42 U.S.C. § 1973b (2000)).

19. The mystery is further compounded by Douglas's citation to recent lower court cases striking down state poll taxes under Section 10. See Harper, supra n. 10, at 665, 666 nn. 2, 4. These citations show that Douglas was perfectly aware of Congress's recent effort but utterly failed to reflect on its larger constitutional significance.

20. Harper, supra n. 10, at 684–85.

21. Id. at 685–86 (emphasis added).

22. Id. at 678 (Black, J., dissenting).

23. Hugo Black had initially voted to affirm *Breedlove* without a full hearing, but he changed his mind in response to Goldberg's initial draft. Memorandum for the Conference from Hugo Black, Associate Justice to William Brennan, Associate Justice, March 4, 1965, Hugo Black Papers, Box I: 128, Folder 6, Library of Congress. Once Douglas replaced Goldberg as opinion writer, Black's commitment to *Breedlove* reasserted itself.

24. See Schwartz, supra n. 4, supra.

25. Katzenbach v. Morgan, 384 U.S. 641 (1966).

26. For insightful variations on this theme, see Pamela Karlan, "The Supreme Court 2011 Term, Foreword: Democracy and Disdain," 126 *Harv. L. Rev.* 14–27 (2012).

27. Lassiter v. Northampton County Board of Elections, 360 U.S. 45 (1959).

28. "Congress hereby declares that to secure the rights under the fourteenth amendment of persons educated in American-flag schools in which the predominant classroom language was other than English, it is necessary to prohibit the States from conditioning the right to vote of such persons on ability to read, write, understand, or interpret any matter in the English language." Voting Rights Act of 1965, Pub. L. No. 89–110, § 4(e)(1), 79 Stat. 437, 439 (codified as amended at 42 U.S.C. § 1973b (2000)).

29. Morgan, supra n. 25, at 650

30. Id. at 836.

31. Id. at 669.

32. Id. at 668.

33. Id. at 652, n. 10.

34. The importance of this point was immediately recognized. See Robert Burt, "Miranda and Title II: A Morganatic Marriage," 1969 *Sup. Ct. Rev.* 81.

35. See Chapter 4.

36. 110 *CR* 13319–20 (1964).

37. Compare Dirksen's speech with the excerpts from King's "I Have a Dream" speech in Chapter 3 and Johnson's "We Shall Overcome" speech in Chapter 5.

38. See, e.g., E. W. Kenworthy, "Senate Invokes Closure on Rights Bill, 71 to 29, Ending 75-Day Filibuster," *NYT,* June 11, 1964, at 1, 25; Edwin A. Leahy, "Dirksen, Rejected by Negroes, Makes Civil Rights Bill Possible," *WP,* June 11, 1964, at 9.

7. Spheres of Humiliation

1. For an admirable exercise in demystification, see Reva Siegel, "Equality Talk, Anti-Subordination and Anti-Classification in Constitutional Struggles over Brown," 117 *Harv. L. Rev.* 1740 (2004). I depart from Siegel's essay in emphasizing the fundamental contributions of the landmark statutes to the constitutional solution worked out in the 1960s and early 1970s. For another insightful account, see Ian Haney-Lopez, "Intentional Blindness," 87 *NYU L. Rev.* 1779 (2012).

2. Brown v. Board of Education, 347 US 483, 495 (1954).

3. Id. at 490.

4. See Jack Balkin, *Living Originalism* 221–26 (2011).

5. For a philosophical development of this theme, see Michael Walzer, *Spheres of Justice* (1984).

6. Brown, supra n. 2, at 493.

7. Id. at 494.

8. Karl Llewellyn, *The Common Law Tradition: Deciding Appeals* 121–57 (1960).

9. Plessy v. Ferguson, 163 U.S. 527, 551 (1896).

10. Brown, supra n. 2, at 494 (emphasis added).

11. See Charles Black, "The Lawfulness of the Segregation Decisions," 69 *Yale L. J.* 421, 424 (1960). On Black's view, the "social meaning of segregation" was clear: "I was raised in the South, in a Texas city where the pattern of segregation was firmly fixed. I am sure that it never occurred to anyone, white or colored, to question its meaning." On Black's view, the proper response to somebody who denied the obvious was "to exercise the sovereign prerogative of the philosophers—laughter."

12. See Muller v. Oregon, 208 U.S. 412, 419 (1908).

13. Siegel, supra n. 1, at 1489–1497 (summarizing academic discussion).

14. "Civil Rights Icon Rosa Parks Dies at 92," CNN.com, October 25, 2005, at http://edition.cnn.com/2005/US/10/25/parks.obit.

15. Gayle v. Browder, 352 U.S. 903 (1956).

16. Martin Luther King Jr., "Letter from Birmingham City Jail," in James Washington ed., *A Testament of Hope* 292–93 (1986).

17. Id. at 292.

18. See 110 *CR* 6531–32 (March 30, 1964).

19. 110 *CR* 7799 (April 13, 1964).

20. Humphrey's argument is worth reporting at greater length:

> With due respect for all Senators, after a man has worked hard to get an education in high school, perhaps a college or technical education, and has re-

ceived this blessing of enlightenment, it means more to him that he will be accepted as a desired member of the community than the fact that he exercises that acceptance.

After a man of color has received a degree from a great university, if he is to be rejected at a lunch counter, or at an ordinary drugstore because of his color, it is an insult to him.

What he needs is freedom of dignity or freedom from indignity.

I spoke at a dinner the other night called the Four Freedoms Foundation Award dinner. We remember Franklin Roosevelt's four freedoms: freedom of speech, freedom of conscience, freedom from fear, and freedom from want. I believe there is a fifth freedom—that is, freedom of dignity.

It is not so much that the individual may want to go into every hotel, or will go into every restaurant. If he should want to do that as a human being, he should not have a hand put out and have someone say, "Stop. The reason you cannot come in here is the color of your skin."

A Negro has no control over the color of his skin. He did not select his color at birth. He did not select the country of his birth. But he is an American. He is a citizen.

110 *CR* 6091 (March 24 1964).

21. 1 Lyndon Johnson, *Public Papers of the Presidents of the United States, 1963–64,* 482–83 (emphasis added) (April 24, 1964).

22. For other eloquent statements, see Robert Kennedy, House Judiciary Committee, Hearings: Civil Rights—The President's Program, 88 Cong., 2 Sess. 93–94 (July-September 1963); Thomas Kuchel, 110 *CR* 6556–57 (March 30, 1964); Ted Moss (D-Utah), 110 *CR* 6746–48 (Apr. 1, 1964); Jacob Javits, Civil Rights: Hearings Before Sen. Commerce Committee, 88 Cong., 2 Sess. 257 (1963).

23. I have developed these reflections in response to two important books: Avishai Margalit, *The Decent Society* (1996), and William Miller, *Humiliation* (1993). Philip Petitt has also made an important recent contribution in his book, *On the People's Terms* (2012). But this is not the place to elaborate upon the similarities and differences in my approach to our common subject.

24. 110 *CR* 6534 (March 30, 1964).

25. Sec. 201(a).

26. Civil Rights Cases, 109 U.S. 3 (1883).

27. Id. at 24–25.

28. See Chapter 6.

29. See, e.g., Smith v. Allwright, 321 U.S. 649 (1944); Shelley v. Kraemer, 334 U.S. 1 (1948); Burton v. Wilmington Parking Authority, 365 U.S. 715 (1961).

30. Peterson v. City of Greenville, 373 U.S. 244 (1963); Avent v. North Carolina, 373 U.S. 375 (1963); Lombard v. Louisiana, 373 U.S. 267 (1963); Gober v. Birmingham, 373 U.S. 374 (1963); Suttlesworth v. Birmingham, 373 U.S. 262 (1963); Wright v. Georgia, 373 U.S. 284 (1963). Bell v. Maryland, 378 U.S. 226 (1964), was the lead case for four other companion sit-in cases: Griffin v. State of Maryland,

370 U.S. 935 (1962); Barr v. City of Columbia, 378 U.S. 146 (1964); Robinson v. State of Florida, 378 U.S. 153 (1964).

31. Transcript of Oral Argument at 194, Bell v. State of Maryland, 378 U.S. 226 (1964) (No. 12).

32. More particularly, the liberals wanted to reassert the very broad doctrines of Shelley v. Kraemer to sweep away classical understandings of the state action limitation. Del Dickson ed., *The Supreme Court in Conference (1940–1985)*, 720–27 (2001).

33. See Hugo Black, Draft Opinion in Bell v. Maryland, March 5, 1964, Black Papers, Box 377, Folder 1, p. 11, Library of Congress.

34. Dickson, supra n. 32, at 722–23.

35. Seth Stern & Stephen Wermiel, *Justice Brennan: Liberal Champion* 218 (2010).

36. See Stewart Papers, Group No. 1367, Series No. I, Box No. 199, Folder No. 2034, Yale University. The government's supplemental brief argued that institutionalized humiliation should trump limited notions of state responsibility:

> We deal here not with individual action but with a community-wide, public custom of denying Negroes the opportunities of breaking bread with their fellow men in public places in order to subject them to a stigma of inferiority as an integral part of the fabric of a caste system woven of threads of both State and private action.

Griffin v. State of Md., 378 U.S. 130 (1964), Supplemental Brief 36 (Jan. 17, 1964) in *U.S. Supreme Court Records and Briefs,* at http://galenet.galegroup.com/serv let/SCRB?uid=0&srchtp=a&ste=14&rcn=DW100200355.

37. See Bernard Schwartz, *Super Chief* 504–24 (1983), though I depart from Schwartz's account in a few particulars. A paragraph from one of Brennan's drafts provides a sense of the four dissenters' dismay:

> We of the Court are not so removed from the world around us that we can ignore the current debate over the constitutionality of Title II if enacted. Of course the Court properly limits its decision to the cases before it, which present the constitutional question in the absence of such a statute. But we cannot be blind to the fact that today's opposing opinions on the constitutional question decided will inevitably enter into and perhaps confuse that debate. My colleagues thus choose the most unfortunate time to commit the error of reaching out to decide the question.

Draft Dissenting Opinion in Bell v. Maryland, May 1964, Brennan Papers, Box I: 97, Folder 8, at 1–2, Library of Congress. The draft does not contain a precise date, but it must have been circulated between April 14, when Brennan first announced that he would write a dissent, and May 27, when Brennan began to write an opinion for a five-judge majority—only to lose his majority to Clark in early June.

38. See Hugo Black & Elizabeth Black, *Mr. Justice and Mrs. Black* 92 (1986) (Elizabeth Black reporting her husband's "hop[e]" that his opinion for the Court "will come down on Monday the 18th").

39. See Tom Clark, Draft Opinion in Bell v. Maryland at 9, Douglas Papers, Box 1312, Folder 4, Library of Congress.
40. See text accompanying n. 23, supra.
41. Earl Warren, handwritten note to Tom Clark, Clark Papers, Box 151, Folder 3, Tarlton Law Library, University of Texas.
42. Schwartz, supra n. 37, at 523. Warren wrote his colleagues, "In view of the discussion at our Conference today, at which time Justice Clark stated that he and four other Justices had agreed to an opinion in No. 12—Bell v. Maryland—and inasmuch as he has now circulated an opinion in No. 12, this case and the other sit-in cases controlled by it are assigned to Justice Clark." Earl Warren, Memorandum to the Brethren in Bell v. Maryland, June 11, 1964, Douglas Papers, Box 1313, Folder 16, Library of Congress.
43. See Tom Clark, draft opinion, supra n. 39, at 14.
44. Howard Ball & Phillip J. Cooper, *Of Power and Right* 168 (1992) (quoting from personal interview with William Brennan, October 29, 1986).
45. William Brennan, Opinion in Bell v. Maryland, June 16, 1964, Warren Papers, Box 511, Folder 4, Library of Congress. It was easy for Brennan to move quickly since he had written a usable draft at a much earlier stage in the deliberations, when Black still had his majority intact, and the liberals were trying to deflect his momentum. Draft Dissent in Bell v. Maryland, May 1964, Brennan Papers, Box I: 97, Folder 8, Library of Congress. Brennan's desertion provoked Douglas to express his "real shock" in a personal letter explaining to Brennan why he could not sign his new majority opinion. See letter to William Brennan, June 3, 1964, Douglas Papers, Box 1313, Folder 16, Library of Congress. In a strongly worded memo to his files, Douglas described Brennan's final opinion as "the product of his [Brennan's] plan to keep the Court from deciding the basic constitutional issue of the Fourteenth Amendment." Memorandum for the Files, Bell v. Maryland, June 20, 1964, Douglas Papers, Box 1313, Folder 16, Library of Congress.
46. U.S. v. Darby, 312 U.S. 100 (1941); Wickard v. Filburn, 317 U.S. 111 (1942).
47. Section 201 (d) defines state action broadly to include any public place of accommodation where "discrimination or segregation (1) is carried on under color of any law, statute, ordinance, or regulation; or (2) is carried on under color of any custom or usage required or enforced by officials of the State . . . or (3) is required by action of the State."
48. "Section 201 (b)(3) provides:
    The operations of an establishment [are governed by] this title if . . . it serves or offers to serve interstate travelers or a substantial portion of the food which it serves, or gasoline or other products which it sells, has moved in [interstate] commerce; . . . it customarily presents films, performances, athletic teams, exhibitions, or other sources of entertainment which move in commerce; [or if] . . . it is physically located within the premises of, or there is physically located within its premises, an establishment the operations of which affect [interstate] commerce."

49. See Chapter 4, n. 24.

50. Owen Fiss was among the first to note the significance of this turn in his "The Fate of an Idea Whose Time Has Come: Antidiscrimination Law in the Second Decade After Brown v. Board of Education," 41 *U. Chi. L. Rev.* 742, 747 (1974).

51. See 110 *CR* 6531–32 (March 30, 1964).

52. See Chapter 6, which concludes with an excerpt from Dirksen's speech that displays the artful way in which the Senator combines his two points in making the case for fundamental constitutional change.

53. See Chapter 6.

8. Spheres of Calculation

1. For the larger implications of this intellectual revolution, see Mary Morgan, *The World in the Model* (2012) (economics); Bruce Ackerman, *Reconstructing American Law* (1984) (law).

2. See Michael Les Benedict, *A Compromise of Principle* 241 (1974).

3. *Cong. Globe,* 39 Cong., 1 Sess. 3148 (June 13, 1866).

4. See *WP: T* 160–251. Richard Valelly's outstanding book *The Two Reconstructions* 23–121 (2004) complements my constitutional emphasis with a political analysis of the disintegration of the Republican coalition.

5. For the classic statement of New Deal theory, see James Landis, *The Administrative Process* (1938).

6. See Ronald Dworkin, *Law's Empire* (1986).

7. For a systematic comparison of the new act with the earlier statutory scheme, see Brian Landsberg, *Free at Last to Vote* 148–89 (2007); see also Steven Lawson, *Black Ballots* 234–35 (1976).

8. Chief Justice Warren provides a clear description of these complex provisions in his opinion upholding their constitutionality, South Carolina v. Katzenbach, 383 U.S. 301, 317–19 (1965). See also Steven Lawson, *In Pursuit of Power* 25–8 (1985).

9. The seven states covered by the 1965 act were Alabama, Georgia, Louisiana, Mississippi, South Carolina, Virginia, and twenty-six counties in North Carolina. A few other places were initially included, but except for one county in Hawaii, they all made use of the escape hatch described in the text. U.S. Civil Rights Commission, *The Voting Rights Act: Ten Years After* 13–14 (1975).

10. Voting Rights Act of 1965, Pub. L. No. 89–110 § 4(a).

11. H. R. Rep. No. 439, 89th Cong., 1st Sess. 45 (1965). Liberal Republican John Lindsay also found the trigger proposal "shockingly frozen and inflexible" since "Congress cannot be certain about the scope of discrimination." Voting Rights: Hearings Before Subcommittee No. 5 of the Committee on the Judiciary on H. R. 6400 and other proposals to enforce the 15th Amendment of the Constitution, 89th Cong. 367 (1965).

12. 111 *CR* 9265 (1965).

13. Voting Rights: Hearings Before Committee on the Judiciary on S. 1564 to Enforce the 15th Amendment of the Constitution of the United States, 89th Cong. 537 (1965).

14. Northern Republicans such as Clark MacGregor (MN), Carleton King (NY), Edward Hutchinson (MI), and Robert McClory (IL) joined McCulloch's alternative bill, which would have rejected the administration's technocratic approach. House Hearings, supra n. 11, at 37 (1965).

15. South Carolina v. Katzenbach, 383 U.S. 301, was decided on March 7, 1966; Harper came down on March 24, and Morgan on June 13.

16. Lassiter v. Northampton Bd. of Elections, 360 U.S. 45 (1959).

17. South Carolina, supra n. 15, at 326.

18. Id. at 360.

19. See James Alt, "The Impact of the Voting Rights Act on Black and White Voter Registration in the South," in Chandler Davidson & Bernard Groffman eds., *Quiet Revolution in the South* 350, 374 (Table 12.1) (1994).

20. Allen v. State Board of Elections, 393 U.S. 544 (1969).

21. Id. at 569.

22. See Gomillion v. Lightfoot, 364 U.S. 339 (1960).

23. More precisely, § 4 (a) required the county to establish that its literacy test did not have "the purpose or . . . the effect of denying or abridging the right to vote on account of race or color."

24. Gaston County v. United States, 395 U.S. 285 (1969). Only Justice Black dissented, continuing to assert that the act was treating the South as "conquered provinces." Id. at 297.

25. See Chapter 4.

26. See Lawson, supra n. 7, at 334–39. Given Gaston County, "[t]he only course available to the President consistent with his position against regional legislation is to propose a nationwide ban on literacy tests"—or so Jerris Leonard, assistant attorney general for civil rights, explained to Nixon's senior counsel, John Ehrlichman. Memorandum from Leonard to Ehrlichman, June 9, 1969 (on file with author).

27. The Voting Rights Act: Hearing Before the Subcomm. on the Judiciary of the U.S. House of Representatives, 91st Cong. 266 (1969) (statement of Atty. Gen. Mitchell).

28. The Mitchell plan imposed a nationwide ban on residency tests for presidential elections and provided new authority for the Attorney General to dispatch voting registrars on a national basis. S. 2507, 91st Cong. § 3 (1969). See Hearings Before the Subcommittee on Constitutional Rights of the Committee on the Judiciary on S. 818, S. 2456, S. 2507, and Title IV of S. 2029, Bills to Amend the Voting Rights Act of 1965, 91st Cong., 1st & 2d. Sess. 537–39 (1970).

29. S. 2507 § 3, supra n. 28.

30. See Senate Hearings, supra n. 13, at 2591.

31. See House Hearings, supra n. 28, at 3–4. McCulloch also made a second supportive statement at id. 270–71.

32. The three New York boroughs initially used the escape hatch in 1972, but the district court returned them to federal supervision in 1974—and they did not escape until 2013. See Daniel Brook, "New York Should Hate the Voting Rights Act," *Slate,* Feb. 21, 2013, at http://www.slate.com/articles/news_and_politics /jurisprudence/2013/02/voting_rights_supreme_court_case_why_is_new_york _defending_the_voting_rights.html.

33. J. Morgan Kousser, "The Strange, Ironic Career of Section 5 of the Voting Rights Act, 1965–2007," 86 *Tex. L. Rev.* 667, 686 (2008).

34. See Hugh Graham, *The Civil Rights Era* 361 (1990).

35. Joan Hoff-Wilson ed., *Papers of the Nixon White House,* H. R. Haldeman meeting notes, June 19, 1970, Microfiche 25 (1989).

36. Id., Richard Nixon to H. R. Haldeman, Jan. 11, 1970, Haldeman Files, Box 230.

37. When the Mansfield provision reached the Supreme Court the following year in Oregon v. Mitchell, 400 U.S. 112 (1971), the majority upheld its constitutionality for federal elections—which was the politically important case for Nixon in his pursuit of reelection in 1972. But by a 5-to-4 vote, it struck down the provision as it applied to state and local elections, thereby giving some substance to the constitutional concerns expressed by Pollak and others. Congress responded to this split decision with the Twenty-Sixth Amendment, which guaranteed eighteen-year-olds the vote in all elections.

38. See Rowland Evans Jr. & Robert D. Novak, *Nixon in the White House: The Frustration of Power* 131 (1971).

39. Memorandum from Raymond K. Price, Jr., Speechwriter for the President, to Leonard Garment, Special Counsel to the President, June 18, 1970 (on file with author).

40. Id.

41. Id.

42. Richard Nixon, Statement on the Signing of the Voting Rights Acts Amendments of 1970, June 22, 1970, *Public Papers of President Nixon,* available at www .presidency.ucsb.edu/ws/index.php?pid=2553.

43. See Dean Kotlowski, *Nixon's Civil Rights* 90–91 (2001).

44. See Howard Ball, Dale Krane, & Thomas Lauth, *Compromised Compliance* 78 (1982).

45. See Brian Landsberg, *Enforcing Civil Rights* 66 (1997), characterizing the Department's mode of operation as "administrative."

46. I am adapting the term from William Eskridge & John Ferejohn, *A Republic of Statutes,* see especially 102–04 (2010), but using it in a narrower way. I am focusing on the role of "administrative constitutionalism" during "constitutional moments." Professors Eskridge and Ferejohn are more broadly interested in the ways in which administrative deliberation helps define and entrench the social norms and public values expressed by a much broader class of "super-statutes." Their general discussion, however, usefully informs my more focused inquiry, as do some of their case studies. See also Sophia Lee, "Race, Sex, and Rulemak-

ing: Administrative Constitutionalism and the Workplace, 1960 to the Present," 96 *Va. L. Rev.* 799 (2010).

47. This is a bit of a simplification, as Title II does envision administrative agencies playing an ancillary role. If a state or locality has established an antidiscrimination agency, plaintiffs must give the agency thirty days to solve the problem, according to § 204(c); if one doesn't exist, the federal court may also give a new federal Community Relations Service, established by the act, up to 120 days to try to obtain voluntary compliance, according to § 204(d). Finally, the Justice Department is authorized to bring a lawsuit to challenge a prevailing "pattern or practice," § 206 (a).

9. Technocracy in the Workplace

1. § 703, 78 Stat. 241, 255 (1964).
2. Section 702 granted a series of limited exemptions, most notably one that allows religious organizations to discriminate on denominational grounds.
3. See NLRB v. Jones & Laughlin Steel Corp., 301 U.S. 1 (1937).
4. See §703 (j).
5. See §706 (g).
6. For a concise summary of the most important modifications, see Paul Moreno, *From Direct Action to Affirmative Action* 219–22 (1997).
7. 110 *CR* 12723–24 (1964).
8. See § 706 (a), 78 Stat. 241, 259 (1964).
9. See John Skrentny, *The Ironies of Affirmative Action* 121 (1996).
10. See § 709 (c), 78 Stat. 241, 263 (1964). Senators Joseph Clark and Clifford Case were co-managers of Title VII, and their interpretive memo made it clear that statistical analysis of racial hiring patterns was essential:

> Requirements for the keeping of records are a customary and necessary part of a regulatory statute. They are particularly essential in title VII because *whether or not a certain action is discriminatory will turn on the motives of the respondent,* which will usually be best evidenced by his pattern of conduct on similar occasions. (110 *CR* 7214 (1964), emphasis added)

The Dirksen-Mansfield compromise introduced a new subsection (d) that tried to prevent EEOC and state anti-discrimination agencies from burdening employers with duplicative reporting requirements. But it explicitly authorized the EEOC to impose additional reports when it was "necessary because of difference in coverage or methods of enforcement between the State or local law and the provisions of this title." 79 Stat. 241, 263 (1964).

This language amply justified the EEOC's reporting requirements. While leading political scientists and historians provide the best accounts of this episode—see John Skrentny, *The Minority Rights Revolution* 104–05 (2002) and Hugh Graham, *The Civil Rights Era* 193–97 (1990)—they conclude that the statute and legislative history was "vague" (Skrentny) or that it "clear[ly]" prohibited the EEOC from imposing reporting requirements (Graham).

To the contrary, the commission's statutory mandate was entirely unproblematic. The point was further elaborated in a colloquy between Dirksen and Clark on the floor. Dirksen noted that his home state, Illinois, "explicitly prohibits [its anti-discrimination agency from making] any reference to color or religion. . . . Are we now to force an employer to violate a State law in order to comply with a Federal statute, each of which has the same purpose?" Clark provided a standard legal reply: "[S]tate laws would yield to the supremacy of the federal law, since it is necessary to have this data to determine if a pattern of discrimination exists."

When Dirksen then asked whether Congress should itself specify the appropriate EEOC form in the statute, Clark again provided the standard administrative law answer: "Congress cannot set definite recordkeeping requirements and should not try to write them in the statute, because it is not yet known what records will be needed." 110 *CR* 7214–16.

What could be clearer?

11. Some scholars have claimed that Dirksen's deal with Mansfield involved "cosmetic changes" that did not amount to anything important. But this is a mistake. See Daniel Rodriguez & Barry Weingast, "The Positive Political Theory of Legislative History: New Perspectives on the Civil Rights Act of 1964 and Its Interpretation," 151 *U. Penn. L. Rev.* 1417 (2003). Yet it is also important to recognize, as Rodriguez and Weingast do not, that Dirksen's bargain served as the beginning, not the end, of a larger constitutional process that significantly strengthened the EEOC in 1972.

12. Skrentny, supra n. 9, at 122–24.

13. The EEOC appropriation for the 1966 fiscal year was $2.75 million, "putting the EEOC below the Office of Coal Research and the Federal Crop Insurance Program in terms of budget and staff." Id. at 123.

14. James Harwood, "Rights Groups May Ask Stiffening of '64 Law's Employment Provisions," *WSJ,* May 28, 1968, at 1.

15. Skrentny, supra n. 9, at 124.

16. Id. at 122–24.

17. Graham, supra n. 10, at 422.

18. Id.

19. Alfred Blumrosen, *Black Employment and the Law* 68 (1971).

20. Id. at 73.

21. See Graham, supra n. 10, at 199.

22. See Skrentny, supra n. 9, at 128.

23. See id. at 128–131, describing the conference and the further administrative steps taken by the EEOC to launch the program.

24. Nicholas Pedriana & Robin Stryker, "The Strength of a Weak Agency: Enforcement of Title VII of the Civil Rights Act and the Expansion of State Capacity, 1965–1971," 110 *Am. J. of Soc.* 709, 721 (2004).

25. Id.

26. John Skrentny, supra n. 9, calls this "administrative pragmatism," at III–44, and I am indebted to his account. My contribution, such as it is, locates this pragmatic impulse within the larger constitutional framework. From a constitutional perspective, Skrentny's "pragmatism" represents the agency's effort to redeem the claim to expertise that is central to its legitimacy within the New Deal–Civil Rights regime.

27. Id. at 132–33.

28. Richard Nathan, *Jobs and Civil Rights* 30 (1969) (address by Clifford Alexander, October 6, 1967, emphasis added).

29. See note 10, supra.

30. Federal district court filings only began to take off during the Nixon years, quintupling from 344 in 1970 to 1787 in 1973. See Paul Burstein & Kathleen Monaghan, "Equal Employment and the Mobilization of Law," 20 *Law & Soc. Rev.* 333, 361 (Table 1) (1986).

31. See Graham, supra n. 10, at 448.

32. See Dean Kotlowski, *Nixon's Civil Rights* 120 (2001).

33. Nixon's secretary of labor, George Schultz, revived a proposal that the Johnson administration had abandoned. When Congress tried to repudiate the initiative, Nixon personally intervened to preserve the Philadelphia Plan. See Skrentny, supra n. 9, at 193–209.

34. Myart v. Motorola is reprinted at 110 *CR* 5662 (1964).

35. Arthur Krock, "In the Nation: A Pilot Ruling on Equal Employment Opportunity," *NYT,* March 13, 1964, at 32. See Graham, supra n. 10, at 149–50.

36. 110 *CR* 13,492 (June 11, 1964). Tower explained, "My amendment is quite simple. It provides that an employer may give any professionally developed test to any individual seeking employment or being considered for promotion or transfer or to act in reliance upon the result of any such test." Id.

37. 110 *CR* 13505 (June 11, 1964).

38. The final text of the Tower Amendment provided that the "test, its administration or action upon the results" should not be "designed, intended, *or used* to discriminate because of race, color, religion, sex, or national origin." 110 *CR* 13,724 (June 13, 1964, emphasis added).

39. Id.

40. See American Psychological Association, *Standards for Educational and Psychological Tests and Manuals* (1966).

41. See Griggs v. Duke Power Co., 401 U.S. 424, 433 n. 9 (1971).

42. See Rueul Schiller, "The Era of Deference: Courts, Expertise, and the Emergence of New Deal Administrative Law," 106 *Mich. L. Rev.* 399 (2007).

43. Some believe that Griggs's interpretation of the statute "conflicts with the working and legislative history of title VII." See, e.g., Graham, supra n. 10, at 389, citing Gary Bryner, "Congress, Courts, and Agencies: Equal Employment and the Limits of Policy Implementation," 96 *Pol. Sci. Q.* 411 (1981). But these authors fail to confront the Court's discussion of the relevant legislative history;

see Griggs, supra n. 41, at 434–36, which does indeed provide the support they claim is lacking.

44. Griggs, supra n. 41, at 431.

45. To make my discussion manageable, I have been focusing on two especially revealing aspects of the EEOC's policy-making response. For more comprehensive treatments, see Skrentny, supra n. 10, at 111–44; Graham, supra n. 10, at 124–42.

46. The critical role of personnel professionals in revolutionizing anti-discrimination practices is insightfully analyzed by Jennifer Delton, *Racial Integration in Corporate America* (2009) and Frank Dobbin, *Inventing Equal Opportunity* (2009). See also Gavin Wright, *Sharing the Prize* 137–39 (2013).

47. See United States Civil Rights Commission, *Federal Civil Rights Enforcement: A Reassessment,* chap. 2, 88 (1973); Skrentny, supra n. 9, at 124.

48. Graham, supra n. 10, at 420–21.

49. Id. at 423 (quoting letter from Leonard to Richard Kleindienst, Deputy Attorney General, March, 1969). Nixon's new chairman of the EEOC, William Brown, also initially endorsed the NLRB model for his agency, id. at 429, before backtracking when the administration rejected this approach.

50. Id. at 424–25. Everett Dirksen had also come to the view that his 1964 compromise didn't work in practice and that the EEOC should gain the power to prosecute violators in court. But he died in September 1969, leaving the scene before the debate over the EEOC's powers began in earnest.

51. Hugh Graham provides a skillful analysis of the political dynamics. Id. at 429–45. For a more legally oriented account, see George Sape & Thomas Hart, *Title Seven Reconsidered,* 40 *George. L. Rev.* 824, 832–46 (1972).

52. Editorial, "Banishing Job Bias," *NYT,* February 24, 1972, at 38. At earlier stages in the debate, the *Times* had favored the NLRB model. See e.g., Editorial, "Enforcing Equality," *NYT,* Jan. 25, 1972, at 34.

53. 118 *CR* 294 (Jan. 19, 1972).

54. 118 *CR* 1663 (Jan. 28, 1972).

55. Id. at 1661.

56. Id. at 1676. The vote was 44 to 22, with almost all the nays from the South.

57. Speaking for Motorola at the House hearings, Robert Nystrom couldn't have been clearer:

> As you know last week the U.S. Supreme Court, in a case of first impression, in Griggs versus Duke Power Co . . . construed the meaning of section 703(h) [the Tower Amendment]. . . . Now that the U.S. Supreme Court has construed section 703(h) let us leave well enough alone. We now have legal precedence and guidance. We now have guidelines. Nothing further needs be done.

House Subcommittee on Labor, Equal Employment Enforcement 424 (91 Cong., 2d sess., 1971).

58. 118 *CR* 7166 (March 6, 1972) and 7564 (March 8, 1972). This sweeping endorsement did not cover cases in which the new statute "explicitly" revised the law

set down by the courts, but these revisions did not alter the basic principles established in *Griggs* and the leading cases in the lower courts.

59. See Kotlowski, supra n. 32, at 120–21.

60. For insightful discussions, see Delton, supra n. 46, and Dobbin, supra n. 46.

61. See Wright, supra n. 46, at 117–26; John Donohue & James Heckman, "Continuous Versus Episodic Change: The Impact of Civil Rights Policy on the Economic Status of Blacks," 29 *J. Econ. Lit.* 1603 (1991).

62. The partisans of "rational choice" dominate the study of American politics at present, but the most profound exponent of this view remains William Riker, and especially his *Liberalism Against Populism* (1982).

63. See *WP: F* chap. 7.

64. For a classic statement, see Gerald Gunther, "The Supreme Court 1971 Term—Foreword: In Search of Evolving Doctrine on a Changing Court: A Model for a Newer Equal Protection," 86 *Harv. L. Rev.* 1 (1972).

65. See generally, Desmond King & Rogers Smith, *Still a House Divided* (2011).

66. See Chapter 8.

10. The Breakthrough of 1968

1. Charles M. Lamb, *Housing Segregation in Suburban America Since 1960* 33 (2005).

2. John Herbers, "Javits Gives Up His Demand for a Rights Bill Time Limit," *NYT,* May 4, 1966, at 28.

3. Allen Matusow argues that Johnson backed away from an executive order because of the "political risks" posed by a massive white backlash. On his account, the president was "shirking responsibility while appearing to fulfill it" by calling for landmark legislation. *The Unraveling of America* 266 (1984, 2009 ed.) But Matusow fails to consider that a legislative effort also carried big "political risks" for the president. If he tried and failed to push a housing bill through Congress, this would dramatize the extent to which his fabled political mastery was disintegrating. His decision to put his reputation on the line was an act of courage, not cowardice—especially since he could have issued a weak executive order that would have allowed him to declare a symbolic victory.

4. Ben Franklin, "Wilkins Presses for Open Housing: Warns of 'Heartbreaking' and 'Ugly' Developments if Rights Bill Is Cut," *NYT,* Jul. 26, 1966, at 1.

5. See Darren Miles, "The Art of the Possible: Everett Dirksen's Role in the Civil Rights Legislation of the 1950s and 1960s," 1 *West. Ill. Hist. Rev.* 111, 112 (2009); "Dirksen Assails Fair Housing Plan," *NYT,* May 3, 1966, at 34 ("If you can tell me what interstate commerce is involved in selling or renting a house fixed to the soil, or where there is Federal jurisdiction, I'll go out and eat the chimney off the house.").

6. See 114 *CR* 4574 (Feb. 28, 1968).

7. See Hugh Graham, "The Surprising Career of Federal Fair Housing Law," *J. Pol. Hist.* 215, 218 (2000).

8. Richard L. Lyons, "Nixon, Rocky Push GOP on Civil Rights Bill," *WP*, Mar. 21, 1968, A1.

9. Dean Kotlowski, *Nixon's Civil Rights* 46 (2001).

10. See, e.g., John Herbers, "Panel on Civil Disorders Calls for Drastic Action to Avoid 2-Society Nation," *NYT*, Mar. 1, 1968, A1.

11. Jean Dubofsky, "Fair Housing: A Legislative History and a Perspective," 8 *Washburn L. J.* 152, 158 (1969).

12. This provision was initially sponsored by Senator Howard Baker of Tennessee (Dirksen's son-in-law). He tried to expand a relatively narrow exception that exempted homeowners from the act so long as they sold or rented their homes on a personal basis, without any assistance by real estate professionals. Under Baker's amendment, homeowners would have retained this exemption even if they used real estate agents so long as they "indicat[ed]" to the real estate professional "any preference . . . based on race, color, religion, or national origin" 114 *CR* 5214 (1968). This massive escape hatch was closed by a vote of 48 to 43 after a heated debate. Id. at 5221–22.

13. Marjorie Hunter, "Rights and Votes: The House on Housing," *NYT*, Mar. 17, 1968, at E6.

14. See Marjorie Hunter, "House G.O.P. Eases Rights Bill Stand," *NYT*, Mar. 21, 1968, 28.

15. See "Effective Lobbying Put Open Housing Bill Across," 24 *CQ Almanac* 166, 168 (1968), reporting that Republican votes for the Senate bill moved from 35 in mid-March "to 57, then 65 . . . [e]arly in April." Carl Albert, the House majority leader, emphasized that "[t]he speaker of the House, John W. McCormack, advised me some time ago that he was assured of the votes necessary for House passage," confirming Representative Olsen's comment that "the great contribution Dr. King made to passage of this legislation resulted from the work of his life; it did not result from his tragic death." 114 *CR* 9280 (Apr. 9, 1968).

16. See, e.g. Lamb, supra n. 1, at 42; Matusow, supra n. 3, at 208. Neither author considers the contrary evidence presented here. My view is also supported by Graham, supra n. 7, at 219 (2000) ("King was murdered on April 4. But by then the bill's passage was no longer in doubt.").

17. Roy Wilkins, "History of Open-Housing Bill," *NYT*, May 10, 1968, at 46.

18. 114 *CR* 2279 (1968).

19. Mondale borrowed this formulation from Algernon Black, a leading civil rights advocate. See 114 *CR* 2281 (1968).

20. See Chapter 7.

21. Mondale developed the humiliation theme from the very opening of the debate. His initial speech presented down-to-earth stories about the failures of black college professors, doctors, and naval officers "to buy decent housing in all-white neighborhoods":

> Lt. Carlos Campbell . . . was ordered to report for duty with the Defense Intelligence Agency at Arlington, Va. The story he told as he tried time and

time again to find decent housing, which he was able to pay for, within reasonable distance of the post to which he was assigned by the U.S. Government, is a story of shame . . . that should be a burden on the conscience of every decent American. (114 *CR* 2277–78 [1968])

Mondale's link between the military and housing echoes Warren's link between public schooling and military service in Brown's earlier effort to establish the centrality of the sphere of public education.

22. 114 *CR* 3421 (Feb. 20, 1968).
23. Id. at 3422.
24. Brooke also explicitly reaffirmed his co-manager's point in his speech introducing the bill:

> Fair housing does not promise to end the ghetto; it promises only to demonstrate that the ghetto is not an immutable institution in America. It will scarcely lead to a mass dispersal of the ghetto population to the suburbs; but it will make it possible for those who have the resources to escape the stranglehold now suffocating the inner cities of America. (114 *CR* 2279 [1968])

25. See Fair Housing Act, Pub. L. 90–284, § 808 (e)(5). As Charles Lamb emphasizes, Mondale did hope that HUD would ultimately replace ghettos with "truly integrated and balanced living patterns." See Traficante v. Metropolitan Life Insurance Co, 409 U.S. 205, 211 (1974). But I part company when he claims that "it is not clear whether Mondale was referring solely to racial integration in housing or to economic integration as well." See Lamb, supra n. 1, at 10. To the contrary, Mondale was perfectly clear that the statute did not aim for "economic integration," and focused solely on assuring blacks that they could buy housing on equal terms with whites. See also supra n. 24 for the identical point made by Mondale's Republican co-manager, Edward Brooke.
   Lamb rightly suggests that George Romney tried to embrace economic integration as a national goal when he was Nixon's secretary of HUD. But he fails to note that Romney explicitly stated that the Fair Housing Act did not provide an adequate legal basis for this more ambitious goal and that a new statute would be required to legitimate his larger initiative. See n. 56, infra.
26. 114 *CR* 2708 (Feb. 8, 1968).
27. See Richard Nixon's rationale for signing the renewal of the Voting Rights Act in 1970, elaborated in Chapter 9.
28. "Civil Rights: The President's Message to Congress," 4 *Weekly Comp. Pres. Docs.* 113 (Jan. 24, 1968). This point was broadly understood at the time: "Despite the satisfaction expressed by the legislators and the President, it appeared doubtful that the legislation by itself would satisfy the civil rights groups or solve the basic social problems of the Negroes. At best [it] opened slightly the door out of the ghettos; for the Negro there still remained the problem of earning enough money to take the path to the suburbs." John W. Finney, "Conflicting Pressures on Congress," *NYT,* Apr. 14, 1968, at E2.

29. Senator Mondale borrowed these provisions from a fair housing bill he had previously submitted in 1967. See 114 *CR* 2271 (Feb. 6, 1968) (restating relevant provisions).

30. See § 810 and § 812, 82 Stat. 85–88 (1968).

31. See § 813 (a), 82 Stat. 88 (1968).

32. See "Statement by President on Rights Bill," *NYT,* Apr. 12, 1968, at 18 (transcribing remarks in full); also available at www.presidency.ucsb.edu/ws/index.php?pid=28799&st=&st1=.

33. 392 U.S. 409 (1968).

34. See Chapters 4 and 7 for further elaboration of this theme.

35. See generally Darrell Miller, "White Cartels, the Civil Rights Act of 1866, and the History of Jones v. Alfred H. Mayer Co.," 77 *Ford. L. Rev.* 999 (2008).

36. Act of April 9, 1866, ch. 31, § 1, 14 Stat. 27. This language was revised later in the nineteenth century and now reads:

    All citizens of the United States shall have the same right, in every State and Territory, as is enjoyed by white citizens thereof to inherit, purchase, lease, sell, hold, and convey real and personal property. (42 U.S.C. 1982)

37. Jones v. Mayer, 255 F. Supp. 115, 119 (E.D. Mo. 1966).

38. Jones v. Mayer, 379 F.2d 33, 34 (1967). As Linda Greenhouse explains, "Blackmun's sympathies were with the plaintiff . . . but he felt constrained to follow precedent. He noted that a 'change of course' may be imminent, but that he was bound as a lower court." *Becoming Justice Blackmun* 29–30 (2005).

39. See Bernard Schwartz, "Rehnquist, Runyon, and Jones—The Chief Justice, Civil Rights, and Stare Decisis," 31 *Tulsa L. J.* 251, 259–60 (1995).

40. Del Dickson ed., *The Supreme Court in Conference (1940–1985)* 730 (2001).

41. Jones v. Mayer, 392 U.S. 409, 450 (1968).

42. Professor Louis Henkin was typical in expressing puzzlement at "why the Court could not resist the temptation to find in the [1866 act] what, by a fair reading, no Congress ever put there." Henkin, "Foreword: On Drawing Lines," 82 *Harv. L. Rev.* 63, 84 (1968). See also Gerhard Casper, "Jones v. Mayer: Clio, Bemused and Confused Muse," 1989 *Sup. Ct. Rev.* 89; Earl Malz, *Civil Rights, the Constitution, and Congress,* 1863–69, 70–78 (1990).

43. Civil Rights Cases, 109 U.S. 3, 24–25 (1883).

44. Jones, supra n. 41, at 443.

45. See, e.g., United States v. Hunter, 459 F.2d 205 (4th Cir. 1972), *cert. denied,* 409 U.S. 934 (1972); United States v. Bob Lawrence Realty, Inc., 474 F.2d 115 (5th Cir. 1973), *cert. denied,* 414 U.S. 826 (1973), upholding provisions of the Fair Housing Act on the basis of Jones without relying on the Fourteenth Amendment or the Commerce Clause.

46. Robert Semple, "The Nixon Strategy: Unity and Caution," *NYT,* Aug. 11, 1968, at 1.

47. The backlog quintupled between 1969 and 1973, moving from 301 to 1,830. Compare 1970 *HUD Statistical Yearbook* 85 with 1973 *HUD Statistical Yearbook* 4.

48. See John Herbers, "New Job Panel Tracks Down 'Biased' Computer," *NYT*, December 14, 1965, at 46.

49. HUD referrals to the Justice Department only led its Civil Rights Division to bring three lawsuits during the period ending in April 1970. In 1973, the division was only acting "upon approximately 20 referrals from HUD" during the entire year. See United States Commission on Civil Rights, *Federal Civil Rights Enforcement Effort* 142 (1971), and 129 (1974).

50. See James Kushner, "The Fair Housing Amendments Act of 1988: The Second Generation of Fair Housing," 42 *Md. L. Rev.* 1049, 1080 (1989).

51. The first specific proposals to strengthen the enforcement provisions of Title VIII were presented to Congress in 1976 by HUD secretary, Carla Hills. Equal Opportunity in Housing: Hearing Before the Subcomm. on Civil and Constitutional Rights of the H. Comm. on the Judiciary, 94th Cong. 116–17 (September 30, 1976) (urging that HUD be authorized to enforce the act through civil actions). It was only in 1978 that civil rights groups began proposing specific changes to the statutory framework. See, e.g., Fair Housing Act: Hearing Before the Subcomm. on Civil and Constitutional Rights of the H. Comm. on the Judiciary, 95th Cong. 138 (1978) (statement of Edward Holmgren, Executive Director, National Committee Against Discrimination in Housing). This began a ten-year effort culminating in a fundamental revision of the Fair Housing Act in 1988, which provided HUD with enforcement authority. See Kushner, supra n. 50.

52. In contrasting the development of housing and employment policy, I am following Christopher Bonastia, whose *Knocking on the Door* (2006) inaugurated this comparative approach. But I reach different conclusions. In Bonastia's view, the contrast shows that a single-issue agency such as the EEOC was a more congenial organizational home for policy entrepreneurship than the multiple-function mega-agency at HUD.

    I am unpersuaded. As Part Three will show, other mega-agencies did manage to play crucial roles in policy development. Most notably, HEW was a mega-agency like HUD—but this did not prevent it from breaking the back of southern resistance to school desegregation. In developing his analysis, Bonastia fails to recognize the point emphasized here: Jones's role in deflecting the political priorities of black civil rights groups. As the following pages suggest, George Romney's political blunders as secretary of HUD were also extremely important in accounting for the agency's failure to redefine the meaning of fair housing—more important, I think, than HUD's organizational shortcomings.

53. Lamb, supra n. 1, at 71; John Herbers, "Romney Making His Greatest Impact Outside Government by Challenging U.S. Institutions," *NYT*, May 15, 1969, at 32.

54. See Lamb, supra n. 1, at 63–68; Kotlowski, supra n. 9, at 49.

55. Kotlowski, supra n. 9, at 56.

56. In campaigning for new legislation, Romney emphasized that the 1968 act did not "permit us to take action in the case local communities use the zoning authority to discriminate against low- and moderate-income housing." Hearing

Before the S. Select Comm. on Equal Educational Opportunity, 91st Cong. 2770–71 (Aug. 26, 1970); see also id. at 2784–86.

57. Open Communities would have authorized "any person denied the benefits" of HUD-subsidized housing to sue for lost benefits; and it also permitted the Justice Department to go to court to open up the suburbs. See Lamb, supra n. 1, at 83.

58. Kotlowski, supra n. 9, at 52. While Nixon was personally opposed to economic integration of the suburbs, he also believed that there was a "need[] to leapfrog the Democrats on the Great Society issues and get ahead of them" to erase the Republicans' "public image as a 'negative' party" and the "'reckless and racist' taint inherited from the Goldwater campaign." Richard Nixon, *RN: The Memoirs of Richard Nixon* 267–68 (1978). White House advisors such as Leonard Garment and Patrick Moynihan were often successful in persuading Nixon to put aside his personal reactions and adopt more liberal positions as part of his larger effort to move beyond Goldwaterism. See generally Kotlowski, supra n. 9. A particularly apt example is provided in Chapter 11's discussion of Nixon's decisions to support an all-out effort campaign against southern school segregation. We will never know, of course, whether liberal advisors might have succeeded in the case of housing as well—Romney's secrecy made it impossible for them to try.

59. Lamb, supra n. 1, at 85–90.

60. For the best account of the Warren affair, see David Riddle, "HUD and the Open Housing Controversy of 1970," 24 *Mich. Hist. Rev.* 1 (1998). See also Kotlowski, supra n. 9, 56 (2001); Lamb, supra n. 1, at 85–89 (2005).

61. See Richard Nixon, "Statement About Federal Policies Relative to Equal Housing Opportunity," at www.presidency.ucsb.edu/ws/index.php?pid=3042 &st=&sti=.

62. The government's case was ultimately upheld by a court of appeals decision, which also blurred the distinction between purpose and effect. See United States v. City of Black Jack, Missouri, 508 F.2d 1179, 1186 (8th Cir. 1974), *cert. denied,* 422 U.S. 1042 (1975).

63. Conservatives took issue with Nixon's broad understanding of racial discrimination. See Lamb, supra n. 1, at 67–68. At the same time, many civil rights groups condemned him for creating "artificial distinctions" between economic and racial segregation. Paul Delaney, "Nixon Criticized on Housing Policy," *NYT,* July 14, 1971, at 39. But the NAACP refused to join this chorus, with Roy Wilkins and Stephen Spottswood giving the president their muted support. See Earl Caldwell, "N.A.A.C.P. Softens Anti-Nixon Stand," *NYT,* July 6, 1971, at 1; Earl Caldwell, "Wilkins Discerns Chance for Nixon," *NYT,* July 10, 1971, at 13.

64. Lamb, supra n. 1, at 141.

65. 114 *CR* 3421 (Feb. 20, 1968).

11. Brown's Fate

1. U.S. Commission on Civil Rights, *Survey of School Desegregation in the Southern and Border States 1965–66* 1–2 (Feb. 1966).

2. Briggs v. Elliot, 132 F. Supp. 776, 777 (D.S.C. 1955).

3. See Shuttleworth v. Birmingham Board of Education, 358 U.S. 401 (1958).

4. Cooper v. Aaron, 358 U.S. 1, 18 (1958).

5. See Michael Klarman, *From Jim Crow to Civil Rights* 326 (2004).

6. See id., at 399–403.

7. See Griffin v. County School Board, 377 U.S. 218, 234 (1964).

8. So far as the judiciary was concerned, the statute says that "nothing herein shall . . . enlarge the existing power of the court to insure compliance with constitutional standards," and it particularly refused to endorse busing "to achieve . . . racial balance." See § 407 (a) (2), 78 Stat. 241 (1964); see also 401 (c). But as Chief Justice Burger would rightly emphasize, "these provisions were designed to foreclose any interpretation of the act as expanding the *existing* powers of federal courts. . . . There is no suggestion of an intention to restrict those powers or withdraw from courts their historic equitable remedial powers." See Swann v. Charlotte-Mecklenburg Bd. of Educ., 402 U.S. 1, 17–18 (1971).

9. See § 407, granting Justice the right to initiate litigation, and § 902, granting it the right to intervene in other lawsuits.

10. Gary Orfield, *The Reconstruction of Southern Education* 41 (1969).

11. See David Brady & Barbara Sinclair, "Building Majorities for Policy Changes in the House of Representatives," 6 *J. Pol.* 1033 (1984).

12. See Dean Kotlowski, "With All Deliberate Delay: Kennedy, Johnson and School Desegregation," 17 *J. Pol. Hist.* 155, 167 (2005).

13. See U.S. Department of Health, Education, and Welfare, *Projections of Educational Statistics to 1975–76* 58 (table) (1966).

14. See G. W. Foster Jr., "Title VI: Southern Education Faces the Facts," *Saturday Review* 60, 76 (table) (Mar. 20, 1965).

15. For a detailed account of HEW policy development between 1964 and 1966, see Stephen Bailey & Edith Mosher, *ESEA: The Office of Education Administers a Law* (1968).

16. The Office of Education allowed some school boards facing the heaviest local resistance to open only two grades to "freedom of choice" as a first step toward fuller compliance. 45 CFR § 181.5 268 (CFR 1966 Supp).

17. Orfield, supra n. 10, at 111.

18. Id. at 97–98. See Kotlowski, supra n. 12, at 171–73. The president also failed to sign more stringent versions of the guidelines prepared in later years. Id. at 175.

19. The precise percentage was controversial. HEW claimed it was 7.5 percent, civil rights groups 5 percent. By any reckoning, this more or less tripled the previous year's percentage. See Civil Rights Commission, *Survey of School Desegregation in the Southern and Border States,* 26–28 (1966).

20. Orfield, supra n. 10, at 146. See 45 CFR § 181.54 407–08 (1967).

21. See Gary Orfield & Chungmei Lee, *Historic Reversals, Accelerating Resegregation, and the Need for New Integration Strategies* 23 (2007). U.S. Commission on Civil Rights, *Southern School Desegregation* 101 (1967) (doc. no. ED 028 876)

provides broadly comparable statistics, estimating an increase from 6–7.5 percent in 1965 to 12.5 percent in 1966.

22. See generally, Orfield, supra n. 10, at 274–304.

23. Orfield & Lee, supra n. 21, at 23.

24. United States v. Jefferson County Bd. of Education, 372 F.2d 836 (December 29, 1966); affirmed en banc, with minor changes, at 380 F.2d 385 (1967).

25. Id. at 847.

26. Id. at 849.

27. Wisdom quotes at length from Harlan Fiske Stone's New Deal paean to the administrative agency, "The Common Law in the United States," 50 *Harv. L. Rev.* 1 (1936). See Jefferson, supra n. 24, at 857–58.

28. Id. at 858.

29. Id. at 859.

30. I am quoting here from the court's en banc decision, not Wisdom's original opinion. See 380 F. 2d 385, 390 (1967).

31. Jefferson, supra n. 24, at 866.

32. I present more elaborate discussions of the anti-subordination principle, and its relationship to anti-humiliation, in Chapters 7 and 14.

33. Green v. County School Board, 391 U.S. 430 (1968).

34. Id. at 431.

35. All quotations come from Justice Brennan's unpublished draft opinion in *Green* 5–7 (circulated May 16, 1968), Brennan Papers, Box I: 174, Library of Congress. Brennan also took up the anti-humiliation theme in a companion case, *Monroe v. Board of Comm'rs of City of Jackson:* "Only by dismantling the dual system, to purge the racial identity ingrained in the system by years of discrimination, *can the stigma of inferiority that works to deny the negro child equal educational opportunity be effectively eliminated*" (emphasis added), at 7 (circulated May 16, 1968) (Box I: 175).

36. My account follows the memo filed by Brennan's law clerks, Francis M. Gregory & Raymond C. Fisher, as part of their Case Histories, October Term 1967, xxix, Brennan Papers, Box II: 6, Folder 10, Library of Congress.

37. Bernard Schwartz, *Super Chief: Earl Warren and His Supreme Court* 704–5 (1983); Gregory & Fisher, Case Histories, supra n. 36, at xxx.

38. Black only exacted some minor verbal modifications as his price for signing on, with Brennan remarking that "they left the opinion virtually unchanged." Fisher, Case Histories, supra at xxx.

39. Green, supra n. 33, at 439.

40. This failure of principle was noted at the time, though the inner dynamics were then invisible. See, e.g., Owen Fiss, "The Charlotte-Mecklenburg Case—Its Significance for Northern School Desegregation," 38 *U. Chi. L. Rev.* 697, 699 (1971).

41. See Green, supra n. 33, at 442, n. 6.

42. See Green, draft opinion, supra n. 35, at 6–7.

43. This time, Black signed on to the majority opinion without great difficulty.

44. When Reagan's last-minute convention challenge became serious, Nixon met with southern delegations to prevent their defection. Even at this crucial moment, he defended his public support of the recently enacted Fair Housing Act, and emphasized the need to move beyond regional appeals if the Republicans wanted to mount a winning national campaign in November. See Kevin McMahon, *Nixon's Court* 18–36, and especially 30–32 (2011).

45. See, e.g., Ben A. Franklin, "Wallace Calls His Opponents Unfit for President Because of Rights Stand," *NYT,* Oct. 29, 1968, at 23.

46. McMahon, supra n. 44, at 47.

47. Id. at 25–26.

48. See Gareth Davies, "Richard Nixon and the Desegregation of Southern Schools," 19 *J. Pol. Hist.* 368, 369 (2007).

49. Id.

50. Richard Harwood, "Agnew Is 'Simpatico': Agnew Choice a Compromise," *NYT,* Aug. 8, 1968, at A1.

51. See Leon Panetta & Peter Gall, *Bring Us Together: The Nixon Team and the Civil Rights Retreat* (1971).

52. See James Rosen, *The Strong Man* 129–31 (2008).

53. At an early news conference, Nixon had already gestured in the direction of a compromise:

> As far as school segregation is concerned, I support the law of the land. I believe that funds should be denied to those districts that continue to perpetuate segregation. I think that what we have here is a very difficult problem, however, in implementing it. One is our desire . . . to keep our schools open, because education must receive the highest priority. The other is our desire to see to it that our schools are not segregated.
>
> That is why I have, in discussing this with Secretary Finch . . . urged that before we use the ultimate weapon of denying funds and closing a school, let's exhaust every other possibility to see that local school districts do comply with the law.

Richard Nixon, News Conference, February 6, 1969, at www.presidency.ucsb.edu/ws/index.php?pid=2208&st=&st1=. Nixon's remarks are confused, since withholding federal funds did not imply the closure of schools—states and localities were the principal source of money for education. Nevertheless, it's plain enough that Nixon wanted to reserve funding cutoffs as the weapon of last resort. This was not very different from the Johnson administration's position while in office—Johnson's HEW only imposed tough deadlines on the next administration while retaining flexibility for itself.

54. "Text of Statement by Finch and Mitchell on School Desegregation," *NYT,* July 4, 1969, at 7.

55. Id.

56. See generally, Dean Kotlowski, *Nixon's Civil Rights* 27–30 (2001).

57. Willard Edwards, "Capitol Views: Stennis Works Out a Deal," *Chicago Tribune,* Sep. 11, 1969, at 18.

58. Stennis's personal letter to Nixon asserted that "HEW integration plans . . . will destroy the public school system of the state . . . [and] are on their face ridiculous and absurd. . . . As Chairman of the Senate Armed Service Committee I have major responsibilities here in connection with legislation dealing with our national security, *but I will not hesitate one moment to leave my duties here . . . to go to Mississippi or do whatever else may be required to help protect . . . and to preserve our public school system*" (emphasis added). Letter, John Stennis to Richard Nixon, August 11, 1969; folder 105A (Whitten Amendment: Busing), Box 34, White House Special Files: Staff Member and Office Files: John D. Ehrlichman; Richard Nixon Presidential Library and Museum, Yorba Linda, CA. If Stennis had left town, Senate leadership would fall to Stuart Symington, "one of the severest critics of defense spending . . . Entrusting the bill to his tender mercies might mean its mutilation." Edwards, supra n. 57. After Nixon received Stennis's letter, Mitchell and Finch approached the senator to reach a "workable solution." Panetta & Gall, supra n. 51, at 263–65. According to a senior staffer, "It was the closest thing to a quid pro quo situation that I ever saw Senator Stennis involved in." Interview with Charles Overby (conducted by Jeff Broadwater), John C. Stennis Oral History Project, Mississippi State University, March 11, 1991, 15–16. See also Jack Rosenthal, "Stennis Linked to Desegregation Delay," *NYT,* Sept. 19, 1969, at 36; James Rosen, supra n. 52, at 137–38.

59. Panetta & Gall, supra n. 51, at 256.

60. Id. at 259–62.

61. Alexander v. Holmes County Board of Education, 396 U.S. 1218–19 (1969) (Black J., Circuit Justice).

62. Alexander Polikoff, *Waiting for Gautreaux* 129 (2006).

63. Id. at 129–30.

64. Alexander v. Holmes County Board of Education, 396 U.S. 19 (1969).

65. Green v. County School Board, 391 U.S. 430, 439 (1968).

66. See Bernard Schwartz, *Swann's Way* 67–87 (1986), for a blow-by-blow description of the litigation and dynamics of decision.

67. Rowland Evans and Robert Novak, *Nixon in the White House* 156 (1971).

68. Davies, supra n. 48, at 373.

69. Id.

70. Nixon fired Panetta without even telling him first—allowing him to learn of his fate when Ronald Ziegler, White House press secretary, announced it at a news conference. See Panetta & Gall, supra n. 51, at 352–55.

71. Nixon and Finch framed the resignation as a promotion: "Nixon told Robert Finch that he wanted his old political associate to join him in the White House as a key counselor . . . 'I feel very comfortable' about the switch, [said Finch] and . . . it is 'categorically untrue' that he has been removed or ousted, as one

wire service report stated." Haynes Johnson, "Nixon Pressed Him, Finch Says," *WP*, Jun. 7, 1970, at 1.

72. 4 Congressional Quarterly Service, *Congress and the Nation: 1969–1973* 297 (1973).

73. Except where explicitly noted, my account of Nixon's response to *Alexander*, together with all the quotations in the text, relies on the archival work presented by Davies, supra n. 48, at 374–78.

74. See Leonard Garment, *Crazy Rhythm* 206 (1997).

75. As Nixon explained to Ehrlichman and Garment, it was "in our interest, politically, to get the issue behind us now," and to have the "confrontations this year rather than '72." Davies, supra n. 48, at 377 (citing Ehrlichman's notes and Garment's memo from the Nixon archives).

76. See A. James Reichley, *Conservatives in an Age of Change* 190–192, 305 (1981); James Bolner & Robert Shanley, *Busing: The Political and Judicial Process* 145 (1974).

77. Richard Nixon, "Statement About Desegregation of Elementary and Secondary Schools," (March 24, 1970), *American Presidency Project*, at www.presidency. ucsb.edu/ws/?pid=2923.

78. Roy Reed, "Both Sides in South Mistrust Nixon Actions on School Integration," *NYT*, July 17, 1970, at 22 (noting that both Justice and the IRS made their announcements simultaneously). Only two months earlier, the Justice Department had been arguing that the tax break for private schools should not qualify as a federal subsidy for segregation. Linda Mathews, " 'Racist' Schools to Lose Tax Break," *LAT*, July 11, 1970, at 1.

79. See Lawrence McAndrews, "Segregated Schools Lose Tax Breaks," *Chi. Trib.* July 11, 1970, at 1.

80. See Kotlowski, supra n. 56, at 25. See generally Lawrence McAndrews, "The Politics of Principle: Richard Nixon and School Desegregation," 83 *J. Negro Hist.* 187, 195–96 (1998).

81. Kenneth Crawford, "Thurmond Threatens," 76 *Newsweek* 25 (Aug. 3, 1970).

82. Spiro Agnew was initially put in charge of the Cabinet Committee, but he refused to play an active role, and Nixon soon turned to Schultz to provide the necessary leadership. See George Schultz, "How a Republican Desegregated the South's Schools," *NYT*, Jan. 8, 2003, at A23; Rosen, supra n. 52, at 142.

83. Davies, supra n. 48, at 383.

84. See Schultz, supra n. 82. Over the next two months, Schultz went through "much the same process" with five other state delegations. Id. The last state on Schultz's list, Louisiana, proved particularly difficult to organize. But just before the school year opened, he convinced Nixon (over Spiro Agnew's dissent) to seal the deal at a highly publicized meeting in New Orleans, which all seven state committees attended. Emerging from their joint conclave, here is what the president told the Deep South:

> Let me be very direct and very candid with regard to where we stand on the problem of school desegregation.

The highest court of the land has spoken. The unitary school system must replace the dual school system throughout the United States. The law having been determined, it is the responsibility of the President of the United States to uphold the law. And I shall meet that responsibility.

However, in upholding the law, a law which requires a very significant social change . . . in the Southern States involved, there are different approaches.

One approach is simply to sit back and wait for school to open and for trouble to start, and then if trouble begins, to order in the Federal enforcers to see that the law is complied with.

I rejected that approach from the beginning. . . .

[L]eadership in an instance like this requires some preventive action . . . and we are getting magnificent cooperation from dedicated people in the seven States involved.

These are civic leaders serving without pay and many of them serving even though some of their friends and neighbors suggest that they, too, should sit on the sidelines and not borrow trouble by trying to give advice or to develop public opinion so that this orderly transition can be made. . . . Time will tell how successful we have been, but I do know this: As a result of these advisory committees being set up, we are going to find that in many districts the transition will be orderly and peaceful, whereas otherwise it could have been the other way. And the credit will go to these outstanding Southern leaders, more credit to them actually than to the Federal officials who were there to help them.

See Richard Nixon, "Remarks Following a Meeting in New Orleans with Leaders of Seven State Advisory Committees on Public Education," (August 14, 1970), at www.presidency.ucsb.edu/ws/index.php?pid=2628&st=Cabinet+Committee+on+Education&st1=#ixzz1SqnLHtUA.

85. See Reed, supra n. 78.

86. Davies, supra n. 48, at 387–388, collects a representative sample of liberal critiques.

87. Gary Orfield, *Public School Desegregation in the United States, 1968–1980* 4 (1983), and Orfield & Lee, supra n. 21, at 23. See also n. 90 for additional data.

88. See Schwartz, supra n. 66, at 73.

89. Burger described the resulting order as "the proverbial 'horse put together by a committee' with a camel as the end result." In the end, he rejected the Cooper v. Aaron model, explaining that "there is some view, which I now tend to share, that a recital of all names at the head of the order has a tendency to give it undue emphasis. I will therefore have this entered as a routine order and a decree letting the contents convey their own urgent message." Justice Burger, Memorandum for the Conference Regarding Alexander v. Holmes County (Oct. 29, 1969), Harlan Papers, Box 606, Folder 12252, Princeton University. Over the past forty years, the absence of a formal opinion has made it easy to forget *Alexander*'s "urgent message."

90. In 1968, 77.8 percent of black students in the South were in schools with 90 percent minority enrollment, while the national average was 64.3 percent. By 1972, the southern number dropped to 24.7 percent, one-third below the national average of 38.7 percent. Gary Orfield, *Public School Desegregation in the United States, 1968–1980* 4 (1983). For other data conveying the same message, see text accompanying n. 87, supra.

91. As Burger himself noted in a confidential memorandum, "a good many judges anticipated that this Court would command racial balance in all schools, 'so that there will be no basis for contending that one school is racially different from others.' In some respects both [lower] courts correctly anticipated Swann, but on the racial balance aspect they erred if indeed they thought that was the way the wind would blow." Justice Burger, "Memorandum to Conference Re: Wright v. City of Emporia," 19–20 (March 16, 1972), Stewart Papers, Box 80, Folder 703, Yale University.

92. Swann, supra n. 8, at 23.

93. Justice Brennan, Memorandum of Justice Brennan in *Swann,* March [n.d.] 1970, Brennan Papers, Box I: 243, Folder 1, National Archives. The March date is misleading, since certiorari was only granted on June 29, 1970. The mystery is resolved by a memo reviewing the 1970 term written by Brennan's law clerks— which indicates that Brennan prepared his draft in July 1970 in response to a memo of June 27, circulated by Douglas in connection with the grant of certiorari. See Loftus Becker, Richard Cotton, and Michael Moran, "Opinions of Justice Brennan: 1970 Term," xxvi, Brennan Papers, Box II:6, Folder 6, Library of Congress.

94. Burger's initial draft supported optional busing for black students "to relieve particular hardship cases for those who find the posture of being a part of a school racial majority a 'badge of inferiority.' " Swann draft circulated Jan. 11, 1971, at 29, Black Papers, Box 436, Library of Congress. Justice Black immediately objected: "[T]he quote 'badge of inferiority' would, in my judgment, lead to all kinds of trouble. No court should, I think, order a state to provide an 'optional transfer' of pupils because those pupils suggest that they have a psychological feeling of a 'badge of inferiority.' Such a suggestion would, in my judgment, only serve to perpetuate more and more law suits and simply prolong indefinitely any hope for a permanent settlement of the school problems as it affects races." Justice Hugo Black, Letter to the Chief Justice (Jan. 13, 1971), Box 436, Black Papers, Library of Congress.

95. See Loftus Becker, Jr., Richard Cotton, & Michael Moran, "Opinions of William J. Brennan Jr. October Term 1970," xxvi, Case Histories, Brennan Papers, Box II:6, Folder 6, Library of Congress. This case history by law clerks simply reports that Brennan did not circulate his draft and does not speculate about the reasons—though, as I suggest in the text, they are rather obvious.

96. See Swann, supra n. 8, at 12.

97. Burger suggested that overwhelmingly black schools were acceptable "until new schools can be provided" or "neighborhood patterns change[d]"—this latter

condition implying that they would be an enduring fixture in some cases. Id. at 26.

12. The Switch in Time

1. Keyes v. Denver School District, 413 U.S. 189 (1973).
2. In fact, the district court's sweeping order in Crawford v. Bd. of Educ. generated "very little progress in actually desegregating Los Angeles's public schools," since it only succeeded in provoking extended litigation for more than a decade. Jack Schneider, "Escape from Los Angeles: White Flight from Los Angeles and Its Schools," 34 *J. Urb. Hist.* 995, 999–1000 (2008). Nevertheless, the decision generated widespread anxiety, as did integration campaigns in other northern cities even when they did not lead to court orders but used the threat of litigation to induce school boards to create busing plans on their own initiative. See generally David Kirp, "The Bounded Politics of School Desegregation Litigation," 51 *Harv. Ed. Rev.* 395 (1981).
3. See A. James Reichley, *Conservatives in an Age of Change* 190–192, 305 (1981); James Bolner & Robert Shanley, *Busing: The Political and Judicial Process* 145 (1974).
4. Richard Nixon, "Statement About Desegregation of Elementary and Secondary Schools." March 24, 1970, *American Presidency Project* at www.presidency.ucsb .edu/ws/index.php?pid=2923.
5. Id. This sentence appears in a remarkably philosophical section, "A Free and Open Society":

> An open society does not have to be homogeneous or even fully integrated. There is room within it for many communities. Especially in a nation like America, it is natural that people with a common heritage retain special ties; it is natural and right that we have Italian or Irish or Negro or Norwegian neighborhoods; it is natural and right that members of those communities feel a sense of group identity and group pride. In terms of an open society, what matters is mobility: the right and the ability of each person to decide for himself where and how he wants to live, whether as part of the ethnic enclaves or as part of the larger society—or, as many do, share the life of both. We are richer for our cultural diversity; mobility is what allows us to enjoy it.
>
> Economic, educational, social mobility—all these, too, are essential elements of the open society. When we speak of equal opportunity we mean just that: that each person should have an equal chance at the starting line.

Id. The statement then goes on to list a series of Nixon initiatives inspired by this aim—including the Philadelphia Plan for affirmative action in employment, and Nixon's revolutionary family assistance program, which would have replaced traditional welfare with a guaranteed annual income but was ultimately rejected by a curious congressional coalition of conservatives and liberals. See generally Daniel Moynihan, *The Politics of a Guaranteed Income* (1973).

6. Nixon, supra n. 5.

7. Nixon does invoke ethnic "pride"—the opposite of "humiliation"—in making his case. See id.

8. Id.

9. Id. Nixon also specified two other priorities for the new federal money. This part of his agenda targeted special problems involved in the southern transition to unitary school systems.

10. For example, Nixon emphasized the problem of white flight and the practical impossibility of ending all racially imbalanced schools given the concentration of black children in urban ghettos. But my text emphasizes the more philosophical and legal aspects of the president's position.

11. Whitten's language changed from year to year, but his overriding aim was the same. Senate versions of the Whitten initiative also changed annually, but the ultimate result was also the same: the House-Senate conference deprived Whitten's rider of effective legal significance. The changing formulations are traced in Bolner & Shanley, supra n. 3, at 63–92 (1974). For a penetrating view of the political dynamics driving the legislative process, see Gary Orfield, "Congress, the President, and Anti-Busing Legislation," 4 *J. Law & Educ.* 81 (1975).

12. 116 *CR* 2933–4 (1970) (containing text of Stennis Amendment).

13. 116 *CR* 2892 (1970).

14. Here are Senator Dominick's precise words: "It seems to me that when there is a fair housing law which permits people, in a reasonable manner, whenever they have the economic means and desires, to move where they want to, we have solved the basic problem of whether or not there has been intentional segregation as far as schools are concerned." Id. at 2900. Variations on this theme were developed in the debate that followed.

Senator Mondale took a different tack. He also opposed Ribicoff on spherical grounds, but then argued that the Senate should create a special committee to investigate interspherical impacts and come up with a new set of reforms. 116 *CR* 3577–8 (1970). This never happened.

15. 116 *CR* 3577–81 (1970). The speech had an immediate impact:

> Ribicoff's speech made the front pages in newspapers across the country. Liberals quickly denounced Ribicoff and the Stennis amendment for converting "liberal guilt into segregationist glee" and "[t]he cumulative effect of the debate sparked by the Stennis amendment had been to call into question liberal policies that had all but been taken for granted since the passage of the 1964 Civil Rights Act."

> Joseph Crespino, "The Best Defense Is a Good Offense: The Stennis Amendment and the Fracturing of Liberal School Desegregation Policy, 1964–1972," 18 *J. Pol. Hist.* 304, 314–16 (2006).

16. 116 *CR* 3576 (Feb. 17, 1970) and 116 *CR* 3779–88 (Feb. 18, 1970). Stennis-Ribicoff initially called for a uniform standard when dealing with "conditions of segregation." Scott-Mansfield responded by limiting the proposal's scope to

"*unconstitutional* conditions of segregation," thereby limiting its application to the types that were condemned by the Supreme Court. Ribicoff immediately grasped this point and denounced this one-word addition because it would apply only "to the States in the South, and the States in the North will be home free." Id. at 3580. To make his contrary intentions clear, he changed the Stennis-Ribicoff amendment to require a uniform approach to "conditions of segregation by race *whether de iure* [*sic*] *or de facto.*" 116 *CR* 3590 (1970) (emphasis supplied).

17. See 116 CR 2892 (1970).

18. As late as February 12, the White House was gesturing in Stennis's direction: "The President has consistently opposed, and still opposes, compulsory bussing of school children to achieve racial balance . . . To the extent that the 'uniform application' amendment offered by Senator John Stennis would advance equal application of law, it has the full support of this Administration." Nixon Administration Statement, Feb. 12, 1970; reprinted in 116 *CR* 3562 (Feb. 17. 1970). Two days later, the administration was still professing neutrality in the Senate debate (Spencer Rich, "White House Neutral on Stennis Plan," *WP*, Feb. 14, 1970, A1), only to repudiate Stennis three days later.

19. The key portion of the White House letter, signed by Bryce Harlow, reads:

DEAR SENATOR SCOTT:

This confirms that the following language was prepared by the Administration and furnished to you for possible use in the Senate . . . :

Sec. 2. It is the policy of the United States (1) that guidelines and criteria . . . shall be applied uniformly in all regions of the United States in dealing with *unconstitutional* conditions of segregation by race in the schools of the local educational agencies of any State; and (2) that no local educational agency shall be forced or required to bus or otherwise transport students in order to overcome racial imbalance. (Emphasis added)

Since the Supreme Court had condemned only de jure discrimination, the provision approved by the administration applied just to "unconstitutional" systems of the type prevailing in the South—until such time as the Justices condemned northern segregation as well. See 116 *CR* 3785 (1970) (entering White House letter in the record).

20. 116 *CR* 3800 (1970). For the vote breakdown, see www.govtrack.us/congress/votes/91–1970/s285.

21. As Senator Pell explained, "[T]he Stennis Amendment was hard fought in the conference. . . . [T]he conference . . . broke up 2 or 3 days due to our standing pat on it. The [compromise] language . . . was offered by a House Member." 116 *CR* 8874 (March 24, 1970). In addition to requiring a uniform policy in all cases of de jure segregation, the final version of Scott-Mansfield also required uniformity in the application of "such other policy as may be provided pursuant to law . . . to de facto segregation." But, as Senator Pell explained, "no laws presently apply because de facto segregation has not been ruled unconstitutional." Id.

22. See Chapter 11.

23. Reichley, supra n. 3, at 204.

24. John Ehrlichman, *Witness to Power: The Nixon Years* 221–22 (1982) (emphasis supplied).

25. George Gallup, 3 *The Gallup Poll* 2328 (1972). Southerners led the opposition, with 82 percent, with midwesterners at 77 percent and both easterners and westerners in the low 70s. Even blacks opposed it by a margin of 47–45 percent on a national basis, with 8 percent expressing no opinion.

26. David Riddle, "Race and Reaction in Warren, Michigan, 1971 to 1974: Bradley v. Milliken and the Cross-District Busing Controversy," 26 *Mich. Hist. Rev.* 1, 11 (2000).

27. Bradley v. Milliken, 338 F. Supp. 582 (September 27, 1971).

28. See Riddle, supra n. 26, at 48.

29. James O'Hara and William Ford, for example, had been serious liberal candidates for House leadership positions, but they became fervent anti-busers in 1971. See Orfield, supra n. 11, at 102, 104 (1975).

30. See n. 9, supra.

31. When Congressmen Collins (Texas) denounced Nixon's proposal as a massive "busing bill," he was supported by Congressmen Ford (Michigan), Gross (New Jersey), and Scherle (Iowa). See 116 *CR* 42218–20 (1970).

32. The Broomfield amendment provided that "any order . . . of any United States district court which requires the transfer or transportation of any student . . . for the purpose of achieving a balance among students with respect to race . . . shall be postponed until all appeals . . . have been exhausted." 117 *CR* 39302 (1971). It was approved by a vote of 235–125, with 56 northern Democrats voting yes. See generally, "Busing Opponents: New Friends in the House," 118 *CR* 5719–20 (1972). For the vote breakdown, see www.govtrack.us/congress/votes /92–1971/h236.

    Paradoxically, Nixon's ambitious description of his initiative may well have helped provoke this strong counterattack. In calling for a major funding effort, he emphasized the scale of the integration effort: "Some 220 school districts are now under court order . . . ; 496 districts have submitted, are negotiating or are likely to be negotiating desegregation plans . . . ; another 278 districts are operating under plans begun in 1968 or 1969; more than 500 Northern districts are now under review or likely soon to be under review for possible violations of Title VI of the Civil Rights Act of 1964." Richard Nixon, "Special Message to the Congress Proposing the Emergency School Aid Act of 1970" (May 21, 1970), *American Presidency Project* at www.presidency.ucsb.edu/ws/index.php?pid=2509.

33. The Ashbrook amendment prohibited the use of federal funds for busing "to overcome racial imbalance in any school." The Green amendment banned HEW from "urg[ing]" schools to use local and state funds for busing. It also forbade the agency from conditioning any federal grants on the system's busing decisions and barred the use of federal funds to "acquire or pay the use of equipment for the purpose of transporting children to or from any school." Sec. 2117.

Finally, it stipulated that "[n]othing in this title shall be construed as requiring" the assignment of "students to schools on the basis of geographic attendance areas drawn on a racially non-discriminatory basis . . . *whether or not the use of such geographic attendance areas results in the complete desegregation of the schools of such agency.*" Sec. 2118 (emphasis added). See 117 *CR* 39072 (1971). Southern senators delayed passage of the Emergency School Aid Act while *Swann* was pending before the Supreme Court, leaving final decisions for later.

34. Senate liberals barely managed to reject (48–47) the toughest anti-busing amendment offered by Robert Dole of Kansas, which would have banned all busing orders that "require[d] that pupils be transported to or from school on the basis of their race, color, religion, or national origin." 118 *CR* 6276 (1972). But they could not prevent the Senate from accepting the Ashbrook and Broomfield amendments already passed by the House. Eventually the Emergency School Aid Act was incorporated into the Education Amendments of 1972 and signed into law on June 23, 1972 (P.L. 92–318). The neighborhood school clause—sec. 2118, supra n. 33—was watered down by deleting the words "whether or not the use of such geographic attendance areas results in the complete desegregation of the schools of such agency." The funding prohibitions were amended to allow the provision of funds "on the express written voluntary request of appropriate local school officials." The Broomfield Amendment, supra n. 32, was also weakened before it was completely eviscerated by Justice Powell in Drummond v. Acree, 409 U.S. 1228 (1972).

35. H.J. Res. 620 (May 6, 1971). See also Reichley, supra n. 3, at 197.

36. See Orfield, supra n. 11.

37. School Busing: Hearings Before Subcom. No. 5 of the Committee on the Judiciary, House of Representatives, 92nd Congress, 2nd session (1972). There were eleven days of hearings between February 28 and March 16, and nine more during the two months ending May 24. Of the sixty-six congressmen opposed to busing, fifteen came from the North. The three pro-busing representatives were James Corman (Calif.), at 1714, Augustus Hawkins (Calif.), at 461, and Charles Whalen (Ohio) at 850.

38. Of the forty-four representatives testifying during the first ten days of the hearings, thirty-seven were for a constitutional amendment, three expressed no preference between an amendment and a statute, and four opposed busing without addressing the issue. As the hearings proceeded, Nixon came out for a statutory solution, and the remaining representatives tended to endorse this option, though many backed an amendment also.

39. Rhodes Cook, *United States Presidential Primary Elections 1968–1996* 127 (2000).

40. See Robert Semple, "Nixon Asks Bill Halting New Busing Orders; Seeks Education Equality," *NYT,* March 17, 1972, at 1.

41. See Reichley, supra n. 3, at 197. At no time, however, did Nixon approve the sweeping language of the Lent Amendment that was the focus of the first round of Celler's committee hearings.

42. Id.

43. Id. at 198.
44. See Bolner & Shanley, supra n. 3, at 156.
45. See Robert Bork, *The Constitutionality of the President's Busing Proposals* 11 (1972).
46. See Arthur Goldberg, "The Administration's Anti-Busing Proposals—Politics Makes Bad Law," 67 *Nw. U. L. Rev.* 319 (1972); Alexander Bickel, "What's Wrong with Nixon's Busing Bills?" *New Republic* 221 (April 22, 1972). Bickel's critique did not confront Bork's claim that Katzenbach v. Morgan grants Congress very broad remedial powers under Section 5 of the Fourteenth Amendment. Goldberg gave this claim short shrift, supra at 339–41, relying on Justice Harlan's dissent to limit the thrust of Justice Brennan's opinion. Goldberg's reliance on Harlan was surprising, since he would have undoubtedly voted with Brennan, not Harlan, if he had stayed on the Court—undermining the credibility of his critique.

    I do not suggest that Bork's analysis was unanswerable. See Chapter 6, and especially text accompanying nn. 33–34. But to put it mildly, the leading critics of the Nixon initiative did not decisively refute his arguments.
47. Letter from Professor James Vorenberg to Senator Claiborne Pell, April 12, 1972, 2 Davison Douglas, *The Public Debate over Busing* 232, 233 (1994). Another professorial statement expressed "grave reservations about the constitutionality" of the proposal but did not directly confront Bork's arguments. 120 CR 14430 (May 13, 1974) (reprinting statement).
48. "How the Candidates Stand on Busing," *Life,* March 3, 1972 (containing statements by all Democratic and Republican candidates).
49. Here is a typical Muskie comment: "The problem is the question of equality of educational opportunity for all our people. . . . Busing isn't going to solve that problem. . . . Housing patterns, employment patterns, local governmental jurisdiction problems—all of these are all involved. Nevertheless, busing is a legitimate tool that has been endorsed by the courts, . . . and I think we have to be willing to use it in a common-sense way." Joel Havemann, "The Busing Issue," 4 *Natl. J.* 635 (April 15, 1972). Note how Muskie emphasizes the court's constitutional leadership on the issue, putting himself in the position of a loyal court follower, urging commonsense cooperation with the judiciary's acts of leadership.
50. "McGovern Attacks Speech for 'Fear and Opportunism,'" *NYT,* March 17, 1972, at 22.
51. The Green Amendment also authorized the immediate termination of prior busing decrees—going beyond Nixon's proposal, which allowed termination only after five years. 118 *CR* 28888 (1972). Green's bill passed the House by a 282–102 vote. 118 *CR* 28906–7 (1972).
52. Richard Nixon, "Labor Day Message," September 3, 1972, *American Presidency Project,* at www.presidency.ucsb.edu/ws/index.php?pid=3557&st=&st1=#axzz-1TikT7HxD. Two days before the election, Nixon closed his campaign with a speech that proclaimed the neighborhood school as one of the "birthrights" of

every American child. Richard Nixon, "The Birthright of an American Child," November 5, 1972, *American Presidency Project,* at www.presidency.ucsb.edu/ws /index.php?pid=3700&st=&sti=#axzz1TikT7HxD.

53. Douglas Kneeland, "Senator Accuses Rival of Exploiting School Issue," *NYT,* September 23, 1972, at 1. While McGovern defended busing, he did not make it a centerpiece of his campaign. See Gary Hart, *Right from the Start* 278–79 (1973), where Hart, McGovern's campaign manager, lays out seven priority issues without any mention of busing.

54. See Kneeland, supra n. 53.

55. See Kevin McMahon, *Nixon's Court* 233, 236 (2011) (reviewing the studies).

56. Here is a leader of the anti-busing bloc, Senator Allen of Alabama, feigning incomprehension at the recalcitrant behavior of the northerners: "I am distressed and perplexed by the fact that some liberal members of the Senate continue to block a vote on its merits. It seems to be conceded that the bill would pass if it could be brought to a vote. Yet, there is a determined effort to thwart the will of the House and the overwhelming sentiment of the people against excessive busing." 118 *CR* 34780 (1972). When the final cloture vote came up on October 12, "every Southern Senator except J. W. Fulbright, the Arkansas Democrat, voted for closure. At the same time, Hugh Scott, Republican of Pennsylvania, and Philip A. Hart, Democrat of Michigan, northerners who have consistently opposed the use of filibusters, voted against stopping the debate." David E. Rosenbaum, "Bill to Bar Busing Killed in Senate as Closure Fails," *NYT,* October 13, 1972, at 17.

Sen. Griffin, fighting hard for reelection in Michigan, warned his filibustering colleagues: "If those who are going to ignore the will of the majority of the Senate and the will of the overwhelming majority of the American people persist in this course, then I predict that next year there will be the two-thirds vote in the Senate, not only to invoke cloture, but possibly to adopt a constitutional amendment." 118 *CR* 34782 (1972).

57. On Oct. 10, Nixon "summoned five anti-busing senators to the White House [led by Senator Griffin] . . . to assure them of his full backing and to urge action on the House-passed bill." Eric Wentworth, "Cloture Bid Fails for 3d Time," *Boston Globe,* October 13, 1972, at 2. Following this meeting, Senator Griffin said that "representatives of the White House are in the process of contacting members of the Senate now and letting them know how strongly he [Nixon] feels about it." "Nixon Vows to Push Vote on Busing," *Chic. Trib.,* October 11, 1972, at 14.

58. The three cloture motions took place on Oct. 10 (vote 45–37), Oct. 11 (49–39), and Oct. 12 (49–38), all falling short of the requisite two-thirds majority. See U.S. Senate, Cloture Motions—92nd Congress, at www.senate.gov/pagelayout /reference/cloture_motions/92.htm.

59. The Senate adjourned on Oct. 18, 1972. 118 *CR* 37323 (1972).

60. Eric Wentworth, "Senate Begins Fight on Busing; Supporters File Cloture Petition," *WP,* October 7, 1972, at A1. Nixon's determination was seconded by Republican moderates such as Howard Baker of Tennessee, who "pledged that he

would continue the effort next year for legislation against busing, which he called 'a grievous piece of mischief.'" David Rosenbaum, "Bill to Bar Busing Killed in Senate as Closure Fails," *NYT,* October 13, 1972, at 1, 17. But Baker was in the midst of a tough reelection campaign, and civil rights leaders professed confidence that "once the elections passed, the pressure for such legislation would be less intense." Id. at 1. As we will see, their confidence was misplaced.

61. Republicans picked up twelve seats in the House but lost two in the Senate. See http://library.cqpress.com/electionsguide/document.php?id=gus6e2–1164 –54406–2200220&PHPSESSID=ftjn6t9an6tptha5tp7g095i44.

62. Wright v. City of Emporia, 407 U.S. 451 (1972).

63. Id.

64. Id. at 462.

65. Id. at 465–66.

66. "We need not and do not hold that this disparity in the racial composition of the two systems would be a sufficient reason, standing alone, to enjoin the creation of the separate school district." Id. at 464.

67. Id. at 476.

68. Karl Llewellyn, *The Common Law Tradition: Deciding Appeals* 121–57 (1960). See also, Bruce Ackerman, *Private Property and the Constitution* 1–22, 88–112 (1977).

69. Christopher Jencks, "Busing—The Supreme Court Goes North," *NYT Sunday Magazine,* Nov. 19, 1972, at 40, 125.

70. Id.

71. Brennan Papers, Keyes v. School District No. 1, No. 71-507, Box I:203, Box I:288, Library of Congress.

72. While the plaintiffs' arguments at trial were wide-ranging, the Legal Defense Fund did not try to prove the existence of pervasive housing discrimination in its presentations to the district court.

73. Certiorari was granted on January 17, 1972, Keyes v. School Dist., 404 U.S. 1036. The brief for petitioners was formally filed and stamped on May 1, 1972. Brief for Petitioner, Keyes v. Sch. Dist., 413 U.S. 189 (1973) (No. 71–507).

74. Id. at v–ix.

75. Transcript of Oral Argument, Keyes v. Sch. Dist. No. 1, 413 U.S. 189 (1973) (Oct. 12, 1972) (No. 71–507), 77 Philip B. Kurland & Gerhard Casper eds., *Landmark Briefs and Arguments of the Supreme Court of the United States: Constitutional Law* 598–99 (1975).

76. William J. Maledon, Gerald M. Rosberg & Geoffrey R. Stone, Opinions of William J. Brennan, Jr., October Term 1972, xxxix–xl, Brennan Papers, Box II:6, Folder 16, Library of Congress.

77. Id.

78. Douglas and Powell went public on this issue in their separate opinions in Keyes, supra n. 1, at 216 (Douglas, J.), and 217 (Powell, J.).

79. Maledon, supra note 76, at xl. Brennan also made this point in a memo of April 3, 1973 to the Conference: "Lewis [Powell] first expressed his view that the de

jure/de facto distinction should be discarded. I told him then that I too was deeply troubled by the distinction. Nevertheless, it appeared that a majority of the Court was committed to the view that the distinction should be maintained, and I therefore drafted Keyes within the framework established in our earlier cases. While I am still convinced that my proposed opinion for the Court is, assuming the continued vitality of the de jure/de facto distinction, a proper resolution of the case, I would be happy indeed to recast the opinion and jettison the distinction if a majority of the Court is prepared to do so." Memorandum, Brennan Papers, Box I:289, Library of Congress.

80. See Milliken v. Bradley, 418 U.S. 717 (1974).

81. Keyes, supra n. 1, at 198.

82. Brief for Petitioners, supra n. 73, at 36–37.

83. See Chapter 11.

84. There is no evidence that Brennan ever entertained this approach in any of the draft opinions that appear in his files—or those of Justices Blackmun, Douglas, Marshall, Powell, and Rehnquist.

85. Keyes, supra n. 1, at 203.

86. See Keyes v. School District No. 1, Denver, 368 F. Supp. 207 (1973).

87. Most famously, federal district judge Garrity approved an extensive busing program for Boston schools in June 1974, culminating a decade-long process of planning and litigation catalyzed by the state's Racial Imbalance Law of 1965. See Morgan v. Hennigan, 379 F. Supp. 410, 417 (D. Mass. 1974).

88. Milliken was argued on February 27. See Milliken v. Bradley 418 U.S. 417 (1974). The House debate began on March 12. 120 CR 6267 (1974).

89. 120 CR 8281–2 (March 26, 1974). The House also approved a provision banning the use of federal funds to "overcome racial imbalance." A similar amendment had been watered down by the Senate in 1972, see supra n. 34, but its sponsor, Representative Ashbrook, insisted that by passing it a second time "we would serve notice on the other body, and to House conferees who are likely to be less than resolute in this matter, that we intend to assert the House position." The House agreed by a vote of 239 to 168. 120 CR 8507–8 (1974).

90. A June 1972 Gallup Poll reported 73 percent opposed to busing, while 27 percent favored it. 1 George Gallup, Gallup Poll 43 (1978). As the 1974 elections approached, the numbers were a bit less lopsided: 65 percent opposed, 35 percent in favor—with levels of support ranging from 30 percent in the Midwest to 37 percent in the South. On a national basis, 28 percent of whites and 75 percent of nonwhites were pro-busing. Id. at 370–71.

91. The vote was 47–46. 120 CR 15076 (May 16, 1974).

92. Griffin's amendment tracked a provision sponsored by Representative Esch, which had already been approved by the House. It imposed an unconditional ban on court-ordered busing "of any student to a school other than the school closest or next closest to his place of residence." 120 CR 15063–4 (1974). But Senator Griffin weakened the parallel House measure in other respects, delet-

ing its draconian provisions requiring the reopening and termination of existing busing orders.

93. Orfield, supra n. 11, at 127.

94. See § 902 (2) (b), 120 *CR* 15076 (1974).

95. 120 *CR* 15079 (1974).

96. The House made its first demand on its conferees even before the conference
started! 120 *CR* 17882 (June 5, 1974). It then followed up with overwhelming
majorities on June 27, 120 *CR* 21599–600, and July 27, 120 *CR* 24449 (1974),
insisting that its conferees hold firm on its tough anti-busing measures.

97. "I am disheartened by the action taken in the Senate Monday on the education
amendments of 1974. I previously indicated my intention to veto the committee
version of S. 1539. . . . I must once again state my unequivocal opposition to
forced busing for the purpose of achieving racial balance. The experience of the
past 5 years across America shows that we can dismantle dual school systems
without resorting to massive forced busing. . . . As I have indicated previously, I
support the busing provision of [the House] over those contained in the Senate
bill. . . . I am hopeful that the difficulties presented by the Senate bill can be
resolved in conference." Richard Nixon, "Statement About Proposed Amendments to the Elementary and Secondary Education Act," May 22, 1974, *American Presidency Project,* at www.presidency.ucsb.edu/ws/?pid=4220.

98. Ford had gone so far as to sign a petition trying to force an anti-busing constitutional amendment out of the Judiciary Committee for a floor House vote. See
David Rosenbaum, "Antibusing Plea Is Signed by Ford," *NYT,* Jan. 26, 1972, at
32. See generally Lawrence McAndrews, "Missing the Bus: Gerald Ford and
School Desegregation," 27 *Pres. Stud. Quart.* 791, 793 (1997).

99. Orfield, supra n. 11, at 130.

100. Conference Report (H. Rept. No. 93–1211), printed in 120 *CR* 24533–93 (dated
July 23, 1974). Milliken, supra n. 88, was handed down on July 25, 1974.

101. Education Amendments of 1974, Pub. L. No. 93-380, 88 Stat. 484 (1974). Sec.
258 (b) forbade any busing order from taking effect until the beginning of the
next school year; Sec. 219 required termination of a busing order if the court
finds that the school system "has satisfied the requirements of the fifth or fourteenth amendments to the Constitution, whichever is applicable, and will continue to be in compliance with the requirements thereof." Neither of these
provisions raised serious constitutional questions. Orfield, supra n. 11, at 136.

102. Id.

103. Under the district court's metropolitan-area-wide plan, minority attendance
would range from 17.5 percent to 30 percent at each school, so as to minimize
the time spent on buses. See Bradley v. Milliken, 345 F. Supp. 914, 917 (1972).

104. The district court concluded that "taking time, distance, and transportation
factors" into account, its metropolitan-area plan was "physically easier and more
practicable and feasible, than desegregation efforts limited to the corporate
geographic limits of the city of Detroit." Id. at 930.

105. Marshall followed up on Burger's initial circulation with a plea for more time: "The great difficulties of these cases, both factually and doctrinally, are evidenced by the amount of time required for the initial draft of the Court's opinion, which was circulated in typewritten form on May 31, three full months after the Conference voted on these cases on March 1." Justice Marshall, "Memorandum to the Conference" (June 13, 1974), Brennan Papers, Box I:328, Folder 3, Library of Congress.

106. The memo was written by Robert Richter in response to Justice Burger's circulation. See Richter, "Milliken v. Bradley, Circulation by the Chief Justice (2nd Draft)," 5 (June 12, 1974), Blackmun Papers, Box 187, No. 73-434, Library of Congress.

107. The conferees were appointed on June 5 and the report was submitted on July 23.

108. "I have been against court-ordered busing to achieve racial balance since the mid-1950s, so that is almost 20 years," President Gerald R. Ford remarked in an interview in 1976. Interview by Nick Clooney of President Gerald R. Ford (June 1, 1976), Ford Presidential Library, White House Special Files Unit Files, Box 4, Folder 4, "Busing Background Book (1)." For Ford's earlier record as a congressman, see n. 98 supra.

109. In arguing for an interdistrict remedy, the Detroit school board made precisely this argument in its brief, contending that a "Detroit-only plan cannot . . . eliminate the human perception that the schools in Detroit are black schools." It insisted that "[r]acial identifiability, and the perceptions condemned in Brown I, are no less invidious in Northern schools than in Southern schools," because black children will fail to understand the role of local governmental boundaries in generating this outcome. Brief for Respondents, No. 73–436, at 83–95. But at no point did Burger take this rationale seriously in framing his draft opinions.

110. Milliken, supra n. 88, at 746. (emphasis added).

111. See Attorney Gen. of Michigan ex rel. Kies v. Lowrey, 199 U.S. 233 (1905), which makes this elementary point in connection with Michigan's relationship to its local public school districts—the very problem confronting the Court in Milliken.

112. Milliken, supra n. 88, at 738.

113. In his opinion for all four dissenters, Justice White also makes passing references to "stigmatization," id. at 779, but Marshall alone presents an eloquent defense of Brown's anti-humiliation principle in his sole dissent.

114. Milliken, supra n. 88, at 804–05.

115. Id. at 808.

116. See supra nn. 105, 106.

117. See generally James Ryan, *Five Miles Away, A World Apart* (2010).

118. See Tomiko Brown-Nagin, *Courage to Dissent* 357–407 (2011).

119. Milliken, supra n. 88, at 814–15.

120. See Owen Fiss, "The Jurisprudence of Busing," 39 *Law & Cont. Probs.* 194, 199–206 (1975).

121. For a broad-gauged view of the problem, see Sofia Behana et al., eds., *Disrupting the School to Prison Pipeline* (2012). For a legal overview, see Catherine Kim, Dan Losen & Damon Hewitt, *The School to Prison Pipeline: Structuring Legal Reform* (2010).

122. *Milliken* returned to the Supreme Court in 1977, when the justices considered whether the district court had the power to supplement its Detroit-only busing order with "compensatory or remedial educational programs for schoolchildren who have been subjected to past acts of *de jure* segregation." See Milliken v. Bradley, 433 U.S. 267, 269 (1977). In upholding this aspect of the decree, Chief Justice Burger recognized that "[c]hildren who have been thus educationally and culturally set apart from the larger community will inevitably acquire habits of speech, conduct, and attitudes reflecting their cultural isolation. They are likely to acquire speech habits, for example, which vary from the environment in which they must ultimately function and compete, if they are to enter and be a part of that community." Id. at 287. This comes close to recognizing humiliation as a constitutional evil, though only at the remedial stage, once intentional discrimination has been established. For another (inadequate) gesture toward the anti-humiliation principle, see Lau v. Nichols, 414 U.S. 563 (1974).

This book does not trace the fate of *Brown* over the half century after the Court's "switch in time" in 1974. It is enough to recapture its centrality in the constitutional politics of the civil rights era. See generally Chapter 14.

13. Spheres of Intimacy

1. See Peggy Pascoe, *What Comes Naturally: Miscegenation Law and the Making of Race in America* 118, 243 & tables (1989). Fourteen states banned white-black marriages, eleven added white-Asian unions, and four more proscribed marriages between whites and Native Americans. South Carolina allowed whites and Asians to marry but banned unions between whites and blacks and/or Native Americans.

2. Kirby v. Kirby, 24 Ariz. 9 (1922); Jackson v. Denver, 124 P. 2d 240 (Colo. 1942); In re Shun T. Takahashi's Estate, 129 P. 2d 217 (Mont. 1942); Davis v. Meyer, 212 N.W. 435 (Neb. 1927); In re Paquet's Estate, 200 P. 911 (Or. 1921). Southern courts had resolved the issue soon after Reconstruction ended. See, e.g., Green v. State, 58 Ala. 190 (1877); State v. Kennedy, 76 N.C. 251 (1877); Lonas v. State, 50 Tenn. 287 (1871). Some border state courts waited longer. See, e.g., Dodson v. Arkansas, 31 S.W. 977 (1895).

3. Pace v. Alabama, 106 U.S. 583, 585 (1883). The particular statute in *Pace* banned interracial fornication and adultery. But its rationale extended to marriage prohibitions as well.

4. See Gunnar Myrdal, *An American Dilemma* 60–61 (2d ed. 1962).

5. Id. at 61.

6. See Michael Klarman, *From Jim Crow to Civil Rights* 321 (2004); Virginia Schoff, "Deciding on Doctrine: Anti-Miscegenation Statutes and the Development of Equal Protection Analysis," 95 *Va. L. Rev.* 627, 632 & n. 19 (2009).

7. See Alex Lubin, *Romance and Rights: The Politics of Interracial Intimacy* 75–76 (2005).

8. See Pascoe, supra n. 1, at 203.

9. Perez v. Sharp, 32 Cal. 2d 711 (1948).

10. See Chang Moon Sohn, "Principle and Expediency in Judicial Review: Miscegenation Cases in the Supreme Court" 129 (1970) (unpublished Ph.D. dissertation, Columbia University) (on file with author):

> The NAACP was fully aware of the test cases that were being formulated by . . . the ACLU and the Interracial Councils. The NAACP was even approached by the ACLU for possible support in these cases, but was willing to go no further than quietly lending its materials on miscegenation to the ACLU.

Sohn cites a March 31, 1948, memo from Constance Baker Motley of the NAACP to support his discussion. I have not been able to inspect this document.

11. See Naim v. Naim, 87 S.E. 2d 749 (Va. 1955).

12. Id. at 756.

13. See Pascoe, supra n. 1, at 202–04, 250; Schoff, supra n. 6, at 632–36.

14. Naim, supra n. 11, at 752.

15. Jackson v. State, 37 Ala. App. 519 (Ct. App. 1954), *cert. denied,* 348 U.S. 888 (1954).

16. See Brief for Petitioner-Appellant in Opposition to Appellee's Motion to Dismiss or Affirm at 2–4, Naim v. Naim, 350 U.S. 891 (1955) (No. 366).

17. Sohn, supra n. 10, at 84 (citing memos to and from ACLU team).

18. See Felix Frankfurter, Memorandum, Naim v. Naim, microformed on *Frankfurter Papers,* pt. 2, reel 17, frames 588–90 (Univ. Publ'ns of Am. 1986). See Dennis Hutchinson, "Unanimity and Desegregation: Decisionmaking in the Supreme Court, 1948–1958," 68 *Geo. L. J.* 1, 95–96 (1979); Schoff, supra n. 6, at 637–40.

19. Frankfurter, Memorandum, supra n. 18. Justice Frankfurter writes: "So far as I recall, this is the first time that I am confronted with the task of resolving a conflict between moral and technical legal considerations."

20. See Bernard Schwartz, *Super Chief* 161 (1983).

21. 350 U.S. 891 (1955).

22. Naim v. Naim, 90 S.E. 2d 849 (Va. 1956).

23. Naim v. Naim, 350 U.S. 985 (1956).

24. Herbert Wechsler, "Toward Neutral Principles of Constitutional Law," 73 *Harv. L. Rev.* 1, 34 (1959).

25. See, e.g., Charles Black, "The Lawfulness of the Segregation Decisions," 69 *Yale L. J.* 421 (1960); Louis H. Pollak, "Racial Discrimination and Judicial Integrity: A Reply to Professor Wechsler," 108 *U. Pa. L. Rev.* 1 (1959).

26. Jack Greenberg, *Race Relations and American Law* 345 (1959); Peter Wallenstein, "Race, Marriage and the Law of Freedom: Alabama and Virginia, 1860s–1960s," 70 *Chi.-Kent L. Rev.* 371, 415 & n. 214 (1994).

27. Alexander Bickel, *The Least Dangerous Branch* 174 (1962).

28. Reva Siegel, "Equality Talk," 117 *Harvard L. Rev.* 1470, 1489–1497 (2004) (summarizing academic discussion).

29. McLaughlin v. Florida came to the court on appeal, so the critical question was whether the Justices would grant plenary consideration or dispose of it summarily. The Court chose the first option on Jun. 15, 1964, 377 U.S. 974—five days after the Senate had finally broken the southern filibuster of the Civil Rights Act, ensuring its success.

30. McLaughlin v. Florida, 379 U.S. 184 (1964). The Court's decision came down on December 7.

31. See Chapter 6.

32. Pascoe, supra n. 1, at 243 & table.

33. Id. at 238–43. At first the ACLU and Japanese American Citizens League spearheaded these efforts, with the NAACP remaining on the sidelines. But over time, the NAACP took a more active role, particularly in California, Nevada and Idaho. Id.

34. Id. at 255.

35. *NORC SRS-Amalgam,* December 1963. Retrieved March 24, 2013, from iPOLL Databank, Roper Center for Public Opinion Research, University of Connecticut, www.ropercenter.uconn.edu/data_access/ipoll/ipoll.html.

36. Since there is no official transcript, here is a transcription of the tape recording of the key exchange at oral argument:

WARREN: Mr. Pollak, weren't both of these people married to others?

POLLAK: Uh, Mr. Chief Justice, uh, there was testimony by some witnesses that uh, that one or, that, I think with respect to each of the defendants, that they had made some such statements, uh. Now I would say as to that, that uh, it would be within the jury's province to believe or disbelieve that portion of the narrator's testimony.

WARREN: Was there any evidence to the contrary?

POLLAK: There was also evidence that, that uh, Mrs. McLaughlin, or Mrs. Hoffman as she's referred to in the record, has described herself as married to uh, McLaughlin. Uh, Mrs. Goodnick so said on page twenty-two of the record.

WARREN: Well that wasn't her testimony, that was the next party's statement—out of court.

POLLAK: But that was true of all the testimony in this case, Mr. Chief Justice. Uh, the testimony with respect to uh, marriage to others was also, uh heresay or ex-parte testimony. There was no testimony in this record forthcoming from the appellants themselves, who were the defendants and who did not take the stand. Uh, so all the testimony is of the same hearsay character, and uh, our position on this is merely, Mr. Chief Justice, that if a jury were permitted to—to consider the testimony, it might have come to either, uh position uh. When—when Mrs. Goodnick says on page thirty, speaking of the appellants, "I know he is husband and wife and they pay me the rent, I didn't bother them," uh I suggest to this Court that that is uh, evidence from which a jury could have concluded that uh, these were people who held themselves out to be, and were thought to be married to one another. Uh, but a jury could have certainly come to the opposite conclusion; I wouldn't begin to challenge.

Oral Argument at 13:54, McLaughlin, supra n. 30.

37. Id., Oral Argument at 33:16.

38. Del Dickson ed., *The Supreme Court in Conference* 694 (2001) (conference of Oct. 16, 1964).

39. Id. The McLaughlins filed an appeal under 28 U.S.C. § 1257 (2)—a provision that requires the Court to accept jurisdiction and render a decision on the merits. But they also "pray[ed] that this statement be regarded . . . as a petition for a writ of certiorari" if the Court "should . . . regard this appeal as having been improvidently taken." Appellants' Juris. St. at 1. Perhaps this explains why Justice Douglas is urging his colleagues to dismiss the case as "improvidently" granted.

40. McLaughlin, supra n. 30, at 191–92.

41. Pace v. Alabama, 106 U.S. 583, 585 (1883).

42. McLaughlin, supra n. 30, at 192.

43. See Chapter 7 for a more elaborate discussion of Brown's five-step logic.

44. Gallup Poll, "Interracial Marriage (Mar. 10, 1965), Jan. 28–Feb. 2 1965," in *The Gallup Poll: Public Opinion, 1935–1997*, at 1928–29 (CD-ROM). The poll addressed only black-white intermarriage. Polls from the National Opinion Research Center (NORC) contained less hopeful findings. NORC's nationwide surveys in 1963 and 1964 found 62 and 60 percent of American whites, respectively, favoring intermarriage bans. Howard Schuman et al., *Racial Attitudes in America: Trends and Interpretations* 106–08 table 3.1b (citing NORC polls). While these numbers declined during the later 1960s, it was only in the early 1970s that Gallup began to report strong national majorities against antimiscegenation laws. Id.; see also *Gallup Poll (AIPO)*, Aug. 1970. Retrieved March 24, 2013, from iPOLL Databank, Roper Center for Public Opinion Research, University of Connecticut, at www.ropercenter.uconn.edu/data_access/ipoll/ipoll.html. Even then, a majority of southern whites still favored interracial marriage bans. Hazel Erskine, "The Polls: Interracial Socializing," 37 *Pub. Op. Q.* 283, 292 (1973) (citing Gallup poll).

45. Siegel, supra n. 28, at 1488–90 (2004).

46. See Chapter 7.

47. Loving v. Virginia, 388 U.S. 1 (1967).

48. Loving v. Commonwealth, 147 S.E. 2d 78, 82 (Va. 1966).

49. See Appellee's Brief, Loving v. Virginia 14–26 (No. 395, October Term, 1966).

50. Loving, supra n. 47, at 9.

51. This section of the appellant's brief is entitled "Anti-miscegenation laws cause immeasurable social harm," and explains, "Throughout this section, we often utilize [the] definitive treatise on the Negro problem in America by the eminent social economist [sic], Gunnar Myrdal." The brief also especially relies on more contemporary work by Thomas Pettigrew. See Loving v. Virginia, Appellant's Brief, at 26 (No. 395, October Term 1966).

52. Id. at 25–26.

53. Interview with Benno C. Schmidt Jr., April 25, 2012. Mr. Schmidt has reviewed and approved the report of our conversation presented here.

54. See Appellee's Brief, supra at n. 49, 41–50. Virginia also relied heavily on quotations from a more recent book by Albert Gordon, *Intermarriage—Interfaith, Interethnic, Interracial* (1964), Brief, supra, at 51–52. This book emerged from the author's counseling experience as a rabbi and used sociological data to support a broad assault on intergroup marriages, especially those between Jews and Gentiles. Gordon's discussion of interracial marriage is particularly weak, consisting of a few interviews. Id. at 263–94.

55. To put the point in terms developed in Chapter 7, my alternative opinion would have stopped at Brown step 4, without moving onward to step 5.

56. Interview, supra n. 53. Warren's view of the wartime cases may have evolved over time. In 1962 he gave them a lukewarm public endorsement: "There is still another lesson to be learned from cases like *Hirabayashi*. Where the circumstances are such that the Court must accept uncritically the Government's description of the magnitude of the military need, actions may be permitted that restrict individual liberty in a grievous manner." Earl Warren, "The Bill of Rights and the Military," 32 *N.Y.U. L. Rev.* 181, 193 (1962).

But in his posthumously published autobiography, he was more critical: "I have since deeply regretted the removal order and my own testimony advocating it, because it was not in keeping with our American concept of freedom and the rights of citizens." Earl Warren, *The Memoirs of Earl Warren* 148–49 (1977). These two remarks are not necessarily at odds: It is perfectly consistent for the latter-day Warren to condemn his own conduct as attorney general while still believing that the Court's decision was appropriate under the grim circumstances. But it is also possible that Warren changed his mind after he left the Court in 1968.

57. United States v. Windsor, 2013 U.S. Lexis 4921 (June 26, 2013).

58. Loving, supra n. 47, at 11.

59. I have been unable to locate a draft in Warren's files that did not contain a version of these final paragraphs. I base this account on my interview with Benno Schmidt, supra n. 53.

60. Loving, supra n. 47, at 12.

61. Meyer v. Nebraska, 262 U.S. 390, 399–400 (1923).

62. Letter from Black to Warren, May 31, 1967, Warren Papers, Box 620, Library of Congress. Justice White also wrote that there was "no reason to reach the due process question." Letter from White to Warren, May 31, 1967, Warren Papers, Box 620, Library of Congress. Warren gained White's consent by making minor textual changes. I emphasize Black's role because, as the Court's only southerner, even a partial dissent from him would have gained wide notoriety.

63. Schmidt interview, supra n. 53. Compare draft of May 25 with draft of June 5 (striking out reference to Meyer). Draft Opinions, Warren Papers, Box 620, Library of Congress. Warren does cite Meyer, together with Skinner v. Oklahoma, 316 U.S. 535 (1942), earlier in the opinion, in support of the innocuous proposition that the Fourteenth Amendment limits the states' power to regulate marriage. Loving, supra n. 47, at 7.

64. Potter Stewart chimed in with a one-paragraph concurrence, joining the Court on a narrow ground that did not detract from Warren's more general pronouncement. Loving, supra n. 47, at 13.

65. While federal courts did intervene to overcome some resistance by a few southern registrars, Loving was ultimately implemented without serious incident. More generally, the Court's announcement provoked "barely a murmur of objection in the land." Richard Kluger, *Simple Justice* 751 (1976).

66. McReynolds emphasized that he was not challenging "the State's power to prescribe a curriculum for institutions which it supports. Those matters are not within the present controversy." Meyer v. Nebraska, 262 U.S. 390, 402 (1923).

67. Windsor, supra n. 57, at 43–44.

68. For Justice Scalia's defense of federal uniformity, see id. at 84–85.

69. See Lawrence v. Texas, 539 U.S. 558, 578 (2003).

70. Brown v. Board of Education, 347 U.S. 483, 494 (1054). Windsor does not cite Warren's great opinion by name, probably for a technical reason: Brown considers state violations of the Fourteenth Amendment, while Windsor avoids this issue and deals only with the federal government's violation of the Fifth Amendment. At one point Justice Kennedy does cite Bolling v. Sharpe, the companion case to Brown that struck down segregated schools in the District of Columbia under the Fifth Amendment—but even here he fails to reflect on his opinion's deeper indebtedness to the Warren Court. Windsor, supra n. 57, at 40.

71. See Chapter 7's discussion of the five steps in Brown-style argumentation, especially the relationship between step four and step five.

72. Windsor, supra n. 57, at 89.

73. Id. at 90.

14. Betrayal?

1. See *WP: T*, chaps. 2–3.

2. See Samuel Rosenman ed., *Public Papers and Addresses of Franklin Delano Roosevelt* 132 (1937). For further elaboration, see *WP: T* 326–27.

3. For some surprising—to me, at least—uses of statistical techniques to test key claims made in earlier volumes, see Daniel Ho & Kevin Quinn, "Did a Switch in Time Save Nine?" 2 *J. Leg. Anal.* 69 (2010); Daniel Young, "How Do You Measure a Constitutional Moment?" 122 *Yale L. J.* 1990 (2013).

4. See especially *WP: T,* chaps. 8–12.

5. Shelby County v. Holder, 133 S. Ct. 2612 (June 25, 2013).

6. Id. at 2616.

7. Id. at 2618 (emphasis in original; internal quotation marks omitted).

8. See *WP: T,* chap. 2, especially the Founders' treatment of Rhode Island during the proposal and ratification of the Constitution.

9. Shelby County, supra n. 5, at 2622. Chief Justice Roberts first expressed the Court's constitutional doubts about the VRA in Northwest Austin v. Holder, 557 U.S. 193 (2009), and he relied on his earlier opinion to support Shelby's "equal state sovereignty" principle. But Northwest Austin's case analysis consisted of little more than brief quotations from a very few cases.

A fuller discussion exposes the weakness of Roberts's case analysis. Begin with the most recent decision that the Chief Justice cited: United States v. Louisiana, 363 U. S. 1, 16 (1960). The Court did not take this case because of its jurisprudential importance but because it was constitutionally obligated to accept original jurisdiction over a lawsuit between five southern states and the federal government over underwater resources. In deciding the case, Justice Harlan made a passing reference to equal sovereignty, but ultimately he *upheld* the federal government's claims against four of the states involved, while granting limited relief to Texas. His "equal sovereignty" language is sheer dicta—yet Roberts invoked it to justify a result opposite to the one reached by Harlan. While *Louisiana* vindicated the powers of the federal government against the states, *Shelby County* cited it to protect the states against the federal government.

Roberts also cited Pollard's Lessee v. Hagan, 3 How. 212 (1845), another water rights case. This antebellum decision is even less relevant to a voting rights dispute under the modern Constitution, since, as I argue in the text, Section 2 of the Fourteenth Amendment fundamentally revolutionized constitutional law on this matter.

The Chief Justice's appeal to Texas v. White, 74 U.S. 700 (1869), is no less puzzling. That case involved a decision by the Confederate legislature of Texas to sell some U.S. bonds provided by the federal government before the Civil War. Writing for the Court, Chief Justice Chase held that the rebel legislature lacked the power to make this sale, declaring that the bonds were now the property of the new Texas government that Congress had reorganized under the Reconstruction Acts, which, as is well known, thoroughly violated the "equal state sovereignty" principle. For a fuller account, see *WP: T* 191–246. When read in historical context, Chase's invocation of "an indestructible Union, composed of indestructible States" stands for the very opposite of an "equal sovereignty" principle. The opinion is a small part of a larger process through which the *unequal* treatment of states was legitimated by the American People. See also Akhil Amar, "The Lawfulness of Section 5—and Thus of Section 5," *Harvard Law Forum*, Feb. 13, 2013, at www.harvardlawreview.org/issues/126/february13/forum_989.php.

This left the Chief Justice with Coyle v. Smith, 221 U.S. 559 (1911), which did indeed strike down a congressional effort to impose a special restriction on the admission of Oklahoma into the Union, and is an appropriate source for Roberts's ringing pronouncements on behalf of state equality. But in writing for the Court in Coyle, Justice Horace Lurton was careful to say that the federal government could impose conditions on admission when they were otherwise "within the sphere of the plain power of Congress." Id. at 574. In enumerating these powers, Lurton didn't mention Section 2 of the Fourteenth Amendment, which authorizes selective sanctions on states that "abridge" black voting rights—undoubtedly because this provision had become a dead letter by the time he was writing in 1911. Nevertheless, Lurton's reasoning undercuts Roberts's use of Coyle to support his version of the "equal state sovereignty" principle in striking down the VRA.

What is more, Justice Ginsburg was right to insist that South Carolina v. Katzenbach explicitly refused to extend Coyle beyond the special problem posed by the admission of new states to the Union. Chief Justice Roberts responded to her critique by claiming that South Carolina v. Katzenbach's deviation from the "equal sovereignty" principle was acceptable only under the egregious conditions prevailing in the Jim Crow South. But a review of Roberts's authorities does not support his claim that "equal sovereignty" *is* a basic principle when states violate the voting rights of minorities.

10. To be more precise, Section 2 orders a proportional reduction in House representation for any state that "denied . . . or any way abridged" the suffrage of "male inhabitants" over "twenty-one years of age" in federal or major state elections. To the dismay of the leaders of the rising women's movement, this formulation imposed its selective sanction only on states that barred blacks from the polls, not those that restricted women's access. See Alexander Keyssar, *The Right to Vote* 143–44 (2000). Section 2 allows the states leeway in a few other areas, but these details are irrelevant for present purposes. The key point is that Section 2 *expressly* authorizes disparate treatment of states based on their discriminatory treatment of black voters.

11. See Stanley Hirshson, *Farewell to the Bloody Shirt* 200–35 (1962) for a blow-by-blow account of the Republicans' last major effort in 1890 to protect black voting rights—which was ultimately defeated by a Democratic filibuster in the Senate.

12. Shelby County, supra n. 5, at 2618. As my discussion of Section 2 of the Fourteenth Amendment shows, the Chief Justice was simply incorrect in calling this "unprecedented."

13. See Richard Nixon's statement upon signing the Voting Rights Act of 1970 in Chapter 8.

14. See Representative William McCulloch's remarks in Chapter 8.

15. In criticizing the VRA's basis in contemporary realities, Roberts highlighted the fact that "African-American voter turnout exceeded white voter turnout in five of the six States originally covered [by the triggering provisions in 1965]." Shelby County, supra n. 5, at 2625. But he gave cursory attention to studies supporting Congress's view that the 1972 formula continued to identify jurisdictions that more frequently used racial gerrymandering and other second-generation techniques to minimize black political power. Instead of taking this evidence seriously, he referred to the critique leveled by Judge Williams in the court of appeals. But Williams's opinion failed to persuade the majority on the three-judge panel, whose more positive assessment was powerfully supported by Justice Ginsburg in her dissent. Given the significance of the issue of second-generation discrimination in convincing President Nixon and Congress to reaffirm the triggering provisions in 1970, the Chief Justice should have analyzed the congressional evidence far more carefully before condemning it as an "irrational[]" basis for retaining the 1972 triggering formula. Id. at 40.

16. See her dissent, Shelby County, supra n. 5, at 2639–44.

17. See *WP: F*, chaps 4–6.

18. For some very different explorations, see Stephen Griffin, *Long Wars and the Constitution* (2013); Alison LaCroix, "Temporal Imperialism," 158 *U. Penn. L. Rev.* 1329 (2010); Gerard Magliocca, *The Tragedy of William Jennings Bryan* (2011) and *Andrew Jackson and the Constitution* (2007); Jed Rubenfeld, *Revolution by Judiciary* (2005) and *Freedom and Time* (2001); Reva Siegel, "She the People," 115 *Harv. L. Rev.* 948 (2002). I am also encouraged by the increasing willingness of scholars committed to the primacy of the Founding and Reconstruction to incorporate twentieth-century developments into their doctrinal discussions. See, e.g., Akhil Amar, *America's Unwritten Constitution* (2012); Jack Balkin, *Living Originalism* (2011).

19. 2 *Public Papers of the Presidents of the United States: Lyndon B. Johnson, 1965* 635–40 (1966).

20. See Stevens's speech in Chapter 8.

21. I elaborate further on the Radicals' failure in *WP: T*, chaps. 6–8.

INDEX